Ken Sakamura (Ed.)

TRON Project 1989

Open-Architecture Computer Systems

Proceedings of the Sixth TRON Project Symposium

With 113 Figures

Springer-Verlag
Tokyo Berlin Heidelberg New York
London Paris Hong Kong

KEN SAKAMURA
Leader, TRON Project
Department of Information Science
Faculty of Science
University of Tokyo
Hongo, Tokyo, 113 Japan

ISBN-13:978-4-431-68104-5   e-ISBN-13:978-4-431-68102-1
DOI: 10.1007/978-4-431-68102-1

Foreword

It is almost six years since the inauguration of the TRON project, a concept first proposed by Dr. K. Sakamura of the University of Tokyo, and it is almost 2 years since the foundation of the TRON Association on March 1988. The number of regular member companies registered in the TRON Association as of November 1988 is 145 which is a new record for the Association.

Some of this year's major activities that I would particularly like to mention are:

– Over 50 TRON project-related products have been or are about to be introduced to the marketplace, according to a preliminary report from the Future Study Committee of the TRON Association. In particular, I am happy to say that the ITRON subproject, which is ahead of the other subprojects, has progressed so far that several papers on ITRON applications will be presented at this conference, which means that the ITRON specifications are now ready for application to embedded commercial and industrial products.

– The TRON Association has been able to issue many English-language specification books aimed at the 6th TRON Project International Symposium, owing to the efforts of the various subproject committees. This issue is designed to invite various opinions, especially those focussing on academic and technological points, from people around the world. All of these documents were produced by voluntary efforts by members of the subproject committees. I would like to invite member companies to join specific subproject committees if they are interested in research and development.

– To date, TRON project activities have been mostly conducted in computer-related areas such as operating systems, microprocessors, and personal computers. From now on, however, it seemes that the focus will shift to R&D activity related to very broad application areas such as TRON-specification houses, buildings, cities, home electronics, and transportation control networks. This clearly indicates that the TRON project is not aimed at simply developing a microprocessor architecture or an operating system, but it is also aimed at developing a totally new computer culture.

I understand that some crities express doubts concerning the economic balance of the TRON project, considering the huge amount of money invested in research, but I don't think much of critics who can only raise economic issues when people like us are attacking a new, challenging field. Since we proposing to create a totally new computer culture suitable for the twenty-first century, I believe that we will be able to conquer the various problems before us by cooperating with and competing against each other.

Actions require far more bravery than simple knowledge—after all, revolutions are never caused by knowledge alone; they are caused by the application of knowledge.

At this opening of the 6th TRON Symposium, I hope that people will come to understand fully the TRON concept through their participation in the symposium, and that the diffusion of this understanding will contribute significantly to the development of the computer industry around the world.

KATSUSHIGE MITA

Chairman, TRON Association
President, HITACH LIMITED

Preface

The TRON Project aims to develop a revolutionary new computer architecture and to establish a vision for the computerized society of the future, when the number of computers in use will outnumber that at present by 100,000 times. It is essential that we begin now to discuss seriously the use and role of computers in a future society, for the reason that computers will occupy an increasingly influential position in people's lives, in the economy and in politics.

The TRON Project is managed by a nonprofit core group, the TRON Association, which monitors specification and validation activities as well as publicity. There are no plans, however, to commercialize the TRON Project. On the other hand, the contents of this book include a number of commercial products, based on TRON specifications, which will be making an appearance in the near future. All in all, the TRON Project has been progressing steadily and a large number of researchers have been making important contributions at the developmental stage.

The Sixth TRON Project Symposium (International) contributions have been compiled in this volume. It is to be hoped that the research findings presented here will serve as a catalyst to spark interest in the computerized society of the future.

KEN SAKAMURA

Table of Contents

Chapter 3: CTRON

Chapter 4: TRONCHIP

Key Note Address

The Computerized Society

Ken Sakamura

Department of Information Science, Faculty of Science, University of Tokyo

ABSTRACT

The TRON Project is being carried out based on a vision of the future computerized society. Already we are approaching that future as computers come to be used in all areas of life, making life without computers seem almost impossible. This paper discusses, from a computer architecture point of view, the infrastructure that must be laid to avoid the problems to which a computerized society is liable, and to enable the society to grow in a more positive direction.

While the TRON Project is a computer development project, it also has an inescapable social responsibility. From this standpoint, the paper looks at the nature of the HFDS (Highly Functionally Distributed Systems) which the project is aimed at realizing. It notes the necessity of standardization in HFDS realization, and discusses the qualities required of that standardization.

Finally, a number of application projects are introduced, which are important means for evaluating the architecture being developed in the TRON Project. These can be seen as small-scale simulations of the future computerized society.

We are confident that through these application projects, it will be shown that the computerized society can grow in a desirable direction, based on the information infrastructure being proposed in the TRON Project.

Keywords: HFDS, Standardization, Computerized society, Computerized home, Intelligent building, Intelligent automobile.

1. INTRODUCTION

A specific aim of the TRON Project is to realize highly functionally distributed systems (HFDS).[1] An HFDS is a system in which extremely large numbers of computers, of many different functional and performance levels, are networked together in a way that allows them to work cooperatively. The result is a system whose functions are greater than the sum of its individual parts.

Computer-embedded systems are now finding their way into all areas of daily life, and personal computers are coming into wide use. The HFDS concept is based on the premise that this trend will intensify even further in the future. The meaning of "home electronics" will extend far beyond items in the local appliance store, as computers and sensors are embedded in furniture and accessories, even clothes, walls and ceilings. These ordinary items will then be endowed with their own power of judgment, and be able to perform various functions automatically. They will become what can be called "intelligent objects."* When these intelligent objects proliferate further, the resulting environment will deserve to be called a "computerized society."

2. THE NEED TO TAKE INTO ACCOUNT HUMAN SOCIETY

Anyone planning the new order of computers based on the premise of a "computerized society" must give full consideration to the human society that will be served by those computers. This is a different situation from that of, say, CIM (Computer Integrated Manufacturing), used in factories where the conditions are largely predictable. Problems in such a controlled environment can be analyzed locally to determine the required network specifications.

The environment of the "computerized society" is a wholly different matter. The largest part of that environment reflects the very complexity of human society itself. The expected circumstances in which computers will be used vary widely, and the various systems are intricately related, making it risky to attempt a localized analysis.

It must be supposed, for example, that in a typical home intelligent objects will continually be added, gotten rid of, or replaced. It is highly unlikely that a manufacturer's representative will be on hand each time to install a new device. Intelligent objects will have to be made so that when a user with essentially no understanding of computers takes them home and plugs them in, they will operate properly. Allowance will also have to be made for the existence in any society of those who deliberately break the rules and commit criminal acts.

3. INSTABILITY OF THE COMPUTERIZED SOCIETY

If the computerized society is looked at from this standpoint of its relation to human society, then the networking of intelligent objects so that they can function cooperatively can be seen as more than simply for the sake of greater efficiency, convenience and comfort. This networking is also inevitable from the standpoint of security.

---

* This term refers to a more advanced decision-making ability than that of a simple control mechanism like a thermostat, but is based on an extension of present-day computer technology and is not comparable to artificial intelligence in its true sense.

The essence of the functions provided by systems embedded with computers is automation. Automation means greater convenience, but on the other hand there is in automation an element of instability, and even danger. In a non-automated environment, human beings have to operate and manage everything, but at the same time it is a world free of surprises, a predictable and therefore reassuring environment.

By contrast, automated devices in a computerized society have two aspects of instability. One is inadequate awareness by each individual intelligent object of the overall situation. The other is not being sure of what changes will take place as the result of mutual interaction among large numbers of intelligent objects.

The first type of instability can also occur when individual automatic devices are installed, and is already being seen as a problem. Examples are equipment starting up automatically and creating a noise just when you are listening to quiet music, or automatic blinds that shut while you are looking out the window. The problem could grow to larger proportions if an intelligent object that breaks down happens to be involved with use of fire, or is tied in with security facilities.

The second type of instability is not yet a major problem, but could easily arise in the future. Take, for example, a case in which more than one intelligent air conditioner is installed in the same room. Their sophisticated programs for adjusting output based on room temperature changes could easily be confused by the combined effect of each other's operation. In that case they might react incorrectly, resulting in wide temperature fluctuations in the room. Because they are each programmed to have sole control over room temperature, they are not able to function cooperatively.

To take an even simpler example, suppose a number of intelligent objects, such as an alarm clock, toaster, air conditioner, washing machine, car heater and many others, are all programmed to operate automatically in time for your departure for the office in the morning. If there is a sudden change in that time or you decide not to go to work, imagine having to change each of those programs individually the night before. This is a clear case of imposing too great a burden on the user.

Problems such as these are less likely to be an issue when automated equipment is introduced at the work place. The reason is that there is less variation in the kinds of situations likely to arise in an office or factory, and most changes can be predicted readily. In the home, on the other hand, there are numerous variations and these are often hard to predict. Moreover, even if it were possible to predict each situation, there is still the difficulty of coordinating the operation of different equipment purchased freely and with random timing.

4. User Interface in a Computerized Society

When intelligent objects are introduced into society in large numbers, another important issue alongside the problem of instability is the user interface.

User interface is an important issue also when personal computers are introduced into the work place; but in the sense that these are equipment for use on the job, a certain amount of training effort is taken for granted, and it is possible to assume that the users will have a minimum required degree of skill. The same cannot be assumed, however, when intelligent objects are introduced into the home and other areas of everyday life.

The home is, after all, a place to relax. Equipment that cannot be operated without the skill and attention of a professional has no place there. Public facilities, likewise, must be able to provide proper service to users who cannot be expected at all to be familiar with their operation.

In either environment, too, the spectrum of users runs much broader than in a typical work place, ranging from children to the elderly. If intelligent objects cannot be used readily by the weaker members of society, then the future "computerized society" will be an even less suitable environment for them than our present society.

Even though it is necessary to achieve an improved user interface, the cost-raising effect on each piece of equipment has to be minimized. It would be nice, for example, if every piece of equipment could be provided with a bit-map display and touch panel, and make use of speech recognition and voice synthesis to give users detailed instructions in a natural language interface. Cost factors, however, make this unrealistic. The user interface must not impose an undue cost burden, especially on the above-mentioned weaker members of society.

As intelligent objects are brought into the home, public facilities and other areas of daily life, making these areas the coming focus of attention as the arena of most intense contact between computers and society, it will be the responsibility of information science to tackle seriously the types of problems mentioned above. These will need to be the premises of future research and development.

When design is carried out from the bottom up, without considering the problems of the weak or other effects on society, many important things tend to get overlooked. Equipment aimed at professional or semi-professional users can be designed from the bottom up, and the initial products still in the rough stages will be bought for their functions alone; by the time the equipment is in wide use, knowhow will have been accumulated. Products for the computerized society, however, will have to be designed from the top down, with full awareness of the social aspects.

5. Necessity of HFDS

HFDS is one answer to the types of problems that can be foreseen when a socially responsible outlook is adopted. By connecting the intelligent objects together in networks that enable them to function cooperatively, it should be possible to avoid the problems touched on above. While HFDS involves a form of distributed processing, at the same time it has the advantage of centralized processing in making possible a comprehensive view of the situation. In cases like the examples given earlier, an HFDS can suppress background noise levels during a musical performance, and, making use of a home security system, can even detect the presence of a person standing by a window and wait before it closes the blinds.**

Another advantage of an HFDS is the possibility of monitoring or cross-checking among a number of devices. This makes it easier to locate faults and automate fault recovery than when individual devices function independently of each other.

Similarly, in an HFDS the cooperation between intelligent objects having an interest in the same type of environmental information can suppress the confusion arising between independent systems, of the kind we saw when multiple air conditioners are installed in the same room. Moreover, when a large number of intelligent objects are involved, it is possible to become aware of the indoor environment in its entirety, solving the problem of uneven temperature distribution caused by local air conditioner setting and localized air flow.

It is also easy in an HFDS to have timer settings be mutually related, so that when the setting for one device is changed, the others will automatically adjust accordingly. Another possibility is hooking up a BTRON-specification personal computer to the HFDS. Its advanced human/machine interface functions, with bit-map display and intuitive input devices, can be used in giving instructions to individual intelligent objects or making requests of the environment as a whole.

** In this latter example, the decision whether to lower the blinds is made not by the security system but by the window intelligent objects. The window system, in other words, is aware that people living in the house are sometimes given to gazing at the scenery outside. It also knows its own place, like any good servant. Before it decides to close the blinds, it gets information from the security system, via the HFDS, as to whether anyone is in a position to be looking out the window.

The information gathered by the home security system has application to systems for turning lights on and off, for directing the flow from air conditioners, or for setting the sound field location of the audio system, and therefore is information that should be sent around through the HFDS.

In cases like the above, information broadcast throughout the HFDS under the heading, "position information, inhabitant," could be taken into consideration by any number of intelligent objects, depending on their own particular interest in this information. Information of less general interest, instead of being broadcast, can be handled in the following way. When an intelligent object is newly installed in the HFDS, it broadcasts a list of the information it needs. Other objects able to provide the requested information then add the new object to their mailing list. Whenever that information becomes available they send it around for reference by all designated intelligent objects. Deliberate queries can also be used when necessary. The HFDS, in other words, must be able to support many different communication patterns, including one-to-one, one-to-many, broadcast, and round robin, just as in an electronic mail system.

Realizing an HFDS will thus require a standard format for expressing qualities of the physical environment such as position, time, temperature, or brightness. Each device, moreover, will need to be aware of its own position. This is a major feature of an HFDS, that each device has the ability and knowledge needed to change the physical environment in which it exists, and that this knowledge is treated as general information for use by other devices as well.

An important point to note here is that the HFDS is an infrastructure aimed at realizing a new level of day-to-day comfort. It is not directly aimed at making possible each of a number of individual applications that might be thought of. People might well ask, for example, why it is necessary to introduce a large-scale system like an HFDS so that a night lamp can go on automatically when you get out of bed in the middle of the night. This, however, is seeing the issue in the wrong perspective. If that's all there were to it, the night lamp could simply be equipped with an infrared sensor. But when you start going beyond that, and have footlights go on in the hallway to the toilet, and then try to continue with further enhancements, you soon reach a stage where the piecemeal approach is no longer cost effective. Besides that, there are the problems mentioned earlier of interference among systems. Trying to make the necessary adjustments to overcome these in an ad hoc manner runs up the cost even further.

In an ordinary living environment, especially in the home, the next level of comfort cannot be achieved simply by tackling each problem (including some which by themselves are rather trivial) on an individual, localized basis. A general request for relief from the heat can be solved by installing individual pieces of equipment, and such equipment is already widely available. Only now we are faced with problems like air conditioning-itis. Achieving a more refined comfort may be possible with independent systems, but this approach faces the law of diminishing returns and is difficult for all but users with money to burn. Even such users will probably not enjoy having their ceilings plastered with sensors for all sorts of different systems.

It seems inconceivable that computers will be able to make their next round of contributions in non-professional arenas without the provision of an infrastructure like the HFDS.

6. STANDARDIZATION

The TRON Project is aimed at realization of the HFDS. The role of standardization in making possible proper HFDS operation cannot be overemphasized. The objects of standardization toward this end in the TRON Project are the interfaces that define a computerized environment at various layers.

An HFDS is a network in which there are hundreds, thousands, or even greater numbers of nodes. It is also an open-ended network, with nodes constantly being added, removed or replaced. In such a network it would be impossible to achieve the necessary cooperation among nodes without interface standardization.

Standardization in the TRON Project is not for the purpose of making everything the same. On the contrary, it is premised on diversity, and is aimed at establishing an infrastructure where diversity can have full play.

One feature of a computer, for example, is that it can be programmed to adapt to a wide spectrum of application needs. If, however, the hardware products do not provide the design latitude of a broad user interface as a "standard model," attempts to take advantage of that feature will require "special-order" models, whose limited demand will drive up their cost. This problem has been pointed out, for example, in the case of equipment for use by handicapped persons.

Trying to optimize functions among a number of different devices by means of software is impossible unless a minimum level of communication is maintained. Requiring in such a case that all the equipment be that of the same manufacturer does not help the cause of diversity.

Standardization in the TRON Project is for the sake of diversity, and to this end a number of deliberate policies and measures are being adopted. These include an open architecture, loose standardization of the BTRON user interface at the operation method level,[2] and TULS allowing redesign of an interface while maintaining compatibility.[3]

7. INFORMATION SCIENCE AS SOCIAL SCIENCE

When standardization is thought about in this context, the attitude of those who propose standards without having a vision of future society is seen to be irresponsible and even dangerous. This is because fundamentally, standardization projects are not simply influenced by movements in society today, but will themselves have a great influence on the computerized society of tomorrow.

When a standardization effort is actually undertaken, a very large number of problems appear. These are not just technological problems, but include many societal problems as well. This matter itself is a social phenomenon; looked at historically, however, international organizations for standardization have traditionally played an important leadership role. More recently, however, their influence has weakened to where their role is largely one of putting their stamp on so-called de facto standards.

Perhaps this is why standardization is now often viewed as unrelated to the essence of science and technology. This is a big mistake, however. Given the huge changes in society being wrought by computers, the involvement of information science with society is a vital theme that cannot be ignored, and standardization issues are representative of this involvement.

In fact, information science should think about starting a research area on "the qualities required of specifications in order to become accepted by society." It is quite conceivable, after all, that a scientific approach will be effective in determining the qualities required of a given kind of information (specification).

Looking at the example of user interface design, many of the functions that have come into being with the introduction of computers differ largely from those of traditional machines and tools based on physical actions. For this reason, physical metaphors with which users are familiar are of only limited effectiveness in making the user interface easier to use. Before designing individual user interfaces, a world model for a series of user interfaces — in other words, a new metaphor — must first be designed.

Unless there is an objective method for evaluating the world model in the background of the metaphor, user interface design will remain in the realm of the senses, and more often than not will end up as design in the sense of art. The result that emerges is likely to lack consistency from beginning to end; what's more, when the attempt is made to expand the design motif over an entire series, it will soon wear thin, especially as other designers besides the original one get into the act. The problem with such an idea is that it lacks the universality required of a new metaphor.

What are needed, then, are first of all standards on which to build an information culture, and then a new design perspective in which the world model itself is evaluated and studied as information — so-called metadesign.

Over the course of information science up to now, such an approach has never been attempted in a deliberate form. As we move toward the computerized society, however, we can expect the social science aspect of information science, as well as metadesign, to become vitally important research fields.

8. APPLICATION PROJECTS

For the sake of top-down development in awareness of social issues, a number of TRON-related application projects have been started, as attempts to reveal a future image of computer use in society. These projects incorporate the kinds of approaches to the future computerized society that have been touched on above, and are seeking to give actual substance to the environments of the future. Because they are building future environments in the present, the facilities of necessity include equipment still under development, products not yet available commercially, and special-order items, not all of which will be on sale immediately. The pilot house introduced below, for example, is costing more than a billion yen to build. In that sense, these projects in their present form can be seen as actual-size simulators of the real future environment.

One of these application projects is a computerized home, planned and being built by the TRON Intelligent House Study Group. Participating in this project are a wide range of firms involved in building, home equipment, furniture and other related fields. The first fruits of their research, a completed pilot house, will be opened to the public at the end of 1989.

Exterior view of TRON-concept Intelligent House
The glass-roofed area includes a semi-open, combination kitchen-patio. Computer-controlled glass panels open and close automatically with changes in the environment. The panels adjust to the precise angle to let in warmth, light and breezes, or to shut out rain, wind, cold, dust and noise. When fully closed, the room becomes a large sunroom.

Glass-enclosed area (including kitchen-patio) as viewed from second-story terrace

*Computer graphics image of the TRON-concept Intelligent Building, where technology and nature go hand in hand
The walls rise in a graceful spiral, wrapping around a daringly open interior. The rounded contours gently embrace the people
who work in the building; strategic use of natural stone and wood add to the feeling of harmony with the outdoors.*

Another project is being undertaken by the TRON Intelligent Building Study Group, consisting of construction firms as well as computer, electrical and communications companies. Work on the first computerized building is expected to begin in two or three years.

On an even more ambitious scale, the Chiba Computer City project will soon see the startup of a TRON-concept city complex on approximately 100 hectares of land. It will be the first project anywhere in the world to extend computer control to the whole range of civic functions. Development work, which is being carried out jointly by local governmental agencies, organizations and corporations from many areas, is expected to last into the next century, with a total investment of $700 million or so.

Still another project is that being undertaken by the TRON Intelligent Automobile Research Committee. Car makers are teaming up with electronics firms to study a new type of automobile. It is planned to apply the research findings to the traffic system in the Chiba Computer City.

Mockup of site where Chiba Computer City is to be built, and building skyline
Making the most of the natural landscape, including canals, the city will offer a rich variety of surroundings.

At the center of the TRON Project is the TRON Association, whose membership now numbers over 132 companies and organizations. These include Nippon Telegraph and Telephone, NTT Data Communications Systems and other telecommunications firms; major computer and electronics manufacturers like Oki Electric, Toshiba, NEC, Hitachi, Fujitsu, Matsushita Electric Industrial, and Mitsubishi Electric; and a growing number of overseas-based corporations, including IBM Japan, Intel Japan, Olivetti Systems Technology, Yokogawa Hewlett-Packard, Motorola, and recently Apple Computer Japan.

The basically society-oriented nature of the TRON Project makes it essential that large numbers of application projects like the above be carried on. Ideally, the ongoing results of these projects can be fed back into the basic TRON architecture, as well as into the ITRON, BTRON, CTRON, and TRON CHIP subprojects. This is the best way for a project like TRON to proceed,making the startup of these application projects extremely significant.

REFERENCES

[1]   K. Sakamura, "The Objectives of the TRON Project," TRON Project 1987 (Proc. of the Third TRON Project Symposium), Springer Verlag (1987), pp. 3-16.

[2]   K. Sakamura, "BTRON Human-Machine Interface," TRON Project 1987 (Proc. of the Third TRON Project Symposium), Springer Verlag (1987), pp. 83-96.

[3]   K. Sakamura, "TULS: TRON Universal Language System," TRON Project 1988 (Proc. of the Fifth TRON Project Symposium), Springer Verlag (1988), pp. 3-18.

Ken Sakamura is currently an associate professor at the Department of Information Science, University of Tokyo. He holds a Ph.D. in Electrical Engineering. Being a computer architect, he has been the leader of the TRON project, which he started in order to build a new computer system architecture for the 1990s, since 1984. His promotion of the TRON architecture now extends to architecture of buildings and furniture. He serves on the editorial board of the Institute of Electrical and Electronics Engineers (IEEE) MICRO magazine and chairs the project promotion committee of the TRON Association. He is a member of the Japan Information Processing Society; the Institute of Electronics, Information and Communication Engineers; ACM; and a senior member of IEEE. He has received best paper awards from IEICE twice, from JIPS, an IEEE best annual article award, and other awards from Japanese and overseas organizations.

Dr. Sakamura may be contacted at the Department of Information Science, Faculty of Science, University of Tokyo, 7-3-1 Hongo, Bunkyo-ku, Tokyo, Japan.

Chapter 1: ITRON

MR3210 Based on ITRON2 Specification Realtime OS

Hideo Tsubota, Osamu Yamamoto, Toru Shimizu, and Kazunori Saitoh
Mitsubishi Electric Corporation

ABSTRACT

M32 (G_{MICRO}) series microprocessors, such as M32/100, M32/200 and M32/300, will be the first commercial 32bit microprocessors based on the TRON specification MPU. MR3210 is a realtime operating system (OS) for these microprocessors based on the ITRON2 specification. The MR3210 makes up a series of realtime OS's with MR3200, which is based on the micro-ITRON specification. Comparing the MR3210 with the MR3200, the MR3210 has better functionality and reliability with some overhead of the code size and the execution time. The MR3210 has a file system called MR3210F, which is based on the ITRON/FILE specification. The ITRON/FILE specification is a subset of the BTRON specification file system.

This paper describes design and implementation of the MR3210, especially implementation techniques for the TRON specification microprocessors. This paper also describes evaluation results of the performance.

Keywords: Real-time operating system, ITRON specification, ITRON2 specification, micro-ITRON specification, TRON specification MPU

1. INTRODUCTION

ITRON operating system (OS) specification has been changed as shown in Fig.1.1, reflecting the evolution of the microprocessor (MPU) technology. First, ITRON1 specification was designed for 16bit MPU's. Then the study of ITRON2 specification was started for 32bit MPU's, because the ITRON1 specification was a little poor to make use of valuable functions of 32bit MPU's. In parallel with ITRON2 design, the study of micro-ITRON specification was started for single chip MPU's with on-chip ROM and RAM. The micro-ITRON specification is for critical realtime embedded systems, and became a slimmed version of the ITRON2 specification.

We developed MR7700 and MR3200 based on the micro-ITRON specification. The MR7700 is for 16bit single chip microcontrollers of MELPS7700 series, and the MR3200 is for 32bit MPU's of M32 (G_{MICRO}) family. They are aimed at the use in critical realtime embedded systems.

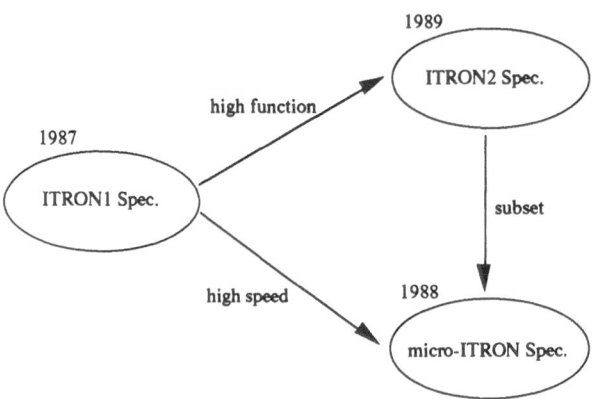

Fig. 1.1 ITRON Specification Series

MR3210, we have recently developed, is an advanced version of the MR3200. The MR3210 is based on the ITRON2 specification, and runs on the M32 family MPU's. Comparing the MR3210 with the MR3200, the MR3210 has better functionality and reliability with some overhead of the code size and the execution time. The MR3210 has a file system called MR3210F, which is based on the ITRON/FILE specification file system. The ITRON/FILE specification is a subset of BTRON specification file system.

This paper describes design and implementation of the MR3210, especially implementation techniques for the TRON specification MPU's. This paper also describes evaluation results of the performance.

2. ITRON2 SPECIFICATION

The ITRON2 specification is a revised version of the ITRON1 specification. Features of the ITRON2 specification are described in this section.

2.1 TASK AND OBJECT MANAGEMENT

In the ITRON2 specification, task execution is scheduled by 272 level priority based queues. Each task is assigned a priority number from -16 to 255 corresponding to the priority levels. Negative priority numbers and priority zero are reserved for system tasks.

A task is thought as object in the ITRON2 specification. A semaphore and a mailbox are also regarded as object. An object is assigned an identification (ID) number of 32bit word. Based on the ID number, object access is managed. A system object that has negative ID number can do access to any object. But positive ID number object used for user object can't do access the negative ID number objects.

Table 2.1 Object Access Management

		Object	
		ID<0	ID>0
Task	ID<0	○	○
	ID>0	✕	○

○ : enable to access
✕ : disable to access

2.2 ALLOCATION OF THE ADDRESS SPACE

TRON specification MPU is based on the memory address space of 4 rings. Each ring has its own stack pointer, and an additional stack pointer is given for interrupt handlers. Therefore the TRON specification based MPU's have 5 stack pointers in total. Table 2.2 shows the allocation of the 4 rings and usage of the 5 stack pointers in the ITRON2 specification.

Table 2.2 Allocation of the Address Space

	Interrupt Handler	OS	Extended SVC Handler	System Task	Task
Ring	0	0	0	1	3
Stack	SPI	SP0	SP0	SP1	SP3

2.3 CHARACTERISTIC FEATURES

Fig. 2.1 shows relationship of the ITRON1, the ITRON2 and the micro-ITRON specification. The ITRON2 specification has some additional functions comparing with the ITRON1 specification. A rendezvous mechanism called port is supplemented for synchronization and communication. A local memory pool and a message buffer are introduced to make use of the MMU functions of MPU's. Some new exception handling functions are added: exception handlers can be defined for interrupt handlers and for user defined system calls independently, an exception handler can be activated by system call, and activation of an exception handler can be suppressed. Debugging facilities are provided for debugger task implementation.

3. MR3210 IMPLEMENTATION

MR3210 is a realtime OS based on the ITRON2 specification. The MR3210 runs on M32(G_{MICRO}) series MPU's, M32/100, M32/200 and M32/300. Implementation techniques of the MR3210 are described in this section.

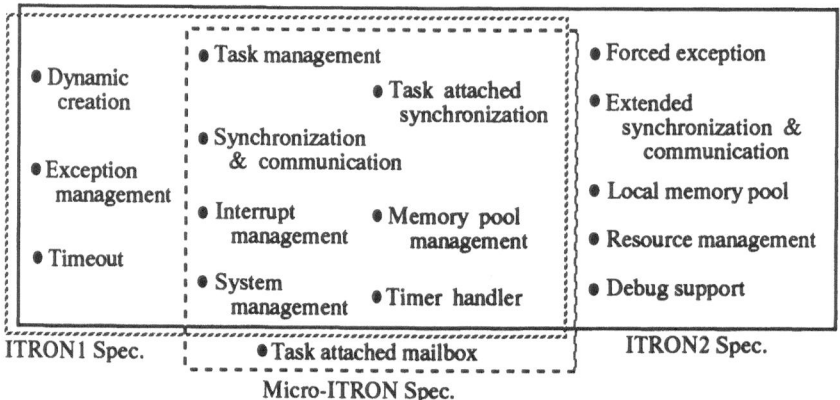

Fig. 2.1 Relationship of ITRON1, ITRON2 and Micro-ITRON Specification

3.1 MR3210 SPECIFICATION

MR3210 is based on the ITRON2 specification as shown in Fig. 3.1. In this figure, basic functions are equivalent to those of the ITRON1 specification, and extended functions and system operation functions are newly introduced into the ITRON2 specification. MR3210 supports all the functions of the ITRON2 specification, except local memory pool functions which use MMU functions of the MPU. Serial I/O functions (for M5L8251) and file system functions for ITRON/FILE specification are provided as utilities.

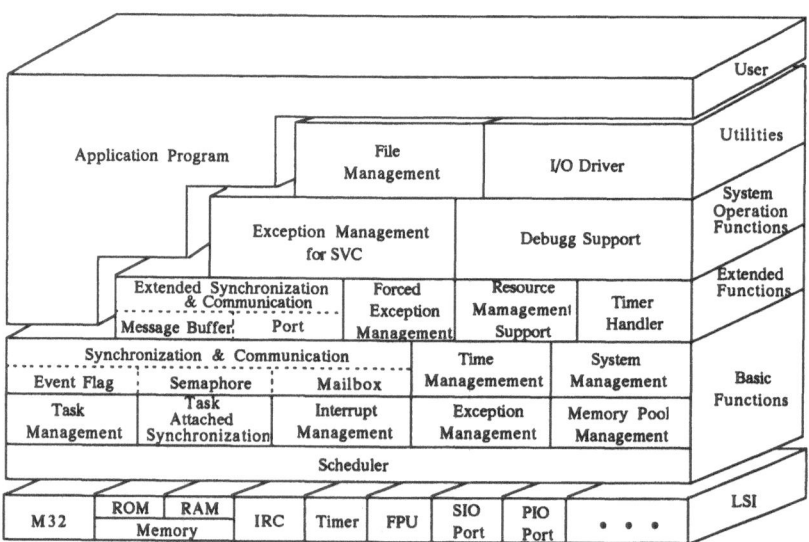

Fig. 3.1 MR3210 Specification

3.2 OS SUPPORT INSTRUCTIONS

The MR3210 was implemented by OS support instructions of the TRON specification MPU's, as follows:

(a) Context switching mechanisms
    · Hardware context block
    · Save/restore the context block (LDCTX, STCTX)
    · Save/restore the values of multiple registers (LDM,STM)
are used for high speed switching of the running task.

(b) Queue manipulation instructions
    · Insert/delete a member into/from a queue (QINS,QDEL)
are used in the implementation of the task queue waiting for some events.

(c) Bit manipulation instructions
    * Single bit set/clear instructions (BSET,BCLR)
    * Bit search instruction (BVSCH)
are effective to implement a priority based queue of ready tasks.

(d) DI (Delayed Interrupt) mechanisms
  DI is a hardware mechanism to activate some specified routine, called DI handler, when all the interrupt handling operations complete. In the implementation of the MR3210, the task dispatcher is registered as the DI handler in order to activate the task waiting for the interrupt.

3.3 OS DATA STRUCTURES

(a) Task Context Block
Task context block is a data structure for storing context block and register values of a task as shown in Fig.3.2. It is prepared for resuming the task and pointed by context block base register (CTXBB). Contents of the context block are saved or restored by the task dispatcher. The task control block (TCB) structure is designed based on the hardware context block. The CPU context switching mechanisms are effective to implement the TCB.

(b) Ready Queue
Ready queue (RDQ) is a data structure for managing tasks in ready state. The RDQ is searched for a task with the highest priority every time when the task dispatcher is called. In the implementation, the RDQ is an array of double linked queues of TCB's as shown in Fig. 3.3. The double linked queues can be manipulated by the queue instructions effectively.

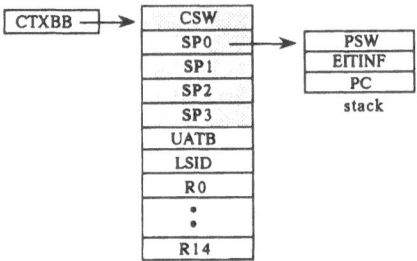

Fig.3.2 Hardware Context Block

In addition to the double linked queues, a block of bits are used to find the target task quickly. Each bit of the bit block is a status flag of the corresponding queue. If the bit is '1', the queue is not empty, and if the bit is '0', the queue is empty. So searching the bit block for '1' in order gives the number of the queue with highest priority and not empty. The top TCB of the queue is of the target task. The bit manipulation instructions are effective to set/reset/search the bit block.

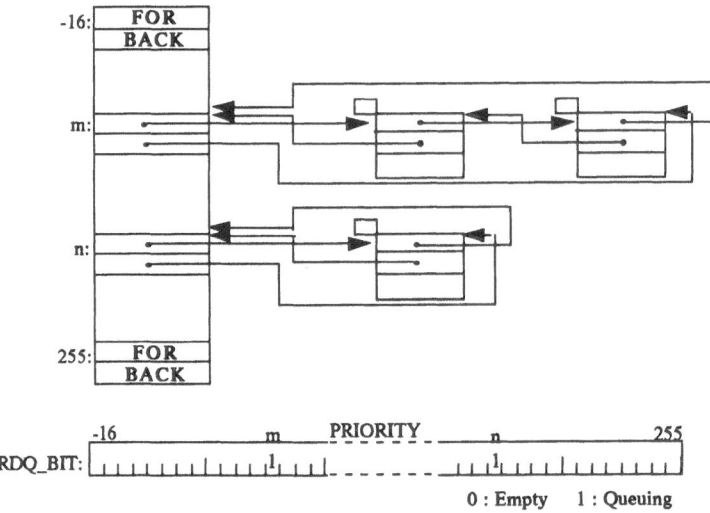

Fig.3.3 Ready Queue Structure

3.4 OS MECHANISM

The MR3210 system configuration is shown in Fig.3.4.

(a) System Call Interface

In the MR3210, system calls are invoked by using a trap instruction TRAPA and OS is executed in ring 0. Function code is passed by a register.

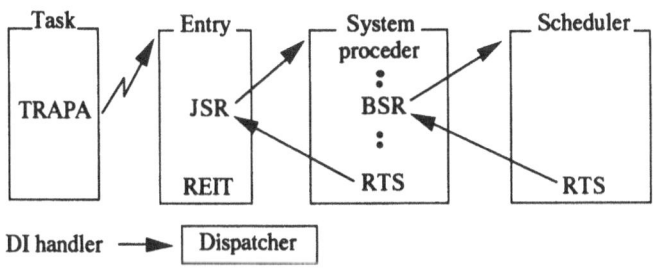

Fig.3.4 MR3210 System Configuration

(b) Task Scheduler

The task scheduler has two kinds of functions. One is to manipulate the RDQ depend on the changing of the task status. The other is to find out the highest priority task in RDQ. Fig.3.5 shows the example of queue manipulation operation with using the TRON based queue instruction.

```
; delete from RDQ                          ; insert into RDQ
     QDEL @@(R1,BACK), @(R1,FOR)              MOV @(R1,TSK_PRI), R2
; request of task dispatcher                  QINS @(R1,FOR), @(RDQ_TBL,R2*8)
     LDC  #14, @DI                        ; request of task dispatcher
; if empty on its priority                    LDC  #14, @DI
     MOV  @(R1,TSK_PRI), R2               ; if new entry on its priority
     BCLR R2, @RDQ_BIT                        BSET R2, @RDQ_BIT
(a) Dequeue Task from RDQ                   (b) Enqueue Task into RDQ
```

Fig. 3.5 Task scheduling

In order to show the effect of the queue instruction, Fig. 3.6 shows the case of using the TRON based queue instruction and using normal instruction. The rate of performance using the TRON based instruction was 18 : 26 (1 instruction executing with 2 machine cycles). And the code size was 1 : 3.

About the finding out the highest priority in the RDQ, Fig. 3.7 shows the comparison of operation using BVSCH instruction and normal instruction. The BVSCH instruction makes it possible to reduce OS's response time and shorter interrupt masking time to the rate of 62:5712. The reason is thought as maximum clock cycle of using BVSCH instruction is shorter than using normal instruction .

```
QINS @(R1,FOR), @(RDQ_TBL,R2*8)          MOV  @(RDQ_TBL+4,R2*8), Rn
                                          MOV  R1, @(RDQ_TBL+4,R2*8)
                                          MOVA @(RDQ_TBL,R2*8), @(R1,FOR)
                                          MOV  Rn, @(R1,BACK)
                                          MOV  R1, @(Rn,FOR)
```

machine cycle = 18   **machine cycle = 26**

code size = 12 bytes   **code size = 36 bytes**

(a)With Using Queue Instruction   (b)With Using Normal Instruction

Fig. 3.6 Queue Manipulation

```
                                          MOV    #0, R2
MOVA @RDQ_BIT, R0                   check: MOVA  @(RDQ_TBL,R2), R0
MOV   #0, R1                               CMP   @(RDQ_TBL,R2), R0
MOV   #272, R2                             BNE   found
BVSCH/F/1                                  ACB   #8,R2,#272*8,check
                                   found:          :
```

machine cycle = 32 + (priority/32)*4   **machine cycle = 21 * priority**

maximum machine cycle = 62   **maximum machine cycle = 5712**

(a)With Using BVSCH Instruction   (b)With Normal Instruction

Fig. 3.7 Manipulation of Finding Out the Highest Priority in RDQ

(c) Dispatcher

Task dispatcher is implemented by a DI handler, and activates the task with the highest priority in the RDQ. The dispatching operations are as follows.

Store contents of the hardware context block in the running task's TCB (STCTX).
Store contents of registers in the running task's TCB (STM).
Load the hardware context block address of the new task's to CTXBB (LDC).
Load the hardware context block with contents of the new task's TCB (LDCTX).
Load registers with contents of the new task's TCB (LDM).

Currently context block is not supported perfectly as mentioned earlier, so LDM and STM instruction must be executed explicitly. When context block is fully supported, these will be absorbed in LDCTX and STCTX instruction.

(d) Interrupt Handling Algorithm

When multiple interrupts occur, the MR3210 should complete handling of the interrupts before calling dispatcher. The DI is an effective mechanism to implement the interrupt handling algorithm. Fig. 3.8 shows an example of the multiple interrupt handling.

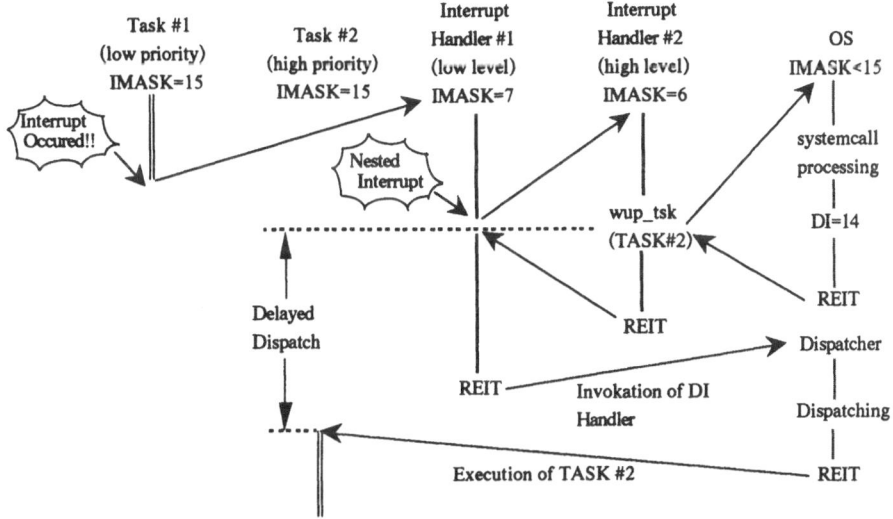

Fig. 3.8 Interrupt Handling by DI Mechanism

3.5 I/O DRIVER DESIGN GUIDELINE

In general, realtime OS users are interested in developing device drivers for peripheral devices such as a serial port, a parallel port, a disk and so on. MR series OS's standardize the development manner of the device drivers. The manner is called request I/O (RIO), and defines a standard system call 'req_io' between device drivers and user application programs. Device drivers following the RIO are compatible on MR series OS's.

(a) Synchronous and Asynchronous I/O Methods

There are 2 methods to perform I/O operations in general, a synchronous method and an asynchronous method. We adopted the asynchronous method for the RIO. One reason is that asynchronous method is commonly used in realtime application fields because it can perform other operations while waiting for the I/O completion. Another reason is that synchronous I/O method can be realized by the asynchronous method as shown in Fig.3.9.

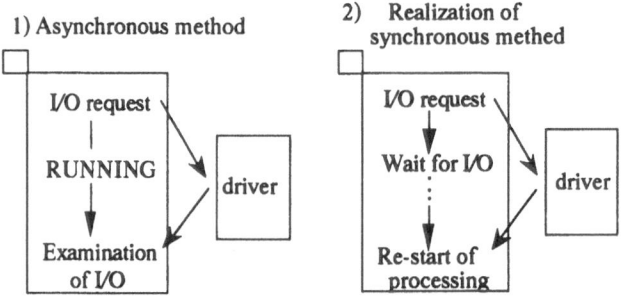

Fig. 3.9 Synchronous and Asynchronous I/O Methods

(b) Device Driver Configuration

A device driver consists of 3 parts, I/O handler, I/O task and interrupt handler as shown in Fig. 3.10. The I/O handler checks parameter of an I/O request and sends it to the I/O task via a mailbox. The I/O task performs the requested I/O operations in cooperation with the interrupt handler.

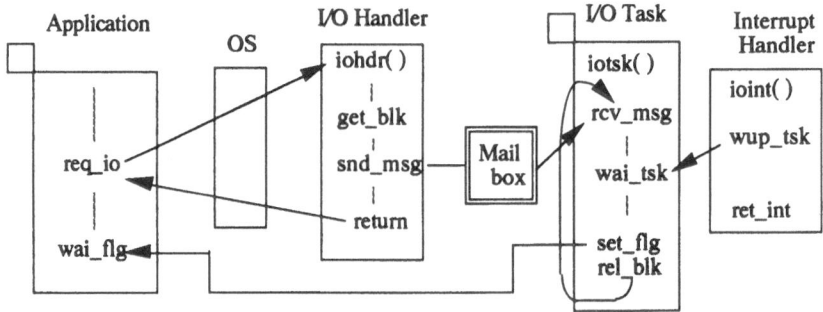

Fig. 3.10 Configuration of the Device Driver

RIO prescribes system calls and operations in device drivers. Req_io system call is used to request I/O operations to the device. Parameters of the req_io are shown in Fig. 3.11. I/O handler receives an I/O request through the req_io interface and copies its parameters into the message area secured by get_blk system call. The message is queued in a mailbox assigned to each device. I/O task receives the message from the mailbox, activates the I/O device operation, and waits for the completion. The interrupt handler is signaled by the device when I/O is completed and wakes up the I/O task. The I/O task informs the application task of the I/O completion by setting an eventflag. The application task can recognize the I/O completion by checking the eventflag.

[Calling Convention]
    req_io (UW iodvn, T_RQIO *pk_rqio) ;

[Parameter Packect]

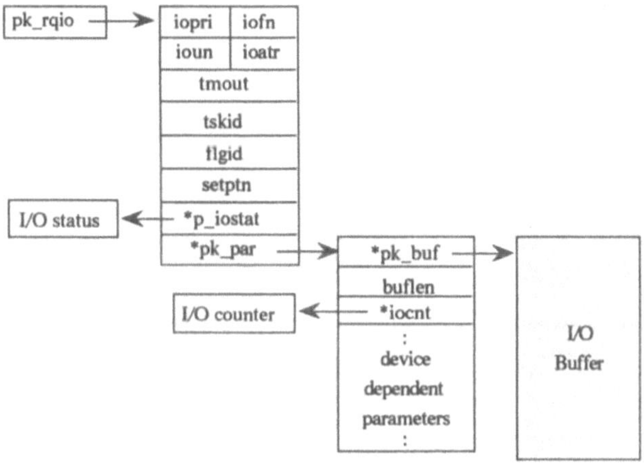

Fig. 3.11 Calling Convention of Req_io

4. THE MR3200 AND THE MR3210

The MR3210 is regarded as an advanced version of the MR3200, which we have already developed based on the micro-ITRON specification. The MR3210 and the MR3200 make up a series of realtime operating systems for the M32 (G_{MICRO}) series MPU's. The both operating systems run on any of the M32 series MPU's, but each of them is optimized according to its own application field.

The MR3200 is an OS for embedded controllers in robots and sensor systems. In order to control robots or get data from sensors, interrupt masking time should be less than 20 micro seconds and task switching time should be less than 30 micro seconds. OS code size and data size should be small, as they influence the total memory size and the execution speed. The MR3200 satisfies the requirements. The interrupt masking time is shorter than 9 micro seconds and a task is waken up by interrupt handler in 18 micro seconds. The size of the memory used by the OS varies 2K byte to 11.6K byte with the OS configuration.

The MR3210 is an OS for systems with human interface. The human interface requires more functionality, such as run-time management of the resource, and more reliability in the operation. The MR3210 satisfies the requirements as described in the previous sections. The relationship of the MR32xx series OS's and their application fields is shown in Fig. 4.1.

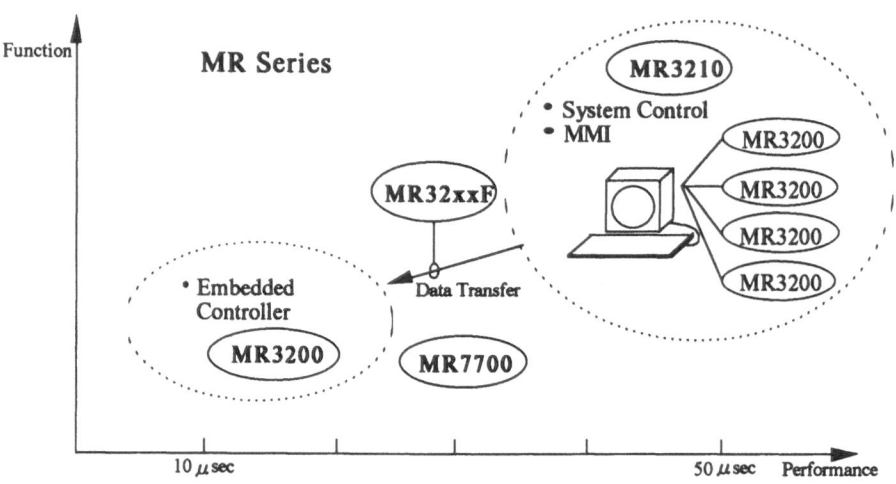

Fig. 4.1 Relationship between MR32xx Operating Systems and Application Fields

5. EVALUATION OF THE MR3210

5.1 MEMORY SIZE

Table 5.1 shows the code size of the MR3210 and the MR3200. The MR3210 is 4 to 20 times larger than the MR3200, as it has more system calls and rich functionality.

Table 5.1 Code Size of the MR3210 and the MR3200

	MR3210	MR3200
OS Spec.	ITRON2 Spec.	micro-ITRON Spec.
number of system calls	131	53
code size	about 40KB	2K ～ 11.6KB

Table 5.2 shows the data size of the MR3210 and the MR3200. The MR3210 requires 3 times larger data area than MR3200, to support dynamic object management, various exception handlers, etc.

Table 5.2 Data Size of the MR3210 and the MR3200

Object	Table Size (bytes)	
	MR3210	MR3200
Task	300+FPU+stack	29+72+stack
Eventflag	48	13
Semaphore	48	10
Mailbox	48	20+buffer
Memory Pool	88+pool	14+pool
Message Buffer	68+buffer	-
Port	56	-

5.2 PERFORMANCE

Table 5.3 is a table of the time for waking up a task by the MR3210 and the MR3200. It is measured by a single board computer of the M32/100 (20MHz,No-Wait). The MR3210 takes 3 times longer time than MR3200 to wakeup a task, as it performs checking of the exception occurrence before dispatching and using TRAP interface to system calls.

Table 5.3 Task Wake-up Time of the MR3210 and the MR3200

	MR3210	MR3200
Wakeup by wup_tsk	57 micro sec.	18 micro sec.
Wakeup by sig_sem	65 micro sec.	21 micro sec.

6. CONCLUSIONS

TRON specification MPU provides effective functions for the implementation of operating systems based on the ITRON specification. Making use of these functions, we have developed the MR3210 based on the ITRON2 specification and the MR3200 based on the micro-ITRON specification. They are tuned to their own application fields, and achieve good performance in their domain.

The authors wish to acknowledge Dr. Ken Sakamura for his helpful discussions.

REFERENCES

[1] O. Yamamoto, H. Tsubota, K. Saitoh "ITRON specification OS and TRON specification chip", TRON PROJECT MONTHLY 1989.9

[2] O. Yamamoto, K. Nakata, H. Tsubota, K. Saitoh "Performance Evaluation of MR3200 : A Realtime Operating System based on the MICRO-ITRON Specification", Proc. of TRON Technical Conference, Vol.2,No.2,pp.39-50,1989(in Japanese)

[3] H.Tsubota, K. Nakata, K. Saitoh "Implementation of MICRO-ITRON Specification on G_{MICRO} series 32 bit Microprocessors", SIGMIC 56-4 1989.6.27(in Japanese)

[4] Y.Kisuki, H.Tsubota, K.Saitoh "Implementation of MR3200F based on ITRON/FILE Specification", Proc. of TRON Technical Conference, Vol.2,No.3,pp.43-51,1989(in Japanese)

[5] K. Nakata, H. Tsubota, T. Shimizu, K.Saitoh, T. Enomoto "MR7700 : Implementation of MICRO-ITRON Specification on 16-Bit Single-Chip Microcontroller,TRON PROJECT 1988, Proc. of the Fifth TRON Project Symposium, Springer-Verlag, pp.55-66

Hideo Tsubota : He received his B.S. degree, in information technology, from Shizuoka University, Shizuoka, Japan, in 1983. He joined Mitsubishi Electric Corporation in 1983. Since then, he has been engaged in research and development of basic software for microprocessors at LSI Reasearch and Development Laboratory.

Osamu Yamamoto : He received his B.S. degree, in information technology, from Kyushu University, Fukuoka, Japan, in 1983. He joined Mitsubishi Electric Corporation in 1986. Since then, he has been engaged in research and development of basic software for microprocessors at LSI Reasearch and Development Laboratory.

Toru Shimizu : He received his B.S., M.S. and Ph.D. degrees, both in computer science, from University of Tokyo,Tokyo, Japan, in 1981, 1983, and 1986, respectively. He joined Mitsubishi Electric Corporation in 1986. Since then, he has been engaged in the research of VLSI microprocessor architecture and basic software for the microprocessor at LSI Research and Development Laboratory. Dr. Shimizu is a member of ACM, IEEE, the Institute of Electronics, Information and Communication Engineers of Japan, and Information Processing Society of Japan.

Kazunori Saitoh : He received his B.S. and M.S. degrees, both in electrical engineering, from Waseda University, Tokyo, Japan, in 1975 and 1977, respectively. He received Ph.D degree in electrical engineering in 1989, from Osaka University, Osaka, Japan. He joined Mitsubishi Electric Corporation in 1977. From 1977 to 1980, he was engaged in the development of CAD and electron beam lithography technology at the VLSI Cooperative Laboratory. From 1980, he has been engaged in research and development of VLSI process technologies and basic software for microprocessors at LSI Research and Development Laboratory.

Above authors may reached at : LSI R&D Laboratory, Mitsubishi Electric Corporation, 4-1 Mizuhara, Itami, Hyogo, 664, Japan.

REALOS/F32: Implementation of ITRON2 Specification on GMICRO F32

Akira Shimohara, Tsutomu Minohara, Kenji Kudou, and Haruyasu Ito
Fujitu Limited

ABSTRACT

REALOS/F32 is the realtime operating system based on ITRON2 specification for the GMICRO F32 series. GMICRO F32 is a microprocessor family based on the TRON architecture. Optimizing the ITRON2 specification to a TRON architecture processor includes adequate usage of Delayed Interrupt (DI) and Delayed Context Trap (DCT) mechanisms and other TRON architecture chip features such as queue manipulation instructions. Such optimization enables the REALOS/F32 to offer both the highest performance and abundant functions.

Keywords: ITRON, Delayed Interrupt (DI), Delayed Context Trap (DCT), Delayed System Call Execution (DSE), Coprocessor Dispatching Mechanism (CDM)

1. INTRODUCTION

The REALOS series is the realtime operating system product family of FUJITSU for industrial embedded systems based on ITRON specification. REALOS/286 [1] is for the 80286, based on ITRON1 specification [3], and REALOS/97 [2] is for the MB89700 series, which is a FUJITSU original single-chip microcontroller, based on μITRON specification [4]. The next product, REALOS/F32 will be available soon. It is for the GMICRO F32 series [6] [7], which is a microprocessor based on the TRON architecture. REALOS/F32 is based on ITRON2 specification [5].

Processors based on the TRON architecture have advantages when implementing operating systems, especially TRON specific operating systems, ITRON, BTRON and CTRON. ITRON2 is the second version of the ITRON specification, adapted to 32 bit high performance microprocessors. The harmony of the TRON architecture processor and ITRON2 specific operating system enables both the highest performance and abundant functions. REALOS/F32 uses new technology adapted to the TRON total architecture, such as Delayed System call Execution (DSE) and Coprocessor Dispatching Mechanism (CDM) mainly for high speed response.

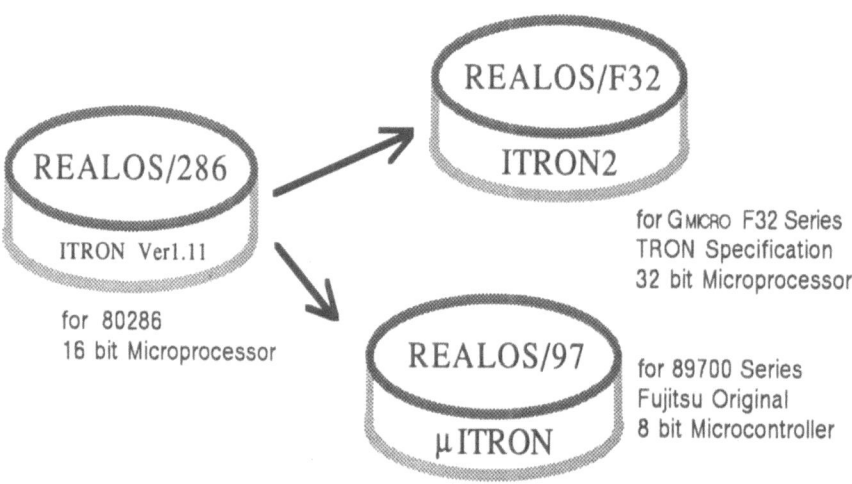

Fig. 1 REALOS Series

2. DESIGN CONCEPT

When designing REALOS/F32 there were two considerations in order to realize the best operating system for industrial embedded systems on high performance 32 bit microprocessors.   The first was prioritizing user demands and the second was making the best use of the total TRON architecture.

Achieving the highest performance will not satisfy most users' needs. User demands should be taken into consideration, but demands must be prioritized. At some technology levels, it is impossible to satisfy all user demands: high speed response, reliability, many functions and so forth. There are technological conflicts in all these user requests. User demands can be prioritized as follows:

1) Interrupt Response Time
2) Task Switch Time
3) Scheduling Time
4) Operating System Throughput
5) Abundant Function

For the realtime embedded system, response time comes first, especially interrupt response time. If an operating system can't start the user task or interrupt handler in time, it can't be used.

However, recent user application systems have become larger and more complex, so providing abundant functions and easy development of application system increases in importance. Technological innovation can solve the problem of demand conflicts. Careful consideration of the chip architecture reveals a suitable platform for implementation of ITRON2 specification. It enables us to improve the technology base.

3. ITRON2 Specification

REALOS/F32 is based on the ITRON2 specification. The ITRON2 specification is the second version of ITRON adapted to 32 bit high performance microprocessors. (See Fig. 2) ITRON2 has added some functions, such as rendezvous, message buffer, timer handler, etc. It has also enhanced definition of the specification for the compatibility of the products based on ITRON specification. For example, handler interfaces, which depend on processor architecture, are defined in ITRON2 specification because all 32 bit processor architectures are so similar to each other that definitions are required.

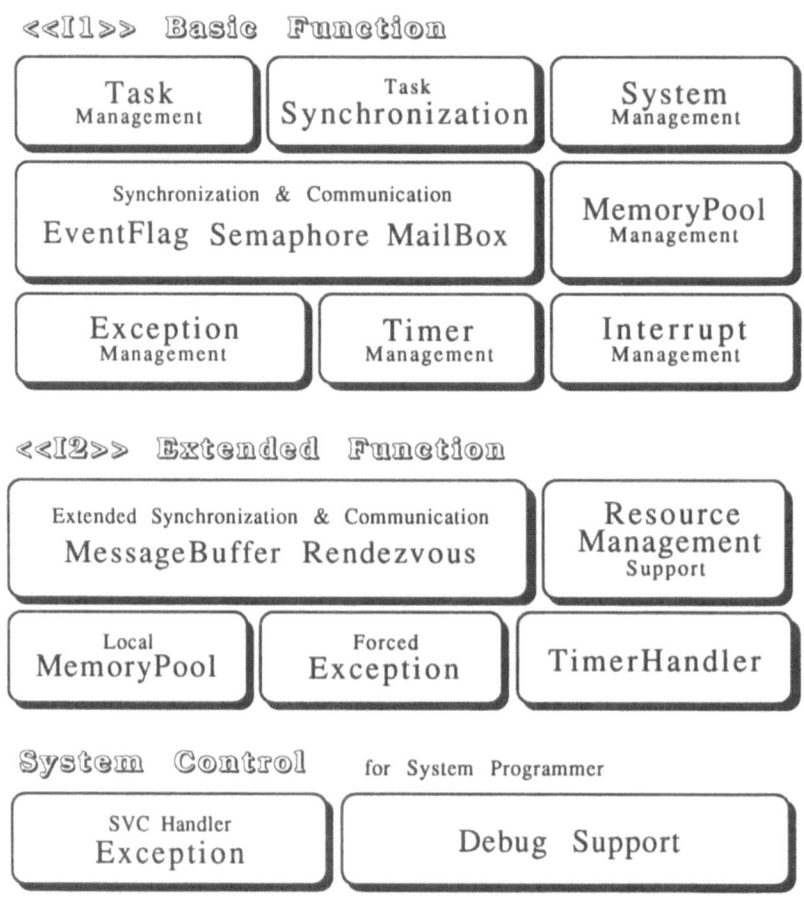

Fig. 2   ITRON2 System Configuration

4. TRON SPECIFICATION PROCESSOR

GMICRO F32 Series is the microprocessor family based on the TRON architecture. The chip architecture of TRON has been determined by analysis of application demands and optimized to execute operating systems, especially TRON specific OS's. REALOS/F32 makes the best of these features. It uses the task switch instruction for task switch handling, queue manipulation function for task scheduling, and so on. Delayed interrupt and delayed context trap are specific features of the TRON architecture and are essential mechanisms for the REALOS/F32 task/interrupt controlling algorithm. The following shows the outline of DI and DCT mechanisms. If you need more information, see [6],[7].

4.1 Delayed Interrupt (DI)

DI is a software interrupt, which can be requested by a program. If a program wants to request DI, it writes the request interrupt level in Delayed Interrupt Register (DIR). Between executing each instruction, the processor compares the DIR and IMASK (Interrupt Mask) in the PSW (Processor Status Word) register. If the request level of DI is higher than IMASK Level, the program is interrupted and the delayed interrupt handler is started. Fig. 3 shows this mechanism. The lower the number is the higher interrupt level.

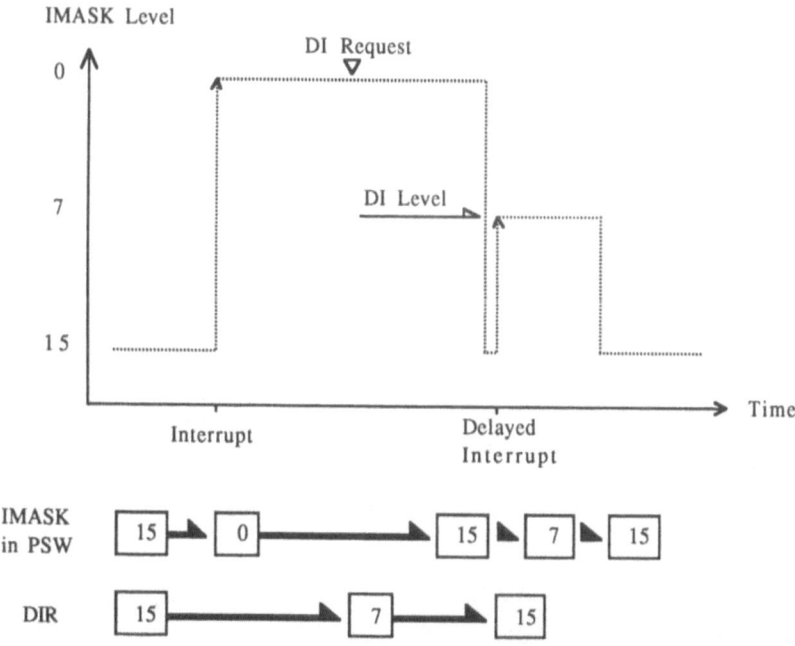

Fig. 3 Delayed Interrupt Mechanism

4.2 Delayed Context Trap (DCT)

DCT is another software interrupt, which occurs at context switching. DCT is requested by writing the request ring level in Context Status Word (CSW) register. If the current ring level is lower than the requested DCT level of CSW, then an interrupt takes place. In TRON architecture, there are ConTeXt control Blocks (CTXB) and each CTXB has the CSW data. So if CSW data is written on CTXB, DCT can occur when the operating system switches the current CTXB for the next task. In Fig. 4 this mechanism is illustrated. RING I is the highest ring level for interrupts, then RING 0, RING 1, RING 2 and RING 3, which is the lowest level.

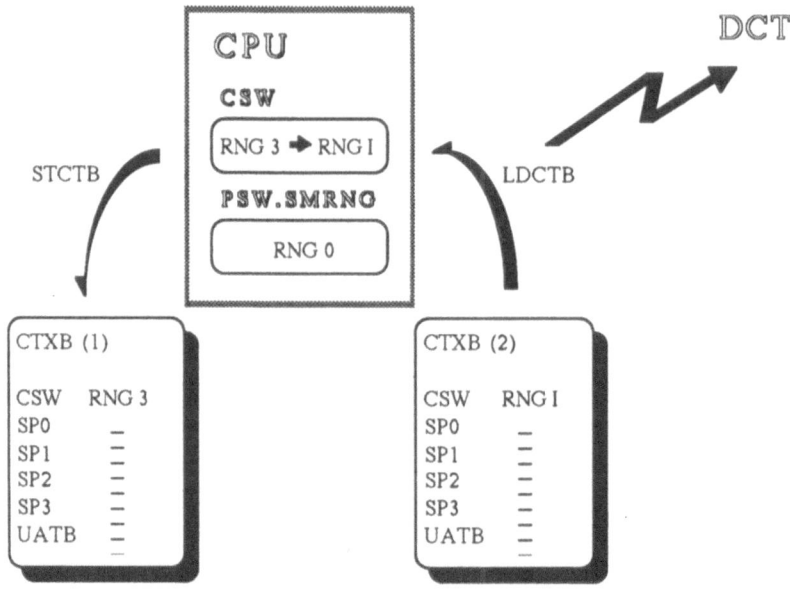

Fig. 4 Delayed Context Trap Mechanism

5. IMPLEMENTATION of ITRON2 on GMICRO

How were features of the GMICRO architecture used to implement ITRON2, provide good performance and yet remain practical in functionality? Not only were specific instructions of TRON architecture, such as queue instructions, used in programming system calls and functions, but new algorithms for executing system calls using Delayed Interrupt and Delayed Context Trap were developed.

5.1 Delayed System Call Execution (DSE)

To minimize the interrupt response time, interrupt latency times have been reduced. Interrupt latency minimization was implemented using the Delayed System call Execution (DSE) with algorithms which took advantage of the DI function of the TRON architecture. In addition DSE provides a mechanism for proper handling of interrupt latency. The primary reason an operating system would prohibit interrupts is to support exclusive data access. Since there is a possibility that an interrupt handler may access the same data of a normal read or write call an access problem exists between normal execution and interrupt handlers. This problem is solved by masking interrupts during data access.

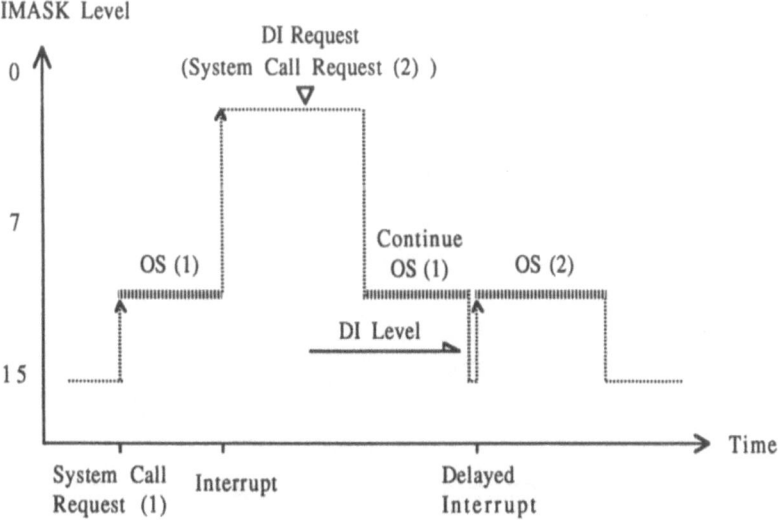

Fig. 5 Delayed System Call Excecution

The TRON architecture features a Delayed Interrupt mechanism. Using this function, the request of data access by interrupt handlers can be delayed and executed after completing the current access. Fig. 5 shows this mechanism, DSE. By using the interrupt masking method, the only way to shorten the interrupt mask time is to complete data access as fast as possible. So the functions called by an interrupt handler must be limited. Using the DSE mechanism, Interrupt mask time is not dependent on the data access time, so it is possible to realize both high performance and abundant functions.

5.2 Coprocessor Dispatching Mechanism (CDM)

Using Delayed Context Trap mechanism, context switching of the coprocessor can be independent of the dispatch time of a task which does not use the coprocessor. In a normal task dispatch process, DCT requests occur if it is necessary to dispatch coprocessor context. Fig. 6 shows the algorithm of CDM.

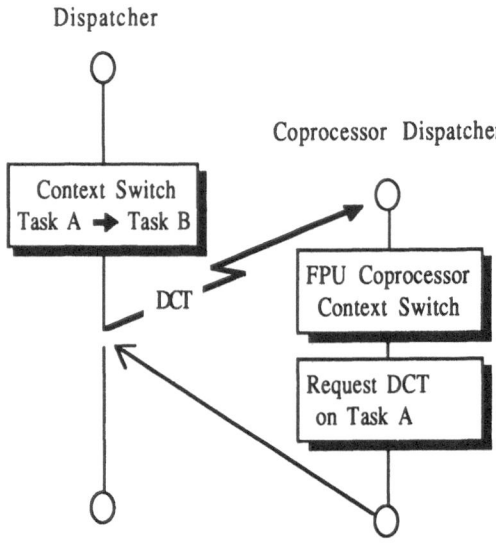

Fig. 6 Coprocessor Dispatching Mechanism

6. REALOS/F32 PRODUCTS

At the first release of REALOS/F32 <<I1>> level functions and System Generator will be available. The next phase, extension <<I2>> Level functions, File System and Task Debugger will be released. Now it is in the program test stage. Estimated performance of REALOS/F32 is: dispatch time is about 10ms and interrupt latency time about 5ms. The program object size is about 15k Bytes.

For the development of application system, REALOS/F32 provides a system generator to make it easier to construct an adequate user system. It is executed on multi-window display environment for the improvement of MMI. Fig. 7 illustrates the display image of System Generator.

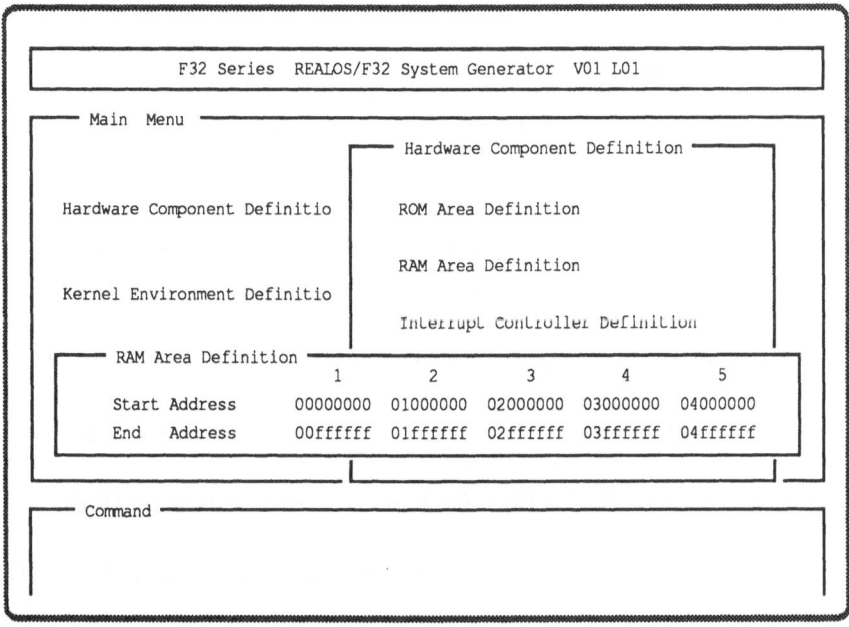

Fig. 7 System Generator Display

7. SUMMARY and CONCLUSION

REALOS/F32 has high speed response and rich functionality of a realtime operating system for industrial embedded systems. The TRON architecture make it possible to solve technological limitation. In the future, industrial realtime systems will be more complex and REALOS/F32 will make full use of its real time capabilities.

ACKNOWLEDGEMENTS

The authors would like to thank Dr. Ken Sakamura, professor of the University of Tokyo, for his helpful suggestions to design REALOS/F32. Also appreciated is the contribution of Richard Jensen, in Fujitsu Microelectronics Inc., who edited this paper.

REFERENCE

[1] A. Shimohara, "REALOS/286: An Implementation of ITRON/MMU on 80286," TRON Project 1987 (Proc. of the Third TRON Symposium), Springer-Verlag, 1987, p45-56

[2] K. Kudo, A. Honda, "An Implementation of µITRON on the F^2MC-8," Proc. of TRON Technical Conference, Vol.1, No.2, 1988, p59-68

[3] K. Sakamura, "ITRON Ver 1.11 Specification," TRON Association, 1987.

[4] K. Sakamura, "µITRON Specification," TRON Association, 1989.

[5] K. Sakamura, "ITRON2 Specification," TRON Association, 1989.

[6] "GMICRO F32/200 Operation Architecture Manual," FUJITSU LIMITED, 1988.

[7] "GMICRO F32/200 Programming Manual," FUJITSU LIMITED, 1988.

Akira Shimohara is an engineer of Software Design Section in Microprocessor Development Department of FUJITSU LIMITED. He joined FUJITSU after graduating from the University of Tokyo in 1984. He has been engaged in development of realtime operating system. He is a member of the Information Processing Society of Japan.

Tsutom Minohara is an engineer of Software Design Section in Microprocessor Development Department of FUJITSU LIMITED. He joined FUJITSU after graduating from Osaka University in 1984. He has been engaged in development of realtime operating system.

Kenji Kudou is a senior engineer of Software Design Section in Microprocessor Development Department of FUJITSU LIMITED. He joined FUJITSU after receiving a B.E. and M.E. degree from the Iwate University in 1976 and 1978. He has been engaged in development of operating system and support software for microprocessors. He is a member of the Information Processing Society of Japan.

Haruyasu Ito is a manager of Software Design Section in Microprocessor Development Department of FUJITSU LIMITED. He joined FUJITSU after graduating from Yokohama City University in 1971. He has been engaged in development of support software for microprocessors.

Above authors may be reached at: Microprocessor Development Department, MOS Division, Semiconductor Group, FUJITSU LIMITED. 1015, Kamikodanaka, Nakahara-ku, Kawasaki, 211 Japan

An Integrated Approach to HI8 System Development

David Wallace
Hitachi Europe Ltd.

ABSTRACT

An efficient multi-tasking Real Time Operating System such as that defined in the ITRON specification can provide a design engineer with a means of reducing the design cycle as well as improving the performance of code written for a particular application. It is important however to acknowledge the fact that, while a good Real Time Operating System can be a real asset to a designer, its inherent complexity can lead to additional problems during the development and debug phases.

In acknowledgement of this fact the European Design and Engineering Support Centre (EuroDESC) of the Electronic Components Division of Hitachi Europe Limited, based in Watford, England, together with Cambridge Beacon Limited of Cambridge, England have developed a fully integrated development environment for the ITRON Specification Operating System. The Hitachi Integrated Development Environment (HIDE) is available for HI8 and HI16 and is based on IBM-PC® embedded Evaluation Boards designed by EuroDESC for H16 and H8/532.

In order to demonstrate the effectiveness of the integrated approach to implementation of a Real Time Operating System on a microcontroller or microprocessor we will consider the specific application, within the automotive sector, of using the H8/500 Series together with HI8 (Hitachi's implementation of the µITRON specification for H8/532) to control the engine of a car. The implementation of the design will be examined at a high level with a view to design with and without HI8 thus giving an overview of the benefits of using a Real Time Operating System for the application. The design and development using HIDE will then be described and discussed.

The importance of HIDE together with the EuroDESC Evaluation Boards as a fully integrated ITRON Specification Development Environment cannot be over-emphasised. It offers potential users, who may not have previously encountered a Real Time Operating System, a simplified design and development path on a familiar host - the IBM-PC® - and as such can help to make implementations of the ITRON specification easily available to a much wider market. Additionally, HIDE is currently only implemented with regard to the ITRON and µITRON specifications but later versions could be helping in other areas of the TRON specification such as the BTRON concept.

Keywords: Real Time Operating System, ITRON Specification, µITRON Specification

INTRODUCTION

As part of its role in Europe, EuroDESC is deeply involved in supporting the introduction of the ITRON specification to European engineers. This is a complex task - a Real Time Operating System is a software component. This makes it distinct from packages such as Cross Assemblers which are software tools. A software tool will typically be very linear in its operation. A Cross Assembler will read in the designer's assembly level source code and convert it into object code (or, of course, produce a string of error messages!). A software component, such as HI8 (Hitachi's own implementation of the ITRON Specification), has considerable flexibility - it is a multi-tasking Real Time Operating System - and hence considerable complexity. An additional problem for EuroDESC to consider in the introduction of the ITRON concept is that the principle of using a Real Time Operating System in a microcontroller environment is still not widely understood. HI8 support is then necessary in two areas - firstly in educating European engineers so that they understand the benefit of HI8 (as a Real Time Operating System) from a practical engineering point of view and secondly to provide engineers with a logical and comprehensible interface into the initialisation of HI8 - the latter being provided by the Hitachi Integrated Development Environment (HIDE) which has been designed and developed jointly by EuroDESC and Cambridge Beacon Limited, an independent design consultancy of Cambridge, England.

HIDE is hosted on the IBM-PC® or compatibles and provides a completely original approach to the problem of designing with a sophisticated Real Time Operating System. Using the graphical capabitilies of the host, HIDE offers multiple windows and menus through which the user can configure the target HI8 or HI16 system and then execute the code on the EuroDESC H8/532 or H16 Evaluation Board.

This paper presents HIDE for the first time and, in order to make its purpose and function clearer, shows its usage in respect of a particular application - in this case that of the engine control system of an automobile. The application will not be considered quantitatively or authoritatively but will be examined at a stylised system level to illustrate how HI8 as a Real Time Operating System can assist with system design.

It should be noted that the version of HIDE described in this paper is targeted to the ITRON and μITRON specifications but that later versions of HIDE could address other parts of the TRON specification such as the BTRON concept.

The next section of this paper will explore some of the details of HI8 which is Hitachi's implementation of the μITRON specification.

HI8

HI8 is a Real Time Operating System which conforms to the μITRON specification. Historically, programmers and software engineers have been inclined to develop their own customised real time handlers. Because of this any attempt to design a general purpose Real Time Operating System had to take into account the necessity of minimising interrupt response time and interrupt masking as these would be two of the prime features which a programmer or software engineer would be seeking in writing a customised real time handler. In any real time development speed of response is critical otherwise it ceases to be real time. The other major consideration was to tailor HI8 to the code and data areas of the target processor - namely the H8/532.

HI8 has been implemented so that it will respond to asynchronous external interrupts and requests for task switches in under a half of a millisecond. It is also possible to eliminate parameter checking during system calls, thereby increasing its speed of operation still further. An advantage of the modular structure of HI8 is that it can be implemented in a number of configurations which range in size from a minimum of 1.9k bytes to 4.7k bytes. The size of workspace (RAM) required depends on the system configuration but is a minimum of 18 bytes. Table 1 shows the memory requirements of the different objects in HI8.

Table 1 - Memory Requirements of HI8 Objects

Object	Size
Task	16 bytes
Event Flag	4 bytes
Semaphore	6 bytes
Mailbox	6 bytes
Memory Pool	8 bytes

Three levels of the µITRON specification are implemented by HI8:-

Level 1 (the minimum set) - ready, wait and run

Level 2 - ready, wait, run and dormant

Level 3 - all task statuses defined by µITRON specification

In fact HI8 supports, in addition to Level 3 System Calls, task termination and exception handler functions that are defined in the ITRON specification, but not in the µITRON specification.

The modular nature of HI8 is illustrated in Figure 1.

The Nucleus of HI8 manages up to a maximum of 64 user tasks and independent programs which are capable of parallel processing. It is therefore in the interest of the user to divide application programs into tasks which are known to the Nucleus through the setup file. Handling of the tasks is carried out by the Nucleus according to individual task priorities in the range 1-32 and their status in the system. Tasks of equal priority are assigned to a ready queue with other tasks of the same priority. Dynamic modification of task priorities and the ready queues is available to the user during the running of HI8. Figure 2 shows the various task states and the means of transition between these states within HI8.

Inter-task communication and synchronisation is achieved using three features of HI8 - event flags, semaphores and mailboxes. The user has the option of single or multiple-bit event flags. The multiple-bit event flags allow for synchronisation on a combination of events while the single bit event flag is obviously restricted to only 1 event. A semaphore is a counter (in the range 0 - 65,535) which indicates the number of resources that a task currently needs. Mailboxes are used for exchanging data between tasks - for example an ASCII string. The sending task will specify the mailbox and write a message to it while the receiving task specifies the same mailbox and reads the data from it.

If an interrupt occurs during the execution of HI8 and the user's application code, the operating system does not interfere in any way. The user's interrupt handler will be executed and the user then has the option of using either the HI8 system call **ret_int** which will simply terminate the interrupt handling routine under the control of HI8 or, alternatively, the **ret_wup** system call which will, as well as handling termination of the interrupt handler, also wake up the specified task.

If an exception occurs during the execution of a task within HI8, the operating system will normally simply terminate the task. The user then has the option of using a customised exception handler to recover the situation.

This then is a very brief overview of HI8, Hitachi's own implementation of the µITRON specification. The next step is to consider a potential application of HI8 and for that we will look in the automotive area and specifically at the nature of engine control within an automobile.

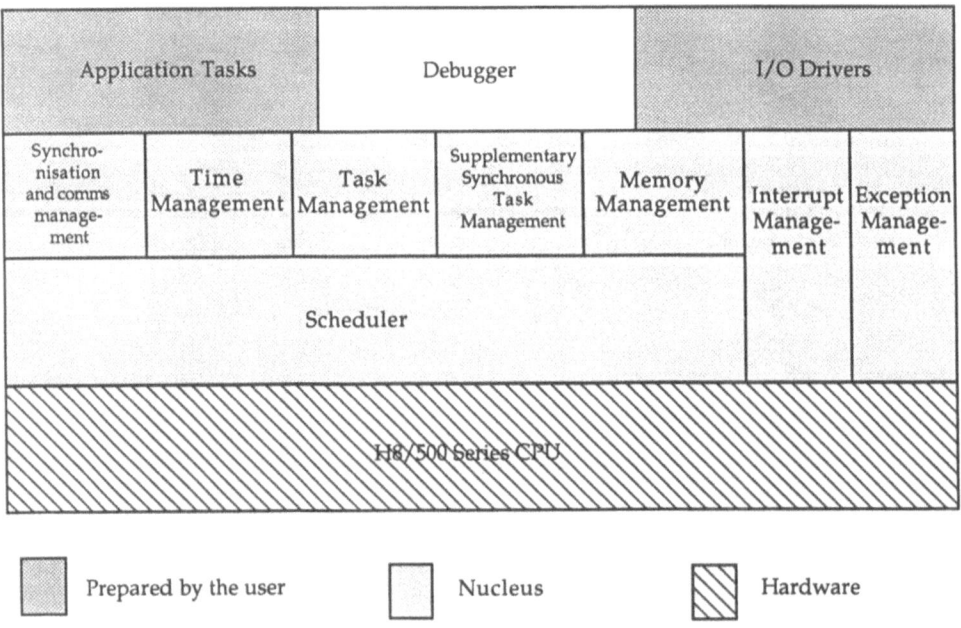

Fig. 1 - HI8 System Configuration

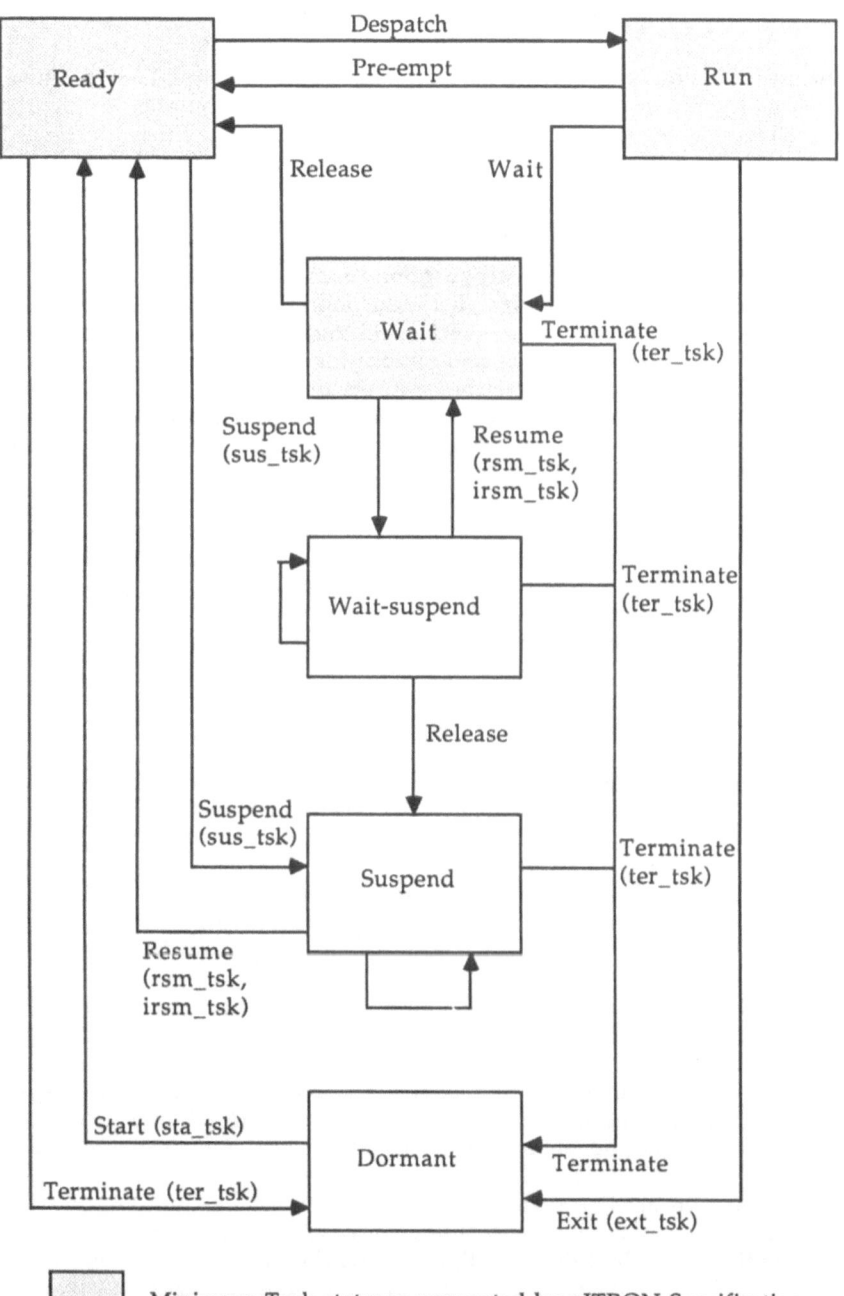

Minimum Task statuses supported by µITRON Specification

Fig. 2 - Task statuses and transitions in HI8

AUTOMOBILE ENGINE CONTROL

The principle of operation of an internal combustion engine is well known - the 4 stroke engine cycles repetitively through the stages of induction, compression, ignition and exhaust (colloquially known as "suck, squeeze, bang, puff"!). The efficiency of this kind of engine depends upon many factors and it is on of these - the air-fuel mixture - that we will consider now.

The air-fuel mixture directly affects the actual fuel consumption of the engine and it is important to note that different air-fuel mixtures are necessary for the different operational modes of the engine. Any fuel induction system must be able to assess the current state of the engine and alter the air-fuel mixture accordingly. For the 4-stroke internal combustion engine there are two options for fuel induction - a carburettor or a fuel-injection system. While carburettors are still the most widely used form of fuel induction, fuel injection offers the opportunity to control the air-fuel mixture very precisely in relation to the current state of the engine with the effect that combustion is much more complete.

Any fuel-injection system must therefore be able to deliver to each of the cylinders exactly the correct air-fuel mixture at exactly the right time. In order to do this, it must process data from many different parts of the engine, assess their effect on the fuel requirements of the engine and adjust the air-fuel mixture accordingly - and do all of this very quickly - if the engine is running at 3000 rpm, each engine revolution takes place in 20ms.

Figure 3 shows the components of a typical fuel-injection system. The quantity of air taken in by the engine when it is running determines the quantity of fuel required. The air flows through the air flow control unit and the intake manifold and into the engine. A sensor in the air flow control unit detects the rate of air flow and passes it back to the control unit. The engine speed is sensed by the ignition system and is then reported back to the control unit. Based on these variables, the fuel injection system can calculate the quantity of fuel required and controls the operation of the injection valves. Flow of fuel is controlled by the fuel pump which feeds it into the fuel distribution line from where it is injected into the cylinders by the solenoid-controlled injection valves.

In addition to the main control variables - air intake and engine speed, further variables must be considered in order to ensure optimum performance. For example, when cold starting, the Start Valve must inject more fuel into the Intake Manifold as when the engine is cold, more of the fuel in the air-fuel mixture condenses and can be lost. The temperature of the engine must therefore be monitored to allow the control unit to assess the quantity of additional fuel necessary as a function of engine temperature.

In conclusion, a fuel-injection system requires a multi-tasking control unit which must respond instantaneously to any one of a number of asynchronous inputs and be able to control several independent outputs. Specifically, the inputs are, for example, engine temperature and engine speed; the outputs are, for example, injection valve switching and fuel flow.

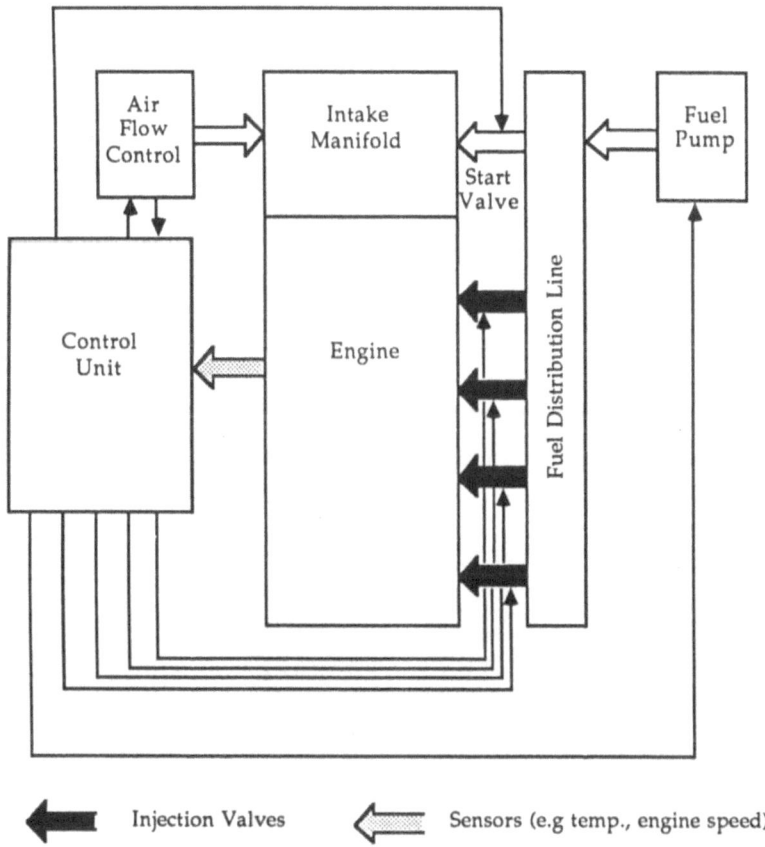

Injection Valves   Sensors (e.g temp., engine speed)

Fig. 3 - Fuel Injection Control Overview

Assuming that a microcontroller such as H8/532 is used as the control device for such a system, and setting aside completely any hardware requirements of the system, there are two options for the software engineer. The logic of an application such as this says that there must be some executive within the application software to co-ordinate the processing of the input data and to handle the control outputs. A simplified high-level software schematic would look like that shown in Figure 4.

Having initialised the hardware and software of the system, the executive needs to poll the control inputs - in this simplified diagram these are Temperature Monitoring, Engine Speed Monitoring and the Air Flow Sensor - and, based on the inputs, calculate the actions required at the outputs - in Figure 4 these are the Fuel Pump Control and the Injection Valve Control. In order to achieve this in real time with true multi-tasking (and multi-tasking is necessary, each of the three control inputs shown in Figure 4 can vary randomly and asynchronously), the software engineer would need to write an application-specific real-time control executive. There would then be two additional considerations in the planning of a project of this nature. Firstly, the design and development of the executive would require a significant amount of engineering effort and secondly, in the nature of software projects, the testing and maintenance of such an executive would require additional engineering effort.

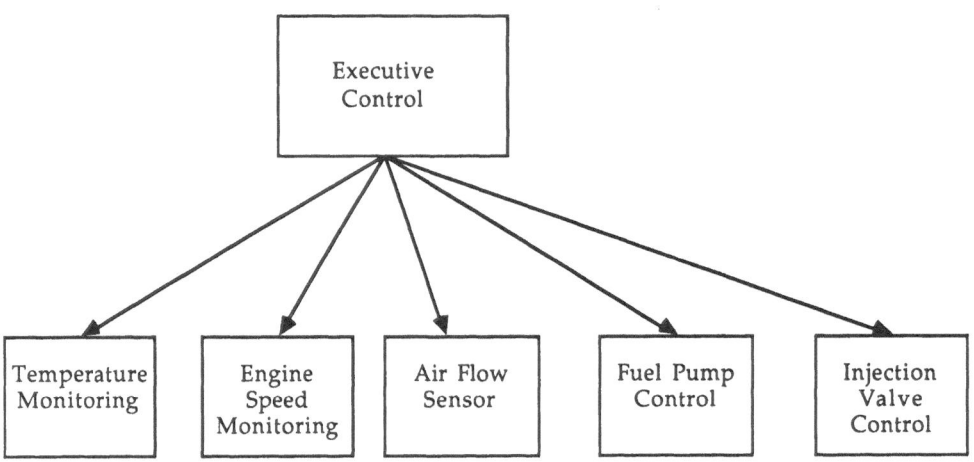

Fig. 4 - Simplified high level software schematic

HI8 is a general purpose, multi-tasking, Real Time Operating System. Obviously, the fact that it is general purpose means that there is likely to be an amount of overhead built in to it. In the same way, programmers must accept an overhead if they decide to use C instead of assembler because C is a general-purpose high-level language. The advantages of using C apply equally to HI8 - faster development times, easier maintenance and the fact that both C and HI8 are industry standards and therefore any applications are likely to be highly portable across host processors.

HI8 has built into it the necessary mechanisms to aid in the design of this kind of real-time system. For example, the user can create 6 tasks which correspond to the control executive, 3 inputs and 2 outputs shown in Figure 4. These can run independently of each other or can use the synchronisation and communication mechanisms such as semaphores, mail boxes and event flags to co-ordinate one another. As an example, the Temperature Monitoring task could pass details of the current temperature of the engine to the control executive through a mailbox. The control executive would then calculate various control parameters based on this data and also on data received from the other input monitoring tasks and then use an event flag to indicate to the Fuel Pump Task that the fuel pump should be turned on. The control executive (or any other task) would be able to use semaphores to request, through HI8, the memory resources necessary for complex mathematical calculations.

Having examined this application from what is admittedly a very high level and a very simplistic point of view, it should now be more apparent that for real-time multi-tasking programs HI8 offers the user an abbreviated design cycle and also the base on which to run multiple tasks with comprehensive inter-task communication and synchronisation. The next consideration must be how to build a HI8 application such as this one.

BUILDING AN HI8 APPLICATION

The HI8 package comprises the following software components:-

a. HI8 Kernel (relocatable object code) - a library file containing all of the kernel of HI8.

b. HI8 Debugger (relocatable object code) - a library file containing all of the debugger for HI8.

c. General purpose I/O Drivers (source code) - the general purpose I/O Drivers are the Console Driver, the Printer Driver and the Timer Handler and are written for the H8/532 Evaluation Board. They can be used if HI8 is to be run on the H8/532 Evaluation Board or can be customised by the user to the application hardware.

d. HI8 Setup File (source code) - it is this file which lists the user tasks, HI8 workspace area, numbers of event flags, numbers of semaphores etc.

e. HI8 Vector table (source code) - all of the vector addresses for H8/500 including those required for HI8.

f. HI8 Definition Table - (relocatable object code) - library file containing all of the definitions for HI8 such as the timer interrupt handler, timer definition table, console driver definition table, etc.

The final component of any HI8 system is the user's application software.

Figure 5 shows how the components of HI8 are combined to generate a typical system.

Because the kernel and the debugger are modular, it is likely that the user will want to vary the number of modules which are linked in when the system is created. The debugger is, for example, entirely optional and only the parts of the kernel which support the ready, wait and run task statuses are compulsory. Other modules such as those which handle priority manipulation and exception management can be excluded before system creation.

The user must also make modifications to the setup table source file before assembling and linking as it is through this file that the kernel of HI8 understands where the user tasks are situated, what their priority is, etc.

When all of the necessary modification has been done, it is then necessary to link all of the modules shown in Figure 5 together to create a combined object file. By passing this through the Object Code Converter, an S-Record file can be created from the SYSROF output of the Linker. The user then has code which can be loaded to a target system such as an Emulator or to an EPROM programmer so that a device can be blown with the HI8 code before being fitted to the target application. It is also possible to compile and link the various components at a later stage if modification is necessary.

This is how a system is generated for the application discussed or for any other application. However, there is an alternate method available for HI8 System building and modification and it is that which we will examine next.

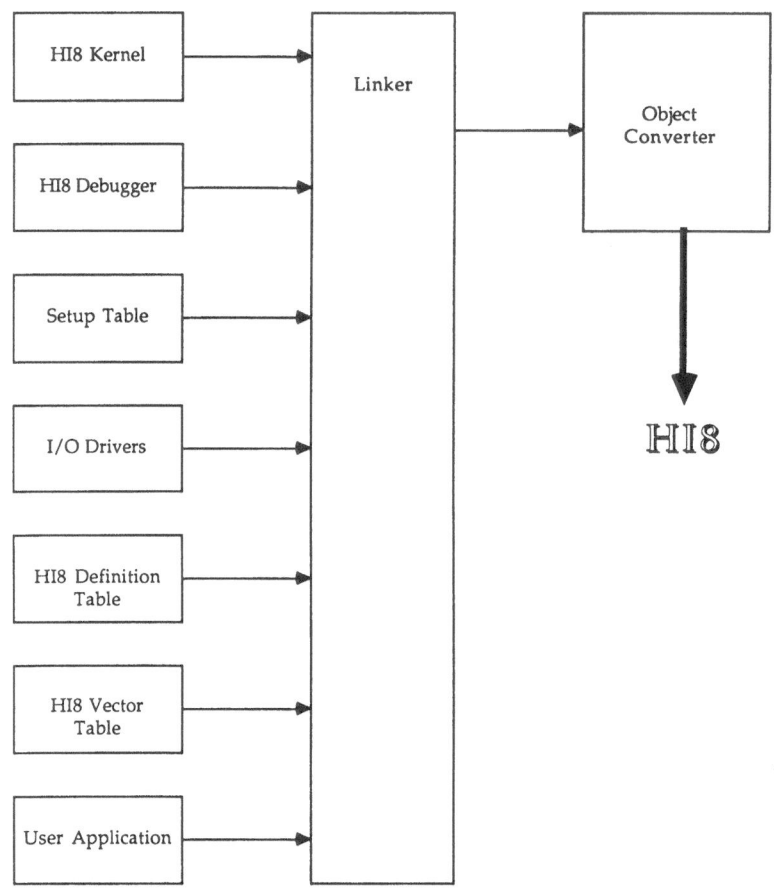

Fig. 5 - HI8 System Generation

HITACHI INTEGRATED DEVELOPMENT ENVIRONMENT (HIDE)

The final part in the HI8 picture is provided by HIDE. HIDE is a development environment which is based on a combination of the IBM-PC® and the EuroDESC H8/532 Evaluation Board - the later being a PC plug-in board.

Behind HIDE, in a logical sense, sit the H-Series support tools (C Compiler, Cross Assembler, Linker, Librarian and Object Code Converter) and the HI8 Configurator. Figure 6 shows how HIDE and the other tools are placed with regard to each other.

When HIDE is run on the a PC, it displays three windows, one is a command window which offers a subset of MS-DOS® commands, the second is a terminal window which can be used to communicate with a monitor on the H8/532 Evaluation board and the third window is a printer window which could be driven by the printer drivers in HI8. The screen layout of HIDE is shown on Figure 7.

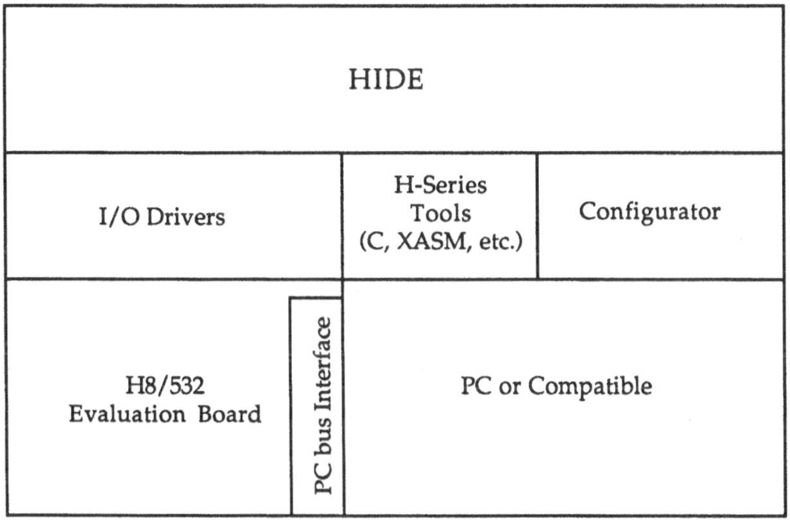

HIDE		
I/O Drivers	H-Series Tools (C, XASM, etc.)	Configurator
H8/532 Evaluation Board	PC bus Interface	PC or Compatible

Fig. 6 - HIDE and associated hardware and software

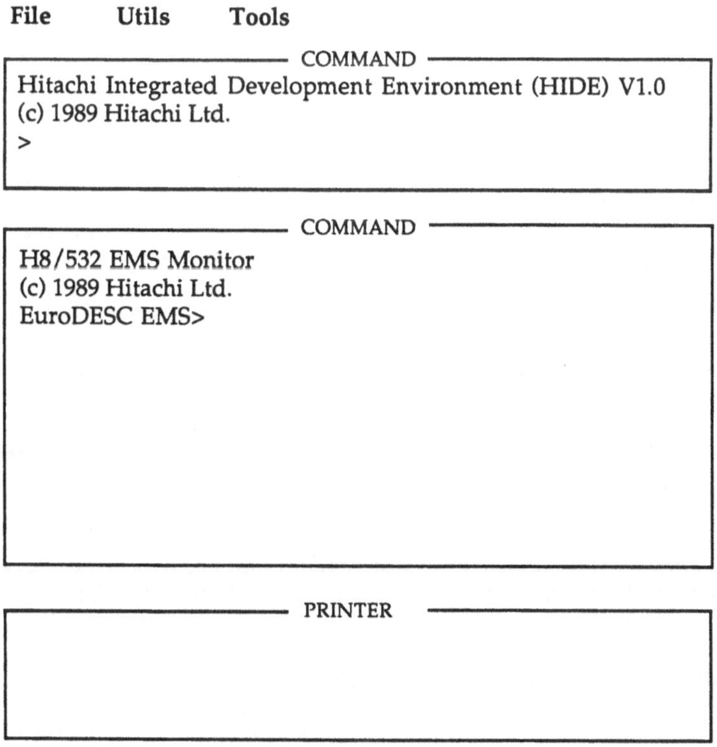

File   Utils   Tools

```
──────────── COMMAND ────────────
Hitachi Integrated Development Environment (HIDE) V1.0
(c) 1989 Hitachi Ltd.
>
```

```
──────────── COMMAND ────────────
H8/532 EMS Monitor
(c) 1989 Hitachi Ltd.
EuroDESC EMS>




```

```
──────────── PRINTER ────────────


```

Fig. 7 - HIDE User Interface

HIDE also offers pull down menus which give the user an extensive set of functions. These include the ability to upload and download files from disc to and from the H8/532 Evaluation Board and manipulation of the Evaluation Board itself (as an example, it is possible to apply a software reset to the board from HIDE). There is full on-line help, access to an MS-DOS® shell, a calculator facility and also the ability to run the H-Series tools and the HI8 Configurator. It is the latter that we will consider next in some detail as it provides the user with a fully comprehensive means of configuring an HI8 system.

HI8 CONFIGURATOR

The basic principle of the HI8 Configurator is that it automates the HI8 configuration process within an MS-DOS® environment. Like HIDE, the HI8 Configurator consists of three basic elements - pull-down menus, interface screens and on-line help. In order to better understand the HI8 Configurator, we will consider the functionality of each of the pull-down menus.

The File menu allows for the upload and download of Configuration files (setup files) and also gives the user an option of exiting from the Configurator.

The Options menu is used to set up the HI8 Configurator system parameters - Library path, Application path, HI8 object path, etc.

The Utilities menu can invoke the MS-DOS® shell and the calculator.

The heart of the HI8 Configurator lies in the Edit and Generate menus - it is directly from these that the HI8 system can be built.

The Edit menu gives access to a set of options which allow the user to modify the configuration file. This is done through interactive interface screens which prompt the user for the required data. It is in this area that memory pools, tasks and event flags are defined (along with many other system-related parameters). If the user modifies the system parameters through the Edit menu, it is not necessary to undertake any textual editing of the configuration file - this will be done automatically by the HI8 Configurator.

The final part of the HI8 Configurator is the Generate menu. It is through the options offered in this menu that the system files - i.e. defined application modules, object modules, library modules and source modules - are used to build two command files - a batch file and a link subcommand file. The generated batch file will automatically perform the preprocessing, assembling and compilation of the appropriate files and will then run the Linker with the link subcommand file. The user can also optionally request that the HI8 Configurator write to a file or the printer port the details of the system configuration.

All of this is done by the HI8 Configurator without any need for user intervention. The only requirement from the user is the generation of the application code and the modification of the configuration file by use of the Edit menu of the HI8 Configurator.

Having created the application version of HI8, the code can be tested by returning to HIDE and downloading the file to the H8/532 Evaluation Board. Debugging can be carried out using the HI8 Debugger, the interface to which can be through the Terminal window of HIDE or via a terminal connected to the serial port of the H8/532 Evaluation Board.

CONCLUSION

In conclusion, it is worth reiterating the ground that has been covered in this paper.

We have seen HI8 as a compact and flexible multi-tasking Real Time Operating System and looked in a simplistic way at how it might be applied to the "real world".

Although we have only looked at one application, it is a fact that there are an enormous number of potential applications for HI8 - any situation in which there are asynchronous inputs which have a real time effect on multiple outputs should be considered.

Size of code should not be a bar to using HI8 - we have seen that a 1.9k byte kernel is possible and that a single-chip implementation is already available for H8/532.

Finally, implementation of HI8 has become much simpler with the introduction by EuroDESC and Cambridge Beacon of the HIDE tools which includes the HI8 Configurator. The user can now concentrate more on the problems that any software engineer has with implementing application code and leave HIDE and the Configurator to build the system.

ACKNOWLEDGEMENTS

Thanks are due to the following:-

Dr.K.Sakamura of the Department of Information Science, Faculty of Science, The University of Tokyo for his work on the TRON Project

Mr.H.Takeyama, Mr.T.Shimizu and the HI8 design and development team at Hitachi Limited, Tokyo, Japan

Cambridge Beacon Limited - developers of HIDE and Configurators for HI8 and HI16

REFERENCES

1. Cambridge Beacon Limited - Hitachi HI8 Configurator Operation Manual

2. Hitachi Limited - H8/500 Programming Manual

3. Hitachi Limited - HI8 User's Manual

4. Sakamura K - μITRON, Vol. 1 No. 1, TRON Study Group, Japan

5. Sakamura K - ITRON Real-Time Operating System, Vol. 3, No. 5, J.Robotics Soc. Japan

6. Sakamura K - (April 8-14 1988) The TRON Project, IEEE Micro

7. Sakamura K - ITRON Real-Time Operating System, Operating System Study Group, Japan

8. Takeyama H, Shimizu T, Kobayakawa M (1988) - HI8: A Realtime Operating System with μITRON Specifications for the H8/500 (K.Sakamura Ed. TRON Project)

9. Vauxhall-Opel Passenger Car Marketing - Fuel Injection: The product explained

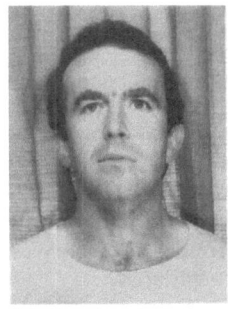

David Wallace is the Applications Engineering Manager of the European Design and Engineering Support Center of Hitachi Europe Limited. He graduated from Bath University in 1977 with an Honours Degree(B.Sc.) in Physics with Physical Electronics.

His career since University has include 4 years with Marconi Avionics as a Design Engineer working on Airborne Radar, 2 years with Multitone PLC designing Radiopaging systems, 1 year with Acorn Computers designing peripherals for Home Computers. He has been with EuroDESC since February 1985.

As Manager of Applications Engineering, He is responsible for the initiation and co-ordination with Hitachi Europe of applications projects which cover the whole Hitachi electronic components product range.

Application of ITRON Specification Based OS in the Mobile Radio Communication System

Naoya Morita, Satoshi Kitajima, Hiroshi Saitoh
Matsushita Communication Industrial Co., Ltd.

Keiichirou Kuwazuru, and Jun Sugano
Matsushita Electoric Industrial Co., Ltd.

ABSTRACT

The IGEM (Industrial Global Environment Manager), which is a real-time operating system with ITRON specifications, has been developed and applied to the mobile radio communication systems. This system is used for AVM (Automatic Vehicle Monitoring) and MCA systems (Multi Channel Access) which uses M68000 (MCP-16 board) CPUs, having several connections to more than one microcomputer. In this system, a general purpose operating system (OS-9)* and real-time operating system (IGEM) coexist ,and they work together. This paper introduces examples of the use of this system and gives an evaluation of its operating system.

Keywords: ITRON specifications, real-time OS, MCA system, AVM system.

1. SYSTEM OVERVIEW

Table 1 shows an overview of the mobile radio communication system. The system has an architecture of a multiprocessor configuration with more than one processor connected with a GPIB-like Communication (described as C-bus, hereafter) bus, and takes advantage of the distribution of both function and processing loads.

Table 1 : Overview of the mobile radio communication System

Type of multiprocessor system	Load decentralization, Function decentralization system
Type of coupling system	Loosely coupled multiprocessor system (LMCP)
The number of processors	1~128
Communication system	Transaction Transfer system
Bus	C-bus (GPIB) Dual
OS	OS-9*, IGEM
Memory Composition	Local Memory Decentralization
Reliability	Duplex (Spare for standby)

* OS-9 is a trademark of Microware System Corp.

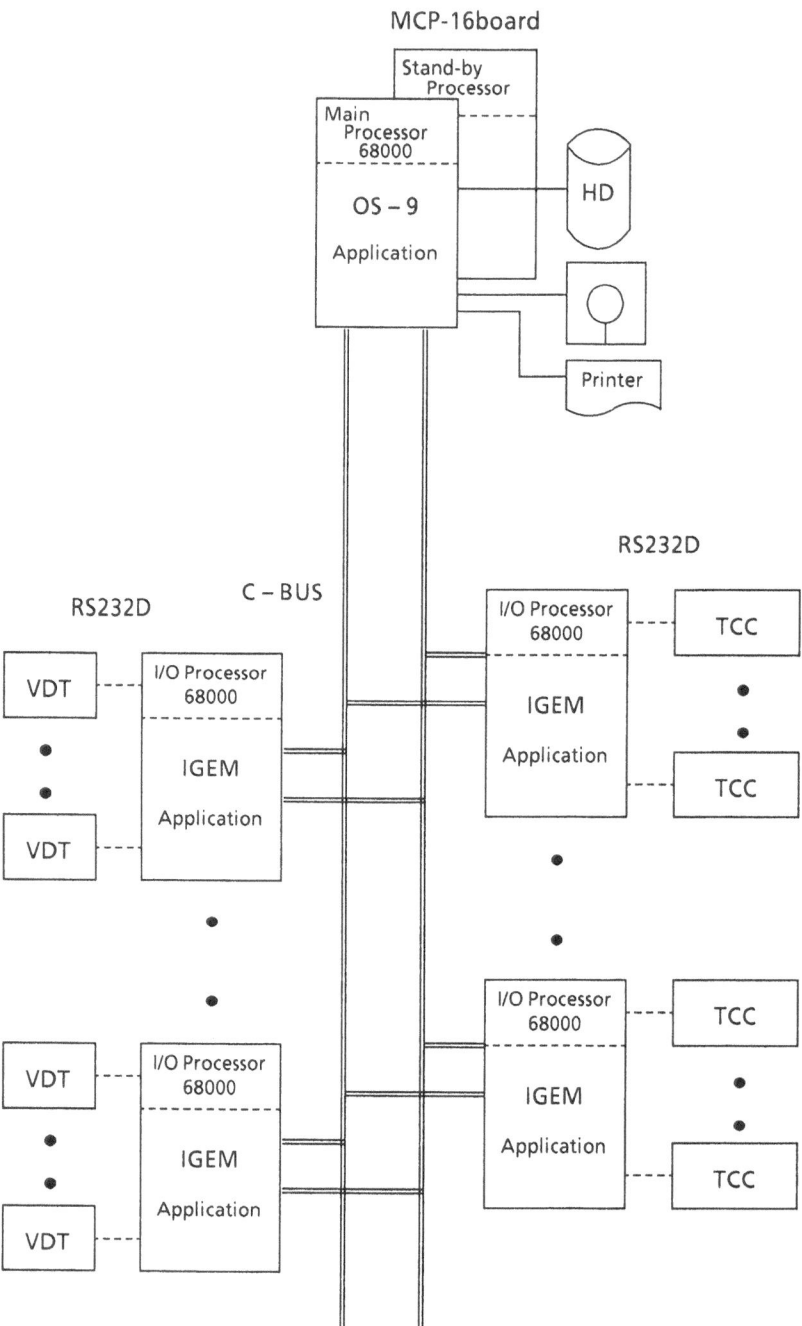

Fig. 1 : System Configuration

Fig. 1 shows the overall system configuration. Each processor is connected with the dual C-buses, so that in the case of failure of a bus, the entire system can continue to operate without interruption.

The main processor has a redundant configuration with a stand-by processor that replaces the main processor in case of emergency; it runs under the control of OS-9, a general-purpose operating system.

The I/O processor controls the VDT (Video Display Terminal) and TCC (Telecommunication Control Circuits) by means of the newly developed real-time operating system, called IGEM, (ITRON specification). For each I/O processor, a maximum of 4 serial ports are available. IGEM has been introduced for the purpose of supporting high speed and high level communication procedures such as HDLC (High level Data Link Control procedure). Here, the appropriate number of I/O processors according to the number of terminals are prepared for distribution of the load.

The program for the entire system is stored in the peripheral memories connected to the main processor. It is transferred to each processor at the time of initial start-up via the C-bus, where it can then be used for a different application.

Both the main processor and I/O processors are configured with the same CPU board (MCP-16). Specifications of the board are listed in Table 2. MCP-16 houses all the basic I/O devices on a single board and the CPU board controls them.

Table 2 : MCP-16 Specifications

Part	Spec.
CPU	68000
CPU clock	12.288MHz
Memory	EPROM 128/256 kbytes SRAM 256kbyte+4Mbyte(option)
Serial	EIA-232D 4 channel
Floppy Disk	4
Hard Disk	SCSI 8
Printer	parallel IF
C-bus	dual 400kbyte/sec

Fig. 3 shows the block diagram of the MCP-16 board.

The CPU bus on the board is configured so that the CPU and memory are connected to the 16-bit bus, and the I/O devices to the 8-bit bus.

Communication between the CPU boards is performed as follows: First, the talker makes a request for the bus, and after obtaining the access right, sends a data packet to the bus, as shown in Fig. 2. The receiver checks the first byte (target CPU number) to see if the data is addressed for it. If so, acknowledgment procedure continues, analyzing the following information. The number of the listener CPUs may be a single, dual, group, or all. The control of send/receive operations is provided by a dedicated gate array LSI.

```
Byte  0 | Listener CPU number                              |
      1 | Listener task number                             |
      2 | Talker CPU number                                |
      3 | Talker task number                               |
      4 | Data length (Maximum 250 bytes or 4kbytes)       |
      5 | Data                                             |
        :
        :
    255 |                                                  |
 (4,096)
```

Fig. 2 : C Bus Data Format

2. MULTI PROCESSOR ENVIRONMENT ADMINISTRATION

In a system with a multiprocessor configuration, system status management has to be performed by managing each processor's operational status in order to achieve normal functioning of the total system.

System status management is configured as a "Centralized Management System" by MCP-16 with a C-bus controller. When there is a change in any one of the processors' status during operation, the controller informs all processors of the status change via the C-bus network. This improves the reliability of the system. (Processor status: stop, IPL, operation, under operational check)

A C-bus networking function provides the "distribution invisible task control" by a user. (OS-9 remote process start-up, file transfer, etc.)

Furthermore, a function under IGEM enables easy start-up of another processor's task and the start-up of an IGEM task from other processors.

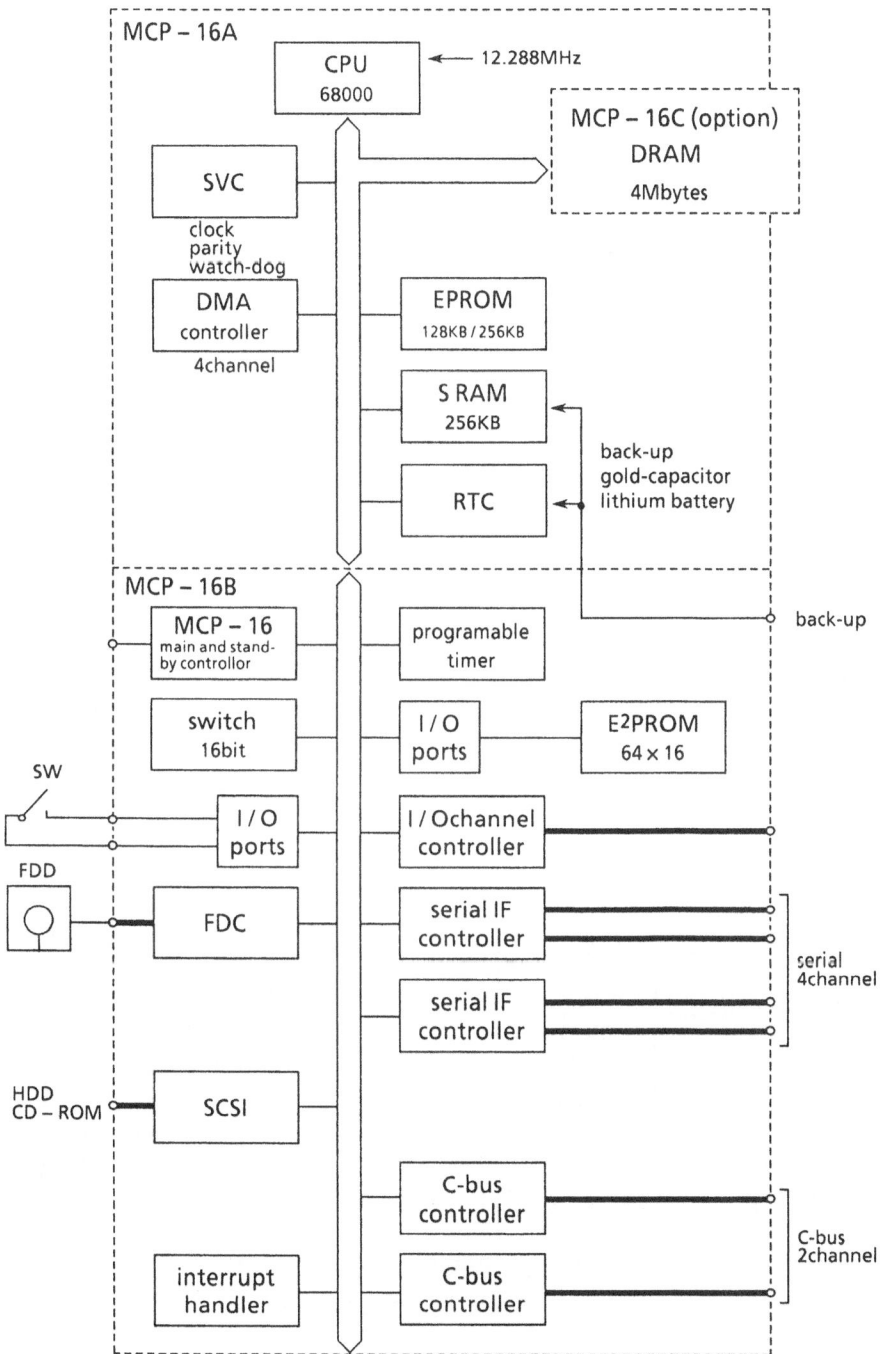

Fig. 3 : MCP-16 Block Diagram

3. EXAMPLES OF APPLICATION

1) MCA (Japanese trunked radio) system

The MCA(Multi Channel Access) system is a communication system in which a large number of users can share a wide bandwidth. It is, therefore, capable of handling a high volume of traffic, allowing more effective use of the bandwidth, compared to the conventional land mobile communication systems in Japan, by providing local and nation-wide services.

2) Summary AVM system

Recently, in the land mobile radio system market, the use of data transmission has been increasing. Furthermore, due to the diversification of the ways people live, and the worsening of traffic congestion, AVM (Automatic Vehicular Monitoring) system has been introduced for its advantages, such as automatic identification of the vehicle's current position and activities.

This system has been designed for a vehicle dispatch system, especially for the taxi industry which has the largest share in the land mobile radio system market. Its objective is to implement more effective methods of vehicle dispatch via radio through automatic identification of dynamic information given by the driver and the status (occupied/empty) of vehicles.

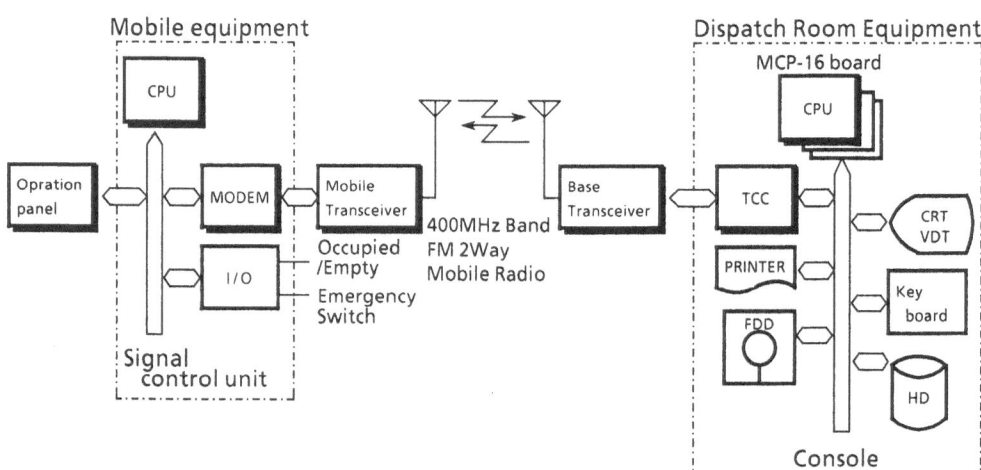

Fig. 4 : Block diagram of AVM.

4. IGEM OVERVIEW

The real-time operating system used in the mobile radio communication system is a newly developed operating system complying with the specifications of ITRON, and is expected to become one of the industry's de facto standard operating systems whose overview is presented in Table 3. Features of IGEM are as follows.

1) Real-time facilities with ITRON specifications. That is, facilities such as task management, synchronized communications, memory management, interrupts, exception handler and clock management, complying with the ITRON specifications.

2) Coexistence with OS-9 general-purpose operating system. While IGEM provides a high-speed, real-time processing environment (difficult to achieve with a general-purpose operating system), it allows the use of general-purpose software services (such as file management) that are difficult to be provided by IGEM.

3) Capable of extracting various statistical information. Allows effective system debugging and maintenance by computing statistical data such as CPU load and memory usage.

4) C language is predominantly used in writing the source programs, and some assembler language is also used.
   We have a plan to introduce 32 bit-cpu for the equipment. Therefore, we have since adapted C-language under serious consideration of easier implement to other cpu, and better maintenability.

Table 3 : IGEM Overview

OS	IGEM (Industrial Global Environment Manager)
CPU	68000
Kernel	25k bytes
Program size	4000 steps
Programming Language	C 90% , Assembler 10%
Developing environment	OS-9 work station (ET8300)
Related software	①Console driver ②Self-debugger ③HDLC driver
Features	①Harmonizing operation with general use OS(OS-9) ②Easier implement to other CPU.

5. HOW TO EVALUATE A REAL-TIME OPERATING SYSTEM

Some of the criteria usually applied in evaluating real-time operating systems are memory capacity, processing time of system calls, and interrupt masking time. However, processing time of system calls and interrupt masking time largely differ, depending on the actual conditions of their use. Therefore, it is not advisable to refer to these specifications in designing applications. The processing time is drastically differs, for example, when the length of the message wait queue and task vary.

In the development of the mobile radio system, evaluation of the operating system has been made by counting the send/receive error frequency of high traffic HDLC data stream, that is,the quality of interrupt handling at high send/receive speed of HDLC data stream during the performance of a real application. Table 4 shows the results. Here, both the new and old versions of IGEM are used as the operating system. System calls in both versions are invoked repeatedly and their durations are recorded. Furthermore, approximately 200 bytes of data are used as the HDLC send/receive data, and run in parallel from three ports. Sending/receiving speed was 19200 baud (approximately 420 μsec. of interrupt interval) and 9600 baud (approximately 830 μsec. of interrupt interval). The number of send/receive errors which occurred during 10 minutes for the former and 30 minutes for the latter were recorded. According to the results of this testing, it was found that when the processing time of a system call is improved by about 30%, interrupt response in terms of HDLC processing significantly improves.

Table 4: IGEM Performance Evaluation

(12.288MHz clock with 1 wait cycle)

		New Version	Old Version
System Call Processing Time (μsec.)	slp_tsk/wup_tsk	615	872
	wai_flg/set_fig	833	1241
	rev_msg/snd_msg	754	1077
HDLC error frequency (times)	19200 baud (10 min.)	450	950
	9600 baud (30 min.)	2	1400

The differnces between new and old versions of IGEM are as follows.
1) Improvement for processing speed of Kernel. The codes of the
   scheduler dispatch routine for the system calls have been
   rewritten in Assembly language from C-language.
2) Reduction of interruption masking time.
   Interruption-handling have been enabled in most of the processing
   time for the system call.

6. CONCLUSION

     This paper presents examples of IGEM application, a newly
developed real-time operating system with ITRON specifications, to the
mobile communication system. In addition, an evaluation of the
operating system in the form of application benchmarks were performed
and the results were presented. We estimate that IGEM is satisfied
with the performance required in this mobile communication system.
The mobile communication system is a multiprocessor system with
network facilities. It is expected that ITRON specifications based
system will establish a reputation as a standard architecture.

REFERENCES

[1] K. Nakada et al., "Performance Evaluation of MR7700", Proc. of TRON Technical
Conference, Vol. 2, no. 1, pp31~40(1989) (in Japanese)
[2] K. Sakamura (1988) Introduction to ITRON, Iwanami-shotem, Japan
                                                        (in Japanese)
[3] K. Sakamura (1988) Tron Project 1988, Springer-Verlag

68

Naoya Morita : He received his B.E. degree from Tokyo University in 1972.
He has been engaged in the development of Redio Telecommunications Systems, including the Mobile Radio Communication system, as the manager of Data Communication Engineering, Radio Telecommunication Division in Matsushita Communication Industrial Co., Ltd. Yokohama, Kanagawa, Japan.

Satoshi Kitajima : He received his B.E. degree from Chuuou University in 1985.
He has been engaged in the development of the basic software and the mobile radio communication systems in Data Communication Engineering section, Radio Telecommunication Division in Matsushita Communication Industrial Co., Ltd. Yokohama, Kanagawa, Japan.

Hiroshi Saitoh : He received his B.E. degree from Aoyama-gakuin University in 1975.
He has been engaged in the development of the basic software and the mobile radio communication systems in Data Communication Engineering section, Radio Telecommunication Division in Matsushita Communication Industrial Co., Ltd. Yokohama, Kanagawa, Japan.

Keiichirou Kuwazuru : He received his B.S. and E.S. in Physics Kyushu University, Fukuoka, Japan, in 1980.
He joined Matsushita Electric Industrial Co., Ltd. (MEI) in 1985. He has been engaged in the research and development of Network System Engineering.
He is currently with MEI Tokyo information and Communications Researcih Laboratory, Kawasaki, Kanagawa, Japan. He is a member of the IPSJ

Jun Sugano : He received his B.S. degrees from University of Electronics and Communications, Tokyo, Japan, in 1972.
He joined Matsushita Electric Industrial Co., Ltd. (MEI) in 1972. He has been engaged in the research and development of the basic software, and in product planning for microcomputer systems. He is currently with MEI Tokyo information and Communications Research Laboratory, Kawasaki, Kanagawa, Japan. He is a member of the IPSJ, IEICEJ and JCEA.

Above author may be reached at : Radio Telecommunication Division in Matsushita Communication Industrial Co., Ltd. 4-3-1 TsunashimaHigashi, Kouhoku-ku, Yokohama, Kanagawa 223 Japan.

The Design of a Real-Time Operating System Kernel for the Gmicro Family of Processors

Theodor Nissim, and Jim Ready
Ready Systems Corporation

ABSTRACT

The challenge of designing a real-time operating system kernel includes meeting the critical require-ments of deterministic behavior, interrupt latency time, speed and overall performance. This paper presents the design of the VRTX32 real-time operating system kernel for the Gmicro family of processors, emphasizing the architectural features of these processors that make them high perform-ance real-time VRTX32 based engines. A possible implementation of the ITRON operation system on the top of the VRTX32 kernel is also presented.

Keywords: Gmicro processor, real-time operating systems, VRTX32/G

INTRODUCTION

A real-time kernel provides a virtual machine layer on the top of the "real hardware," in which the real-time designer can develop an application. This allows the application to be designed and devel-oped independently, using the virtual machine primitives as higher level machine instructions. The real-time kernel should also guarantee that the whole system will behave in a deterministic way, i.e. the system will respond to external stimuli within strict time limits.

Although the goals of real-time software engineers include the run for absolute best case performance, the optimization of the worst case performance and predictability of the response time to external events is required to meet "hard" deadlines. The VRTX32 real-time operating system kernel was originally designed to respond to these "hard" real-time environment requirements. Although VRTX32 was designed to be generic, its ability to port to different computer architectures implies a fine tuning of the kernel design to the specific features of the processor.

In this paper, we present the design of the VRTX32/G, a real-time kernel for Gmicro processors. The discussion emphasizes the architectural features which make this processor well suited for real-time applications and the ways in which the design takes advantage of these features to help turn the Gmicro into a high performance real-time engine.

THE VRTX MODEL OF REAL-TIME APPLICATIONS

The philosophy behind the VRTX32 generic design is to provide a complete answer to the hard real-time environment requirements. The most important requirement is the deterministic behavior of the system, i.e. the guarantee of the system's response to external events within a strict time limit, constant in the ideal case. In order to achieve such a behavior, all the internal kernel algorithms must have constant or low complexity. This is achieved in VRTX32 by using internal sophisticated data structures and by optimizing algorithm speed. Another requirement for a hard real-time system is the interrupt latency time, i.e. the maximum period the interrupts are disabled within the kernel. A low interrupt latency time contributes to a "more deterministic" behavior of the system, since external stimuli are linked to the real time software using interrupt mechanisms.

The functional model of VRTX32 includes sophisticated tasking management with specific real-time optimizations (task priority management, voluntary self-preemption, etc.), various interprocess communication and synchronization mechanisms (queues, semaphores, mailboxes, event flags), memory management, the possibility of extending the kernel with user- or system- defined components, and extensive interrupt processing support. (See Fig.1.)

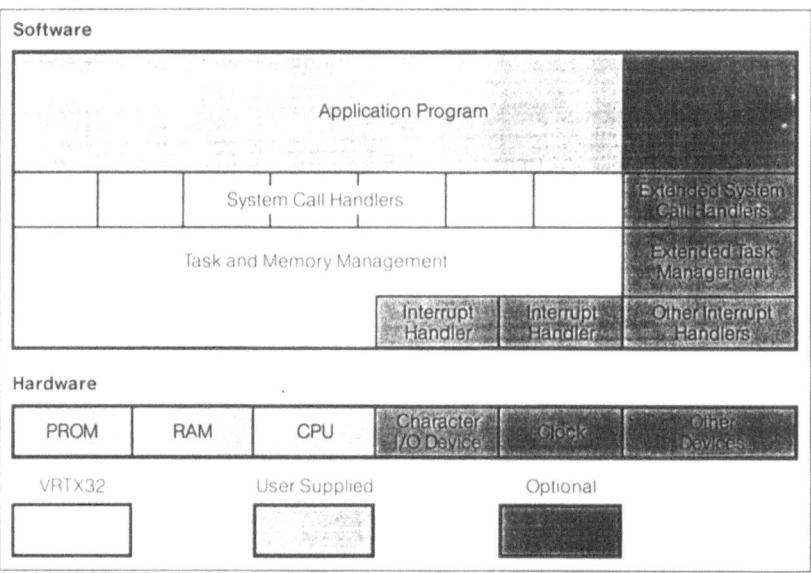

Figure 1. VRTX32-Based System Structure

THE GMICRO PROCESSOR AS A VRTX ENGINE

Porting VRTX32 to a new architecture produces a kernel which is optimized for using the specific architectural features of the processor, while inheriting the functional and behavioral characteristics of the generic design. This is achieved by coding VRTX32 completely in assembly language, and optimizing every code module according to the processor's architecture. However, architectural features of the processor, such as stacking scheme, number of registers, and exception processing capabilities, may affect the performance of the real-time kernel. The Gmicro family of processors has architectural features which make them good platforms for real-time VRTX32 based systems. These features were used in the development of VRTX32 in two basic domains:

- The optimization of the basic design of VRTX32 (task management, interrupt and exception processing).
- Local optimizations in specific modules at the implementation level.

The main optimization performed on the VRTX32 basic design is the task switch time minimization. VRTX32 tasks are viewed as "lightweight processes," i.e. running in the same address space. Thus, the context to be saved includes the general purpose registers of the CPU and the context registers, as defined by the Gmicro architecture.

VRTX32/G uses the STM instruction for atomically saving all the general purpose registers of the currently running task on its ring O stack. The context registers are atomically stored in the task control block using the STCTX instruction. Thus, the actual task switch consists of only a few STCTX and LDCTX instructions. These instructions switch the tasks between the pre-empted task and the next scheduled task. As a result, the task switch is performed with a few "atomic actions," implying a small interrupt latency in an extreme time critical area. The overall performance is very good. Since the same VRTX32/G system call may or may not result in a task switch, an important issue is to make the execution time for these two cases as close as possible in order to achieve a more deterministic behavior of the system. (See Appendix A.)

VRTX32/G saves and restores the general purpose registers regardless of the system call result (a task switch or not), and in an atomic and very fast way. The only overhead required by the task switch operation are the LDCTX/STCTX instructions. Therefore the timing behavior of the VRTX32/G system calls is more deterministic and has a good overall performance.

The stack mechanism of the Gmicro architecture makes it a good base for multitasking systems in real-time and non-real-time applications. The important addition for real-time systems is the possibility of flexible stack switching when executing an exception or interrupt handler, or performing a system call. The fact that the hardware itself switches to the "specified by user" stack avoids the inclusion of the same functionality in the operating system, thus eliminating a serious overhead in a time critical section. The elimination of an entire interrupt processing system call improves the performance of a time critical section.

The large number of vectors reserved for software traps allow the introduction of "fast entries" in the kernel for time critical system calls. In the original design, all the system calls are performed via a single trap entry, and the function decoding is performed internally. VRTX32/G isolates time critical system calls in separate trap entries, eliminating another time overhead in a time critical section.

The larger number of registers and the orthogonality of the Gmicro instruction set allow efficient coding of the kernel software. For instance, frequently used variables can be kept in registers during the execution of a complete path within the kernel.

The queue management instructions of the Gmicro architecture allow complete management of the internal kernel queues via atomic actions. This implies a minimization of the interrupt latency time, since queue management is a critical section of code and must be protected. Moreover, the resulting code is more compact and faster.

The context switch instructions provide a strong support for multitasking activity in hard real-time environments. In VRTX32/G, a task may have more than one active stack; therefore the atomic switch of all the stack pointers (regardless of the number of active stacks or the number of the stack pointers implemented by the hardware) minimizes the length of a critical section of code and reduces the interrupt latency time.

Another important performance optimization issue is the minimization of the "search for the highest priority ready task" time. VRTX32/G keeps bit lists to indicate which of the priority levels contain ready tasks. VRTX32/G can quickly mark or find a priority level in an atomic way by using the powerful bit field operations defined by the Gmicro architecture. The data structures and the related algorithms are simplified. Consequently, the search for the"task to be scheduled" in VRTX32/G is extremely fast, atomic, and does not affect interrupt latency.

In general, the Gmicro architecture can be defined as a "Super CISC" machine, which provides complex instructions at the machine level. The fast execution times for complex instructions allows the use of instructions for building "atomic actions." These are not expensive (from the timing point of view) and are self-protected in the code critical sections often met in real-time kernel code.
The debugging of multitasking kernel based real-time applications is a complex job, even for experienced programmers. In order to ease this activity, RTscope, a system level debugger for VRTX32 based applications, was developed. RT scope's built-in hardware debugging capabilities add data and code address breakpoints functionality for debugging complex systems. (See Appendix B.)

VRTX32/G is built as a common kernel for all Gmicro processors. Only instructions common to all current processors were used in the VRTX32/G implementation. Thus, applications may migrate between different Gmicro processors without any change, even at the binary level (from the VRTX32 point of view).

A POSSIBLE SOLUTION FOR AN ITRON IMPLEMENTATION:
The VRTX32 kernel may be viewed as a subset of the ITRON standard for a real time industrial operating system. The objects manipulated by ITRON are also found in VRTX32 based systems, and their management is based on similar event-driven, priority based strategies. However, the ITRON functionality includes a wider choice of options than VRTX32, which is only an operating system kernel. Thus, by adding the missing functionality to VRTX32, an ITRON system may be implemented. The advantages of this solution are:

- The basic VRTX32 object management remains unchanged, and the resulting ITRON system will inherit the high real-time performance of the kernel.

- The extension of the VRTX32 to ITRON is orthogonal. The original features and performance of VRTX32 will be unaffected by the changes.

- The new features of the system are built using the same fast algorithms and special data structures as VRTX32, guaranteeing a high real-time performance.

- Any application written for an ITRON/VRTX32 based system has access to the primitives of the both systems, without any performance penalty.

- The resulting system is an open one, with the possibility of adding customized extensions according to the application's needs.

CONCLUSION

The primary objectives of real-time design are to develop an operating system kernel that is predictable and deterministic in behavior, that optimizes interrupt latency and time critical sections, and improves overall performance. The characteristics of such a system are strongly influenced by the architecture of the processor running the kernel. The Gmicro processors' architectural features were intensively used in the VRTX32/G design and implementation. The resulting "VRTX32 - Gmicro" virtual machine has an excellent real-time performance, making it a good platform for hard real-time applications.

Appendix A
VRTX32 System Calls

Systems Call	Communication And Synchronization	Real-Time Clock
		SC_GTIME
Task Management	SC_ACCEPT	SC_STIME
SC_TCREATE	SC_PEND	SC_TDELAY
SC_TDELETE	SC_POST	SC_TSLICE
SC_TSUSPEND	SC_FCLEAR	
SC_TRESUME	SC_FCREATE	**Character I/O**
SC_TPRIORITY	SC_FDELETE	SC_GETC
SC_TINQUIRY	SC_FINQUIRY	SC_PUTC
SC_LOCK	SC_FPEND	
SC_UNLOCK	SC_FPOST	**Interrupt Servicing**
	SC_QACCEPT	UI_ENTER
Memory Management	SC_QCREATE	UI_EXIT
SC_GBLOCK	SC_QECREATE	UI_TIMER
SC_RBLOCK	SC_QINQUIRY	UI_RXCHR
SC_PCREATE	SC_QJAM	UI_TXRDY
SC_PEXTEND	SC_QPEND	
	SC_QPOST	
	SC_SCREATE	
	SC_SDELETE	
	SC_SINQUIRY	
	SC_SPEND	
	SC_SPOST	

Appendix B
RTscope Command Set

VRTX32 SYSTEM CALLS

syscall	Interactive System Call
sysbreak	Set/Display System Call Breakpoint*
nosybreak	Remove System Call Breakpoint*

VRTX32 OVERVIEW COMMANDS

dtask	Display Task
dmbox	Display Mailboxes
dflag	Display Event Flag Group
dsem	Display Counting Semaphores
dsystem	Display System Status
dpart	Display Memory Partitions
dqueue	Display Queues
dout	Display Output Buffer
din	Display Input Buffer

EXECUTION COMMANDS

go	Start Execution*
task	Switch to Task Mode
cmd	Switch to Command Mode
ttrace	Single Step*
next	Single Step at Same Level*
brach	Go Until Branch*

MEMORY COMMANDS

show	Display Memory*
fill	Fill Memory*
search	Search Memory
move	Move Memory*
set	Modify Memory*
cmp	Compare Memory
follow	Display Linked Lists
list	Disassemble Memory
asm	Assemble into Memory

REGISTER COMMANDS

regs	Display General-Purpose Registers
setreg	Set General-Purpose Registers*
creg	Display Control Registers
setcreg	Set Control Registers*
hreg	Display Hardware Breakpoint Registers
sethreg	Set Hardware Breakpoint Registers*

BREAKPOINT COMMANDS

break	Set/Display Breakpoints*
nobreak	Remove Breakpoints*
gotill	Set Temporary Breakpoint*

HOST COMMUNICATION COMMANDS

dload	Download*
tmode	Transparent Mode*
upload	Upload*

SPECIAL COMMANDS

alias	Alternate Command Name
unalias	Delete Alias
call	Call User Supplied Routine
eval	Calculator
symbol	Define Symbol
nosymbol	Remove Symbol

SPECIAL FOR GMICRO

hreg/sethreg	Hardware Breakpoint Commands
asm command	Assemble Into Memory
cregs/setcreg	Display Control Registers
list command	Disassemble Memory
cregs/setcreg	Display/Set Specific Control Registers for Gmicro/100/200/300
hregs/sethreg	Hardware Instruction breakpoint Display/Set

Jim F. Ready is the Executive Vice President at Ready Systems Corporation. He has more than a decade of experience in mini- and microcomputer based real-time embedded systems. In 1981 he co-founded Ready Systems and pioneered the concept of off-the-shelf real-time operating systems software. Previously he had held marketing and engineering positions at Advanced Micro Devices and Rolm's Mil Spec Computer Division. He holds a B.S. degree from the University of Illinois and an M.A. from the University of California, Berkeley. He may be reached at Ready Systems, 470 Potrero Avenue, Sunnyvale, California, 94086.

Theodor Nissim is a Project Manager at Ready Systems Corporation, Operating Systems Group, He is in change of the design of real-time operating system kernels. Prior to joining Ready Systems, he headed up real-time software development at Motorola Israel. His research interests include parallel and distributed computing, computer architecture, and operating systems. He holds a B.Sc.E. (Cum Laude) and is currently completing his work towards an M.Sc.E., both from Technion, Haifa, Israel. He may be reached at Ready Systems Israel, Kiryat Weizmann, Einstein Street, P.O.Box 2048, Rehovot 76120, Israel.

HI32: An ITRON-Specification Operating System for the H32/200

Shinjiro Yamada, Kenichi Horikoshi,
Tsuyoshi Shimizu, and Hiroshi Takeyama
Hitachi Ltd.

ABSTRACT

One part of the TRON (The Realtime Operating System Nucleus) project is the ITRON (Industrial TRON) specifications, which describe operating systems for embedded control. Hitachi, Ltd. is implementing the ITRON specifications for the HD68000 and the H Series (H8/500, H16, H32) of Hitachi-original microprocessors and microcomputers. Development of the HI68K, HI8, and HI16 operating systems has been completed, and these are being supplied to users of the HD68000, H8, and H16.

At the high end of the H Series is the H32 family which includes the H32/200: a 32-bit microprocessor based on the TRON specification. For this chip Hitachi is currently developing HI32, a realtime operating system conforming to the ITRON2 specification. The ITRON2 specification, an upgraded version of the original ITRON1 specification, is designed specifically for high-performance processors, such as microprocessors based on the TRON specification. This paper describes the functions, implementation methods, and performance of HI32.

Keywords: HI32, H32/200, ITRON2, 32-bit microprocessor, realtime operating system

1. INTRODUCTION

The ITRON specifications include the ITRON1 specification targeted at general-purpose 16-bit microprocessors, the μITRON specification, and the ITRON2 specification.

The μITRON specification is a trimmed-down version of the ITRON specification tailored for 8-bit microprocessors and single-chip microcomputers, with standardization deemphasized in favor of adaptability. The ITRON2 specification is a functionally enhanced version of the ITRON specification designed for 32-bit microprocessors conforming to the TRON specification, featuring a greater degree of standardization (interoperability).

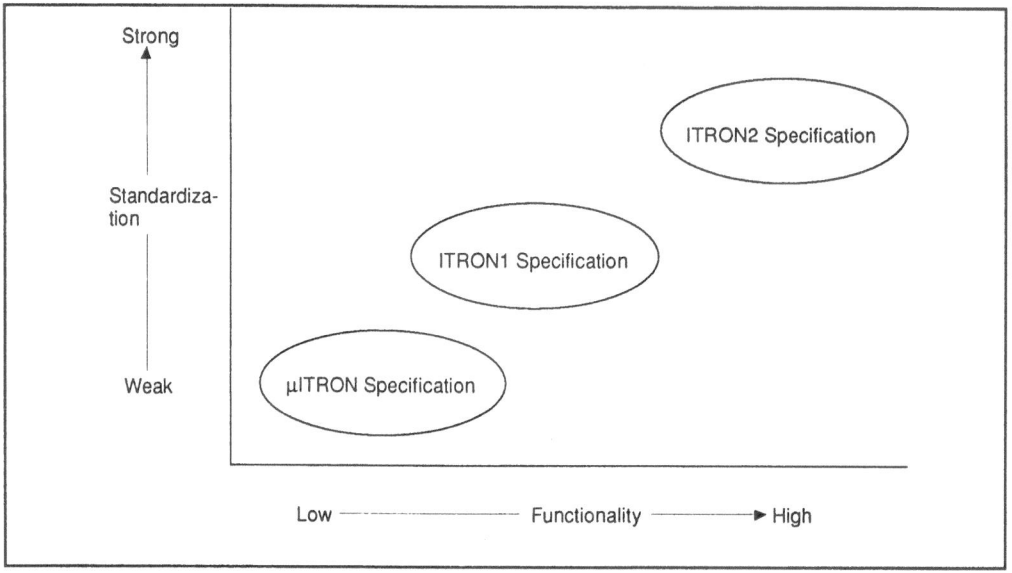

Figure 1 ITRON Specifications

Hitachi, Ltd. is implementing the ITRON specifications for the HD68000 and the Hitachi-original H Series microprocessors (H8/500, H16, H32), taking advantage of the features of each chip.

The H8/500 Series is a high-performance single-chip microcomputer series built around a high-speed CPU core with an internal 16-bit architecture. Abundant on-chip supporting hardware includes timers, I/O, ROM, and RAM. Conforming to the μITRON specification, the HI8 operating system for the H8/500 Series is both fast and highly compact, so that it can operate in the single-chip mode (using only on-chip ROM and RAM).

The H16 is a 16-bit microprocessor with on-chip DMA, timers, and serial I/O and a maximum of 16 register banks. The HI16 operating system, which implements the ITRON1 specification, uses the H16's register banks to achieve very fast context switching.

The H32/200 is one of several chips in the H32 family of 32-bit microprocessors based on the TRON specification. Its instruction set includes high-level instructions designed to speed up execution of OS functions. HI32 is an implementation the ITRON2 specification for the H32/200.

The ITRON specifications also cover file management compatible with the BTRON specification. Hitachi is implementing these file specifications as HI68KA, HI16A, and HI32A for the HI68K, HI16, and HI32 operating systems.

Table 1 HI Series of Operating Systems

OS Name	Processor	Specification	File Management
HI68K	HD68000	ITRON1 Specification	HI68KA
HI8	H8/500	µITRON Specification	—
HI16	H16	ITRON Specification	HI16A
HI32	H32/200	ITRON2 Specification	HI32A

2. H32/200 FEATURES

The H32 32-bit microprocessor family is positioned at the high end of the H Series and implements the TRON specification.

The H32 family includes three processors: the H32/100, H32/200, and H32/300. The H32/200 is designed for engineering workstations, advanced machinery control, and communication control. Table 2 lists its specifications.

For operating systems, the H32/200 offers the following features.

(1) High-speed 32-bit architecture

The H32/200 has sixteen 32-bit general registers and a six-stage pipeline. External memory access is reduced by a distributed set of caches, including an instruction cache, branch window, stack cache, and store buffer. Running at 20 MHz, the H32/200 achieves a peak performance of 10 MIPS and executes EDN benchmarks in the 6- to 7-MIPS range.

(2) High-level instructions

The H32/200 instruction set provides high-level instructions for rapid execution of OS functions. These include queue manipulation instructions, context switch instructions that enable task switching by a single instruction, string manipulation instructions for high-speed text processing, and variable-length bit field instructions for high-speed graphics.

Table 2 Outline of H32/200

Process	CMOS 1.0 μm
Resident transistors	about 730,000
Package	135 pin PGA
Performance	6 – 7 MIPS (EDN Bench mark)/20 MHz 4 MIPS (whetstone)/FPU 20 MHz
General register	32 bit × 16
Address/data bus	32 bit, separated
High speed coprocessor interface	Short time communications with exclusive control signal Maximum 8-coprocessors are connected
Number of basic instructions	100
Addressing mode	General format: 14 types, Short format: 12 types
Data type	Integer/ single-bit/ Bit-field/ BCD Floating-point/ string/ queue entry
Endian	Big Endian
Address space	4G bytes (Physical)/4G bytes (logical)
I/O space	Memory mapped I/O
Memory protection	4 level: Ring structure Protection in page/section units
Minimum bus cycle	2 clock-cycle
Resident cache memory	Instruction cache: 1kbytes Stack cache: 128 bytes Branch window: 4 entries Store buffer: 1 entry
Interrupt level	7 levels
MMU	Resident (virtual memory with demand paging method is supported Page size: 4 kbytes
Pipeline	6-stage

3. FROM THE ITRON SPECIFICATION TO THE ITRON2 SPECIFICATION

The ITRON2 specification is an upgraded version of the ITRON1 specification designed for use with advanced 32-bit microprocessors, including microprocessors based on the TRON specification. A major objective of the ITRON2 specification is to assure a high degree of compatibility among systems conforming to ITRON specifications. Its design philosophy differs from that of the ITRON1 specification in the following two points:

• Higher level of standardization

  Due to the higher performance of the processor, standardization and virtualization are carried to higher levels to improve interoperability.

• Closer affinity with other operating systems in the TRON project

  Terminology and nomenclature are more closely aligned with the BTRON specification and CTRON specification.

The ITRON2 specification consists of basic functions equivalent to those of the ITRON1 specification, additional functions, and system control functions for debugger implementation and improvement of the execution environment.

(1) Basic functions

  The basic functions are equivalent to the ITRON1 specification, with the following improvements:

a) System objects

  Objects such as tasks, event flags, and mailboxes are divided into system objects and user objects so that system objects can be protected from user tasks.

b) Abolishment of access addresses and access keys

  For high-speed processing, objects were formerly accessed using an access address or access key assigned dynamically when the object was created, but to simplify program coding and improve compatibility, access is now performed using ID numbers assigned before the start of execution.

c)   Exception management

Exception handlers for processing exceptions that occur during program execution can be created and registered dynamically for individual tasks, for all tasks in common, for extended SVC handlers, and for interrupt handlers.

In ITRON2 specification exceptions are divided into detailed classes, exception handlers are made reentrant, and to promote the standardization of exception-handling programs, more explicit specifications are given for exception management by extended SVC handlers.

d)   Event flag

Event flag function is fulfilled so that more than one task can wait for an event flag.

(2)   Additional functions

The major additional functions are the following:

a)   Rendezvous

This is a task synchronization function that was introduced in the Ada programming language. This function can be achieved by the combination of mailbox functions. However in the case of inter-task communication with acknowledge processing, overheads are reduced by the use of the rendezvous.

A queuing or buffering of data (message) is unnecessary for the user.

b)   Message buffering

Messages are sent and received by tasks through a message buffer held by the operating system. In the case of inter-task message communication using the mailbox function (basic function) in the MMU supported system, it is necessary to have an environment in which both tasks can access the same page, for transferring the message address. Using this function no environment setup is required.

c)   Forced exception

This function enables a task to force an exception in another task so that a task can request process to another task asynchronously.

d) Resource management

It's possible for the resource management to exchange the contents of specified memory indivisibly with get and release functions. This enables a task to manage its resource. This function, moreover, has no critical sections so no problem can occur with forced termination and suspend operating system function. A multi-user operating system usually releases a resource by itself at the time of task termination. Although the ITRON2 specification operating system does not release resources in order to be compact and high speed, the user can easily design a program to release all resources allocated by this function.

e) Local memory pool

Memory block obtained from memory pool of basic functions can be accessed by all tasks. Local memory pool function is for MMU system, and memory block of local memory pool can be accessed by only task that obtained a memory block.

(3) System control functions

Functions for debugger implementation are provided, as well as functions for extending the operating system.

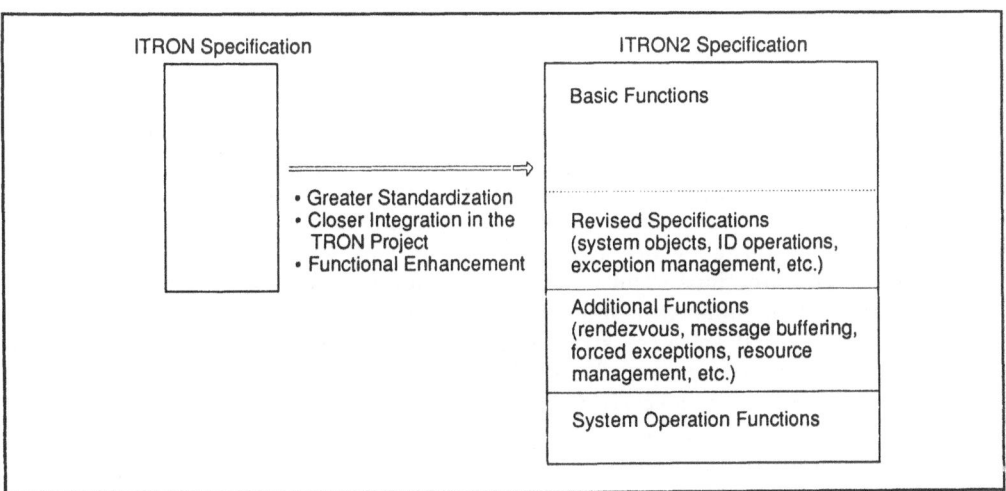

Figure 2 ITRON Specification and ITRON2 Specification

4. HI32

4.1 HI32 DESIGN PHILOSOPHY

The HI32 design philosophy comprises the following points.

(1) Compliance with the ITRON2 specification.

(2) High speed through use of the H32/200's high-level instructions. Particular efforts were made to minimize the worst-case external-interrupt response time, interrupt mask time during OS processing, and context-switch time.

(3) Modular structure, adaptable to both large and small application systems by selection of required modules.

(4) Simple system structuring, for efficient debugging.

4.2 IMPLEMENTATION OF HI32 FUNCTIONS

The first version of HI32 implements a superset of the basic functions of the ITRON2 specification. The level of implementation is detailed below.

(1) HI32 Structure

Figure 3 shows the layered structure of HI32. The system is divided into a chip kernel and a chip kernel shell. The chip kernel, which is the central part of a realtime operating system, has its own context and executes indivisibly until a requested function has been completed. Supplementing the chip kernel is an extended chip kernel, which is located in the chip kernel shell and carries out extended OS functions. These include file management and the execution of extended system calls. Although the extended chip kernel belongs to the non-task part of the overall software structure, it executes under the control of the chip kernel, and has the same set of execution statuses as defined for tasks. Table 3 lists the layers of HI32 and the corresponding H32/200 execution modes.

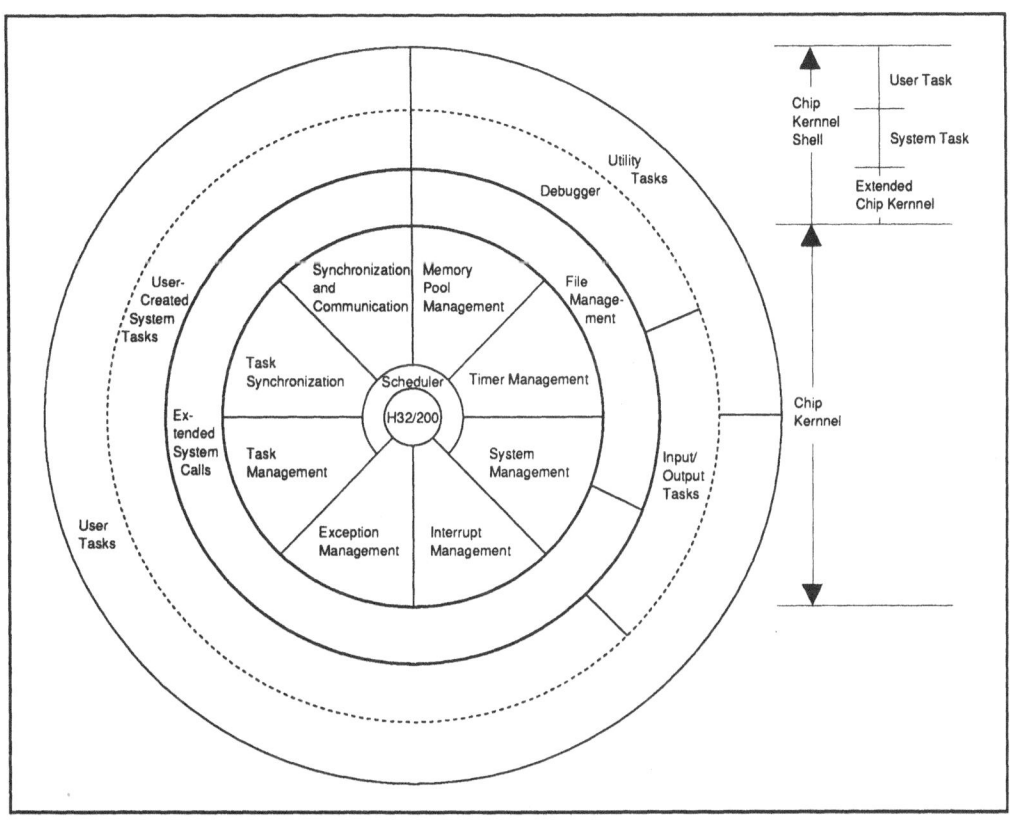

Figure 3 Structure of HI32

Table 3 HI32 and H32/200 Execution Modes

HI32 System		H32/200 Execution Mode	
Layer	Ring Level	Stack Pointer	Privilege Level
Chip kernel	RNG0	SPI	Most privileged level
Extended chip kernel		SP0	
System tasks	RNG1	SP1	Privilege level 2
(Reserved)	RNG2	SP2	Privilege level 3
User tasks	RNG3	SP3	Least privileged level

The H32/200 has four ring levels of memory protection, each with its own stack pointer (SP). Another, context-independent stack pointer (SPI) is provided for use with external interrupts. The ring level of the code currently executing is indicated in the processor status word (PSW). Ring level 0 has the highest privilege level, and can issue privileged instructions. The H32/200's memory management unit (MMU) allows reading, writing, and execution to be enabled and disabled on a page-by-page basis by means of the ring levels. Address translation using the MMU is not a standard feature of HI32, but if the user creates an address translation table, the MMU functions enable memory protection to be specified separately and in detail for the chip kernel, file management, system tasks, and user tasks. Even when the MMU functions are not used, the RNG signal output by the H32/200 can be employed to protect memory areas used by rings 0 and 1 from programs executing in rings 2 and 3.

Task management

Tasks are identified by ID numbers, and their execution is controlled by their status and priority. System tasks have IDs from −16 to −5; user tasks have IDs from 1 to 32767. HI32 applies the same classification to other objects as well (event flags, semaphores, mailboxes, and memory pools), assigning IDs from −16 to −5 to system objects and IDs from 1 to 32767 to user objects. System objects are thereby protected from user tasks.

When a system call is issued the task in question is specified by its task ID (TID). HI32 must determine which TCB is associated with the specified task in the shortest possible time and this is done by the use the hash method.

In the hash method a hash table with 64 entries is accessed by a hash function

H(X) Where   H is the Hash function and X is the Task ID of the specified task

The hash functions consists of a combination of shift and addition operations and is executed in 0.5 μs.

For a given resultant H(X) there may be more than one TCB and so TCBs are chained in a double linked list. The cases of both random and ordered assignments of TIDs have been considered so that the search time is minimized. In the case where there are less than 65 tasks search time becomes constant.

For other objects (event flags, semaphores, mailboxes and memory pools) HI32 applies the same method.

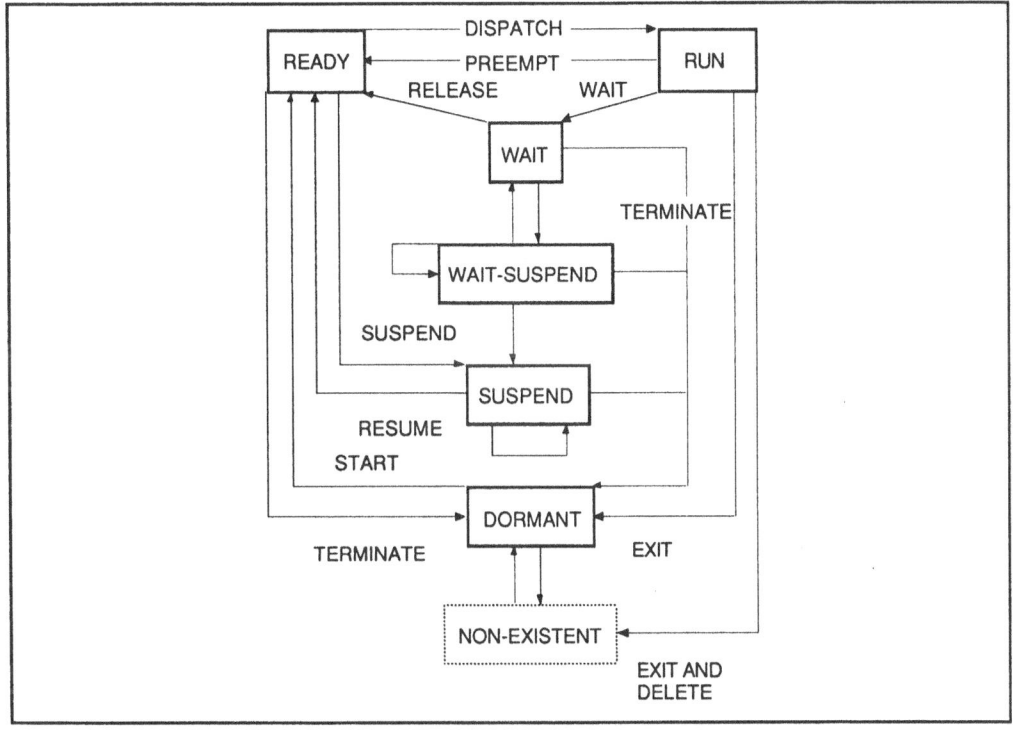

Figure 4 Task Status Transitions

Figure 4 shows the task status transitions in HI32. The ITRON2 specification designates the same task status transitions as the ITRON specification. Task execution scheduling is based on task priorities, which run from –16 to –5 and 1 to 255, smaller numbers indicating higher priorities. If two or more tasks with the same priority are ready for execution (in the READY state in figure 4), execution is controlled on a first-come-first-served basis.

To achieve high speed ready queue operation each priority has a unique ready queue. To keep processing time down the H32/200 has a queuing instruction and all queues are constructed from double linked lists.

In order that the next task in the ready queue be dispatched as quickly as possible HI32 uses a bit map table to search for the specified TCB in the shortest possible time. Each bit in the bit map table corresponds to a ready queue of a specified priority where a bit value of 0 indicates that the queue is empty and a bit value of 1 indicates that the queue contains one or more TCBs.

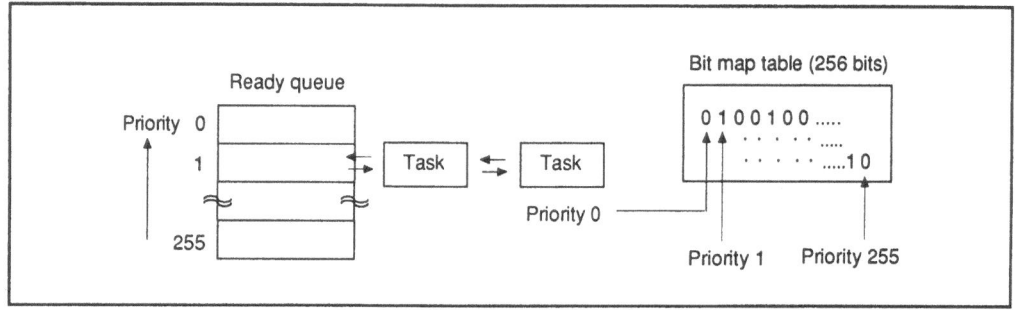

Figure 5 Relationship of Ready Queue and Bit Map Table

The H32/200 has a BVSCH instruction which optimizes bit search speed in a variable length bit field and returns the bit position in a general register. Using the BVSCH instruction it is possible to locate the bit in a time between 0.7 μs and 2.1 μs.

Co-processors are managed as part of task management. When a task is created, up to eight co-processors can be assigned for its use.

(3) Interrupt management

The user can create interrupt handlers for external interrupts and enter them dynamically in the H32/200's interrupt vector table, using a system call. Then when an interrupt occurs, the interrupt handler is started quickly without OS intervention.

If a request for context switching occurs during execution of an interrupt handler, due to a wup_tsk system call for example, execution of the interrupt handler is given priority and the context switch is postponed until the the return from the handler. This is referred to as the delayed dispatching rule.

HI32 implements delayed dispatching with a hardware function of the H32/200 provided explicitly for this purpose. The H32/200 has a delayed interrupt request register (DI), the value in which can be set by software. The DI value is compared with the interrupt mask value (IMASK) in the PSW at breakable points in instruction execution, and a delayed interrupt request is issued when IMASK > DI.

Figure 6 illustrates the delayed dispatching process. When task switching is requested from an interrupt handler, the operating system sets the value 14 in the delayed interrupt request register. On return from the interrupt handler a delayed interrupt request is automatically accepted and the task switch is carried out.

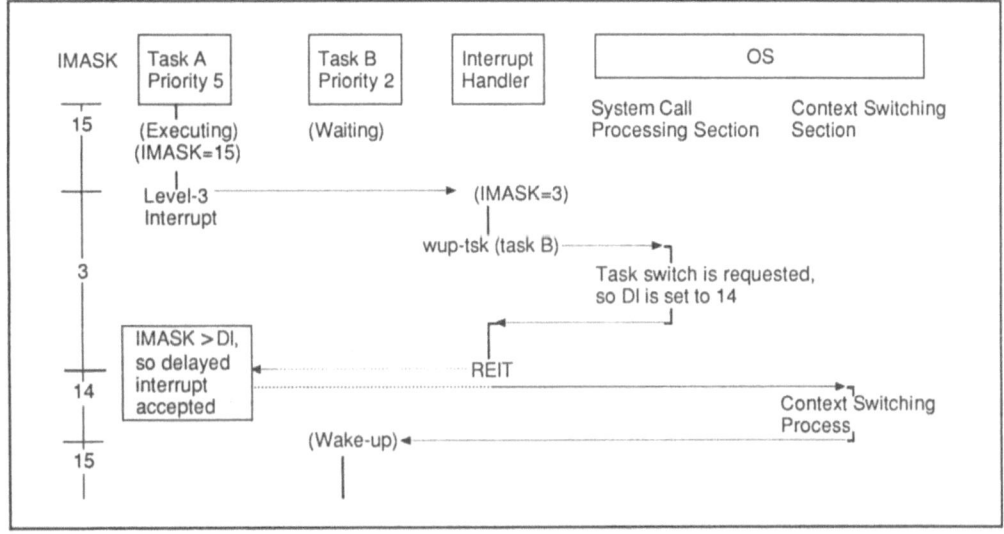

Figure 6 Delayed Dispatching

(4)   High-level language service

For tasks and handlers coded in high-level languages such as C, it was formerly necessary to set up the high-level language execution environment for each task or handler separately (by saving registers, setting parameters, setting the stack pointer, etc.). HI32 dispenses with this requirement by bringing these functions into the operating system.

When a task or handler coded in a high-level language is invoked, instead of being invoked directly, it is invoked through a high-level-language service routine that establishes the high-level-language execution environment. The operating system has one such routine for each type of task or handler: one for tasks, one for supervisor call handlers, one for interrupt handlers, one for exception handlers, and so on. When created and installed, every task or handler is assigned an attribute specifying whether intervention of the high-level-language service routine is required.

Different compilers may follow different parameter-setting procedures. HI32 permits the user to cope with such differences by making easy modifications to the high-level-language service routine, without having to modify application programs.

(5)   Debugger

The debugger executes as a system task under HI32. Application tasks can be debugged in realtime multitask environment. Table 4 lists the debugger commands.

Table 4 Debug Commands

Command	Function
CRE-TSK	Create task
STA-TSK	Start task
SUS-TSK	Suspend task
RSM-TSK	Resume task
FRSM-TSK	Forcibly resume task
TER-TSK	Terminate task
DEL-TSK	Delete task
FLG-STS	Get event flag status
SEM-STS	Get semaphore status
MBX-STS	Get mailbox status
MPL-STS	Get memory pool status
RM	Modify task register contents
TSK	Display task control block information
STS	Display all tasks in specified status
ASM	One-line assemble
DASM	Disassemble memory contents and display
PRA	Attach printer
PRD	Detach printer
F	Initialize memory
D	Display memory contents
M	Modify memory contents
MOV	Move memory contents
SCH	Search memory contents
BS	Set breakpoint
B	Display breakpoint
BC	Clear breakpoint
GO	Execute task stopped at breakpoint
TSCST	Start system call trace
TSCED	End system call trace
TSCDP	Display system call trace
TSCPT	Move system call trace display pointer
S-SVC	Issue SVC
DT	Set or get date and time
HLP	Help function
EXIT	Terminate debugger

Table 5 HI32 System Calls

- **Task Management**

System Call	Function	Function Level*
cre_tsk	Create task	I1
sta_tsk	Start task	I1
del_tsk	Delete task	I1
ext_tsk	Exit self task	I1
exd_tsk	Exit and delete self task	I1
abo_tsk	Abort task	I1
ter_tsk	Terminate task	I1
ras_ter	Raise terminate request	I1
chg_pri	Change task priority	I1
rot_rdq	Rotate ready queue	I1
rel_wai	Release from wait state	I1
get_tid	Get task identifier	I1
tsk_sts	Get task status	I1
hdr_sts	Get handler status	I1

- **Task Synchronization**

System Call	Function	Function Level*
sus_tsk	Suspend task	I1
rsm_tsk	Resume task	I1
frsm_tsk	Force resume task	I1
slp_tsk	Sleep task	I1
wai_tsk	Wait for wakeup task	I1
wup_tsk	Wakeup task	I1
can_wup	Cancel wakeup task	I1

- **Synchronization and Communication**

System Call	Function	Function Level*
cre_flg	Create event flag	I1
del_flg	Delete event flag	I1
set_flg	Set event flag	I1
clr_flg	Clear event flag	I1
wai_flg	Wait event flag	I1
flg_sts	Get event flag status	I1
cre_sem	Create semaphore	I1
del_sem	Delete semaphore	I1
sig_sem	Signal semaphore	I1
wai_sem	Wait on semaphore	I1
sem_sts	Get semaphore status	I1
cre_mbx	Create mailbox	I1
del_mbx	Delete mailbox	I1
snd_msg	Send message to mailbox	I1
rcv_msg	Receive message from mailbox	I1
mbx_sts	Get mailbox status	I1

- **Interrupt Management**

System Call	Function	Function Level*
def_int	Define interrupt handler	I1
ret_int	Return from interrupt handler	I1
chg_ims	Change interrupt mask	I1

- **Exception Management**

System Call	Function	Function Level*
def_ext	Define exit handler	I1
def_cex	Define CPU exception handler	I1
def_sex	Define system call exception handler	I1
ret_exc	Return from exception handler	I1
end_exc	End exception handler	I1
clr_ems	Clear exception mask	I1
set_ems	Set exception mask	I1
idef_ext	Define exit handler for non-task	I1
idef_cex	Define CPU exception handler for non-task	I1
idef_sex	Define system call exception handler for non-task	I1

- **Memory Pool Management**

System Call	Function	Function Level*
cre_mpl	Create memory pool	I1
del_mpl	Delete memory pool	I1
get_blk	Get shared memory block	I1
rel_blk	Release shared memory block	I1
mpl_sts	Get memory pool status	I1
blk_sts	Get shared memory block status	I1

- **Timer Management**

System Call	Function	Function Level*
set_tim	Set time	I1
get_tim	Get time	I1
dly_tsk	Delay task	I1
cyc_wup	Cyclic wakeup task	I1
can_cyc	Cancel cyclic wakeup task	I1

- **System Management**

System Call	Function	Function Level*
def_svc	Define supervisor call handler	I1
ret_svc	Return from supervisor call handler	I1
get_ver	Get version No.	I1
psw_sts	Get processor status word	I1

- **Exception Management for Extended SVC**

System Call	Function	Function Level*
sdef_cex	Define CPU exception handler for extended SVC	System control

* Function level: I1 indicates a basic function of the ITRON2 specification.

5. HI32 PERFORMANCE

Two key indices of realtime operating-system performance are the time taken to respond to an external interrupt, and the time taken to process a system call that switches task execution.

Except under special conditions, the interrupt response time of HI32 (interrupt mask time) is 8 μs at a 20-MHz clock rate.

The special conditions occur when an entry is inserted in a user-specified, priority-based semaphore, mailbox, or memory-pool queue. The high-level QSCH instruction provided by the H32/200 greatly speeds up the search for the insertion position in the priority queue, but to assure queue integrity, interrupts are masked while the QSCH instruction code is executing. Figure 7 compares the time required for queue insertion with and without the QSCH instruction.

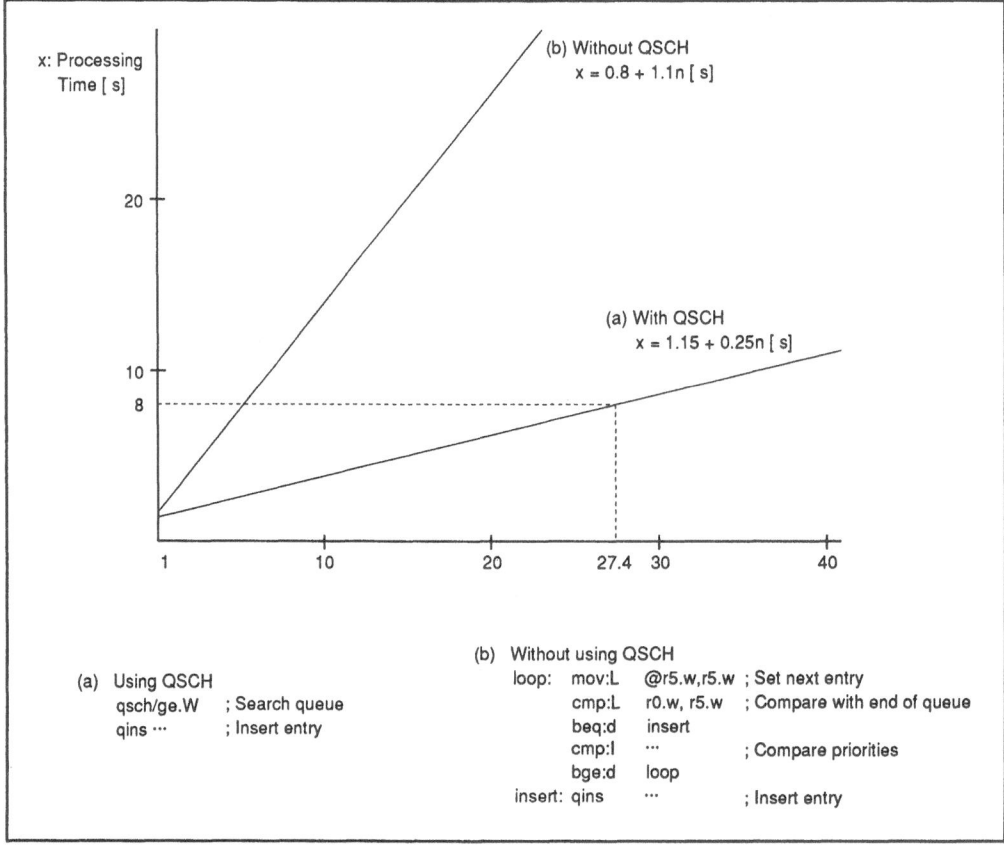

Figure 7 Insertion Time for Priority-Based Queue

In case (b) if interrupts are enabled the algorithm becomes more complex as it is necessary to monitor events form interrupt handlers to keep a consistency between queue status and object status.

Therefore HI32 makes use of the QSCH and QINS instructions.

However in the case of QSCH and QINS instructions it is still necessary to disable interrupts in order to achieve the required consistency during pre and post processing stages.

If there are less than 20 entries in a priority based queue HI32 guaranties an interrupt inhibit time of less than 8 μs.

Such special cases can be disregarded in realistic system designs. They are clearly outweighed by the speed-up of system call processing gained from the QSCH instruction.

Task switching is typified by the wup_tsk (wakeup task) system call, which is processed in 22 μs for an environment with less than 65 tasks.

6. CONCLUSION

The HI32 realtime operating system implements the ITRON2 specification for the H32/200 32-bit microprocessor, which is based on the TRON specification. HI32 offers a high level of functionality and speed, including an interrupt mask time of 8 μs and a task switching time of 22 μs. Its extensive functionality is modularized so that it can be tailored to both large and small systems, with a minimum size of 68 kbytes.

The authors would like to express their gratitude to Dr. Ken Sakamura of The University of Tokyo for his guidance in the development of HI32.

Acknowledgement

The authors would like to thank the members of the TRON Association for their cooperation in standardizing external specifications.

References

1. Ken Sakamura, TRON Project 1987, Springer-Verlag, 1987

2. Ken Sakamura, TRON Overview, Kyoritsu Shuppan, 1988, p. 150 (in Japanese)

3. Ken Sakamura, (Ed.), Introduction to ITRON, Iwanami Shoten, 1988, p. 271 (in Japanese)

4. Ken Sakamura, (Ed.), TRON Project '87 – '88, Personal Media, 1988, p. 400 (in Japanese)

5. Saito et al., "Structure and Performance of ITRON for the NS32000, " Proceedings of 1st TRON Realtime OS Research Panel, TRON Realtime Operating System Provisional Research Committee, IECE of Japan, Apr. 1987, pp. 40 – 52 (in Japanese)

6. Monden et al., "ITRON" (technical paper), TRON Committee Report, TRON Assoc., Vol. 1, No. 2, Sept. 1988, pp. 59 – 76 (in Japanese)

7. Ken Sakamura, TRON Project 1988, Springer-Verlag, 1988

8. Hiroshi Monden, "Introduction to ITRON the Industry-oriented Operating System," IEEE Micro, Vol. 7, No. 2, pp. 45 – 52, April 1987

9. Ken Sakamura, "The TRON Project," IEEE Micro, Vol. 7, No. 2, pp. 8 –14, April 1987

10. Ken Sakamura, "BTRON The Business-oriented Operating System," IEEE Micro, Vol. 7, No. 2, pp. 53 – 65

11. Ken Sakamura, "μITRON Design Directions," TRON Study Group, TRON Assoc., Vol. 1, No. 1, June. 1988, pp. 1 – 17 (in Japanese)

12. Nakata et al. "MR7700: An Implementation of μITRON Specification on 16-bit Single-chip Microcontroller," TRON Project 1988, Springer-Verlag pp. 55 – 66

13. Takeyama et al. "HI8: A Realtime Operating System with μITRON Specification for the H8/500," TRON Project 1988, Springer-Verlag, pp. 35 – 54

14. Takeyama et al. "Design Concept and Implementation of μITRON Specification for the H8/500 Series," Compcon Spring '89, IEEE Computer Society Press, February 1989, pp. 48 – 53

15. Akito Honda, "Implementation of μITRON for the F2MC–8," TRON Technical Study Group, TRON Assoc., Vol. 1, No. 2, Oct. 1988, pp. 59 – 68 (in Japanese)

16. Ken Sakamura et al. "Chapter 5: TRON CPU," TRON Project 1987, Springer-Verlag, pp. 199 – 308

S. Yamada joined Hitachi, Ltd. in 1988 and now an engineer in the Microcomputer System Engineering Dept. at the Semiconductor Design & Development Center of Hitachi's Semiconductor Division. He is currently engaged in research and development of realtime operating systems for microcomputers. He received his BA in electronic engineering from the University of Kansai in 1988.

H. Takeyama joined Hitachi, Ltd. in 1969 and is now a senior engineer in the Microcomputer System Engineering Dept. at the Semiconductor Design & Development Center of Hitachi's Semiconductor Division. Since 1983 he has participated in research and development of realtime operating systems for microcomputers and in-circuit emulation software, and in product planning for microcomputer support tools. He received his BA electronic engineering from Fukuoka institute of technology in 1969.

T. Shimizu joined Hitachi, Ltd. in 1978 and now an engineer in the Microcomputer System Engineering Dept. at the Semiconductor Design & Development Center of Hitachi's Semiconductor Division. He is currently engaged in research and development of realtime operating systems for microcomputers. He received his BA in informatics from the University of Osaka in 1976 and his master's degree from the same school in 1978.

K. Horikoshi joined the Hitachi Yonezawa Electronics Co., Ltd. in 1975 and is now an engineer in the Electronic System Design Section. His current work is in research and development of real time operating systems for microcomputers. He was graduated from Yonezawa Polytechnic Institute in 1975.

Above authors may be reached at: Semiconductor Design & Development Center, Hitachi, Ltd., 5-20-1, Jousuihon-cho Kodaira, Tokyo 187 Japan.

Chapter 2: BTRON

The µBTRON Bus: Functions and Applications

Ken Sakamura
Department of Information Science, Faculty of Science, University of Tokyo
Kazushi Tamai, Katuya Tanaka, Shigeo Tsunoda
Fourth Laboratory, Applied Electronics R & D Laboratories, Yamaha Corporation
Kanehisa Tsurumi
Center for Musical Instrument and Software Development, Yamaha Corporation
Makoto Kaneko
System Laboratory, Semiconductor R & D Laboratories, Yamaha Corporation

ABSTRACT

In addition to the BTRON bus which is used as a heavy-duty LAN, the BTRON standard includes the µBTRON bus, which is a simple LAN used to connect a BTRON-based workstation with electronic stationery goods. The µBTRON bus is intended to be a low-cost LAN which takes advantage of the following features of TRON.

1) Realtime response

2) Ease of use

3) Compatibility

In order to provide realtime response, the µBTRON bus is a token ring type LAN, but from considerations of ease of use, cable routing has been simplified so that it can be done by non-technical users. Standardization is expected to bring cost reductions of the basic devices.

It is expected that the use of systems such as Home Bus system and ISDN will continue to spread. By interconnecting with these systems, we expect that BTRON will find even wider application as the home network for the 1990s.

Keywords:µBTRON bus,electronic stationery goods,token ring,physical layer,MAC sub-layer

1. INTRODUCTION

The BTRON bus and the µBTRON bus are the two network standards which allow BTRON-based machine to function as a communication one. These standards are important architectural elements in the highly functional distributed system (HFDS) toward which TRON aims, and allow connection between machines with ITRON-based operating system (OS) and as a bridge to CTRON-based machines.

Among these standards, the μBTRON bus intends to be a serious LAN standard capable of handling realtime transmission of multi-media data including images. In contrast, the μBTRON bus standard we will be explaining in this paper is intended to be a simple, low-cost LAN that takes advantage of the realtime characteristics which are a central concept of TRON.

2. PURPOSES AND REQUIRED SPECIFICATIONS

The μBTRON bus is a simple master/slave type LAN which connects BTRON-based workstations and electronic stationery goods. The required specifications of the μBTRON bus are as follows.

1) Capable of simultaneously controlling multiple devices. In a typical application, a single BTRON-based workstation will control several electronic stationery goods. In a more specialized example, it is also possible for electronic stationery goods to communicate each other.

2) Bandwidth of several Mbits/second.

3) Use in an office or home is assumed, and the physical cable should be thin and flexible.

4) The system control functions should be distributed to the various devices so that the system will function regardless of whether or not a device is connected, or whether or not the power of a device is turned on.

5) The cable, connectors, and controllers should be inexpensive.

6) The system should be able to interface with the Home Bus via a gateway.

7) The system should be able to transmit audio or musical data in realtime. In particular, realtime transmission should be possible even while high volume bulk data transmission such as file transmission is taking place.

8) The LAN cable should be extensible to a distance of several hundred meters.

9) It should be possible to connect up to 100 nodes.

The specification of the μBTRON bus is based on the IEEE802.5 that is a standard for a token ring. Table 1 is a comparison of the various LAN systems.

Existing LAN systems were originally designed for industrial use. If we are to make such systems suitable for the type of personal network for which the μBTRON bus is intended, we must deal with the following problems.

- The physical connectors are large.
- Handling is difficult since the cable is thick and inflexible.
- Performance is not sufficient for realtime transmission of music or voice data.

The μBTRON bus specification is made in order to deal with the above problems. Details will be given in the following chapter.

Table 1: Comparison Chart of LAN Systems

Item	StarLAN	Ethernet	TokenBus	TokenRing	μBTRON bus
Specification	IEEE802.3 1BASE5	IEEE802.3 10BASE5	IEEE802.4	IEEE802.5	—
Media access control method	CSMA/CD	CSMA/CD	Token passing	Token passing	Token passing
Transmission (rate)	1Mbps (base band)	10Mbps (base band)	1Mbps,5Mbps, 10Mbps,(base/ broad band)	4Mbps,16Mbps (base band)	4Mbps (base band)
Transmission medium	unshielded twisted pair	coaxial cable (50 ohms)	coaxial cable (75 ohms)	Shielded twisted pair	Shielded twisted pair (optical fiber cable)
Priority management	none	none	none	yes(8 level)	yes(4 level)
Realtime ability	× (not during high load)	× (not during high load)	△ (long token rotation time, depending on data length)	○ (short token rotation time, depending on data length)	◎ (short token rotation time, independing on data length)

3. INTRODUCTION TO SPECIFICATIONS

We will be explaining the characteristics of the μBTRON bus physical layer and MAC (Media Access Control) sub-layer.

3.1 Physical Layer

The μBTRON bus has a transmission speed of 4 Mbps, and uses Differential Manchester Encoding. The wiring system of the μBTRON bus has been designed in order to meet the requirements of personal appiications. Provision has also been made for supplying power to connected equipment.

(a) Wiring method

Wiring cost and handling ease were the primary considerations when planning the μBTRON bus wiring method. The result was that the connectors were simplified, and that provision was made

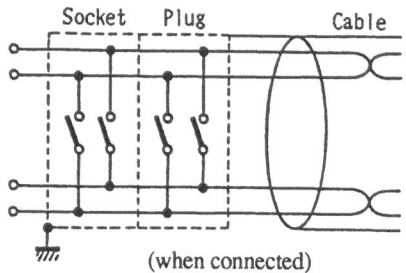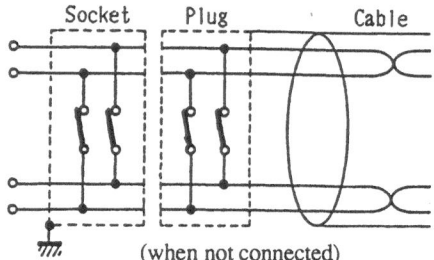

Fig.1: Connectors

for allowing non-technical users to easily and correctly connect devices. The main features of the μBTRON wiring method are as follows.

- Cable: In order to make bus-type connections, the cable includes a return path.
- Connectors: We use mechanical connectors. When this connector is not connected, the send and return signal lines are mechanically shorted, and return the signal at that point. This function allows the rest of the network to continue operating even when a station is cut off from the transmission line, as shown in Fig.1. When a station is connected to the cable and is not supplied with power, the signal is returned at a relay in the station, as shown in Fig.2.
- Connection method: As shown in Fig.4, two methods of connection are possible; branching from a concentrator unit, and directly daisy-chaining stations. The two methods can be used in conjunction, and concentrators can be connected to each other. In this type of system, daisy-chaining stations to a concentrator in a disorderly fashion can result in two or more rings separated from each other, as shown in Fig.3. To prevent this from happening, the μBTRON bus uses four types of connector and two types of cable as shown in Fig.4. This way, cable connections which would result in a loop returning to the concentrator are impossible.

The actual shape of the wires and connectors are currently under consideration by the BTRON hardware standardization committee.

(b) Power supply

To allow small electronic stationery goods to operate without a separate power cable, power can be supplied from the transmission line to stations connected to the μBTRON bus cable.

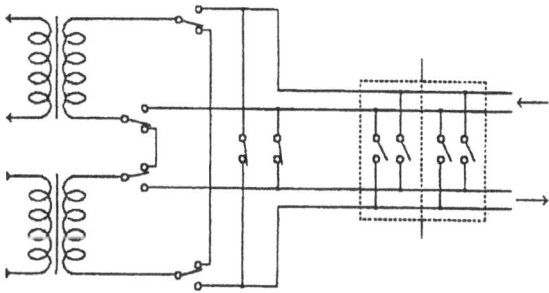

Fig.2 A relay in a station (Insertion Control Relay)

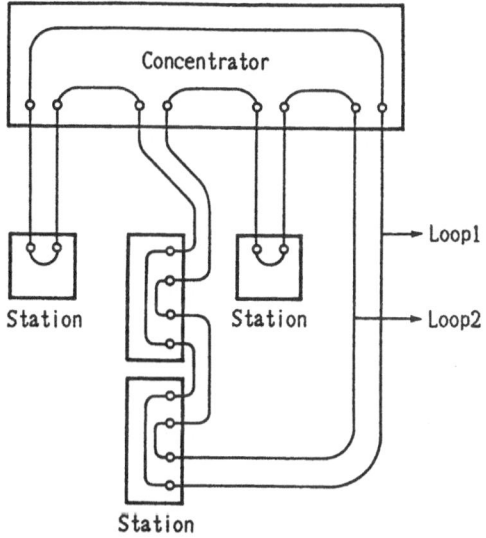

Fig.3 An example of faultly connection

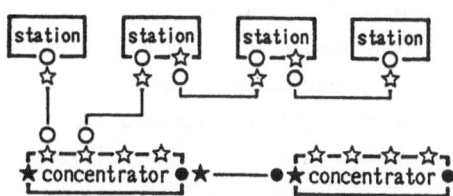

○☆●★ : connector (only ○--☆ and ●--★ can be connected)
○--☆ : cable (connection is possible only between stations and from
        station to concentrator)
●--★ : cable (for connection between concentrators)

Fig.4 Wiring of the μBTRON bus

3.2 MAC Sub-layer

The frame format of the μBTRON bus is shown in Fig.5. The basic format is made to improve realtime performance. Also, special MAC frames that were thought to be useful for implementing electronic stationery goods have been defined.

Details are given below.

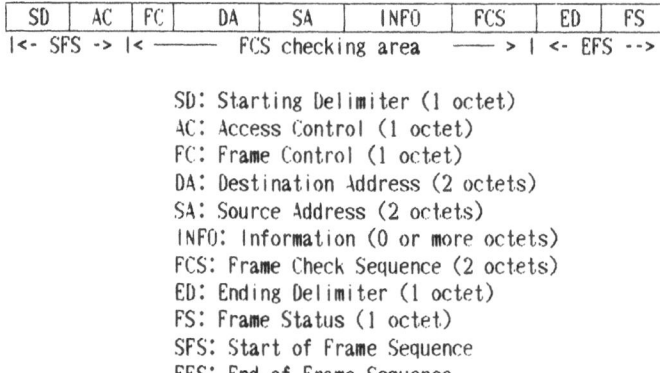

SD: Starting Delimiter (1 octet)
AC: Access Control (1 octet)
FC: Frame Control (1 octet)
DA: Destination Address (2 octets)
SA: Source Address (2 octets)
INFO: Information (0 or more octets)
FCS: Frame Check Sequence (2 octets)
ED: Ending Delimiter (1 octet)
FS: Frame Status (1 octet)
SFS: Start of Frame Sequence
EFS: End of Frame Sequence

Fig.5 μBTRON bus frame format

(a) Improving the realtime performance

Data transmitted in the network is divided into Batch data (non-realtime data such as file transfers) and Realtime data (data which must be sent in realtime). Batch data is transmitted in a low priority frame, and realtime data is transmitted in a high priority frame.

To determine the transmission delay time for realtime data, we consider a condition of high load where low-priority frames are occupying 100% of the network's effective bandwidth. In this condition, high-priority frames should be able to keep the transmission delay to a fixed value (a few milliseconds). If the frame length of high-priority frames is short enough,the worst case of transmission delay between transmitting and receiving stations will be as follows.

(transmission delay) = (token waiting time) + (ring circumferential delay)

The token waiting time will be the greatest in the following cases.

1) The high-priority frame originates from a station immediately after the token reservation bit in the header of a low-priority frame has   just passed that station, so that the station can not make a   reservation to transmit. In addition, the length of the low-priority   frame is the maximum frame length.

2) Following this, suppose that another station takes the token and transmits a low-priority frame before the token returns to the station which is waiting to send the high-priority frame of case 1). Further suppose that low-priority frame is also of the maximum length. The station that wants to transmit the high-priority frame of case 1) will take the token after this low-priority frame has passed, and then transmit its own high-priority frame.

The transmission delay in these cases will be approximately as follows.

(transmission delay) = (maximum length frame transmission time) x 2
+ (ring circumferential delay) x 2

These results show that with a data transmission speed of 4 Mbps, a delay time of 3 bits per station, 100 stations, and a maximum frame length of 200 bytes, the transmission delay can be kept to about 1 msec.

On the other hand, if we decrease the maximum frame length, the overhead of the software transmission processing becomes relatively high, and the effective transmission speed of batch data is lowered. To solve this problem, we added a function to the MAC sub-layer that allows split frame transmission. Details are as follows.

- Split transmission is possible only for lowest-priority data.
- If the data does not fit into one frame, it is split at the transmitting source, sent into the network as two or more frames, and reassembled into the original data at the receiver.
- All the split frames which make up a single piece of data can be transmitted during a single capture of the token.
- If a station wishes to transmit high-priority data, it can make a reservation to interrupt the sequence of split frames, and transmit a high-priority frame.
- If a high-priority frame has interrupted the transmission of split frames, transmission of the remaining frames will resume after the interrupt.

We restricted this split frame transmission to only the lowest-priority data because we expect that this function will be implemented in hardware, and therefore the reassembly process at the receiving side has to be kept relatively simple. This means that the receiving station will not have to handle the reassembly of multiple data received simultaneously.

In the μBTRON bus, the address length is fixed at 2 bytes, and the FCS is also 2 bytes. From the number of nodes (maximum 100) one byte would be sufficient, but since the function address is bit mapped, 8 bits were not sufficient, and 2 bytes were used.

The measures explained above allow the μBTRON bus to achieve realtime response without sacrificing batch data transmission efficiency.

(b) Special MAC frames

The μBTRON bus defines TICK, I/O, and several watch-related MAC frames.
Details are as follows.

1) TICK MAC frame

TICK frames are used as synchronization signals within the network. Stations in the network
a functional address to periodically   transmit TICK frames, and supply a synchronization
clock to two or more reception stations. This function can be used when two or   more
devices must operate in synchronization with a single device;   for example, instruments and
a sequencer. 8 bits of the 13 bit   functional address are assigned to the TICK, meaning that
a single   network can simultaneously have eight clocks.

2) I/O MAC frame

I/O MAC frames are used as simple input and output. By directly   supporting two pairs
(input and output) of 8 bit terminals at LSI level, the μBTRON bus can be used as if you
were accessing an IO port. Once the transmission path is set appropriately, this allows data
transmission to take place without passing through software.

3) Watch-related MAC frames

A network contains one master watch, and these frames are used to   adjust the watches of all
stations to this master watch. Defining   MAC frames allows us to minimize the time
differences between   stations. Watch-related MAC frames are as follows.

AMW = Assign Master Watch
DMW = Deassign Master Watch
RW = Reply Watch
QAW = Request to Adjust Watch
AW = Adjust Watch
QMW = Request Master Watch
RMW = Reply Master Watch

4. AN EXAMPLE OF AN APPLIED SYSTEM

The μBTRON bus is in the form of a LAN, but has the essential characteristics of a high-speed
external bus that connects peripherals to BTRON. Thus, it can be used in applications similar to
SCSI or GP-IB. It is possible to connect devices in series to each other in a simple layout as
shown in Fig.6. A power supply is provided for small electronic stationery goods, and even
smaller handy-type devices can be used as part of a wireless system using infrared rays, etc.

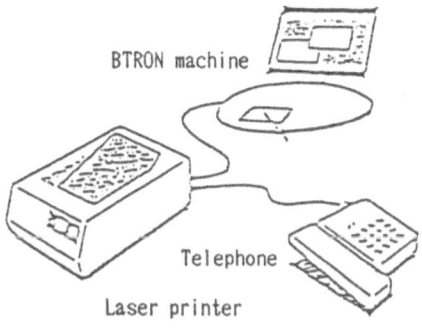

Fig.6: Series connection

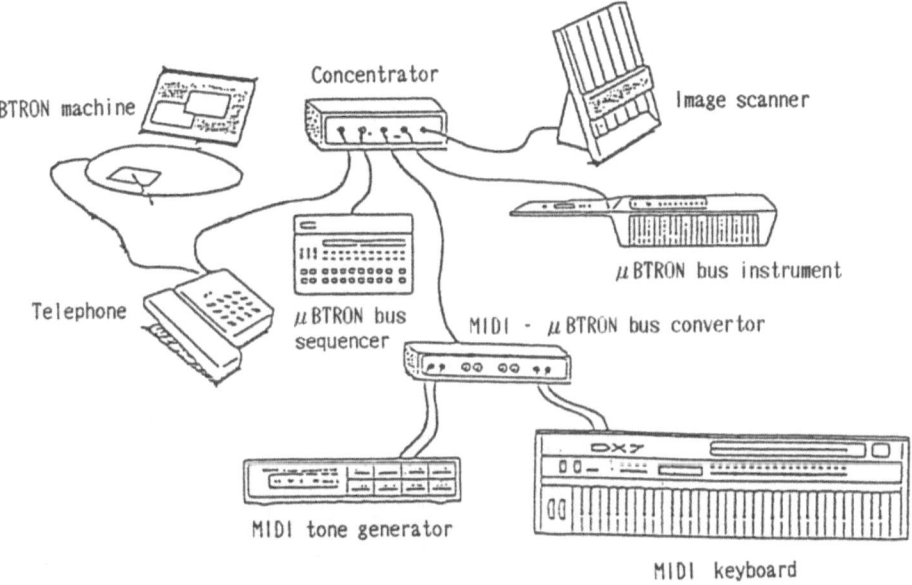

Fig.7: Combination of star and series connections

It is also possible to use a concentrator to connect the various devices in a star topology, and also possible to combine star and series connections. Fig.7 shows a next-generation music network that utilizes the realtime characteristics of the μBTRON bus. This makes it possible to construct a system that is compatible with the MIDI standard currently in wide use, yet with the advantages of high speed and high reliability.

Recently, there is growing interest in making home networks such as the Home Bus System (HBS) practical. Some home control or security systems such as those specialized for AV or air conditioning are already in operation. There are also ambitious plans for home control systems that are completely networked including amenities, such as the TRON-based intelligent house project being constructed in the Roppongi district of Tokyo. It is highly possible that the µBTRON bus will be used as the network connecting the various devices, sensors, and control centers used in such systems. By using the µBTRON bus, the various devices will be able to communicate in greater detail, and will provide a user-friendly system with consistent operability unified by the BTRON concept. When this network using µBTRON bus is interconnected via gateways with existing networks such as ISDN and HBS, we can expect applications to extend to an even broader area (Fig.8).

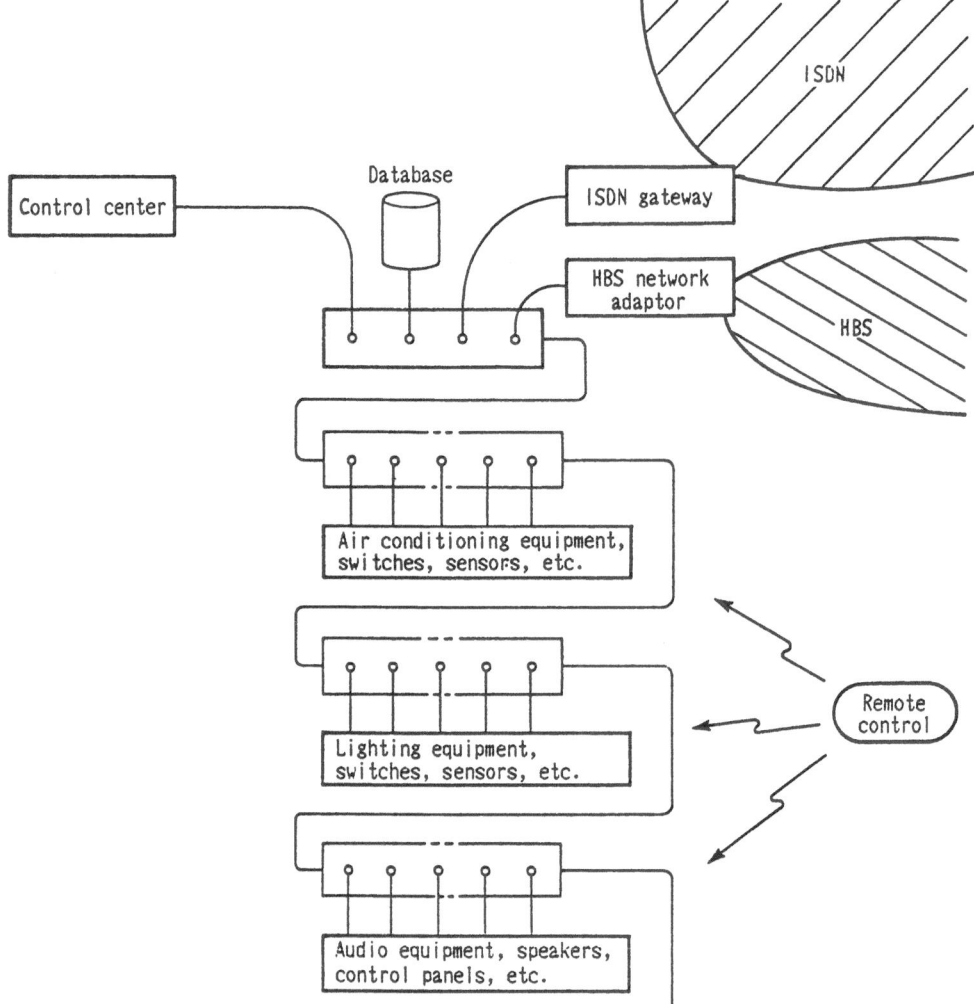

Fig.8: Home control using the µBTRON bus

5. CONCLUSION

To determine the μBTRON bus specifications, we took into account the needs of a network to connect the electronic stationery goods of the 1990s, and made several additions and modifications to the IEEE802.5 standard.

At present, the transmission control LSIs central to this plan are being designed. In the simplest configuration, basic transmission control can be achieved by adding an external single chip CPU with μITRON-based OS and a pulse transformer.

In the future, various activities aimed at the popularization of this standard will be necessary. These include defining the transmission protocol for higher level or for gateways, establishing validation standards for testing, and preparing protocol testers etc. as part of a developmental environment.

In closing, we would like to take this opportunity to express our thanks to the members of the BTRON hardware standardization working group of the TRON association for their help in the writing of this paper.

REFERENCES

[1] K.Sakamura, K.Tsurumi, H.Kato, "μBTRON bus : Design and Evaluation of Musical Data Transfer",TRON Project 1987 (Proc. of the Third TRON Project Symposium),1987.

[2] K.Sakamura, K.Tsurumi, H.Kato, "Applying of μBTRON bus to Music LAN",the Fourth Realtime Architecture TRON Study Group,1988(In Japanese).

[3] K.Sakamura,"New Concepts from the TRON Project" ,Iwanami-Shoten,Tokyo,1987(In Japanese).

[4] K.Sakamura, "Making of TRON",Kyoritsu-Syuppan,Tokyo,1987(In Japanese).

[5] ANSI/IEEE Std 802.5-1985,ISO/dp 8802/5, "An American National Standard IEEE Standards for Local Area Networks:Token Ring Access Method and Phisical Layer Specifications",IEEE,1986.

Katsuya Tanaka: He is an engineer/researcher of Forth Laboratory, Applied Electronics R&D, YAMAHA Corporation. He received his B.S. degree from Shizuoka University in 1988.

Kazushi Tamai: He is an engineer/researcher of Forth Laboratory, Applied Electronics R&D, YAMAHA Corporation. He received his B.S. degree from Nagoya University in 1980.

Shigeo Tsunoda: He is a manager of Forth Laboratory, Applied Electronics R&D, YAMAHA Corporation. He received his B.S. and M.S. degrees from Waseda University in 1972 and 1974.

Kanehisa Tsurumi: He is a software engineer/ researcher of Center for Musical Instrument and Software Development, YAMAHA Corporation. He received his B.S. and M.S. degrees from Nagoya University in 1979 and 1981.

Makoto Kaneko: He is a Senior Engineer of Semiconductor R&D Laboratories, YAMAHA corporation. He received his B.S. and M.S. degrees from Shizuoka University in 1973 and 1975.

Ken Sakamura: He is an associate professor at the Department of Information Science, University of Tokyo. He holds Ph. D. in EE. He has been the leader of the TRON project which he started to build a new computer system architecture for 1990's since 1984.

Implementation Issues of the TACL/TULS Language System on BTRON

Noboru Koshizuka, Hiroaki Takada, Masaharu Saito, Yasushi Saito, and Ken Sakamura
Department of Information Science, Faculty of Science, University of Tokyo

ABSTRACT

In the computer systems of the TRON Project, many interfaces are described with TULS (TRON Universal Language System). TACL (TRON Application Control-flow Language) is a language based on TULS which defines the protocol between the end user and the BTRON system. TACL can describe various programs such as batch programs, home automation control programs, and some application programs of BTRON. This TACL/TULS language system consists of four components: the TACL/TULS Manager, the Dictionary Manager, the TACL/TULS interpreter task, and the TACL/TULS program editor.

Keywords: TAD, BTRON, macro language, programming environment, language interpreter

1. INTRODUCTION

The ultimate goal of the TRON Project is to create an HFDS(Highly Functional Distributed System), for which TULS (TRON Universal Language System) defines various interfaces to realize. TULS is not one simple language, but rather a language system which indicates guidelines of TRON standard language specifications. BTRON, CTRON , ITRON, and MTRON use TULS to realize common data representation formats, network protocols, user programming interfaces, and system program interfaces [1] .

TACL (TRON Application Control-flow Language) is a language based on TULS, which provides protocol between the end-user and BTRON. TACL can invoke various functions provided by the BTRON environment. Thus, TACL is a CLI (Command Language Interpreter) language, batch language, and database retrieval language. A simple application program can also be described using only TACL. These TACL programs can be mixed with every data processed by BTRON. This makes it possible to call BTRON's functions in everywhere automatically and forms the basis of data exchange with other machines, too. This purpose is a little over the sphere of TACL. It is rather TULS' purpose than TACL's.

In this paper, our object of study contains this function. Therefore, our language system is named *TACL/TULS* language system.

From the standpoint of language features, TACL is defined as follows [2],

- It is an interactive language and some parts of it are compilable
- It has multiple foci of control
- It is a typeless macro language
- It does not distinguish between data and program
- It has two types of storage - real object and dictionary
- A TACL macro can be defined anywhere in TAD (TRON Application Databus [1]) data
- User events are handled as macro invocations
- Input arguments to a macro can be picked up from data such as a text object

As mentioned above, TACL uses two storage systems. Real objects form a global persistent storage in TACL, while dictionaries form a local temporary storage. A dictionary, in which TACL macro definitions are described, consists of three parts: macro-name entry, arguments, and macro-body. Dictionaries are referred to while interpreting a TACL program. They exist in correspondence with data units in main memory of BTRON, such as data segments and shadow objects [2]. As such data units are constructed in tree structure, dictionaries are also constructed in tree structure.

TACL is a macro language, which executes by expanding macros. During evaluation of TAD data, a macro occurrence in TAD data (it is called macro invocation) causes a macro search in the dictionaries. This search is executed in an order from leaf to upper. When a macro entry is found, the search terminates and the macro is expanded to a macrobody. A user event is also considered as a macro, called an event macro.

Macro call may be accompanied with arguments. TACL has two types of arguments. One is a normal argument (*in-macro-argument*), the other is a *display-area-argument* [2], which is applicable only to TAD data in a real object or a virtual object. This display-area-argument is one of the important features of TACL. The method to expand TACL macros and to evaluate arguments follows the one level expansion rule. It will be discussed later.

A TACL program has two user views. One is an ordinary text program view. The other is a panel program view. In this paper, only the former is considered.

TAD (TRON Application Databus) is a common data exchange format among TRON specification computers. This is also one of the applications of TULS. From another viewpoint, displaying TAD data is the same as executing TAD as TULS. Any TACL/TULS macro can be embedded in TAD data.

In this paper, we present some concrete example of TACL/TULS programs in section 2 and discuss implementation issues of the TACL/TULS interpreter in section 3 and 4. In the section 5, the execution mechanism of TACL/TULS programs is presented.

2. EXAMPLES OF TACL/TULS PROGRAMS

TACL/TULS has two types of usage in general. One is batch type usage (TACL application), the other is embedded type usage (TULS application). In this section, examples of TACL/TULS programs corresponding to each usage are described in text format.

2.1 Examples of The Batch Type Usage of TACL/TULS Program

This type of TACL/TULS program is edited by the TACL/TULS program editor and executed directly by a TACL interpreter task (see section 4).

Ex. 1 TACL/TULS Program in Office

The processes to translate statistical data of office documents into graph data and to send the document to someone can be programmed in TACL/TULS easily.

program 2-1

```
#SequentialExecution(
#Open_RO_To_VO("/SYS/USR/mail_1", #Temp),
        ;Open Real Object to Virtual Object

#Set(#TableList,#CAR(#Search(#Temp, #STATISTIC_DATA))),
        ;Information of the statistic data segment found first in
        ;Virtual Object pointed by #Temp is substituted for
        ;#TableList

#Set(#Top, #CAR(#TableList)),
        ;The position of the segment head
#Set(#Length, #CDR(#TableList)),
        ;The length of the segment

#Set(#Table, #GetSegment(#Temp, #Top, #Length)),
        ;Get the segment body
#Replace(#Temp, #Top, #Length, #TransToGraph(#Table)),
        ;Replace the segment by segments of graphic data which
        ;represent the graph of the statistic data

#Execute(#MailSend, #Temp)
        ;Send the Virtual Object as a Mail
)
```

Notice:

```
#FUNCTION_NAME(arguments.....)
==> return value
            ;comments

#Execute(execution_function_FUSEN, reference)
==> error value
            ;execute reference with application indicated by execution_function_FUSEN

#Open_RO_To_VO( the path name to the real object,
                the name of virtual object)
==> error value
            ;open real object to virtual object

#Search(   pointer to real/virtual object,
           kind of segment to be searched)
==> list of (top of the segment, the segment length)
            ;search in real/virtual object

#GetSegment(   pointer to real/virtual object,
               top of the segment to be get,
               the segment length)
==> segment body
            ;get a segment body from a virtual/real object

#Replace(  pointer to real/virtual object,
           top of the segment to be replaced,
           the segment length,
           segment body to be replaced to)
==> TRUE/FALSE
            ;replace segment in the virtual/real object

#TransToGraph(statistic data segment)
==> graphic data of the graph
            ;translate statistics data to a graphic data that represent the graph of the statistic data
```

Ex. 2 TACL/TULS Program in TRON House

BTRON is also designed to control home automation systems, which are to be experimented within the TRON House. The description of actions of electric appliances in such houses while no one is at home is thought of as a batch. Those who write programs of such actions are end users. So, home automation programs can be programmed by TACL/TULS.

We consider the following program example here.

When one leaves the house, the following operations are executed in order:

- check window locks, and lock them if there are any unlocked,

- check water and gas outlets, and shut off all open outlets,

- check predefined electric power switches, and turn off switches if there are some switches turned on,

- check mail box, and notify the user if there is any mail,

- set answering machine,

- send a message to the elevator to come,

- watch the door and lock it if one has gone out of the door.

program 2-2

```
#SequentialExecution(
    #ElementExecution(#Lock(#X), #X, #OpenedLock()),

    #ConditionalExecution(
        #NOT(#Null(#OpenedOutlet())),
        #SequentialExecution(
            #DisplayScreen("There's opened outlet"),
            #ElementExecution(  #CloseOutlet(#X),
                                #X,
                                #OpenedOutlet()
            )
        ),
        NULL
    ),

    #ElementExecution(  #TurnOff(#X),
                        #X,
                        #OpenedSwitch()
    ),

    #ConditionalExecution(#Mail?(),
        #DisplayScreen("You have Mail!"),
        NULL
    )

    #SetAnswerMachine(),

    #CallElevator(),

    #MessageExecution(#GoOutOfDoor(), #LockDoor())
)
```

Notice:

```
#OpenedOutlet()
#OpenedLock()
#OpenedSwitch()
==> list of opened outlets, locks, or switches
            ; return list of opened outlets, locks, and switches.

#TurnOff()
==> error value
            ; turn off a switch

#CloseOutlet()
==> error value
            ; close an outlet

#LockDoor()
==> error value
            ; Lock a door

#ConditionalExecution(condition, macro_A, macro_B)
==> return value of macro_A or macro_B
            ; if condition is TRUE then macro_A is executed. Otherwise, macro_B is
            ; executed.

#ElementExecution(application program, Data, DataList)
==> error value
            ; executes each elements of DataList with application.
```

```
#MessageExecution(#Message, #Application)
==> error value
              ;executes #Application if #Message comes.
```

2.2 Example of The Embedded Type Usage of TACL/TULS Program

TACL/TULS macros can be defined anywhere in TAD data that is processed by graphic editors or text editors. An application program executes TACL/TULS macros by cooperating with the TACL/TULS Manager when it displays TAD data on the screen, in other words, when it executes TAD as a TULS program.

Ex. 3 Example of The Hyper-Text Application by TACL/TULS Program

Embedding TACL/TULS macros into TAD data could make any graphic objects behave as parts which react upon input events from the user. With this function, it is possible to write a program, such that a pen-down event which occurs on a circle in a BTRON window opens the real object named "step_B" with its default application program. Such a program is described as follows and behaves like illustrated in Fig. 2.1:

program 2-3

```
        :
        :
  <<part of TAD data>>
   #CreateDictionary (
   #Set(PenDown,##ReferenceLaunching("step_B"),
   @circle[attr:XOR, ....., RECT(50,50,60,60)]
   )

        .
```

Notice:

```
@circle[attr:....]
          ;"@" means TAD graphic data primitive segment. So, @circle[attr:...] means the
          ; graphic primitive data segment of a circle with the arguments of [attr:...].
```

The data format in a shadow object depends on the application that manages it. However, when a shadow object is referred to by another application or is stored in a real object, the managing task must be able to translate it into TAD data format.

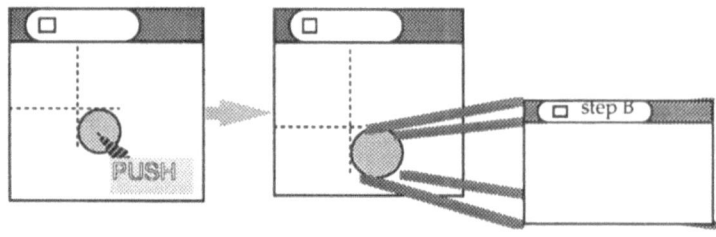

Fig. 2.1   A Hyper-Text like Application

3. SHADOW OBJECT [2]

A shadow object is defined as the information in a task's memory area or a part of the information which can be handled equivalently with the information in the real object . A shadow object is managed by the task that has created it.

This enables tasks to handle shadow objects and real objects in the same context with the same procedure. Communication between tasks in a TACL/TULS program is based on this mechanism. This mechanism is more generalized than the pipe mechanism in conventional operating systems because it allows random accesses to shadow objects as well as to real objects. The following batch program written in a conventional command language is one example to describe that result of task_A is directly read by task_B, then that task_B begins to run.

program 3-1

```
task_A | task_B
```

The TACL/TULS system realizes this kind of procedure by launching task_B referring to the shadow object managed by task_A. The relations among a real object, a task which manages a shadow object, and another application task which refers to the shadow object or the real object are presented in Fig. 3.1.

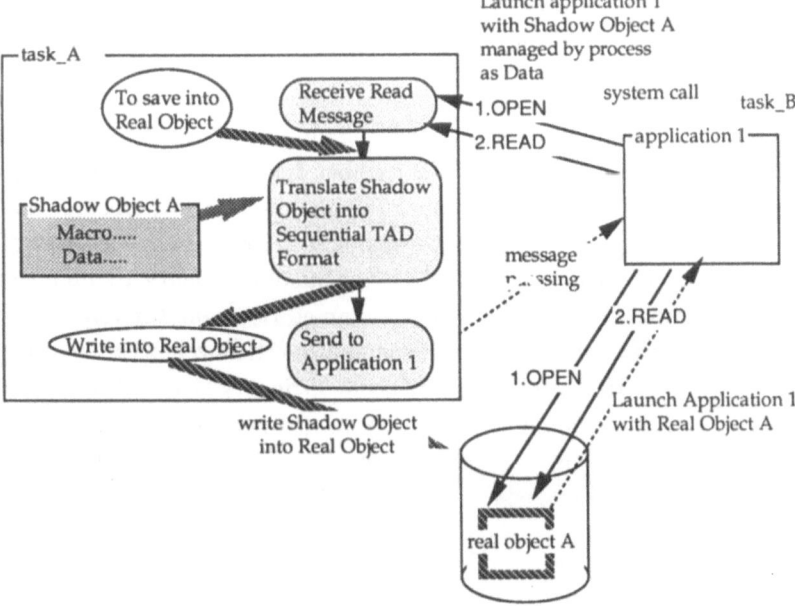

Fig. 3.1   *Shadow Object*

4. STRUCTURE OF TACL/TULS INTERPRETING SYSTEM SOFTWARE

This section discusses the module structure of the TACL/TULS interpreting software system and roles of each component. Mechanism to execute or interpret a TACL/TULS program is presented in section 5.

In BTRON architecture, there are five components which relate to the TACL/TULS system. The TACL/TULS Manager is the main component to interpret and execute TACL/TULS macros. The Dictionary Manager manages all dictionaries in the system and all relationships among them. The TACL interpreter task, which is created by the TACL/TULS Manager for background execution, is a standard application task to execute batch type TACL programs. The TACL/TULS program editor is used to edit batch type TACL programs. An application task is required to interpret and execute TACL/TULS macros mixed in TAD data handled by the application. In the following, the role of each component and relation among them are discussed in more detail.

4.1 The Dictionary Manager

A dictionary of the TACL/TULS system exists corresponding to a data unit in a shadow object which constitutes the scope of the dictionary. Dictionaries form a tree structure with the inclusion relations of their scopes, and the dictionary corresponding to the whole shadow object is defined to be a child of the dictionary corresponding to the shadow object from which the former is launched. Therefore, dictionaries in whole system form a single tree structure (Fig. 4.1). The Dictionary Manager has all dictionaries in a common memory area.

In order to find the definition of a TACL/TULS macro in dictionaries, it is necessary for the TACL/TULS system to get dictionary ID number from which the dictionary search starts, to access dictionary items, and to follow the parent-child relationships among the dictionaries. To manage these operations, three tables are required. The first is a table that maps ID numbers of shadow object data segment to dictionary ID numbers corresponding to the segment. This table, which is named *Segment-Dictionary Mapping Table*, is obtained by each application task managing the shadow object. The second is a table that maps dictionary ID numbers to pointers to dictionary bodies. The last is a table holding parent-child relationships among dictionaries. Each tables of the latter two is necessary only one for each system. The Dictionary Manager also manages these tables in one table together, which is named the *Dictionary Management Table*.

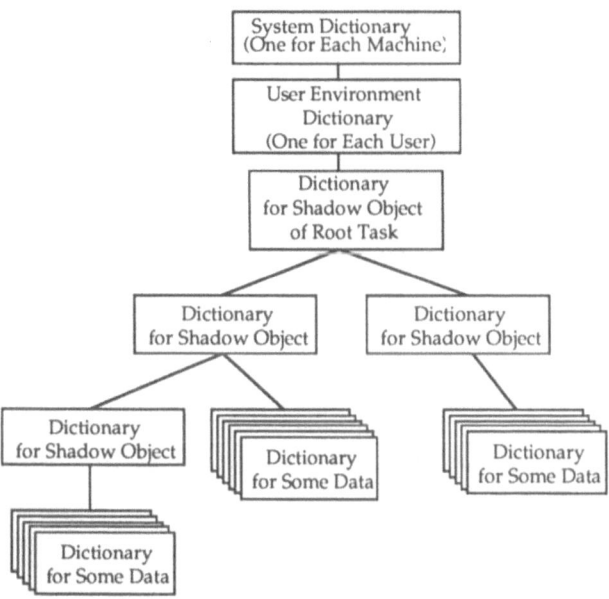

Fig. 4.1   *Tree Structure of TACL/TULS Dictionaries*

4.2 The TACL/TULS Manager

The TACL/TULS Manager is called by application tasks in order to interpret and execute TACL/TULS macros. Only the application task knows from which dictionary the macro definition should be searched for. Therefore, the application task calls the TACL/TULS Manager with the TACL/TULS macro to be interpreted and the dictionary ID from which searching starts.

As stated before, TACL/TULS has two types of usage. As the purpose and feature of each usage are different, we have two execution mechanisms for each usage. In embedded type usage, the processing time of each macro is short. This execution is performed by the TACL/TULS Manager, and the result is returned to the application task synchronously (foreground execution). In batch type usage, the processing time of each macro is long. If the TACL/TULS Manager executes this macro by itself, it cannot accept other TACL/TULS Manager calls from the task for a long period of time. To prevent this case, the user can specify background execution of a TACL/TULS macro. Then the TACL/TULS Manager creates a new task called the TACL interpreter task, asks it to execute the macro, and return immediately (Fig. 4.2). The TACL interpreter task executes the macro by cooperating with the TACL/TULS Manager like other application tasks do, and terminates when it finishes the execution.

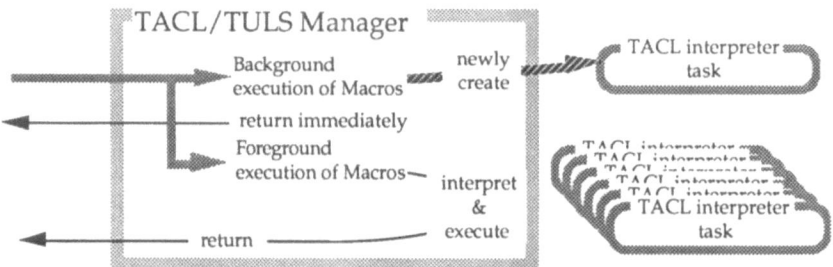

Fig. 4.2   *The TACL / TULS Manager*

4.3 The Application Task

Application tasks such as a graphic editor or a text editor deals with TAD data mixed with TACL/TULS macros.

Special codes are to be added to the application programs to cooperate with TACL/TULS system.

The application task must manage the Segment-Dictionary Mapping Table, which maps data segment IDs to dictionary IDs. If some data segments are moved or copied by CUT&PASTE operations, the application task must change the structure of dictionaries according to the structure of data segments. It must also have an ability to handle TACL/TULS macros. If it encounters a TACL/TULS macro while interpreting TAD data, it calculates the data segment in which the macro call occurs, looks for the dictionary ID corresponding to the segment, and calls the TACL/TULS Manager to evaluate the macro with the TACL/TULS macro and the Dictionary ID.

4.4 The TACL/TULS Program Editor

The TACL/TULS program editor is a tool to edit TACL/TULS programs or TAD data directly. This editor is a little different from other graphic editors or text editors.

In an ordinary editor, data in a shadow object is evaluated and displayed on the screen, but in this TACL/TULS program editor, data in a shadow object is only displayed on the screen, but not evaluated as a TULS program. The TACL/TULS program editor interprets the data differently. This feature is necessary for the TACL/TULS editor.

TACL/TULS programs edited with this editor are executed by a TACL interpreter task, which is a standard application task that executes TACL/TULS programs.

4.5 The TACL Interpreter Task

A TACL interpreter task deals with TACL/TULS macros by cooperating with the TACL/TULS Manager as other application tasks do. A TACL interpreter task must satisfy the following conditions.

1) It can interpret any TACL/TULS macro by referring to the TACL/TULS Manager.

2) It can display all TAD data.

3) It can handle an event as an event macro.

A TACL interpreter task serves in two ways. One is that it is created by the TACL/TULS Manager to perform background execution. The other is that it is launched to provide a dictionary environment when a batch type TACL/TULS program is directly executed from the TACL/TULS editor.

The relationship among these five components in the TACL/TULS system is illustrated in Fig. 4.3 .

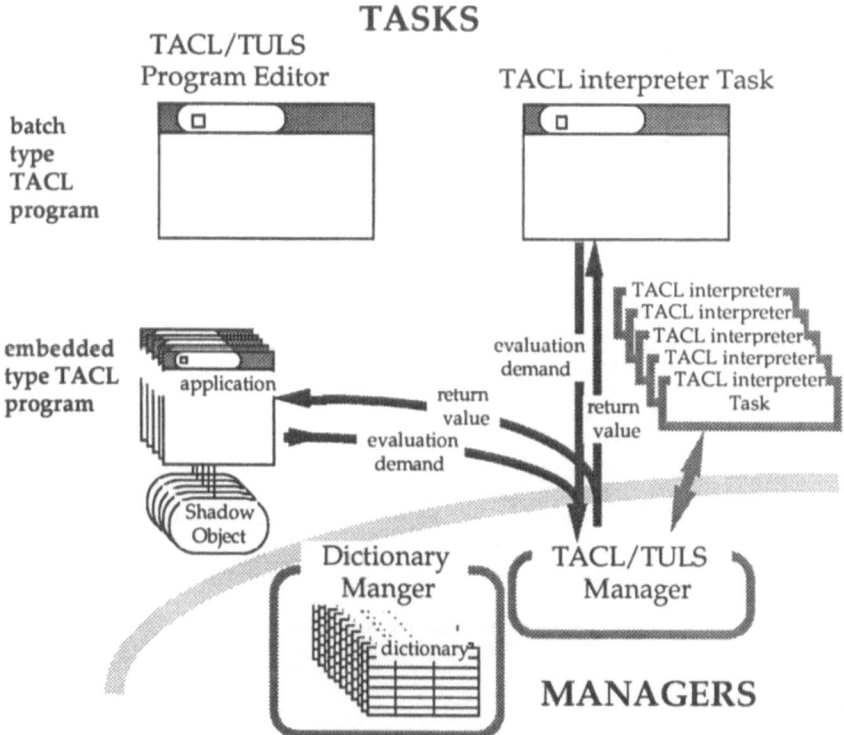

Fig. 4.3   The Complete TACL/TULS System

5. TACL PROGRAM EXECUTION MECHANISM

5.1 Basic Concept of TACL Program Execution

A TACL/TULS program is always mixed with TAD data. The application task reads the TAD data, and evaluates it from the top to the end of the data. TAD data can be evaluated by the application task itself, but a typical application cannot understand TACL/TULS macros mixed in TAD data. Then, the application task calls the TACL/TULS Manager to evaluate a TACL/TULS macro, with the information of all arguments and ID of the dictionary in which the macro search should starts.

Then, macro is expanded by the TACL/TULS Manager. This macro expansion follows the one level expansion rule. In this rule, in-macro-arguments are evaluated from the inner expression and their return values are given to the macro of the outer. But a display-area-argument is not evaluated and the argument itself is given to the outer expression. With these argument values, the macro is expanded.

In order to expand the macro, dictionaries are searched for the item matching it. This search is executed from the dictionary specified by the application, and if the item is not found in it, its parent dictionary is searched next. This search continues until the item is found or search of the root dictionary is completed (Fig. 5.1).

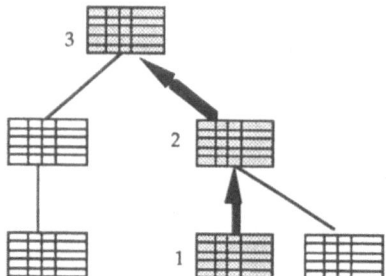

Fig. 5.1   *Dictionary Searching Order*

If such a item is found and it is a user defined macro, the TACL/TULS macro is substituted by the macrobody of the item and the TACL/TULS Manager returns it (Fig. 5.2). If it is a primitive macro, the code designated in the macrobody is executed. Then, a return value is sent to the application task.

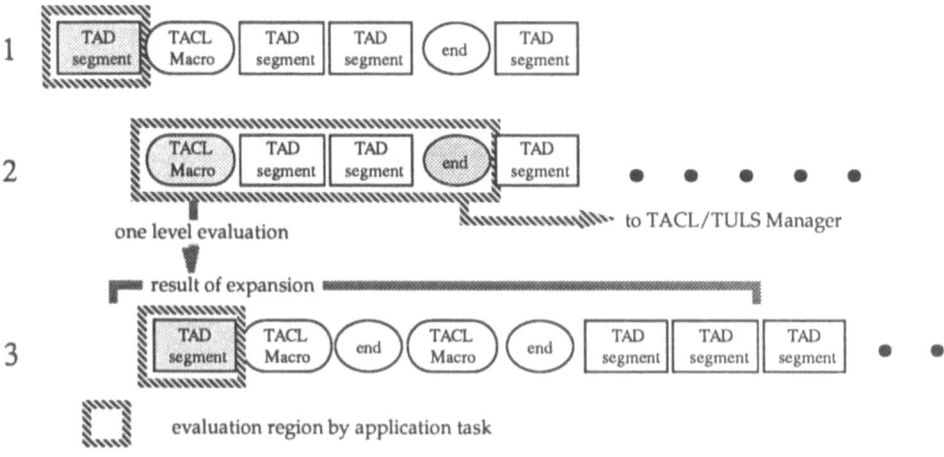

Fig. 5.2   *The One Level Macro Expansion*

5.2 Execution Mechanism of Embedded TACL/TULS Program

In the execution model of an embedded TACL/TULS program, a TACL/TULS macro is replaced by TAD data returned from the TACL/TULS Manager as the result of its evaluation. An application task interprets this TAD data, then displays it on the screen.

Execution mechanism of this type of TACL/TULS program is as follows.

1) An application task reads from a real object into its shadow object and evaluates the data in the shadow object.

2) A TACL/TULS macro appears in the shadow object.

3) Find the ID of the inner-most dictionary which has scope including the macro.

4) The TACL/TULS Manager is called with the TACL/TULS macro and the dictionary ID.

5) The TACL/TULS Manager expands the macro by calling the Dictionary Manager (ref. section 5.1).

6) The result of macro execution is returned to the application task.

7) The application task displays the return value on the screen.

8) If the return value contains TACL/TULS macros, the same procedure is applied to them. Otherwise, return to step 1.

5.3 Execution Mechanism of Batch TACL/TULS Programs

A batch TACL/TULS program is executed in the same way as described in section 5.2. But the editing and launching way is different. It is illustrated as below.

1) Edit the program with the TACL/TULS program editor, in which TAD data and TACL/TULS macros are not interpreted normally but displayed in another editable way.

2) The TACL/TULS editor launches a TACL interpreter task by calling the TACL/TULS Manager, and gives the program edited in it.

3) The TACL interpreter task executes this TACL program in the same way as the application task described in section 5.2.

5.4 Execution Mechanism of Event Macro

A user event is handled as an event macro invocation at the data segment in which the event occurs.

The user event is first picked up by an application task, because only the application task can find the data segment related to the event. In the concrete, event macro processing mechanism is as follows:

1) An application task picks up a user event.

2) The application task looks for the data segment on which the user event occurs.

3) Find the ID of the inner-most dictionary which has scope including the data segment.

4) The event macro corresponding to the user event and dictionary ID are sent to the TACL/TULS Manager.

5) The TACL/TULS Manager expands the event macro according to the event macro definition in dictionaries.

6) Return value is sent back to the application task but a typical application task does not use it.

5.5 Example of TACL Program Execution

In this section, the execution and reaction of the program 2-3 illustrated in section 2.2. is described.

At first, an application task, such as a graphic editor task, create a dictionary of the shadow object, to which the contents of the real object are copied. Then, it reads TAD data including this program from a real object and displays it. If the TAD data contains TACL/TULS macros, they are expanded as described in section 5.2.

Execution steps of the program 2-3 are illustrated in detail below. By the
#CreateDictionary() macro, new dictionary is created and given a new dictionary ID.
An item for the new dictionary is added to the Dictionary Management Table by the
Dictionary Manager. The application task also adds a new item to its Segment-
Dictionary Mapping Table. Next, the application task tries to evaluate the #set() macro.
With the help of the TACL/TULS Manager, the new entry is successfully added to the
dictionary. Then, a graphical object segment @circle[], a TAD primitive data segment,
is evaluated by the application task itself and a circle is displayed on the screen.

If a pen-down event occurs after whole data is displayed, the application task calculates
the graphic data segment on which the pen-down event occurs, looks for the dictionary
ID in the Segment-Dictionary Mapping Table, and sends the event macro and dictionary
ID to the TACL/TULS Manager. The TACL/TULS Manager refers to the dictionaries,
and finds that the definition of the event macro is #Ref_start("step_B"). According to
the definition, a real object "step_B" is opened by its default application. It is illustrated
in Fig. 5.3 .

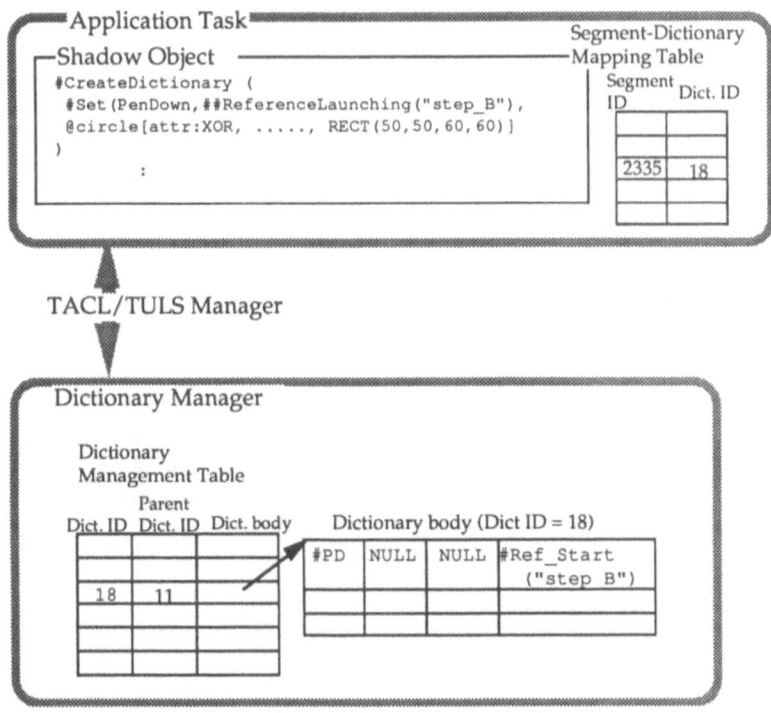

Fig. 5.3   An Execution Example of a Hyper-Text like Application

6. SUPPORT BY THE APPLICATION

Application programs of BTRON must have special routines to cooperate with the TACL/TULS system. Most important one is to enable the application program to call the TACL/TULS Manager, which is described as bellow.

An application must be able to deal with TACL/TULS macros which is read from a real object or shadow object of another task, and to deal with user events as event macros. To evaluate such macros, application must call the TACL/TULS Manager. Application programs call the TACL/TULS Manager in the following cases.

1) If an application meets a TACL/TULS macro in TAD data of real object (or shadow object) which the application handles, it sends the macro to the TACL/TULS Manager. The return value is dealt with as if it appears in the real object.

2) When an application gets an event, it sends the event as an event macro to the TACL/TULS Manager.

3) When a message (interrupt) comes, an application deals with the message as a message macro in the same way as an event macro.

```
event_loop()
{
    ty = wget_evt(.....);

    switch(wevt.type) {
    case ###:
    case $$$:
        :
        :
    default:
    }

    /* calculate segment related to the event */
    /* refer to dictionary ID related to the segment */      TACL/TULS
                                                              manager
    ret = send_TACL(message, dictionary_ID)
}


TACL_message_handler(message)
{
    /* description of message processing   */
    /* from TACL/TULS manager.             */
}

message_handler1(message)
{
    /* general message handler */
    send_TACL(message, dictionary_ID_of ShadowObject)
        :
    /* ordinary message handling description */
        :
}
```

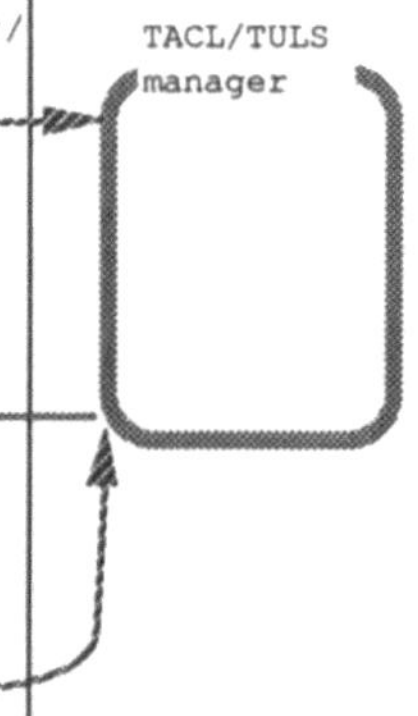

Fig. 6.1   *The Structure of an Application Program Supporting The TACL/TULS System*

There are other application dependent cases to call TACL/TULS Manager. These supporting routines (1, 2, and 3) are described in the C language as Fig. 6.1 .

7. FUTURE WORK

In this paper, we have discussed about implementation issues of the TACL/TULS system base on text user interface. The user interface of the panel programming, which is a kind of Visual Programming [3], is also an important topic and must be discussed.

Application developers will be required to support the TACL/TULS system from the application side when they code applications of BTRON. This enforces application developers to write many fixed function calls according to the TACL/TULS guideline. Application programs of window based computer system like BTRON should obey many guidelines, such as the user interface guideline and the TACL/TULS guideline. This makes it hard to develop application software. Therefore, it is desirable to support software development by using some tool, which is called generally UIMS (User Interface Management System)/UIDS (User Interface Development System) [4].

A UIMS/UIDS helps,

1) development of prototypes,

2) creation of correct programs according to the guidelines, and

3) end-users to program.

It is desirable to develop a UIMS/UIDS and the TACL/TULS system simultaneously.

8. SUMMARY

We have described implementation issues of the TACL/TULS system on BTRON. The TACL/TULS system is constructed from four components. the TACL/TULS Manager, the Dictionary Manager, the TACL interpreter task, and the TACL/TULS program editor.

Application tasks are also an important element of the TACL/TULS system. It is necessary to add special codes to application programs in order to cooperate with the TACL/TULS system.

ACKNOWLEDGEMENT

The authors wish to express sincere appreciation to the members of the Sakamura laboratory for their kind and valuable comments.

REFERENCES

[1] Ken Sakamura, "TULS:TRON Universal Language System," TRON Project
     1988(Proc. of Fifth TRON Project Symposium), Springer-Verlag, 1988, pp.3-18.

[2] Ken Sakamura, "TACL:TRON Application Control-flow Language," TRON Project
     1988(Proc. of Fifth TRON Project Symposium), Springer-Verlag, 1988, pp.79-91.

[3] Shi-Kuo Chang, et al, "Visual Languages", Plenum Press, New York and London,
     1986.

[4] H. Rex Hartson and Deborah Hix, "Human-Computer Interface Development:
     Concepts and Systems for Its Management," ACM Computing Surveys, Vol.21,
     No.1, March 1989.

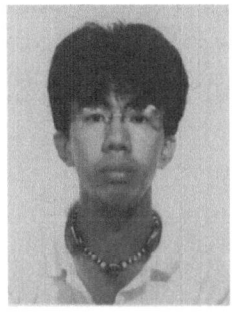

Noboru Koshizuka is a M.S. course student of Department of Information Science at the University of Tokyo. He is now, under the supervision of Dr. Sakamura, engaged in research on TACL, TULS, and software development environment for the TRON project. He received B.S. degree in information science from University of Tokyo in 1989.

E Mail: koshi@spica.is.s.u-tokyo.ac.jp

Hiroaki Takada is an educational staff of Department of Information Science at the University of Tokyo. He is now, under the supervision of Dr. Sakamura, engaged in research on software development environment and programming language for the TRON project. Takada is also interested in hypertext systems. He received B.S. and M.S. degrees in information science from University of Tokyo. He is a member of ACM, IEEE, Information Processing Society of Japan, and Japan Society for Software Science and Technology.

E-Mail: hiro@spica.is.s.u-tokyo.ac.jp

Masaharu Saitoh is a M.S. course student of Department of Information Science at the University of Tokyo. He is now, under the supervision of Dr. Sakamura, engaged in research on TACL, TULS, and software development environment for the TRON project. He received B.S. degree in information science from University of Tokyo in 1987. He is a member of ACM, IEEE, and Information Processing Society of Japan.

E-Mail: saitoh@spica.is.s.u-tokyo.ac.jp

Yasushi Saitoh is a student of Department of Information Science at the University of Tokyo. He is now, under the supervision of Dr. Sakamura, engaged in research on TACL for the TRON project.

E-Mail: yasushi@spica.is.s.u-tokyo.ac.jp

Ken Sakamura is currently an associate professor at the Department of Information Science, University of Tokyo. He holds Ph.D. in EE. Being a computer architect, he has been the leader of the TRON project which he started to build a new computer system architecture for 1990's since 1984. His promotion of the TRON architecture now extends to architecture of buildings and furniture. He servers on the editorial board of Institute of Electrical and Electronics Engineers (IEEE) MICRO magazine and is a chair of the project promotion committee of the TRON Association. He is a member of Japan Information Processing Society, Institute of Electronics, Information and Communication Engineers, ACM, and is a senior member of IEEE. He has received best paper awards of IEICE twice, of JIPS once, IEEE best annual article awards, and other awards from Japanese and over seas organizations.

Above authors may be reached at: Department of Information Science, Faculty of Science, University of Tokyo, 7-3-1 Hongo, Bunkyo-ku, Tokyo, Japan.

Chapter 3: CTRON

Design of General Rules in CTRON Interfaces

Tetsuo Wasano, Yoshizumi Kobayashi, and Takashi Terazaki
NTT Network Systems Development Center

Ken Sakamura
Department of Information Science, Faculty of Science, University of Tokyo

Abstract

The OS interfaces designed in the CTRON subproject are aimed at being applied to various telecommunications network services and at improving software portability. This paper describes the following approach taken to designing interfaces applicable to realtime fields as diverse as switching, communications processing, and information processing.

1) Terminology, concepts, formats of representation, and design rules all have been specified independently of each field.

2) A comprehensive reference model has been devised to assure that all involved in the project have a common understanding of OS functions and configuration.

Keywords: CTRON, general rule, reference model, subsetting, language binding

1. INTRODUCTION

The performance and reliability demands in network services are extremely severe. Up to now, the realtime OSs in main use have been dedicated OSs or oriented to small-scale embedded systems, and have been designed arbitrarily by different vendors. Each has its own interface, so that software portability cannot be guaranteed from one system to another. As a result, software for each network system has had to be implemented separately, even when the functions realized are essentially the same. CTRON[*] is a set of realtime OS interfaces aimed at overcoming this problem by assuring portability of the software that provides the functions required in network service nodes.[1]

Network nodes provide various realtime services such as switching processing, communication processing and information processing, and have employed different

---

[*] The name CTRON was derived as follows. TRON is an abbreviation of "The Realtime Operating System Nucleus." C stands for "Communication" and "Central."

terminology and concepts for each service. Communication field and information processing field have been developed independently. Many experts in each field have to cooperate to design CTRON, because CTRON plays a role of providing common interface applied to both fields. Effective study is also essential, because the range of functions to be designed is very wide. Working groups independent of one another are made up in order to design CTRON interfaces in parallel. In order to give a common understanding of the OS functions and configuration to engineers participating CTRON design and to users employing CTRON specifications, the terminology, concepts and the way in which specifications are written should be standardized. This paper discusses a set of general rules[2] devised for this standardization.

2. DESIGN PRINCIPLES

The following design principles (see Figure 1) have been established in order to meet the requirements for software portability improvement and applicability to different types of network service nodes.[3]

(1) Provision of functions necessary for application to network service nodes

   a. Provision of functions for highly multiple, realtime processing, and for fault tolerance

   b. Permitting a selection of functions as required for each type of nodes

(2) Provision of a common OS interface

   a. Provision of OS interfaces independent of hardware architecture

   b. Provision of OS interfaces independent of applications in the realtime field

   c. Provision of OS interfaces that do not require awareness of resource location in the network

(3) Harmonization with existing standards

   a. Adoption of existing international standards where applicable

   b. Use of standard programming languages

   c.tConformity with the overall TRON architecture

3. GENERAL RULES

When setting out to design an OS interface, first the basic concepts must be determined. Then the range of functions to be included in the specifications must be decided, and the format to be used for their specification. Below are discussed the general rules corresponding to the design principles listed above. These rules cover basic concepts, the function design and the specification format (see Figure 1).

137

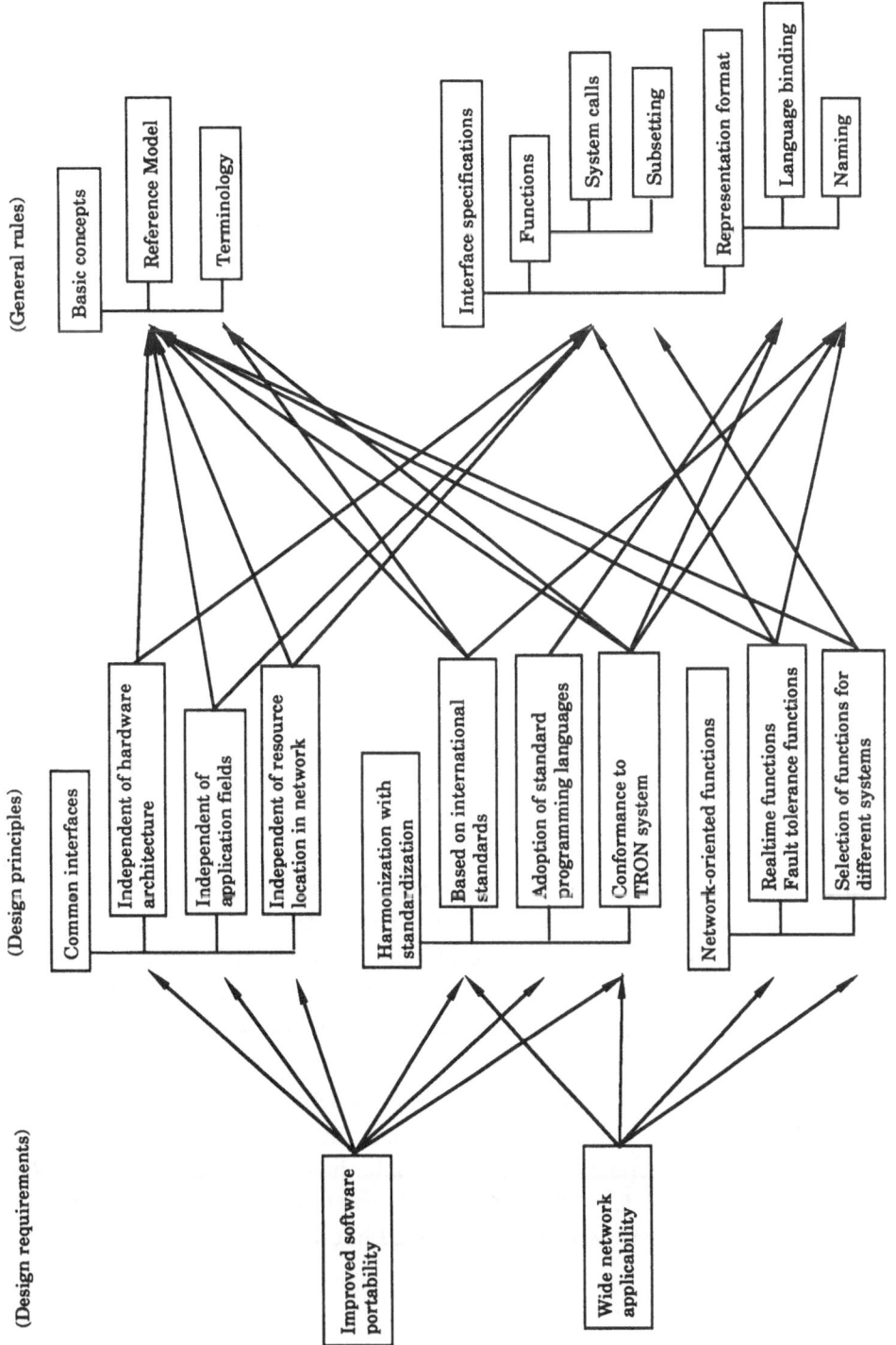

Fig. 1 Relation of design principles and general rules to design requirements

3.1 BASIC CONCEPTS

The basic concepts of CTRON are expressed in a Reference Model,[4] showing the overall OS interface structure and constituent elements, as well as the terminology to be used. The reference model has the following structure, based on the design principles noted above (see Figure 2).

a. Functions geared especially to network systems include realtime functions and fault tolerance functions, as well as the subsetting of OS interfaces so that functions can be selected to meet the performance needs of each system.

b. To make the OS interface independent of hardware architecture, logical interfaces are specified that virtualize physical resources. These logical interfaces are organized hierarchically. One layer, called the Basic OS interface, is directly involved in virtualizing hardware architecture. Extended OS interfaces are located on the Basic OS interface and provide more advanced OS functions. Because of this structure, software portability is not limited to application programs but extends to parts of the OS itself.

c. To design OS interface applicable to different network fields, the functions used in each field are systematized from the standpoint of the physical and logical resources in the network. These functions are organized into a number of interface classes, each of which is corresponding to network resources and independent of one another. It is therefore possible to adjust this classification or add new classes in the future as technology advances.

d. To provide OS interfaces that are independent of actual resource location, the resource management interfaces, which require awareness of this location, are separated from the other interfaces.

e. Conformity to international standards is achieved for the communication control interfaces by basing them on OSI standards and CCITT recommendations,[5] while the database management interface conforms largely to SQL database language standards. The interface specifications include language binding specifications for C, Ada, and CHILL programming languages, since these are standardized for use in writing system programs.

f. Conformity to the overall TRON architecture is achieved by adopting the same terminology, concepts, and specification format. In addition, the kernel and I/O control interfaces conform to ITRON**,[6,7] while the data storage control interface provides an interface for BTRON*** real/virtual file management.[8] Human-machine interface management is also specified in conformity with BTRON.

** ITRON is an abbreviation of "Industrial TRON."
*** BTRON is an abbreviation of "Business TRON."

3.2 GENERAL RULES FOR FUNCTION DESIGN

OS interfaces are specified for each of the classes of functions in the Reference Model. The OS interface specifications prescribe the system calls by which OS functions are called up, and also specify subsets. These subsets define the allowable groups when interface functions are selected.

3.2.1 System Call Specification

For each system call, the specifications give the function, input and output parameters, error information returned, and special precautions to the user. From the standpoint of software portability, all OS interfaces should be specified as system calls. However, standardizing every interface aspect and forcing this to fit all hardware architectures and system configurations would sacrifice performance as well as flexibility of system makeup. Such an approach is not practical in case of application to actual systems. For this reason, CTRON allows for some OS interfaces to omit specification of certain system calls or parameters. Examples of these interfaces are those that are strongly dependent on hardware architecture, or highly system-dependent interfaces such as those for operation administration and maintenance management.

3.2.2 Subsetting

CTRON specifications are intended for use with a wide range of hardware architectures, and include a wide range of interfaces required by a variety of systems. When implementing these specifications for a given system, however, not all of these OS interfaces will be required. It is necessary instead to allow only the required interfaces to be selected for each system. On the other hand, if no rules are set regarding this selection of functions, it will not be possible to guarantee software portability across different systems. Rules are therefore needed that achieve a balance between software portability and applicability to various systems. These rules for selecting and combining interface specifications are called OS interface subsetting specifications.

(1) Definition of terminology

The terminology used in OS interface subsetting specifications is defined as follows.

a. Interface unit

Interface units are sets of OS functions specified corresponding to the resources managed by the OS. Examples are the file management interface, and communication control interface. Interface units are either mandatory or optional, depending on the degree of necessity in each application field.

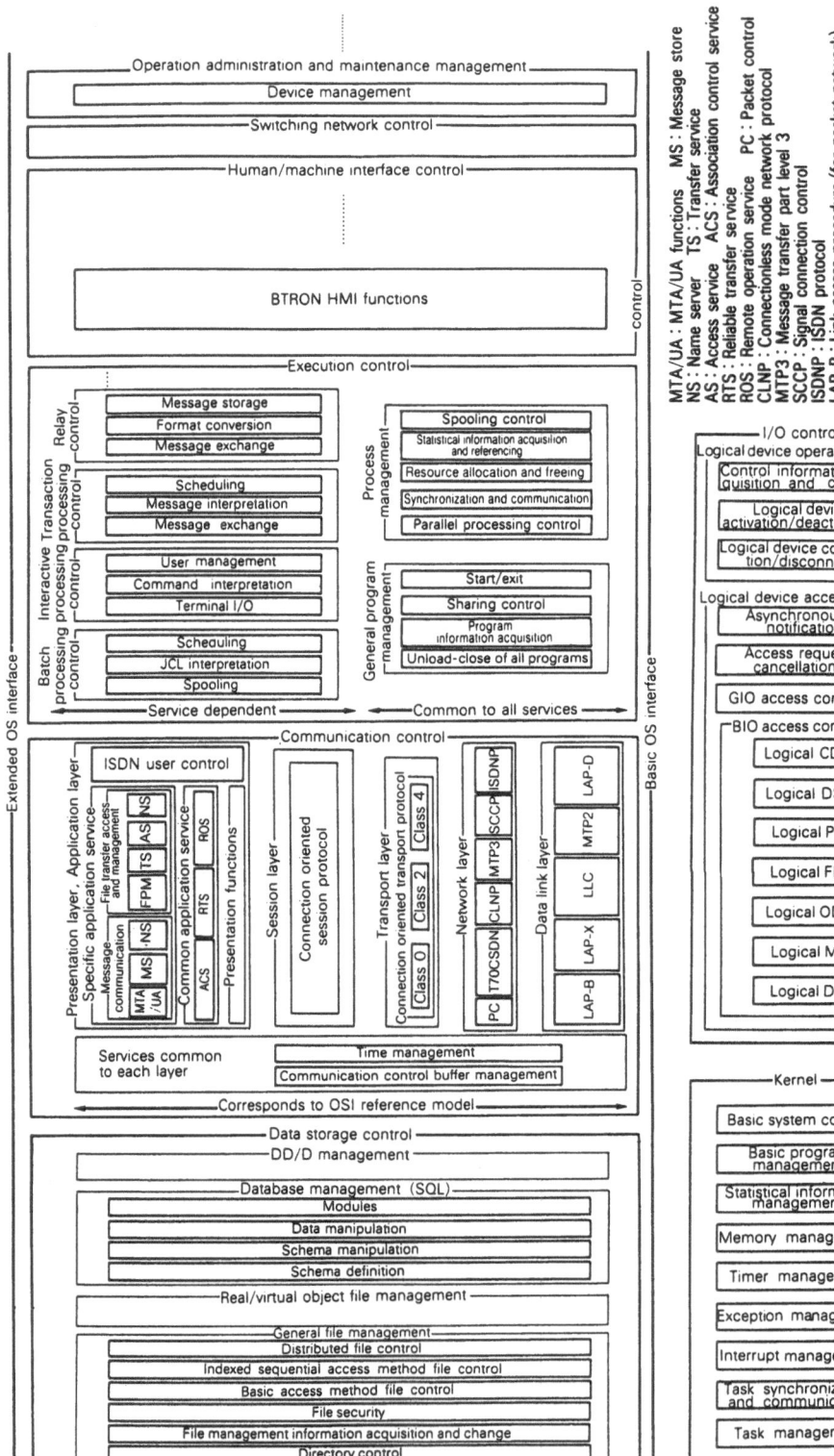

MTA/UA : MTA/UA functions MS : Message store
NS : Name server TS : Transfer service
AS : Access service ACS : Association control service
RTS : Reliable transfer service
ROS : Remote operation service PC : Packet control
CLNP : Connectionless mode network protocol
MTP3 : Message transfer part level 3
SCCP : Signal connection control
ISDNP : ISDN protocol
LAP-B : Link access procedure (for packet network)
LAP-X : Link access procedure (X)
LLC : LAN logical link control
MTP2 : Message transfer part level 2
LAP-D : Link access procedure (for ISDN D channel)

Fig. 2 CTRON reference model

i. Mandatory interface unit

A mandatory interface unit is one that must always be included when a selection of interfaces is made for a particular implementation. Examples are the kernel and I/O control interface units.

ii. Optional interface unit

An optional interface unit does not have to be included in every implementation based on CTRON.

b. Interface primitive

The smallest unit that may be used to configure a subset is an interface primitive. It corresponds to the system call names and parameters that make up a system call. Interface primitives are classified as either mandatory or optional, in order to specify meaningful combinations of system call names and parameters.

i. Mandatory interface primitive

A mandatory interface primitive is required whenever its interface unit is used. The set of mandatory interface primitives in a given interface unit is called the common part of that interface unit.

ii. Optional interface primitive

An optional interface primitive is not necessarily required when its interface unit is used. Sets of optional interface primitives in a given interface unit are called the optional parts of that interface unit.

(2) Subsetting specifications

CTRON interface subsets are allowable combinations of common and optional parts either within an interface unit or across different interface units (see Figure 3).

Within an interface unit, subsets are specified to show how optional parts may be combined with the mandatory common part. Subsets across interface units are specified as combinations of the subsets internal to interface units, so as to ensure inclusion of subsets in mandatory interface units. In CTRON, these subsets are specified in such a way as to include smaller subsets. This is significant for portability of software running on an OS implemented using these subsets, since it indicates whether software developed for a given OS will be portable to another OS, as shown in Figure 4. By arranging OS interfaces in this way, into common and optional parts, a balance is achieved between software portability among OSs and the realization of OSs with functions necessary for different application fields.

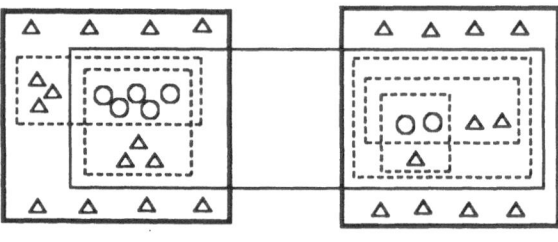

O : Mandatory interface primitives
△ : Optional interface primitives
■ : Interface unit
⌐⌐ : Interface subset (within interface unit)
☐ : Interface subset (across interface units)

Fig. 3   Interface primitives, interface units, and subsets

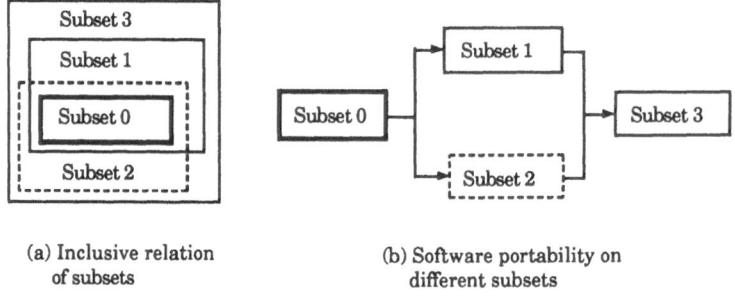

(a) Inclusive relation
of subsets

(b) Software portability on
different subsets

Fig.4   Inclusion of functions in subsets
and software portability

3.3 GENERAL RULES ON SPECIFICATION FORMAT

Rules have been established for use in describing system calls in OS interface specifications, and for giving names to system calls and parameters.

3.3.1 System Call Specification Format

Settling on one standard high-level programming language would be an effective approach to ensuring maximum software portability. Each programming language, however, has its own functional advantages and disadvantages. Programmers have a demand to make use of the particular features of a language for a given application. There are also differences in degree of familiarity with a language, and in the development systems available to a programmer. From the standpoint of wide applicability, CTRON does not restrict any one programming language.

The direct use of system calls takes place in the system program, where a system description language is employed. Here it is necessary to employ a language with standard specifications for the sake of software portability. CTRON specifications at present include system call specifications for each of three standard languages, namely, C, Ada, and CHILL. For other languages besides these, it is possible to add language specifications as necessary.

(1) Language-independent specifications

Examples of standard OS interfaces that provide specifications for use with a number of different programming languages include POSIX* and MOSI.** POSIX first defines its specifications in C, then provides specifications based on these for other languages.[9,10] The approach in MOSI is to write specifications in language-independent form, and then provide specifications based on these for programming languages.[11] CTRON adopts the latter approach of first writing specifications in language-independent form, to avoid the following problems inherent in the former approach.

i. There is a danger that the semantics of the parameter types in the language specifications will influence the OS interface specifications, so that the true scope of the OS functions provided in the interface specifications will not be clear.

ii. If the language specifications themselves are made part of the OS interface specifications, differences in language specifications may make it difficult to specify the OS interface in other languages, and lead to performance problems.

A system call consists of the system call name and parameters. When specifying system calls in programming language-independent form, the problem is what to do with parameter types. In CTRON, data handled by the OS are classified according to their structure, their management by the OS or not, their string attribute, and value range. Parameter types are then determined on this basis (see Figure 5).

a. Data structure

Data structures are classified as either scalar (characterized by a single value) or as sets of scalar items, namely, structures and arrays. A structure or array represents an area, the whole of which is expressed by a storage identifier. The individual elements in them are defined by scalar items.

---

* POSIX is a registered trademark of the IEEE.

** MOSI is a registered trademark of the IEEE.

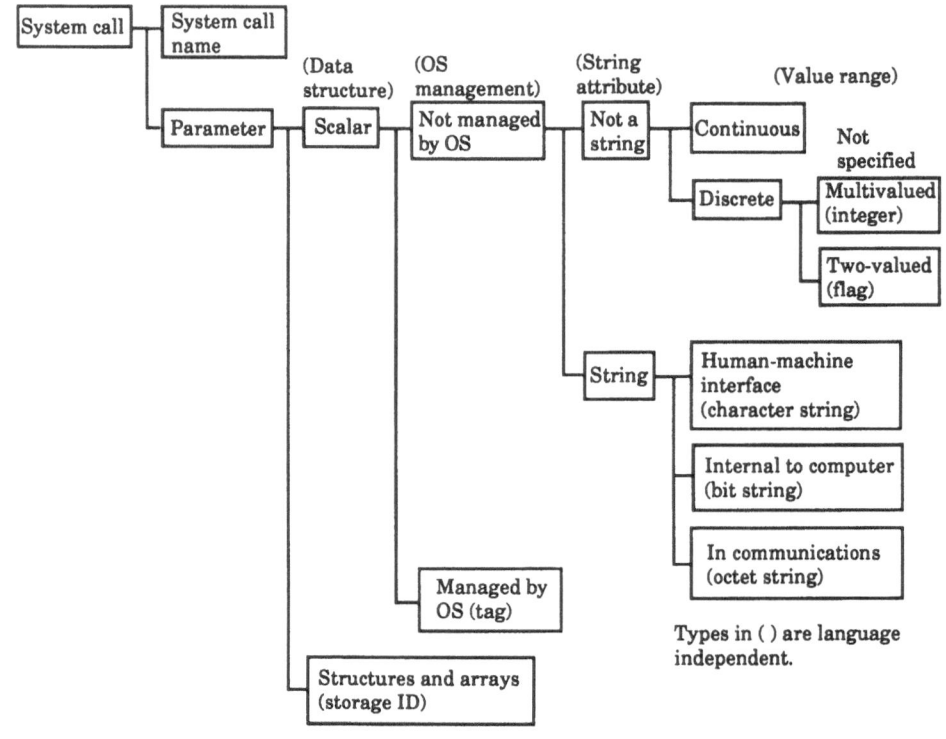

Fig. 5   System call parameter types

b. Management by the OS

Among scalar data, the most important for OS interface specifications are identifiers, which are managed by the OS for each resource and returned with system calls. Since, however, the attributes and range of these identifiers are dependent on the individual system calls that manage OS resources, in the language-independent specifications these are simply called tags to indicate that they are managed by the OS. When specifying each system call, a suitable type of a programming language is selected for the tag.

c. String attribute

Data are expressed internally by computers as bit strings. In a computer environment, data are expressed as character strings for ease of recognition by human beings. In communications there are also octet (byte) strings. There are thus various forms of data in computer systems that must be arranged in rows. In CTRON, data not managed by the OS are classified as string data and non-string data. The above three types are specified for string data.

d. Value range

Non-string data include discrete data (integers, etc.) and continuous data (real numbers, etc.). The OS does not have to deal with real numbers or other continuous data. The integer type is defined for discrete data. Among discrete data, two-valued data can correspond to different OS resources, such as when event flags are used. A flag type is therefore defined for these data.

(2) Language binding specifications

The system call specifications written for each programming language are called language binding specifications. Even in the case of a standardized programming language, matters such as precision of types are dependent on hardware architecture, and therefore differ for each processing system. This means that if the data types to be specified in the language binding specifications are made to correspond directly to the types specified for the programming language, software portability across different processing systems cannot be guaranteed. To get around this problem, CTRON defines virtual types (the type name and the attributes of that type) that are independent of programming languages. The correspondence between the type name and the types in a given processing system is a matter left to the implementor. Figure 6 illustrates language binding specifications and how they are defined in implementation. Types "r1tag_t" and "r2tag_t" are defined and used in CTRON specifications. The same types should be used in implementation. On the other hand, type "int_t" is defined in CTRON specifications, but is replaced by type "int" or "long" suitable in implementation. Independency of processing systems is thus assured.

3.2.2 Naming Rules

The work of determining CTRON specifications for each of the interface units in the Reference Model is carried out in parallel by specialists in each field, for best efficiency. A system is required to prevent duplication of names in the specifications for different interface units. Moreover, since CTRON is a subproject of the overall TRON Project, naming must be carried out in accord with the TRON system as a whole. Naming rules have thus been set for use in assigning system call names, parameter type names, error code symbolic conventions, and the like.

The approach taken in setting these naming rules is given below, using as an example the naming of system calls in the language binding specifications.

In BTRON and ITRON, system call names are assigned as follows.

ZXXX_YYY
    X,Y,Z: alphabet   XXX: operation
    YYY: object of operation   Z: variation (optional)

146

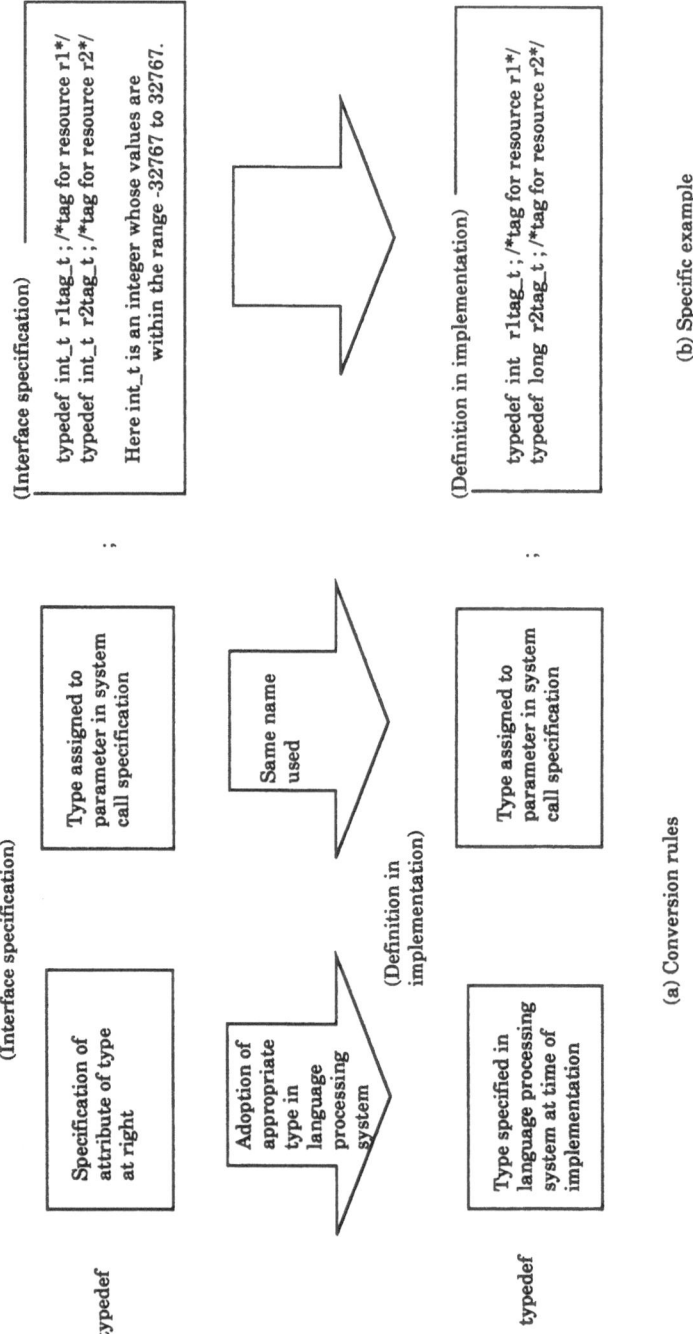

Fig. 6 Language binding specifications, and example (for C) of how they are defined in implementation

System calls are named as combinations of operation and object of operation so as to make clear the object of an operation when a function is designated. Variations express system call classifications, but these are given only when necessary, in order to minimize the burden on users to be aware of such classifications.

CTRON adopts a similar naming scheme, with some alterations reflecting special features of CTRON. These alterations are as follows.

a. Two characters are used to express variations, since there are a large number of classifications. For example, service primitives are specified for each of layers 2 through 5 of the OSI hierarchy, and in the case of layer 7 for MOTIS, FTAM, and other application service elements. Identifiers corresponding to these primitives are assigned to variations (see Table 1).

b. An underbar (_) is inserted to separate the variation from the operation name, since the use of more than one letter to express variations would otherwise make it hard to distinguish these two parts of the name.

CTRON system calls are named as follows.

ZZ_XXX_YYY
   X,Y,Z: alphabet   XXX: operation
   YYY: object of operation   ZZ: variation (optional)

Table 1   Variation in communication control interface

Variations	Layer or service elements
DL	Layer 2 (Data Link Layer)
NL	Layer 3 (Network Layer)
TL	Layer 4 (Transport Layer)
SL	Layer 5 (Session Layer)
AC	Layer 6 (Presentation Layer)
MO	Layer 7 (MOTIS)
FO	Layer 7 (FTAM)
ID	Layer 7 (ISUC DSS)
IC	Layer 7 (ISUC ISUP)
IT	Layer 7 (ISUC TC)
CM	Commonn to all layers

4. GENERAL RULES IN COMMUNICATION CONTROL INTERFACE

General rules applied to the overall CTRON interfaces are described above. Each interface unit cannot be specified, however, only by defining these rules. The concepts and model reflecting characteristics of each interface unit need to be defined as general rules. This chapter describes such rules in communication control interface, which is a key component of CTRON and is essential when CTRON is applied to network services.

4.1 CLASSIFICATION OF COMMUNICATION CONTROL INTERFACE

Each of the layers in communication control interface is made up of the following functional modules (see Figure 7).

a. CCL: Communication Controller

The CCL is a functional module for providing communication services for establishing and releasing connection, data transfer, etc., defined in the OSI model, as well as management services required for implementing the above communication services. A layer n CCL is referred to as (n)-CCL.

b. OAM: Operation Administration and Maintenance

This module consists of management functions, and provides access to the CCL. A layer n OAM is referred to as (n)-OAM.

The interface between the CCLs of two layers ((n)-CCL and (n+1)-CCL) is called an Ia interface, while the interface between the CCL and OAM of a given layer ((n)-CCL and (n)-OAM) is called an Im interface. System calls are specified for both Ia and Im interfaces.

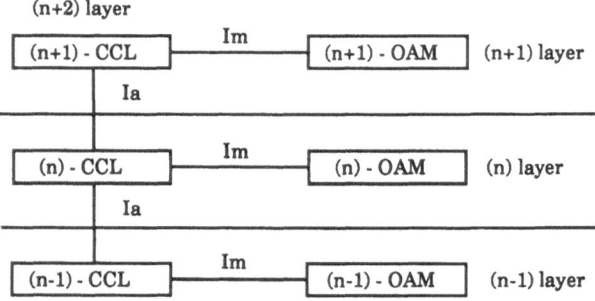

Fig. 7   Communication control interface classification

4.2 SYNCHRONIZATION MECHANISM

The communication control interfaces provided by a CCL are those for (i) requesting services by means of system calls and reporting the results, and (ii) reporting asynchronous events (e.g., incoming calls, or receipt of data). Rules common to these two kinds of interfaces are given below.

a. Synchronization

For system calls requiring synchronization, the communication control interface fundamentally adopts external synchronization making use of a message box in order to assure a high performance processing. Internal synchronization is adopted only as needed by individual layers.

i. Synchronization external to system call

System calls involving exchange of data based on protocol require a certain amount of time before completion. During that time, it must be possible to perform other processing. Accordingly, at the point when the system call has been received, the service provider temporarily returns control to the user. Thereafter, when the operation has actually been completed, notice of this (posting) is made via a message box, using message communication.

ii. Synchronization internal to system call

In the case of internal synchronization, after the system call is received, control is not returned to the user until the operation has actually been completed. Return from the system call is itself the completion indication.

b. Asynchronous indication

The service provider notifies the user of asynchronous events via a message box. The message box for receiving this indication is designated by the user with a system call.

c. Synchronization in the case of data receipt

Two conceivable methods for data receipt indication are synchronous receiving, whereby receipt of data is indicated as READ system call completion information, and asynchronous receiving, whereby asynchronous indication is made in the message box designated at the time of path setting. Communication control interface adopts the latter method. The former method is an option that may be adopted as needed for individual layers.

4.3 ADDRESSING SCHEME

The PSAP (Presentation Service Access Point) addressing scheme is supported by consortia promoting OSI in devising implementation conventions and thus adopted in the communication control interface.

a. Address configuration

The PSAP address consists of a P-selector, S-selector, T-selector, and network address list (see Figure 8).

b. Network layer address

The network address is based on the ISO standards on syntax and semantics for addressing in network layers. The network address is used for addressing the OSI end system.

c. T-selector, S-selector, and P-selector

A T-selector, S-selector, and P-selector are used for addressing the entity within the OSI end system. Based on the premise that each selector will be managed locally in a given end system, only syntax is prescribed for these selectors.

T-selector: 32 bytes and below

S-selector: 16 bytes and below

P-selector: omitted

P-SELECTOR	S-SELECTOR	T-SELECTOR	NETWORK ADRESS LIST

Fig. 8   PSAP address configuration

4.4 CREATING AND DELETING CONNECTIONS

a. Creating a connection

The (n)-CCL conceals a (n-1)-CCL connection from the (n+1)-CCL. In other word, the (n+1)-CCL performs only management (establishment, maintenance and release) of (n)connection, whereas management of (n-1)connection is carried out by the (n)-CCL.

The (n)-CCL, as output information for a connection establishment request, returns a "connection endpoint identifier." After the connection is established and until it is released, the (n+1)-CCL uses this connection endpoint identifier in issuing system calls.

The (n)-CCL requires that message boxes for data receipt indication and for asynchronous indication be designated in a connection establishment request parameter. These message boxes are used thereafter for indication of asynchronous events involving that connection.

b. Deleting a connection

When the (n)-CCL makes a disconnect request, the (n+1)-CCL issues a disconnect response request system call. This system call is not always included in the OSI service primitives, but is required for synchronizing the release of connection endpoint identifiers between the (n)-CCL and (n+1)-CCL.

5. CONCLUSION

The design principles, reference model, and general rules for functions and representation format discussed above are intended to ensure a uniform approach to CTRON design. The design of CTRON interfaces has been proceeding under the auspices of the TRON Association, which is an open organization. The design results are being published in the form of interface specifications, in Japanese and English, and are offered publicly throughout the world for implementation by anyone. As a growing number of companies develop outstanding OS products conforming to these specifications, we can expect CTRON interfaces to come into wide use, leading to greatly improved software portability.

Acknowledgments

The authors are grateful to Dr. Fukuya Ishino for their constant guidance in CTRON development, and also to the members of the CTRON Technical Committee, representing Fujitsu Limited, Hitachi Ltd., Matsushita Communication Industry Corporation, Mitsubishi Electric Corporation, NEC Corporation, NTT Corporation, Northern Telecom Japan Inc., Oki Electric Industry Co. Ltd., and Toshiba Corporation.

References

[1] Wasano, T., M. Ohminami, Y. Kobayashi, T. Ohkubo, and K. Sakamura, "Design of TRON," in TRON Project 1987, Springer-Verlag (1987), pp. 157-172.

[2] TRON Association, Original Series of CTRON Specifications: Outline of CTRON, Ohmsha (1989), pp. 137-198.

[3] Wasano, T., M. Ohminami, Y. Kobayashi, T. Ohkubo, and K. Sakamura, "Design Principles and Configuration of CTRON," Proc. FJCC '87, Dallas (1987), pp. 159-166.

[4] Wasano, T., Y. Kobayashi, and K. Sakamura, "CTRON Reference Model," in TRON Project 1988, Springer-Verlag (1988), pp. 145-155.

[5]   Shimizu, Y., "Design of CTRON Communication Control Interface," in TRON Project 1988, Springer-Verlag (1988), pp. 157-166.

[6]   Ohkubo, T., T. Wasano, and I. Kogiku, "Configuration of the CTRON Kernel," IEEE Micro (1987), pp. 33-44.

[7]   Narimatsu, S., "Design of CTRON Input-output Control Interface," in TRON Project 1987, Springer-Verlag (1987), pp. 183-196.

[8]   Kumazaki, K., "Design of the CTRON File Management," in TRON Project 1987, Springer-Verlag (1987), pp. 173-182.

[9]   Jackson, D.L. (chm.), IEEE Trial-Use Standard Specification for Microprocessor Operating Systems Interfaces, Institute of Electrical and Electronics Engineers, Inc., New York (1985).

[10] Isaak, J. (chm.), IEEE Trial-Use Standard Portable Operating System Environment P1003/D6, Computer Society of the IEEE, Washington, D.C. (1985).

[11] Cragum, D.W., "Portable Operating System Environment," Proc. 5th Annual Phoenix Conf. on Computers and Communications, IEEE, New York (1986).

[12] Wasano, T., and Y. Kobayashi, "CTRON Applicable to Information Communication Networks," Microprocessors & Microsystems, Butterworths (1989).

Tetsuo Wasano:an executive engineer at NTT Network Systems Development Center. He is presently engaged in computer architecture strategy planning. Since joining the laboratory in 1970, he has been engaged in development research on DIPS operating systems and in research into artificial intelligence. He graduated from Tokyo University in 1970 with the BS degree. He is a member of the Institute of Electronics, Information and Communication Engineers of Japanese(IEICE) and of the Information Processing Society of Japan(IPS).

Yoshizumi Kobayashi:a senior engineer at NTT Network Systems Development Center. Since joining the company in 1973, he has been engaged in the research and development of compilers and operating systems. He has played role in construction of principles required for the CTRON design and in the design of program control interface within CTRON. He received the BS degree in 1971 and the MS degree in 1973 at Osaka University. He is a member of the IEICE, the IPS and the Computer Society of the IEEE.

Takashi Terazaki:an engineer at NTT Network Systems Development Center. Since joining the company in 1979, he has been engaged in the development of DIPS computers and the system engineering on DIPS operating systems. He has played role in software portability and validation methodology for the CTRON interface. He graduated from Kurume Technical College in 1979.

Above authors may be reached at:2-1, Uchisaiwai-cho 1-chome, Chiyoda-ku, Tokyo, 100 JAPAN

Ken Sakamura is currently an associate professor at the Department of Information Science, University of Tokyo. He holds Ph.D. in EE. Being a computer architect, he has been the leader of the TRON project which he started to build a new computer system architecture for 1990's since 1984. His promotion of the TRON architecture now extends to architecture of buildings and furniture. He servers on the editorial board of Institute of Electrical and Electronics Engineers (IEEE) MICRO magazine and is a chair of the project promotion committee of the TRON Association. He is a member of Japan Information Processing Society, Institute of Electronics, Information and Communication Engineers, ACM, and is a senior member of IEEE. He has received best paper awards of IEICE twice, of JIPS once, IEEE best annual article awards, and other awards from Japanese and over seas organizations.

Above authors may be reached at: Department of Information Science, Faculty of Science, University of Tokyo, 7-3-1 Hongo, Bunkyo-ku, Tokyo, Japan.

The Basic Concept of CTRON Switching Control

Kazuo Watanabe, Hiroshi Sunaga
NTT Communication Swiching Labs.

Diane Zingale
Bell Northern Research, Ltd.

ABSTRACT

This paper describes the basic concept of switching control in CTRON. As Switching Control Extended OS (EOS), presently specifications for ISDN circuit switching and packet switching are provided. Since the EOS should be commonly used in many applications, protocol processing necessary for them, e.g., Q.931, X.25, etc., and speech path control are specified. The service primitives of the protocols correspond to system calls and asynchronous event notification, which are used by applications that perform translation, routing, billing function etc.. To assure reliability, fault tolerance and management functions are also specified. Switching Control EOS is now developing and expected to be used in vast area of communication.

Keywords: Circuit Switching, Packet Switching, ISDN, OSI Reference Model, Speech Path Control

1. INTRODUCTION

Switching control is an important function in the field of communication, and is expected to be provided in the CTRON extended OS (EOS) specifications for common applications to different switching systems. The field of switching technology is very broad, covering analogue switching to Asynchronous Transfer Mode (ATM) and Intelligent Network (IN), and switching node structure changes as the technology advances. Considering the situation of international standardization, hardware and software technology, CTRON Switching Working Group provides CTRON specifications for packet switching and ISDN circuit switching at the present time.

The construction of an ISDN circuit switching system must realize Digital Subscriber Signaling 1 protocol (DSS1=Q.931) [1] for controlling the users, ISDN User Part (ISUP=Q.761-4) [2]-[5] for the common channel signaling, and speech path control for making a connection. For advanced services and management information transfer Transaction Capability protocols (TC=Q.771-5) [6]-[10] may be required. Since the switching system must be highly reliable and stable, fault tolerant functions such as initialization or saving of calls and management functions such as collection of traffic data are necessary. As for a packet switch, X.25 processing function [11] and other similar functions are needed.

It is important to make an appropriate system-model and to assign the necessary functions properly, in order to make specifications that can be used commonly by many users. From this viewpoint the model of the ISDN circuit switching system and the packet switching system are made with the protocol processing and minimum set of operation and management (O&M) functions defined as EOS. Also speech path control is positioned in EOS layer as a common function to circuit switching systems. In addition in the field of switching control, high throughput and highly multiple processing are required. Several counter measures are also considered in the specifications.

These techniques have been provided and published as CTRON specification [12]-[14]. Now CTRON Switching Working Group is studying the issues to be covered other than packet and ISDN circuit switching, and are also described in the last part of this paper. The functions necessary for the progress of the technology of switching, such as ISDN packet specification, network management function, etc will be specified.

This paper describes a basic concept of CTRON switching control, and it is expected that it would be helpful for constructing a switching system using CTRON.

2. THE MODELING OF SWITCHING SYSTEMS FOR CTRON SPECIFICATIONS

In this chapter the basic concept for modeling switching systems for the CTRON specifications and the positions of the switching control EOSs in CTRON reference model are described.

2.1 THE MODEL OF ISDN CIRCUIT SWITCHING SYSTEM

Circuit switching is a function that performs switching of circuits going into and out of the switch by means of a speech path. Though in ordinary circuit switching nodes, the

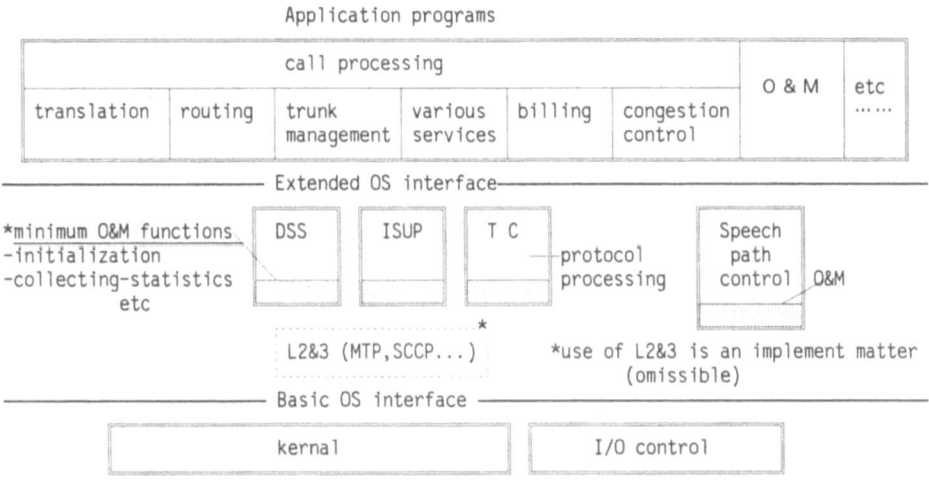

Fig.1 The Model of ISDN Circuit Switching

common channel signaling protocol is generally utilized for inter-office control, subscriber signaling is performed by a simple procedure such as on-hook signal. ISDN switches control the subscriber lines by using the Digital Subscriber Signaling 1 protocol and also use ISDN User Part protocol for controlling inter-office trunks so that various kinds of services can be offered. In addition, Transaction Capabilities may be utilized for advanced services or management information transfer.

Considering this situation, the model of ISDN circuit switching system can be constructed as follows (Figure 1). The important point is what are the common function of all the ISDN circuit switching systems, irrespective of the network providers design policy such as billing, services to be offered, and/or operation method. From this viewpoint, it can be said that the common parts to be provided as EOSs are the protocol processing, speech path control, and minimum sets of operation and management (O&M) functions such as fault tolerant function (initialization) and collection of statistical information. Whereas the other call processing functions, such as translation, routing, trunk management, various service processing, billing, congestion control and the other O&M functions are positioned as application function that CTRON users can design without restrictions.

2.2 THE MODEL OF PACKET SWITCHING SYSTEM

The model of packet switching system using CTRON specifications are as follows (Figure 2). In this case also, the functions common to all packet switching systems should be

Application programs

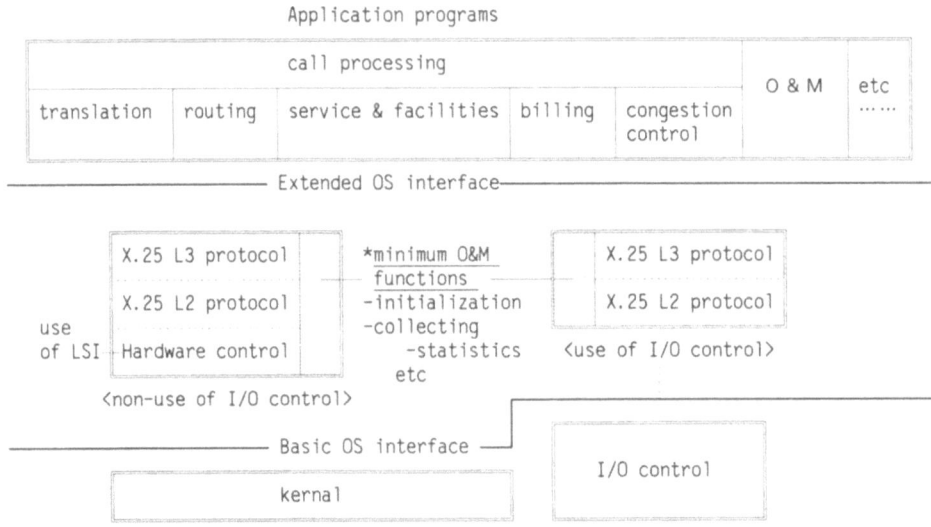

Fig.2 The Model of CTRON Packet Switching

provided as CTRON specifications irrespective of the network providers policy. The common parts are X.25 (network and data link) protocol and also minimum sets of O&M. Translation, routing, various service (or facility) processing, billing, congestion control and the other O&M functions are the application functions.

2.3 CTRON INTERFACE REFERENCE MODEL FOR SWITCHING CONTROL

As mentioned above, the functions to be offered as EOSs for switching control are DSS1 (DSS as the interface name), ISUP, TC, speech path control, network and data link layer protocols. They are positioned in the application layer of Communication Control EOSs basically as shown in Figure 3, since the application programs directly interface with these EOSs. However, the EOS functions necessary for a packet switching system are presently positioned in Network and Data Link layers. Essentially, packet switching control function is also an application function, and therefore the interface should be positioned as CTRON application layer EOS apart from that of terminal equipment. But considering that packet protocol processing functions of both a terminal and a switch are similar enough to be dealt with together (essentially the same), and this way is expected to enhance portability of the EOS and the application programs, if the common interfaces to both are specified.

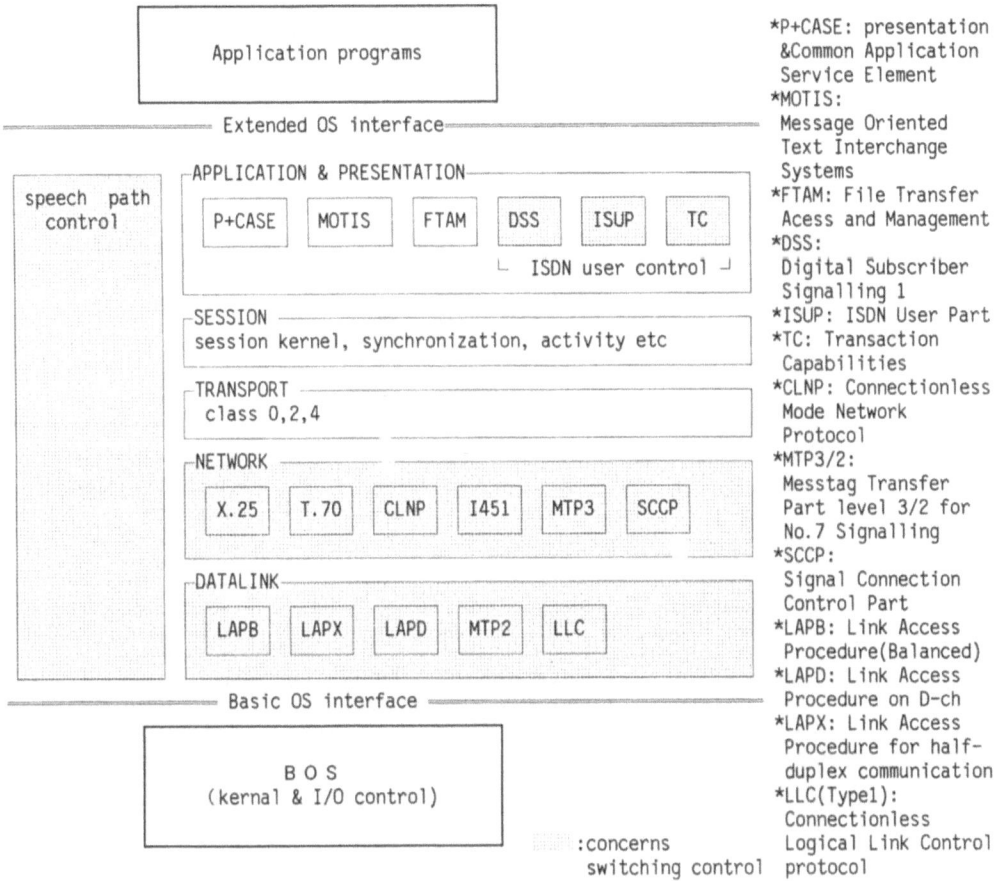

Fig.3 Interface Reference Model

3. ISDN CIRCUIT SWITCHING SYSTEM

CTRON EOSs for ISDN circuit switching nodes consist of the protocol processing interfaces and a speech path control interface. In this chapter the way the EOSs are made and their functions are described.

3.1 PROTOCOL PROCESSING OF ISDN CIRCUIT SWITCHING

The system-calls and asynchronous events notification functions are specified in accordance with the service definition of ISDN protocols. For subscriber protocol processing, the service primitives of CCITT Rec. Q.931 are mapped onto an EOS

Table.1 Main System Calls of ISDN User Control

service	service primitive	system call or asynchronous indication	function
Call setup	SETUP req SETUP ind SETUP resp SETUP conf	ID-SETUP-CALL — MBX:asynchronous ind NL-ESTABLISH-CONNECTION — MBX:system call completion ind	—establish a call
Disconnection	DISC req DISC ind	ID-DISCONNECT-CALL — MBX:asynchronous ind	—clear an access connection
Call release	REL req REL ind REL conf	ID-RELEASE-CALL — MBX:asynchronous ind — MBX:system call completion ind	—release relevant re- sources of the call ie. channel, call reference
Call proceeding	PROC req PROC ind	ID-PROCEED-CALL — MBX:asynchronous ind	—indicate initiation of call establishment
Alerting	ALERT req ALERT ind	ID-ALERT-CALL — MBX:asynchronous ind	—indicate initiation of alerting
Setup acknowledge	MORE INFO req MORE INFO ind	ID-REQUEST-MOREINFO — MBX:asynchronous ind	—require additional inf. after the call set-up
Information	INFO req INFO ind	ID-SEND-ADDITIONAL-INFORMATION — MBX:asynchronous ind	—provide additional user information
Call progress	PROG req PROG ind	ID-PROGRESS-CALL — MBX:asynchronous ind	—indicate the progress of a call for interwor- king or in-band inf.
Suspension (Resumption)	SUSP(RES) req SUSP(RES) ind SUSP(RES) resp SUSP(RES) conf SUSP(RES) REJ ind SUSP(RES) REJ res	ID-SUSPEND(RESUME)-CALL — MBX:asynchronous ind ID-SUSPEND(RESUME)-CALL — MBX:system call completion ind — MBX:system call completion ind ID-SUSPEND(RESUME)-CALL	—suspend a call —resume the suspended call —indicate failure of the resumption
Notification	NOTIFY req NOTIFY ind	ID-NOTIFY-CALL — MBX:asynchronous ind	—indicate information pertaining to a call
User information	USER INFO req USER INFO ind	ID-SEND-DATA — MBX:asynchronous ind	—transfer information to remote user
Initiation/ termination	no corresponding service primitive	ID-INITIATE-LINE ID-TERMINATE-LINE	—intiate/terminate control of line
Activation/ deactivation	no corresponding service primitive	ID-ACTIVATE-CCL ID-DEACTIVATE-CCL	—activate/deactivate the Communication Controller
collecting statis-tical info. etc	no corresponding service primitive	ID-START-COLLECTING-STATISTICAL- INFORMATIONetc	—start collection of statistical inf.

req:request　ind:indication　resp:response　conf:confirm

interface, namely the DSS interface. For common channel signaling, an interface based on Q.76X series (ISUP) is provided, whose users can employ Common Channel Signaling EOS as an underlying service. Also Rec. Q.77x series are mapped as TC interface.

As with the other communication control interfaces, the request and response service primitives correspond to the system calls, which demand a certain action such as call setup or release from the application to the EOS. The indication and confirmation service primitives are the asynchronous events notifications, which inform the application of a certain event occurrence such as reception of protocol data units etc. Examples of this relationship are shown in table. 1.

When the call processing application issues a system call, message boxes are designated to notify various events to the upper layer. Several kinds of message boxes are defined for each event so that the application can distinguish it efficiently or deal with a certain message box preferentially. These details are explained section 4.1.

3.2 THE MECHANISM OF CTRON SPEECH PATH CONTROL

3.2.1. Role of Speech Path Control

Speech path control specifies a standard interface for common application to the different switching systems that employ circuit switching. The necessary functions for controlling the speech path are positioned upon Kernel and I/O control BOS. With above mentioned EOSs and the application programs, an ISDN switch can be constructed, and in addition this interface can also be used for general digital switches other than ISDN switches.

3.2.2. Patterning of Speech Path Configuration and Assumption for the Hardware

A large number of different speech path configurations are possible, depending on the speech path switch structure and the method for connecting the various signaling equipment. If a switching path were designed without restrictions, many kinds of path structures and application programs would be made, so that the portability of application programs would be prevented. Therefore CTRON's approach for speech path control classifies (and confines) speech path switch structures into three patterns as shown Figure 4 : concentration stage only (L), concentration stage + distribution stage (L+D), and distribution stage only (D). These are typical patterns for switching systems, whose application programs differ from one another but can be classified also into only three patterns. By combinations of these with the signaling equipment connected to them,

162

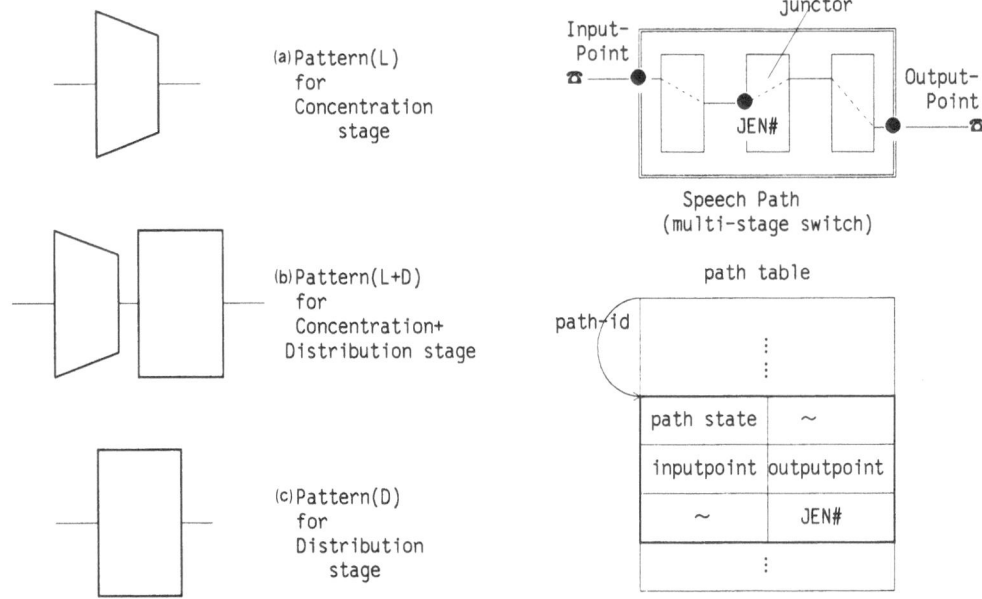

Fig.4 Speech path configuration model   Fig.5 Concealment of Speech Path Structure

basic patterns of speech path configurations can be set. This patterning allows a variety of speech path configurations to be controlled by the same standard interface and enables application programmers to use it without minding path structure.

The assumptions for the hardware are as follows:
-digital switch only ; analogue switches, ATM-switch are outside the scope.
-the switch is required to have the ability to deal with connection of forward and backward direction separately.

Here it should be noted that speech path control EOS hides speech path configurations (T or TST etc.--- T:time switch, TST:time switch + space switch + time switch), but does not hide the above mentioned stage architecture (D, L).

3.2.3 The Function and Features of Speech Path Control Interface

Speech path control provides the interfaces for a speech path connection required for call processing to application programs, such as hunting a speech path and making a connection. When a user construct a system with this EOS, it is appropriate that he need not care about the structure of the speech path. The following items are considered (Figure 5).

(1)Concealment of the junctor number:

When a multi-stage structured switch is used, it is generally not sufficient to input to it only input-position/output-position parameters to connect a certain path. A junctor number (Jen#) is also needed. However it is not suitable that the interface-user input the Jen# because the user (application program) must then be conscious of the hardware structure of the switch on which the junction number is dependent. Therefore, in CREATE_PATH and CONNECT_PATH interface etc, it is specified that the application shall input the input/output-position parameters etc except JEN# and the EOS shall assign and manage the number Jen#, which is not visible to the user.

(2)Introduction of path id:

In addition, it is troublesome for the application to input the input/output-points as parameters every time, which are not required for all the EOS functions. Therefore, an information block called "path table" is introduced. A path table is assigned for each path and contains the input-position, the output-position, the bearer rate, the state of the path, the call_id, the JEN#, and so forth. When a user calls CREATE_PATH, the EOS assigns a path table, sets the information to it and returns the ID of the path table (e.g., the address of the table), which is called "path_id". After that, the user can call DISCONNECT_PATH, RELEASE_PATH, and other system calls for collecting statistical information etc, without using the input-position or output-position etc.---only the path_id is needed. This ID is a so-called system tag, and so the user need not know its contents or internal structure.

Examples are shown below.

    ( ):input parameter, { }:output parameter

-**CREATE_PATH**=hunts a new path between input and output position, and makes it reserved condition

(speech_path_id[1]), (bearer_rate), (call_id[2]), (home_position_no_block[3]),
(mate_position_no_block[4]), (direction_id[5]), (connect_id[6]), (path_state[7])..., {**path_id**}, {return_code}

-**CONNECT_PATH**=connects the path so that the user can commence communication
(**path_id**), {return_code}

-**GET_SPEECH_PATH_INFORMATION**=reads the information concerning the path
(**path_id**), {return_code}

-**DISCONNECT_PATH**=disconnects the path
(**path_id**), {return_code}

<note>1:concentration or distribution stage, 2:identifier of each call, 3:input point, 4:output point, 5:both way/forward/backward, 6:semi-permanent or not, 7:reserved or connected

3.2.4 Fault Tolerant functions

A switching system must be highly reliable. For this reason, speech path control includes an interface that provides functions for fault tolerance, as a way of assuring the necessary reliability. Speech path control specifies interfaces for initialization and maintenance, etc, to assure high reliability. Using these interfaces O&M programs in the application layer performs maintenance functions such as fault detection, fault location, configuration, provisioning and installation.

For example Speech path control specification provides the following system calls:
-**INITIALIZE_SPEECH_PATH_CONTROL**=initializes the speech path hardware
-**FORCE_RELEASE_PATH**=releases the designated speech path connection forcibly
-**SET_SPEECH_PATH_OPERATION_MODE**=changes the operation mode (ACT, SBY, etc) into the designated one
-**SET_CALLSAVE_USER_ID**=makes a list of users to be saved
-**SET_CALLSAVE_PATH_INFORMATION**=releases all the path other than the users to be saved according to the above mentioned list
-**CONTROL_SUPERVISE_PATH**=searches paths that are held for a long time

4. PACKET SWITCHING SYSTEM

4.1 THE INTERFACE FOR PACKET SWITCHING SYSTEMS

Also in case of packet switching, the system calls and asynchronous events notification are specified in accordance with OSI network services, namely Rec. X.213. The relationship between them and the service primitives is almost the same as that of the ISDN protocols. However more message boxes are defined because of processing per logical channel and expedited data processing.

Message boxes are designated by the application so that it can distinguish each event or deal a certain event preferentially. For example, in case of connection establishment, four message boxes are designated for (1)system call completion indication, which notifies success or failure of the system call processing that takes time until the completion, (2)reception of data packets, namely N-DATA indication, (3)other asynchronous events indication, such as N-RESET indication or N-DISCONNECT indication, and (4)reception of expedited data packets (option). Other cases are explained in Figure 6.

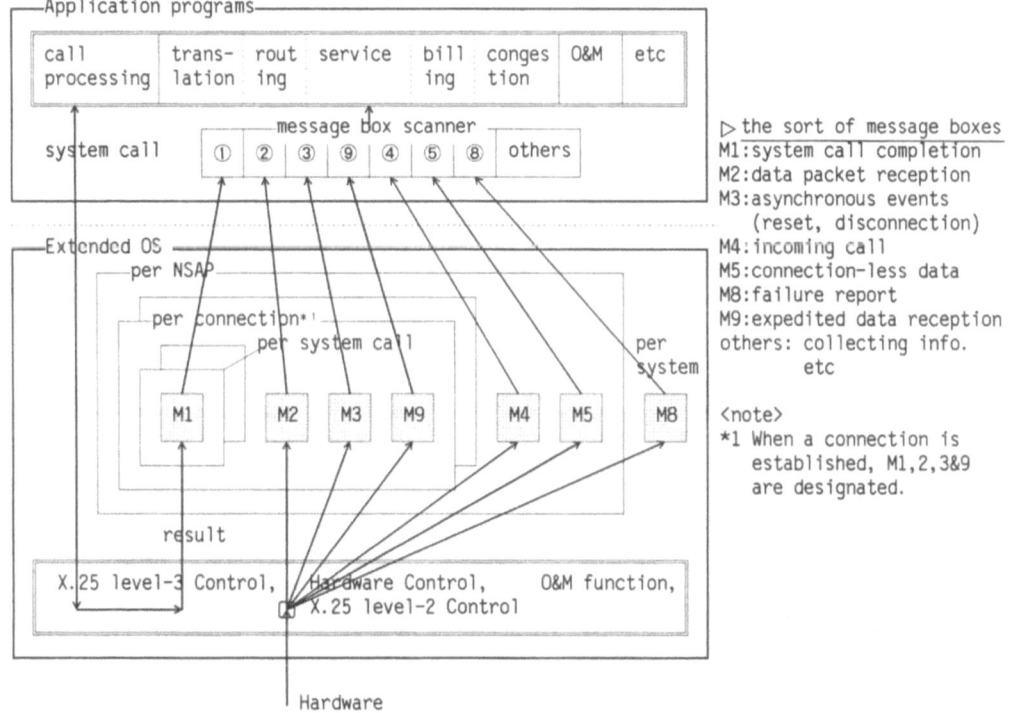

Fig.6 The Way to Use the Message Boxes

4.2 MODELS TO IMPROVE THE PERFORMANCE

In the CTRON model, asynchronous events such as reception of a data packet is notified using a message box as described above. Therefore the processing overhead between two layers is rather high. If layer 2, 3 EOSs and I/O hardware control BOS are separately made, three message boxes are required. To improve the performance the following countermeasures are considered.

(1)Layers 2 and 3 are not separated, but combined into one block.

(2)Input/Output Control Basic OS (BOS) need not be used. This (layer 3) EOS may drive directly line units (layer 2 or 3 LSI). ---But the users may utilize also the BOS, depending on the system configuration.

(3)Although in principle, CTRON system call completion indication should usually be used, this need not be used in the data transfer phase. Confirmation of data transfer can be done by the protocol.

(4)Data packet processing may be performed within the EOS, not in application program, since data packet processing is the dominant factor for performance.

(5)According to item (4), routing and billing functions may also be installed in the EOS.

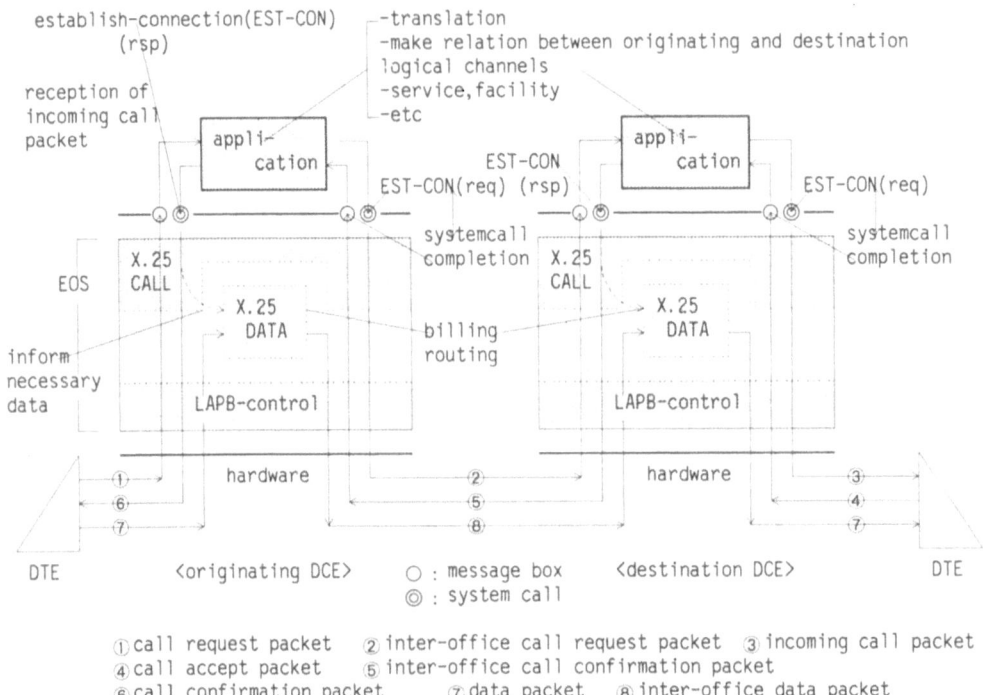

establish-connection(EST-CON)
(rsp)

reception of
incoming call
packet

-translation
-make relation between originating and destination
logical channels
-service,facility
-etc

① call request packet   ② inter-office call request packet   ③ incoming call packet
④ call accept packet   ⑤ inter-office call confirmation packet
⑥ call confirmation packet   ⑦ data packet   ⑧ inter-office data packet

Fig.7 CTRON Packet Processing Sequence

4.3 SEQUENCE OF PACKET SWITCHING PROCESSING

Considering the above mentioned points, a typical set of signal sequence will be explained here (Figure 7).

When a packet switching node receives a call request packet from a data terminal (DTE), the EOS notifies the reception of incoming call packet by a message box after performing X.25 level 2 (LAP-B) and 3 protocol processing. Then the application program translates the destination number, relates the originating DTE's logical channel to that of the destination, processes several services, and issues CONNECTION_ESTABLISHMENT system call to send the packet to the destination office (DCE). The destination DCE similarly performs several processing steps with the DTE and complete the connection establishment. During this phase the EOS gets necessary information to process data packets from the application, and it begins the data packet (and receive ready packet) transfer without using the application. This functional assignment enables efficient data transfer.

4.4 EXTENT OF COMMUNICATION CONTROL SUPPORT

CTRON communication control specifies interfaces for several protocols other than packet switching protocols, which have been set by the ISO and CCITT. Switching Control specifications are concerned with functions relevant to switching nodes, and so the following protocols are specified.

*Data Link Layer :
---LAP-B (Balanced Link Access Procedure), including MLP (Multilink Procedure)
---LAP-D (Link Access Procedure on of D-channel for ISDN)
---LAP-X (half duplex link access procedure based on LAP-B)
---MTP Level 2 (Common Channel Signalling System No.7 Message Transfer Part, for reliable transfer of signalling message between two points)

*Network Layer :
 ---X.25 Packet Level Interface
---CLNP (connection less network protocol)
---MTP Level 3 (No.7 Message Transfer Part, for transfer of signalling message over one signalling data link)
---SCCP (No.7 Signal Connection Control Part, for transfer of information between exchanges and specialized centres)

5. FUTURE WORKS

Remaining issues to be covered include ISDN packet switching, X.75 interworking protocol, network management function, ATM and IN etc. Each of them is thought to be provided as an EOS, when the international standardization are fixed.

Among them, the ISDN packet specification is presently under consideration, and studies on X.75 and network management function will commence soon. For ISDN and X.75 packet switching several items will be added to the existing specifications. As for the network management, concepts of Telecommunication Management Network (TMN), Operation and Maintenance Application Part (OMAP) [15], etc will be introduced to the specifications. ATM and IN will be studied after 1990, when the technical trends are clarified. Thus, service menus will be added according to the needs of CTRON users and international standardization.

6. CONCLUSION

The main techniques employed in CTRON Switching Control Specifications have been described, especially focused on ISDN protocol processing, speech path control and packet switching processing.

The modeling principle is to define the common parts to all the applications that construct ISDN and packet switching nodes. Thus protocol processing (Q.931, Q.76x, Q.77x, X.25) and minimum sets of O&M functions are provided as EOS [12]-[14], whereas in the application program layer, translation, routing, trunk management, congestion control and billing functions etc are positioned. The Speech Path Control specification conceals the hardware (speech path) architecture so as to be controlled by the same standard interface, classifying the speech paths into three structural patterns according to the type of switching nodes. In the switching field it is important to attain high performance and reliability, and some countermeasures are considered in the specifications.

CTRON Switching Control EOSs are useful and their service menus will also be added, e.g., ISDN packet, network management function, and ATM etc. They are expected to be used in many types of switching systems.

ACKNOWLEDGEMENT

The authors wish to express their appreciation to Dr. Ken Sakamura and Dr. Fukuya Ishino for their valuable opinions and guidance in consideration of the CTRON switching control interface. Thanks are due also to the members of Fujitsu Ltd., Hitachi Ltd., Mitsubishi Electric Corporation., NEC Corporation, NTT Corporation, Oki Electric Industry Co. Ltd., and Toshiba Corporation who studied, discussed and wrote the specifications in the CTRON Switching Working Group.

REFERENCES

[1]CCITT Recommendation Q.931 "ISDN user-network interface-network layer specification"
[2]CCITT Recommendation Q.761 "Functional description of the ISDN user part of signaling system No.7"

[3]CCITT Recommendation Q.762 "general function of messages and signals"

[4]CCITT Recommendation Q.763 "Formats and Codes"

[5]CCITT Recommendation Q.764 "Signaling Procedures"

[6]CCITT Recommendation Q.771 "Functional description of transaction capabilities"

[7]CCITT Recommendation Q.772 "Transaction capabilities information element definitions"

[8]CCITT Recommendation Q.773 "Transaction capabilities format and encoding"

[9]CCITT Recommendation Q.774 "Transaction capabilities procedures"

[10]CCITT Recommendation Q.775 "Guidelines for using transaction capabilities"

[11]CCITT Recommendation X.25 "Interface between data terminal equipment (DTE) and data circuit-terminating equipment (DCE) for terminals operating in the packet mode and connected to public data network by dedicated circuit.

[12]Original CTRON Specification Series 1 Outline of CTRON, Ohm-sha, 1989

[13]Original CTRON Specification Series 7 ISDN User Control, Ohm-sha, 1989

[14]Original CTRON Specification Series 5 Communication Control, Ohm-sha, 1989

[15]CCITT Recommendation Q.795 "Operation and Maintenance Application Part"

Kazuo Watanabe is a senior research engineer, supervisor, in the NTT Communication Switching Laboratories. There, he conducts research on advanced switching software technology. Previously, he was engaged in the design of electronic switching system software, and in the developmental research on a packet switching system.

Mr. Watanabe received his B.E. degree from Kumamoto University in 1968. He is a member of the Institute of Electronics, Information and Communication Engineers of Japan, and of the Information Processing Society of Japan.

Hiroshi Sunaga is currently a research engineer in NTT Communication Switching Laboratories, where he is engaged in research on system management of switching nodes. Previously, he was engaged in developmental research on switching systems, especially remote maintenance methods for packet switching systems, network management centres.

He received his B.E. and M.E. degrees in control engineering from Tokyo Institute of Technology (T.I.T) in 1981 and 1983. He is a member of the Institute of Electronics, Information and Communication Engineers of Japan.

Above authors may be reached at: Switching Technology Lab., NTT Communication Switching Labs.,9-11, Midori-Cho 3-Chome, Musashino-Shi, Tokyo, 180 Japan

Diane Zingale was born in Brooklyn, New York, U.S.A. She received the B.S and M.S. degrees in electrical engineering from the Massachusetts Institute of Technology in 1977. She had worked for Digital Equipment Corporation for 10 years in Boston, and for 4 years in Japan. She has been with Bell Northern Research in Tokyo since 1988. Diane has experience in multiprocessor systems, module design, VLSI design, microcode and operation systems. She is a CTRON Technical Committee member and a member of IEEE, Sigma Xi and the Institute of Electronics, Information and Communication Engineers.

Above authors may be reached at: Bell Northern Research, Ltd., c/o NTJI, Oak Minami Bldg., 3-19-23 Minami Azabu, Minato-Ku, Tokyo, 106 Japan

The CTRON Interface Validation System

Ichiro Takenaka, and Hideo Oda
NTT Software Laboratories

ABSTRACT

The CTRON conformance testing was initiated at Dec. 1988 by the TRON Association. The CTRON validation system is designed to assure portability of programs developed to run on a CTRON based OS. There are two types of validation system: document validation system and function validation system.

a. Document validation system: Document validation is based on an examination of user manuals that explain OS functions. The purpose is to determine whether the OS functions either exceed or fall short of those defined in the CTRON interface specifications. Using document validation checksheets provided by the TRON Association, a detailed cross comparison is made between description in the OS manuals and the CTRON interface specifications.

b. Function validation system: Function validation employs special software known as a validation suite. This software is run on the OS being tested to check the functions of each system call, error messages and other aspects of OS operation.

An outline of this CTRON validation system, test case design for function validation and techniques employed to enable the function validation system to run on any kinds of CTRON based OS are described in this paper.

KEYWORDS

CTRON, OS INTERFACE, VALIDATION, CONFORMANCE TESTING, TEST SUITE

1. INTRODUCTION

CTRON interface validation is performed to confirm that the interface specifications of an OS are in accord with CTRON interface specifications, and as a result it guarantees portability of programs running on a CTRON based OS keeping in line with the overall goal of the TRON project.

Since CTRON aims to standardize the interfaces of operating systems used in various fields such as, switching, communications processing and information processing, the CTRON interface validation system should be capable of running on versatile computer systems.

In this paper, the technical aspects of validation such as the principles of validation, the design of the validation system which can be executed on any kind of CTRON based OS and the concept of the validation level are described.

2. PRINCIPLE OF CTRON VALIDATION [1]

2.1 Purpose

The purpose of the validation is to confirm that the interfaces of a given OS are in accord with the CTRON interface specifications and, as a result, to guarantee portability of application programs running on the CTRON based OS.

NOTE 1: If excessive functions are allowed, an application program using those functions provided in one OS will not run on another OS fully complying with the interface specifications. However, since the decision whether to allow or disallow excessive functions is a matter of policy or design principle of the CTRON interface specifications, the discussion here is limitted to technical aspects of validation.

2.2 Scope of Validation

In the interface specifications, some system calls or parameters are defined as implementation dependent. These are not included in the scope of validation. Furthermore, the performance of the system is out of the scope.

2.3 Validation Method

In order to satisfy the above mentioned conditions, two types of validation are employed; Document and Function validation. Both manuals and OS program are tested by means of these validation methods. A product which has passed both validations is approved as a CTRON based OS and allowed to be distributed with the validation mark(Fig.1).

Document validation This is based on an examination of user manuals explaining OS functions to determine whether the functions of the OS subject to validation are excessive or deficient. Using a number of check lists, a detailed cross-comparison is made between the descriptions in the OS manuals and the CTRON interface specifications.

Function validation Confirmation is made as to whether the OS operates as prescribed in the specifications. This process makes use of a set of validation programs (validation suites). The programs are run on the OS to check such the system call inputs and outputs as return codes and error messages.

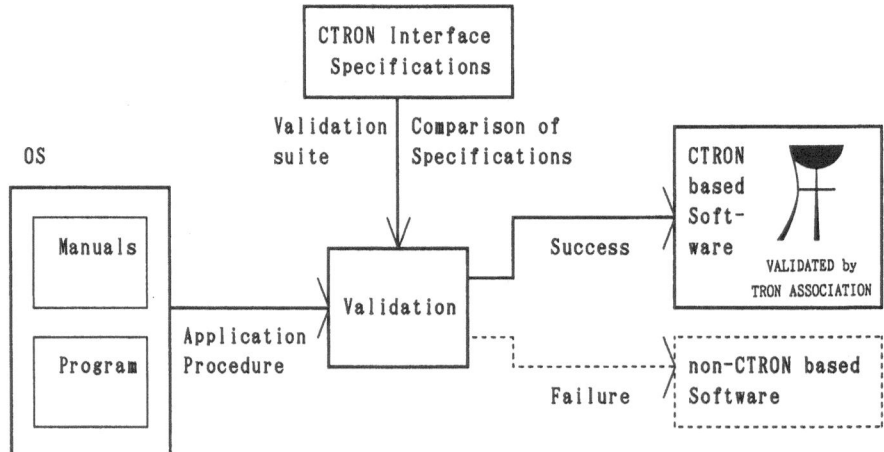

Fig.1 Validation of CTRON interface

NOTE 2: Function validation can check out all fuction shortages but cannot check out excessive functions. Document validation complements this by being able to check out excessive functions. Without the descriptions about the excessive functions in the manuals, those functions can not be used by AP programmers, which means the problem stated in NOTE 1 can be avoided.

3. OUTLINE OF VALIDATION SYSTEM

Two types of validation systems have been developed. The final pass/fail decision for each applicant is made based on the results of both Document and Function validations.

3.1 Document Validation System

This system consists of a set of check sheets as shown in Fig.2 and the manual on how to fill in the check sheets. Each check sheet has a list of validation items, each of which corresponds to a paragraph of the CTRON interface specifications.

The applicant should examine each item one by one if it is described in the user's manual of the product subject to validation. If it is, the applicant should put the volume and page number where the description is in the V/P column so that the TRON Association can easily confirm it.

If any functions excessive to the CTRON specifications are found in the manual, the applicant should submit, together with the completed check sheets, a report as giving the reasons for the excessive functions (Fig.3). The identification number of the report should be given in the note column of the check sheet as a reference. The TRON Association examines each item and checks in the judge column. Pass/fail judgment for document validation is made by the TRON Association after thoroughly examining these results and the excessive function reports.

subset	common unit	classifi cation	CREATE_TASK		code	KC- CA01	page	1/4
class	No.	Validation items			P	V/P	judge	note
syntax	0001	CREATE_TASK [(task_name)] ,(program_name • • •			15			
function	0002	Create a task.			15			
	0003	Set a task to dormant state.			15			
	• • •	• • •						

```
        : entered by applicant
   P    : page of interface specification
   V/P  : Volume and page of manuals
  judge : entered by TRON association
```

Fig.2 An example of check sheet for document validation

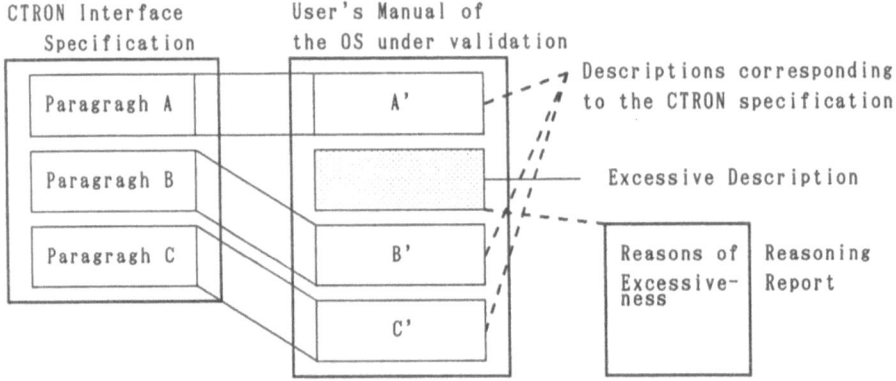

Fig. 3 Document Validation

3.2 Function Validation

This system consists of test suites(a group of test programs controlled by validation management programs) which confirm the functions of a CTRON based OS by issuing system calls sequentially and then comparing the responses of the OS with expected values.

The test suites are managed hierarchically by validation management program. Therefore, the set of test suites to be executed can be selected at any level of the hierarchy as shown in Fig.4.

As mentioned before, the function validation system should be able to run on a variety of computer systems. In order to meet this requirement, the system is in the form of a source program. It is then compiled and linked in the same software development environment as the OS itself. This allows the load module(LM) to execute on the target OS. The flow of function validation is explained below with references to Fig.5:

- The LM of the validation system is created by the applicant and loaded on to the system to be validated.

- The validation control program is initiated and the type of test suites to be executed are specified by the applicant.

- The specified test suites are selected by the control program and executed.

- Test results(Good or No Good; together with reasons of failure) are stored by the suites into the predefined area of main OS memory.

- Execution of the validation system terminates after performing all the specified tests.

- The test results on the memory are dumped onto appropriate media such as FD by means of a memory dump tool. The media is submitted to the TRON Association.

- The validation report is generated by the report output tool in the TRON Association.

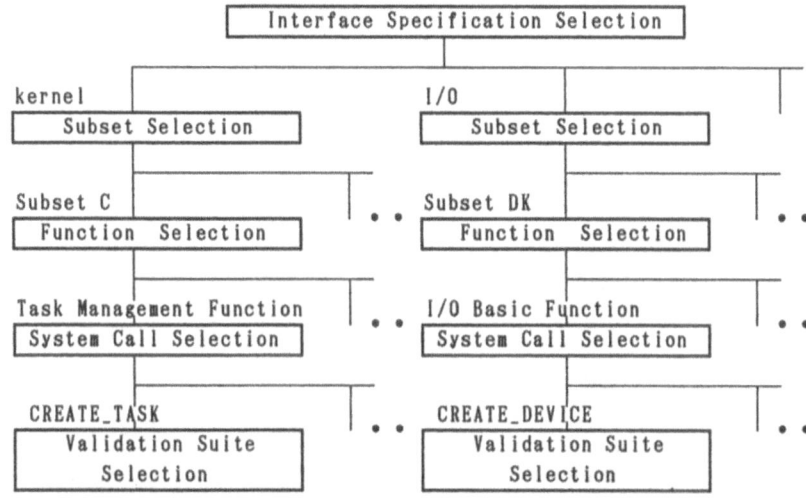

Fig. 4 Hierarchical Selection of Validation Suites

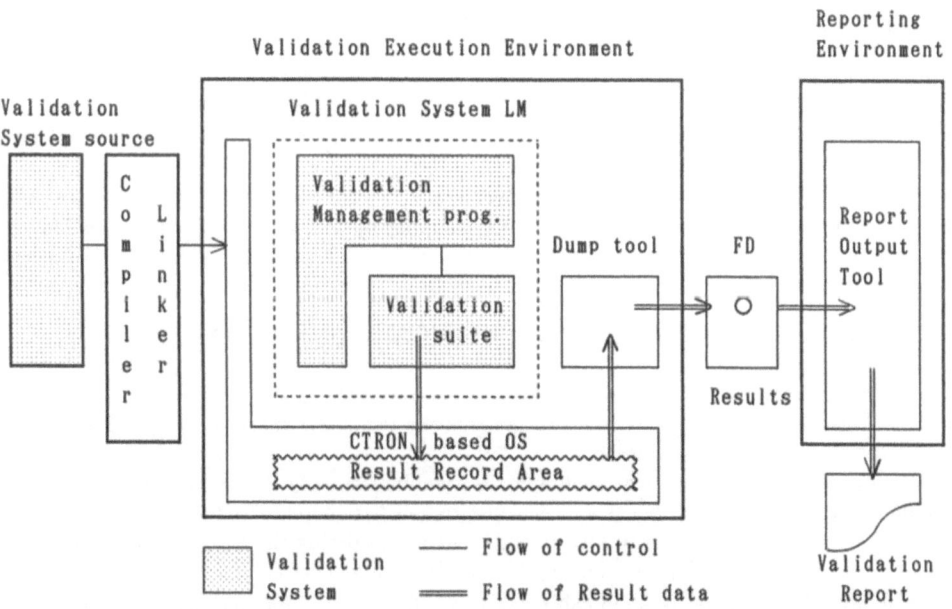

Fig. 5   Structure and operation of
Function Validation system

4. DESIGN OF THE FUNCTION VALIDATION SYSTEM

4.1 System requirements

Input and Output facilities Though it is common for general purpose computers to have some basic I/O facilities, few of the embedded computer systems are provided with them. The validation system should be capable of yielding the output even in the case of a system that has neither external storage equipment nor any I/O facilities.

Memory size An OS subject to validation does not necessarily have ample main memory capacity. Therefore, the validation system should be capable of running under various memory size conditions.

4.2 Implementation of the system

Method for systems with no I/O facilities In order to enable the validation system to run under the worst conditions, such as no I/O facilities, the system was designed to leave the test results on a certain area of main memory which is available in even the smallest CTRON based OS.

This method is based on the assumption that any CTRON based OS has, as a basic tool of its own development environment, some means to dump its memory contents onto various types of recording media. The most commonly used facilities for this purpose is an ICE(In Circuit Emulator).

Method to meet memory requirements In order to cater to various memory capacities, the size of the validation system LM should be variable. The validation management program controls the sequence of test suites based on the contents of a table, namely a table driven system. Therefore, the contents of the table should be modified depending on how the LM is divided. Relationships of the control tables and LM structure are illustrated in Fig.6.

Change of the memory-structure has been realized through compiler option facility. Function modules, which are designated in a compiler option, are combined as one LM. The applicant can adjust the memory size to his own validation environment by this function.

5. TEST CASE DESIGN FOR FUNCTION VALIDATION

5.1 Testing levels

Test cases for function validation are designed by using the check matrix (Table 1) which shows the combination of parameters.

Ideally, all the possible cases, including the combinations of all system calls as well as the combinations of all possible values for each system call parameter, should be tested.

However, it is not practical to test all these cases considering the enormous amount of time required. To cope with this, the following five levels of validation are introduced assuming that the validation is carried out system call by system call; that is, combinations of system calls are not considered.

- LEVEL1(L_1): All the combinations of parameter values are tested.
- LEVEL2(L_2): All the combinations of parameter values are tested except for error cases. Each error case is tested only once.
- LEVEL3(L_3): All the possible valid and invalid values of each parameter are tested at least once.

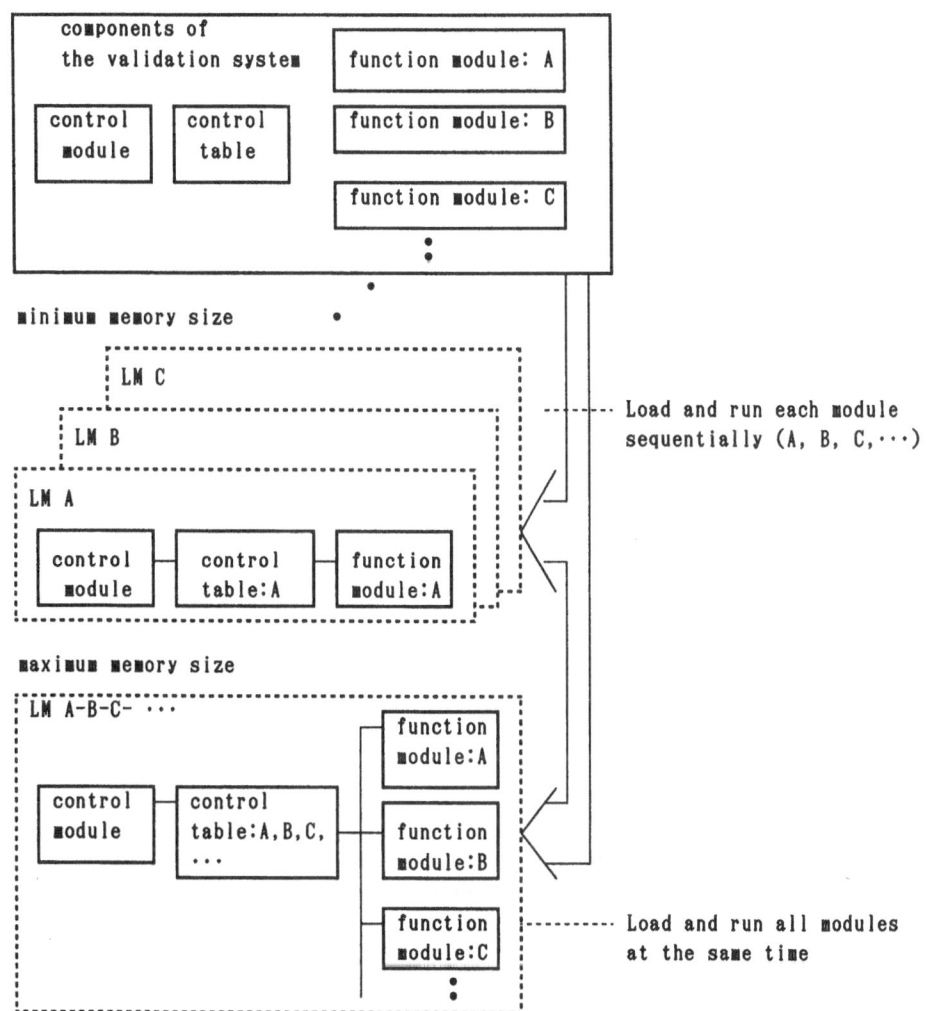

Fig.6 A method to change the memory size

- LEVEL4(L_4): Same as LEVEL3 except for error cases. For error cases, one test item is selected for one system call.

- LEVEL5(L_5): One test program for one system call just to confirm the existence of the specified functions.

The formulas to obtain the numbers of test cases for a system call are given in Appendix.

Table 1 Check matrix

check conditions			check item ID			
contents		ID	1	2	3	4
input	parame ter: A 0	01	●		○	○
	parame ter: A 1	02		●		
	invalid value	03				
	parame ter: B 'A'	04	◎	○	○	○
	invalid value	05				
	parame ter: C 10	06			●	
	default	07	◎	○		○

●: marking point   ◎: marking point already checked on
○: parameter which is checked according to the check of marking point

5.2 The number of test items

The above formulas are applied to the CTRON system calls[2], which are in a common kernel interface unit(84 system calls), to obtain the numbers of test items as shown below. The relationship between validation levels and number of test cases is illustrated in Fig. 7.

$$L_1 = 10{,}709$$
$$L_2 = 1{,}132$$
$$L_3 = 483$$
$$L_4 = 413$$
$$L_5 = 84$$

The function validation system is being built in such a way that it will first meet the level 3 requirements and later grow gradually to a higher level. An evaluation study will be made to clarify the relationship between the validation level and the validation quality, defined as the number of incompatibilities in a validated CTRON system.

6. CONCLUSION

An outline of the CTRON validation system, a test case design for function validation and techniques employed to enable the validation system to run on any type of CTRON-based OS were described.

Conformance tests of the basic OS are being performed now. Research on how to perform the conformance tests of an extended OS and the development of a validation system for it are currently under consideration.

number of test cases

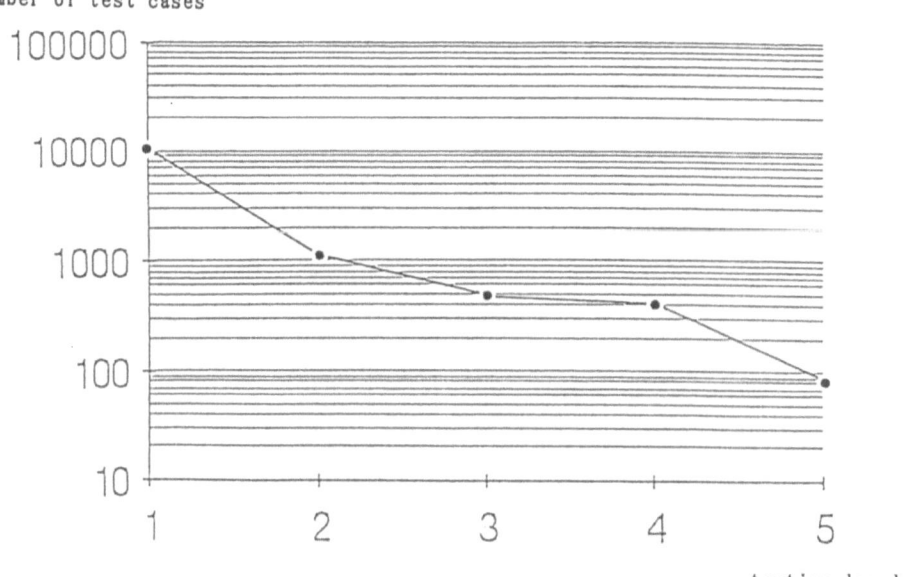

Fig.7 Number of test casese for each testing levels

References

[1] "CTRON SPECIFICATION-KERNEL INTERFACE" by TRON Association, 1981
[2] "CTRON SPECIFICATION-I/O CONTROL INTERFACE" by TRON Association, 1981
[3] I. Takenaka and H. Oda, "Test Cases Design Method for OS Validation System," Information Processing Soc. Japan, 1989, (in Japanese)
[4] I. Takenaka and H. Oda, "CTRON Interface Validation System," The first International Workshop on Software Quality Improvement 1989.2
[5] I. Takenaka and H. Oda, "CTRON Validation System," NTT Technical Journal Vol.1 No.3 1989
[6] I. Takenaka and H. Oda, "Implementation of CTRON Validation System," Information Processing Soc. Japan 1989, (in Japanese).

Appendix

The numbers of test cases in the five levels are given by the following formulas.

$$L_1 = \prod_{i=1}^{p}(n_i + e_i) \tag{1}$$

$$L_2 = \prod_{i=1}^{p} n_i + \sum_{i=1}^{p} e_i \tag{2}$$

$$L_3 = \sum_{i=1}^{p}(n_i + e_i) - p + 1 \tag{3}$$

$$L_4 = \sum_{i=1}^{p} n_i - p + 1 + D \tag{4}$$

$$L_5 = 1 \tag{5}$$

Where,

p : number of parameters of a system call.
n_i: number of valid values for i-th parameter($i = 1$ to p).
e_i: number of invalid values for i-th parameter($i = 1$ to p).

$$D: \begin{cases} 1, & \text{if there is any error case;} \\ 0, & \text{if there is no error case.} \end{cases}$$

ICHIRO TAKENAKA is a senior research engineer, supervisor at NTT Software Laboratories, where he conducts research into software quality assurance and project management. Since joining the company, he has been engaged in developmental research on operating systems, supprot systems for ESS software development and digital communication network configurations. He received the BE degree in 1966 and the MS degree in 1968 at Kyushu University. He is a member of the IEICE.

HIDEO ODA is a senior research engineer, supervisor at NTT Software Laboratories, where he conducts research into software validation systems. Since joining the company in 1973, he has been engaged in developmental research on compilers and CAI systems. He received the BE degree in 1971 and the MS degree in 1973 at Yokohama University. He is a member of the IEICE and the IPS.

The above authors may be reached at: NTT software laboratories, 1-9-1 Kohnan, Minato-ku, Tokyo 108, Japan.

Design of CTRON
Fault Tolerance Functions

Makoto Fukuyoshi, Noboru Furuya, Masaru Ishizuka
Oki Electric Industry Co., Ltd.
Tadashi Ohta
NTT Network Systems Development Center

ABSTRACT

CTRON application fields such as switching node, information processing node, and communication processing node require fault tolerance functions to assure high reliability. In particular, switching system and on-line transaction system are typical fault tolerant system in CTRON application fields. Interfaces for fault tolerance functions are one of the major features of CTRON.

This paper discusses the requirements for fault tolerant system in CTRON application fields, the design principles of CTRON fault tolerance functions, an outline of the CTRON fault tolerant interface specifications, and the relation to OAM (Operation, Administration and Maintenance) which is closely related to the fault tolerance functions. This paper also describes remaining subjects for further study of fault tolerance functions concerning transaction processing and speech path control for switching node.

Keywords : CTRON, Fault Tolerance, Operation Administration and Maintenance

1.INTRODUCTION

With the arrival of the advanced information-oriented society, network systems are becoming more complex and large-scale, and the reliability of network systems is becoming more important. The major application fields for CTRON are the various nodes for switching, for information processing and for communication processing, which are distributed within the network. These nodes are required to provide continuous service 24 hours a day, 365 days of the year, as well as constantly-high reliability [1] [2] . If these services are interrupted due to any breakdown of these systems, society as a whole suffers a huge adverse effect. A fault tolerant system is one which allows faults to occur partially within the system and yet still provides services. There are two approaches to achieving high system reliability: fault avoidance and fault tolerance. The former primarily is a technique at the stage of design and manufacture. According to the latter approach, CTRON interface specifications required for constructing fault tolerant systems are defined.

With respect to fault tolerance functions, the system high reliability technology research committee at the Japan standards association, IEEE Technical Committee and International Federation for Information Processing (IFIP) Working Group 10.4 are investigating standardization for high system reliability technology, including terminology and concepts, in the light of recent trends [3] [5] [8] . In the development of CTRON fault tolerance functions, trends in the establishment of such standardization have been carefully observed.

This paper discusses the position of fault tolerance functions in CTRON, the interface design principles, an outline of fault tolerance interface specifications, and the functional adequacy of fault tolerance functions. In addition, it discusses the requirements for portions of the CTRON interface specifications which have not been established, and the relationships with OAM functions closely associated with fault tolerance functions.

2.REQUIREMENTS OF FAULT TOLERANCE FUNCTIONS

In information communication network systems, high reliability is constantly required and systems are designed to meet this requirement. Consider, for example, the switching system for a telephone office, a typical fault tolerant system. It has been designed on the condition that it will assure high reliability so that the sum of total time of suspended service over 22 years does not exceed one hour [4] .

Meanwhile, with respect to on-line transaction systems, including the recent Tandem's Nonstop computer and Stratus systems, demand for system reliability has been increasing particularly because the volumes of processing have been also increasing and the systems are operated continuously over 24 hours [6] [7] . With information communication network systems, the system designer must consider hardware, software and even network configuration in order to obtain system reliability. Presented below are the major requirements of fault tolerance functions in specifying CTRON interface from these backgrounds.

- It must be possible to detect faults early.
- It must be possible to recover from faults automatically and in a short time period.
- It must be fail-safe.
- It must be possible to guarantee consistency of data and transactions.
- It must be possible to extend or remove system resources without interrupting system operation.
- It must be possible to diagnose, repair and maintain without interrupting system operation and impacting running application programs.

3.FAULT TOLERANCE INTERFACE DESIGN CONDITION

3.1Fault Tolerance Elementary Functions

In investigating CTRON interface specifications, attention is given to fault resistance functions including all types of redundant configurations and recovery techniques for satisfying the requirements mentioned in Chapter 2. In addition, system resource maintenance and extension are considered.

In discussing CTRON, the expression "fault tolerance" includes the meaning not only of fault tolerance in the simple, original sense, but also system extension and maintenance functions without interrupting service as required by non-stop systems. For CTRON, these functions are further subdivided into the 14 functions, which are collectively called "Fault Tolerance Elementary Functions." At each interface class or unit of CTRON, interfaces are specified in consideration of these 14 functions. An outline model of fault tolerance functions is shown in *Fig. 1*, and the fault tolerance elementary functions are indicated below.

1)**Fault preprocessing**
This function gathers information necessary for fault analysis and for recovery prior to the emergence of a fault.

2)**Fault detection**
This function detects faults and notifies a fault to higher-level software.

3)**Fault discrimination**
After notice of fault has been received, this function analyzes the fault and determines its location.

4)**Retry**
This function re-executes processing when a fault occurrs.

5)**Fault confinement and Reconfiguration**
This function removes hardware or software resources which have become the cause of fault and prevents the spread of fault to other modules. Reconfiguration is a function which replaces a faulty unit or device with a spare unit or a substitute device.

6)**Degradation**
If the fault cannot be repaired, this function decreases partial performance or degrade functioning so that the system can continue to operate and provide services.

7)**Recovery processing**
With information collected during fault preprocessing, this function works to restore the conditions prior to a fault or new stable conditions.

8)**Restart**
When a fault can not be recovered by recovery processing, this function initializes the system or uses checkpoint information to restart it from the condition prior to the emergence of the fault.

9)**Synchronization/Matching**
When a portion of multiplexed hardware/software resources has broken down, this function restores the resources under synchronized conditions.

10)**Test/Diagnosis**
This function works to search out and designate the locations of faults.

11)**Preventive Maintenance**
This function confirms normal status of system resources in onder to detect fault early.

12)**Extension/Removal**
This function extend or remove OS control resources.

13)**Protection**
This function works to protect the system from being adversely affected by software bugs or hardware faults.

14)**Status display**
This function displays system operational status to the operator and provides requisite information for load control.

3.2Redundancy

With a fault tolerant system, if a fault occurs within the system there must be some means whereby the system can continue to operate as such and provide service. Some redundancy must be planned for all hardware and software resources in the system so that fault tolerance can be achieved. The system designer must also pay attention to time redundancy, networking and distributed processing [2]. Redundancy techniques as mentioned above for CTRON are discussed below.

(a)Hardware redundancy

An example of a method of hardware redundancy is multiplexed processor and memory. Another method of redundancy configulation is to link a large number of processing units. This can be called a multi-processor structure. Such a structure can come in two forms, depending on how the individual processors are linked; one is the loosely-coupled multiprocessor structure linked by communication equipment, etc., and the other is the tightly-coupled multiprocessor structure linked by shared memory. For redundancy of input/output devices, the multiplexed disk is a typical method. Access paths among these devices are also commonly multiplexed. One method, for example, is to multiplex access buses between CPU and I/O devices. Also in this category is the multi-link in which the communication link is multiplexed. In this way multiplexing all of these OS resources must be considered in the design of CTRON interfaces.

(b)Software redundancy

There are many software resources in the system: files, processes, databases, transactions and soon. By multiplexing these software resources by some method, if the information in these resources should become lost or destroyed, it would be possible to restore the information. It is also necessary to backup the system operation file in case something should go wrong with the system. The method of backup is very closely related to the redundant configuration of hardware. The fault tolerant system is not realized independently with software and hardware. These methods must be integrated so that a more reliable system can be designed.

(c)Time redundancy

Faults within the system are classified into permanent and intermittent fault. In the latter case, retrials can be performed after a fixed time period. If, for example, an error has occurred when the processor accessed an I/O device, access can be attempted again and if normal access is achieved at the second time with no errors, the I/O device can be treated as normal. In the case of a switching system for a telephone office, if a fault has occurred with a multiplexed device, the device can be switched and after a fixed time interval, the device can be re-switched and used. In this case, it is assumed that the fault is an intermittent fault in hardware. It can be recovered by using hardware redundancy and time redundancy.

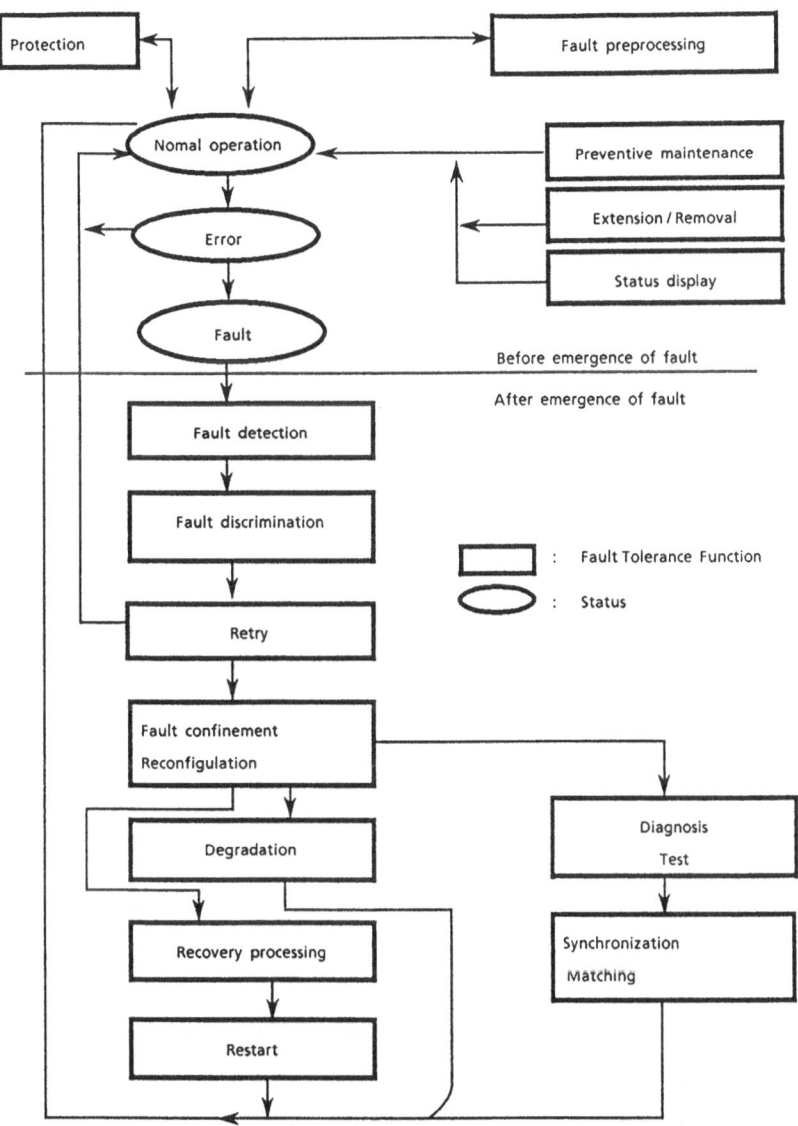

Fig.1 Outline Model of CTRON Fault Tolerance Functions

3.3 Networking and Distributed Processing

Consideration is given to prevent other processing nodes from being adversely affected by a fault in a network processing node or line. In this way, fault tolerance is assured in the information communication network at the network level. At each switching processing and communication processing node, for instance, each communication route is multiplexed so that if a fault occurs in a communication route, communication between each processing node will still be possible. With CTRON, it is necessary to specify the interface for making a high-reliable network .

Moreover, with CTRON it is necessary to consider prevention of loss or overlapped sending of information transmitted and received between each processing node and guarantee of transaction processing.

The distributed database system and the on-line transaction system are typical examples of distributed processing systems in the CTRON application fields.
(For CTRON, distributed transaction processing is an investigative subject of the future.)

4.INTERFACE DEFINITION MODEL AND DESIGN PRINCIPLES

4.1 Interface Definition Model

(a)Interface specification type

CTRON interface can be roughly classified into four categories : Ia, Im, Ii and Iu interface [1]. The Ia interface, the Application Interface is an interface used mainly for general application programs. The Im interface is used mainly for operation, administration and maintenance (OAM). The Iu interface, the Unspecified Interface, is required for system construction, but it is not specified for CTRON because it is difficult to specify the standardized interface for CTRON. The last category, Ii interface, the Internal Interface is required, according to implementing each interface unit. It is not among the specified interfaces for CTRON. We can thus see that for CTRON not only a simple application program interface must be specified for circulation of extended OS as well as that of application program, mutual interfaces among extended OS interface units must also be specified. The fault tolerance functions are realized mainly by using the Im interface. Interface definition model is shown in *Fig. 2* [16].

(b)Interface specification level

With CTRON, in addition to the interface classification presented in (a) above, each interface specification level is also established [1]. The CTRON interface is comprised of operations, objects and parameters, but from the interface specification level, it is divided up into the following four grades.
1) CO level: Object Name Specified
                Only the object name is specified.
2) CS level: System Call Name Specified
                Everything up to the system call name is specified.
3) CP level: Parameter Name Specified
                Everything up to parameter name is specified.
4) CC level: Parameter Contents Specified
                Everything up to parameter contents is specified.
For most realizing fault tolerance functions, it is impossible to completely specify up to parameter, so specification is at the CO~CP level.

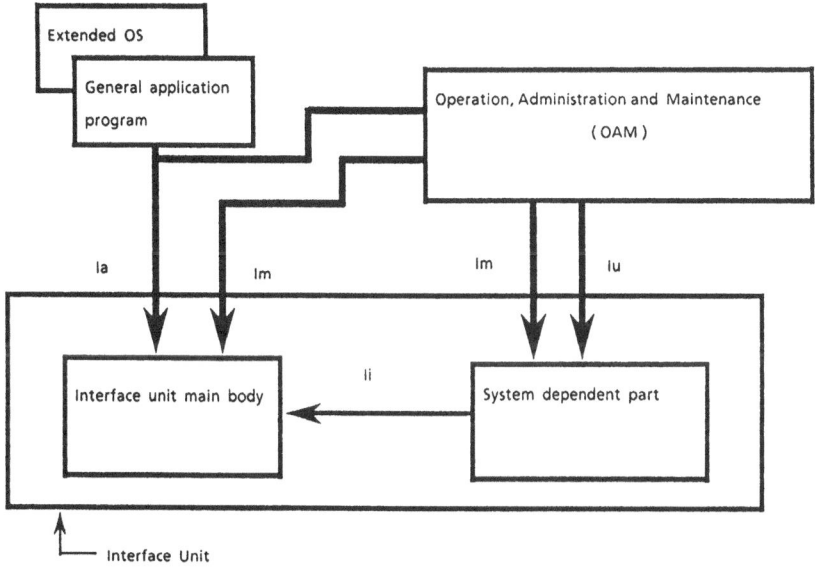

```
Extended OS
    General application
    program
```

Operation, Administration and Maintenance
(OAM)

Ia   Im   Im   Iu

Interface unit main body   System dependent part

Ii

Interface Unit

Ia : Interface for application program
Im : Interface exclusively for operation, administration and
     maintenance
Iu : Unspecified interface
Ii : Internal interface

Fig. 2 Interface definition model

4.2 Position of Fault Tolerance Functions

The relationship between the CTRON fault tolerance functions and each interface unit is shown in *Fig.3*. In order to construct a fault tolerant system based on CTRON interface specifications, functions required for each application system, such as OAM, must be added to the functions within the CTRON interface specification. The functions included in CTRON interface specification are specified by kernel, input output control, data storage control, communication control, execution control, speech path control, and human/machine interface (HMI) control.

Application programs for CTRON are classified into general application programs which are objects of circulation, and special application programs such as OAM and specified support functions for which a common interface cannot be specified and which are highly dependent upon service conditions and system architecture, originally a function of the OS.

Accordingly, these functions must be implemented for each application system and they are considered a kind of application program. In order to implement fault tolerance functions, each CTRON interface unit must provide the interface necessary for the programs implemented for each special application program such as OAM.

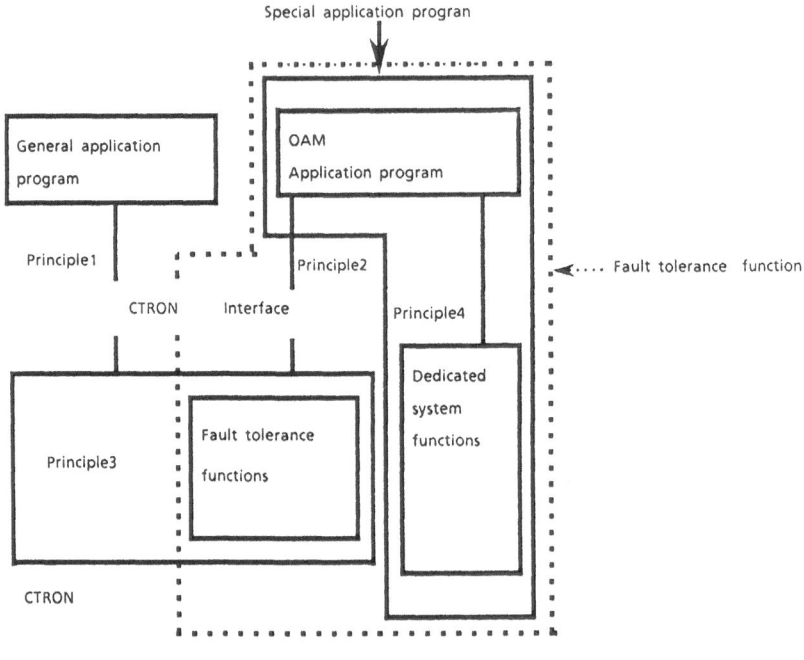

Fig. 3 Positioning of CTRON Fault Tolerance Functions

4.3 Interface Design Principles

CTRON interface for each interface unit in consideration of fault tolerance functions, are specified based on the following four design principles.(Principles 1 to 4 of *Fig. 3*)

1)Principle 1:   Guarantee compatibility with general application programs.
   The same interface must be provided for general application programs regardless of whether or not there are fault tolerance functions in each interface class.

2)Principle 2:   Provide dedicated interface for special application programs.
   Interface shall be provided for implementing special application programs which must be implemented for each application system such as OAM.

3)Principle 3:   Attachment and removal of fault tolerance functions.
   Subsets shall be established so that fault tolerance functions can be attached or removed in accordance with the requirements for each application system.

4)Principle 4:   No specifying of the internal interface of special application programs.
   For special application programs such as OAM, internal interface shall not be specified because system architecture and service/operation conditions strongly depend on each system.

5. OUTLINE OF FAULT TOLERANCE SPECIFICATIONS

For each interface class of CTRON, interface specification takes place with respect to fault tolerance on the basis of the requirements, the interface definition model, and the design principles mentioned in Chapters 2, 3 and 4. This chapter discusses the general outline of fault tolerance interface specifications for each CTRON interface class and the sufficiency of functions.

An outline of the fault tolerance functions specified in each CTRON interface class is presented in *Fig. 4*. In order to implement an OS having fault tolerance functions as described in Chapter 4, an OAM function must be added as an application program implemented for each system. Shown below are the interfaces which must be specified for interface unit so that OAM including fault tolerance functions can be added. Detailed interfaces relevant to fault tolerance or OAM are listed in *table 1* .

5.1 Kernel

(a) Redundancy

At the kernel 〔9〕 , the control units such as CPU and memory must be managed and controlled. In order to construct a fault tolerant system, CPU, memory and other control units must be multiplexed 〔6〕 〔7〕 . Examples of multiplex architecture include dual, majority -voted redundancy, duplex, and pair-and-spare structure. There are also two styles of multiprocessor architecture: the tightly-coupled multiprocessor architecture having a shared memory, and the loosely-coupled multiprocessor where each processor can communicate with other processors by exchanging messages with a communication device. By adopting these redundant configurations, a fault tolerant system can be constructed which is related to the control unit. However, according to the CTRON interface specifications, except for the loosely-coupled multiprocessor, fault tolerance functions can be implemented by using the kernel architecture-dependent portion interface shown in Section (b).

(b) Interface Specifications

In addition to interfaces specified in the kernel main body, including the common part and the optional parts such as task management, task synchronization communication, interrupt management, exception management, timer management and memory management, the interfaces necessary for implementing functions for OAM are also specified in the kernel. These interfaces are specified as the kernel architecture-dependent part. The major specified functions are indicated below. Since these interfaces are highly dependent upon hardware architecture or system configuration, specification of detailed parameters is entrusted to the implementer.

1) Basic system control

— Multiple hardware control
This interface is specified so that CPU, memory and other control devices which have been multiplexed can be switched, reintegrated or removed. The interface specification level is the CS level. Detailed functional specifications such as parameter are implementation dependent.

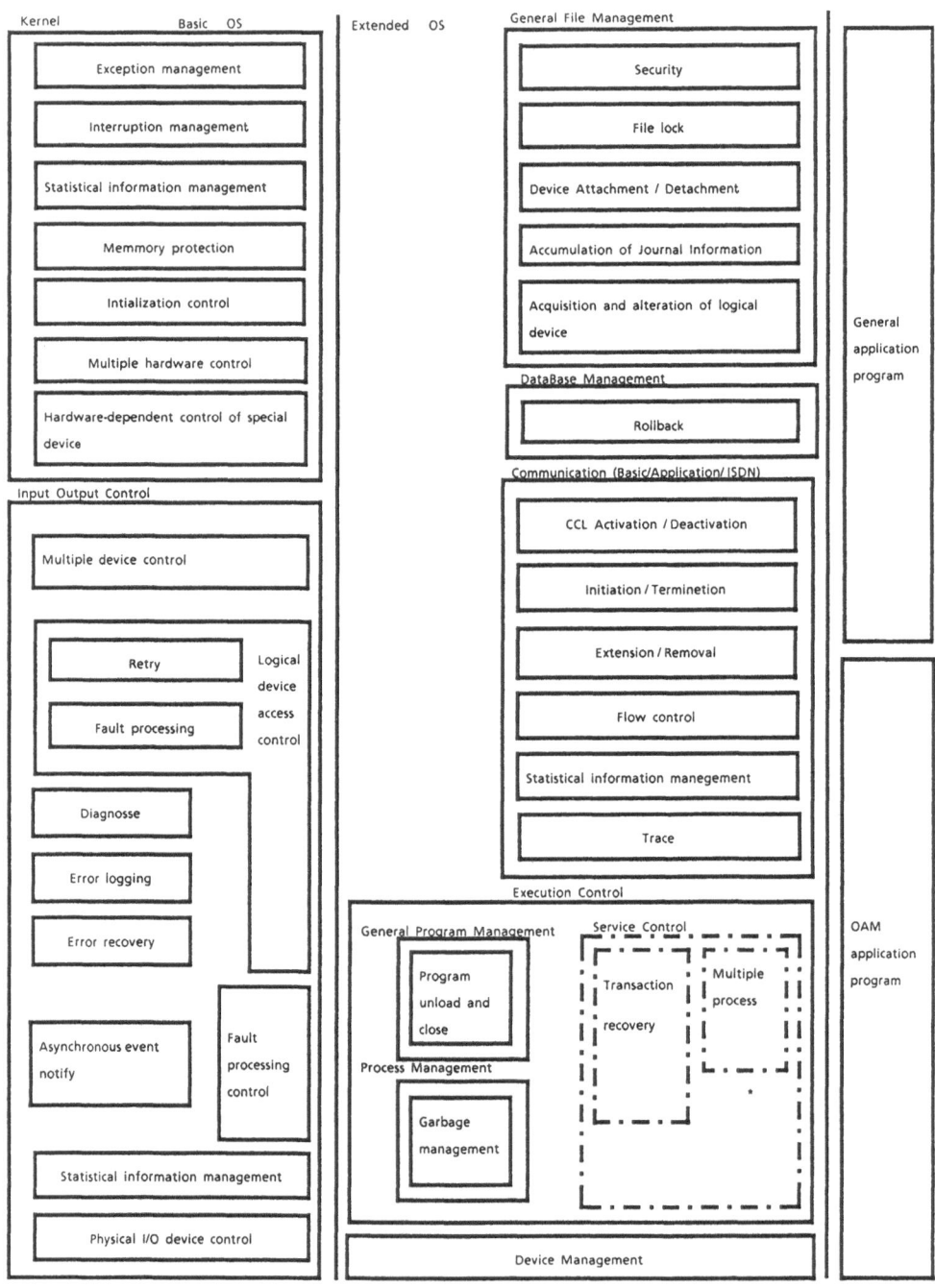

Fig. 4 Reference Model of the CTRON Fault Tolerance Functions

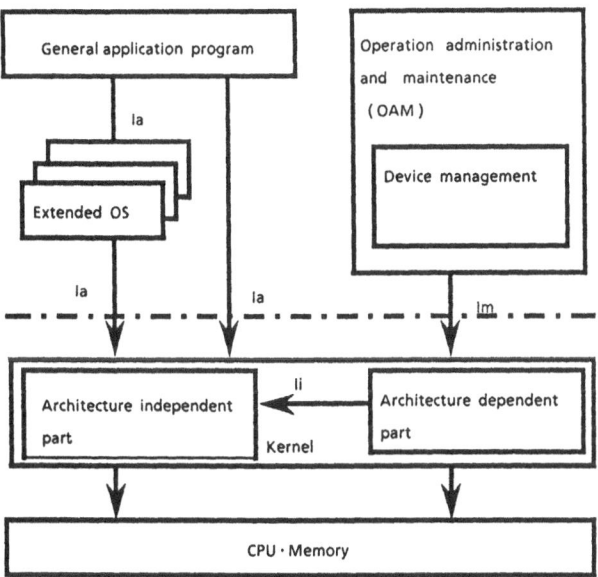

Fig. 5 Relationship between Kernel and OAM

— Hardware-dependent control of special devices
This function is exercised over all special hardware except spare control units such as CPU and memory. (CO level)

— System initialization control
Kernel initialization for system automatic restart are specified with CS level. (CS level)

2)Memory protection

This function provides setting/changing of memory protection, and referencing memory protection status. (CS level)

3)Interrupt management

In addition to an interrupt definition function as the kernel common part, an interrupt detailed information referencing function necessary for control of the point of system return from an interrupt of fault analysis, is specified as an architecture dependent part. (CP level)

4)Exception management

For CTRON, asynchronous events which have an effect on the system are specified as interrupts and asynchronous events which have an effect only on individual tasks are specified as exceptions. Whether a specific fault affects the entire system or task(s) only, however, depends upon system and service conditions. On the other hand, there are two cases in the system execution environment when a fault has occurred: task environment and non-task environment. With CTRON, in the non-task environment an asynchronous event must be treated as interrupt, and thereafter, if an effect is restricted within a task, it must be processed as an exception. Consequently, there are no exceptions in the non-task environment with CTRON. In CTRON kernel interface specifications, interfaces are specified for definition of exception handler, for exception code reference, and for return from exception handler on the basis of the relationships between interruption and exception.

5)Statistical information management

This interface is specified so that the load condition and other information of the CPU or memory can be referenced.

5.2Input/Output Control

For input/output control [10], asynchronous fault notice, diagnosis, recovery, retry, operator intervention, and error logging functions are specified as common functions. The multiplied disk volume control, a typical fault tolerance function, and initialization of the input / output control are specified as optional functions. In addition, the physical I/O devices control function which, for example, control access paths concealed in the input/output control is specified. An outline of specifications for each function is presented below.

(a)Multiplexed device control

Multiplexing of disk devices is normally called disk mirroring and it is a very typical fault tolerance function used in switching systems. For CTRON, the dummy logical device which can be accessed at the general access requestor is defined as the *master device*, and the logical device which is actually multiplexed is defined as the *member device*. (*see Fig. 6*) With I/O control, the interface is specified for definition or cancellation of multiplexed devices, start/stop of multiplexed device recovery and copying of member devices for fault recovery processing. By using these interfaces, multiplexed device recovery processing becomes possible without interrupting service.

(b)Physical I/O device control

Normally, there are physical devices such as a data channel or bus between the CPU and logical I/O devices and they are multiplexed out of consideration for faults. Under CTRON specifications, these physical devices are concealed within the input/output control. The existence of physical devices is concealed from the general input/output requestor, but when a fault occurs, it is necessary for OAM to enable, for example, physical device switching. For this reason, in CTRON input/output control, an interface is specified for control of physical I/O devices.

(c)Retry

Retry in response to I/O device access errors is performed within the input/output control with the designation of the I/O access requestor. Retry can be concealed within input/output control, but the need or not for retry can be designated by higher-level software for I/O access overhead.

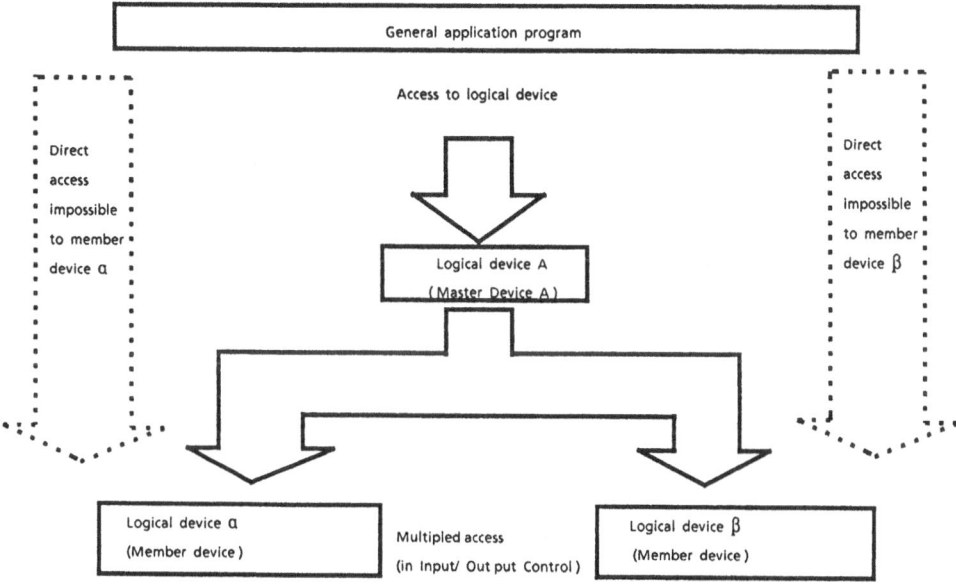

Fig. 6 Configulation of device multiplexing (in Case of Duplexed Device)

(d)Asynchronous error notice

Faults detected within input/output control are notified to the higher-level software via a message box. The detailed contents of fault, however, are implementation dependent because of dependency on hardware.

(e)Fault recovery

It is assumed that input/output devices are managed by device management with CTRON extended OS. When a fault has been detected within input/output control, notice of fault emergence is given to device management by the asynchronous error notice function in input/output control. Recovery processing after the fault has occurred, must be executed in OAM including device management. For this recovery processing, the following functions are provided in input/output control.

- — Change of logical device status
- — Allocation of alternate blocks
- — Creation of defective sector
- — Execution of diagnostic command
- — Collection of hardware log information
- — Initialization of device status

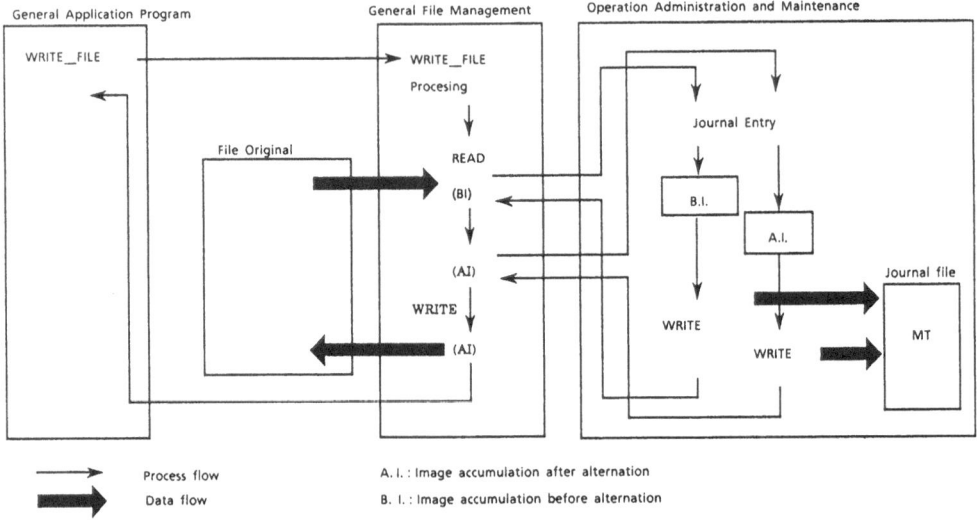

General Application Program   General File Management   Operation Administration and Maintenance

Fig. 7 Accumulation of journal information

5.3 Data Storage Control

(a) General File Management

1) File recovery

There are various methods to assure file safety; for example multiplexing file information, file dump, and recording of updated file information. With these methods, a file can be restored from the information whenever a fault has occurred. In general file management [11], with respect to file redundancy, it is assumed that either the multipled disk volume function is used in input/output control or that logical multiplexing of files is used in the database management or other higher-level software; file multiplexing functions are not specified under general file management per se. Among the various recovery methods available whenever a fault has occurred in a file, are the dump method, rollback or rollforward. Interfaces for the accumulation of journal information is specified in order to utilize any of these methods.

An outline of journal information accumulation with these logical disk recovery preprocessing interfaces is shown in *Fig.7*. First of all, with respect to general file management as fault preprocessing, journal information accumulating processing is registered by the journal data transfer entry register (SET_JOURNAL_ENTRY) system call. When a request for file access is made to general file management by registering this processing in advance, the journal information accumulation processing is called out and journal information is accumulated. Journal information can be accumulated either before and/or after update image, according to the specifications. The detailed contents of journal information, however, depend upon implementation and are not specified. By using this journal function, whenever a file fault has occurred, the file status prior to the fault can be restored by the rollback or rollforward method in accordance with the severity of the fault. Restoration by checkpoint dump will be a subject of future study because of the close relationship with the service control layer of execution control.

2)File garbage processing

When a task is aborted midway because of a fault in the file or process anomaly, processing by the user of file control is abandoned during file access. For this reason, abandoned processes must be treated as garbage in file control. However, the method of garbage processing for CTRON extended OS as a whole is a subject of further study.

(b)Database Management

In transaction processing where database updating takes place, the transaction begins after the application program has first called out the procedure for access to the database. Thereafter, procedures are processed as the same transaction until the transaction is completed. The transaction is terminated by the COMMIT statement or ROLLBACK statement of SQL language. Transactions which is terminated normally are terminated by COMMIT statement, but when a system transaction is terminated abnormally, change of the database is canceled by the ROLLBACK statement and the consistency of database with abnormal termination is guaranteed. In CTRON database management [4] , the rollback function is specified in SQL language.

Furthermore, checkpoint data are accumulated over a fixed time interval in OAM etc., and upon restart, the object of restoration is restricted by using the latest checkpoint data, and the system restart time can be shortened. The accumulation method of checkpoint data method, however, is subject for further study.

5.4Communication Control

CTRON Communication control can be classified into basic communication control from layer 2 to layer 5 of the OSI reference model, application oriented communication control at layer 6 and layer 7 including FTAM, MOTIS, CASE/P layer, and ISDN user control (ISUC) investigated by CCITT. The fault tolerance functions in communication control are discussed below.

(a)Basic Communication Control

In basic communication control [12] , statistical information and trace data collecting functions, the common functions of each communication controller (CCL) of communications control, are provided. Moreover, in basic communication control, a data retransmit recovery function according to the communications protocol is available if a temporary fault or line error due to congestion arises. In addition, an interface is specified for major/minor synchronization and resynchronization during fault recovery at the session layer as a means of data recovery so that the user of basic communication control can implement recovery processing. (Synchronization point service, activity service). Also specified are interface for line activation/deactivation as necessary for extension/removal under on-line status of the line, and interface for line extension/removal so that physical line can be integrated or removed under multi-link

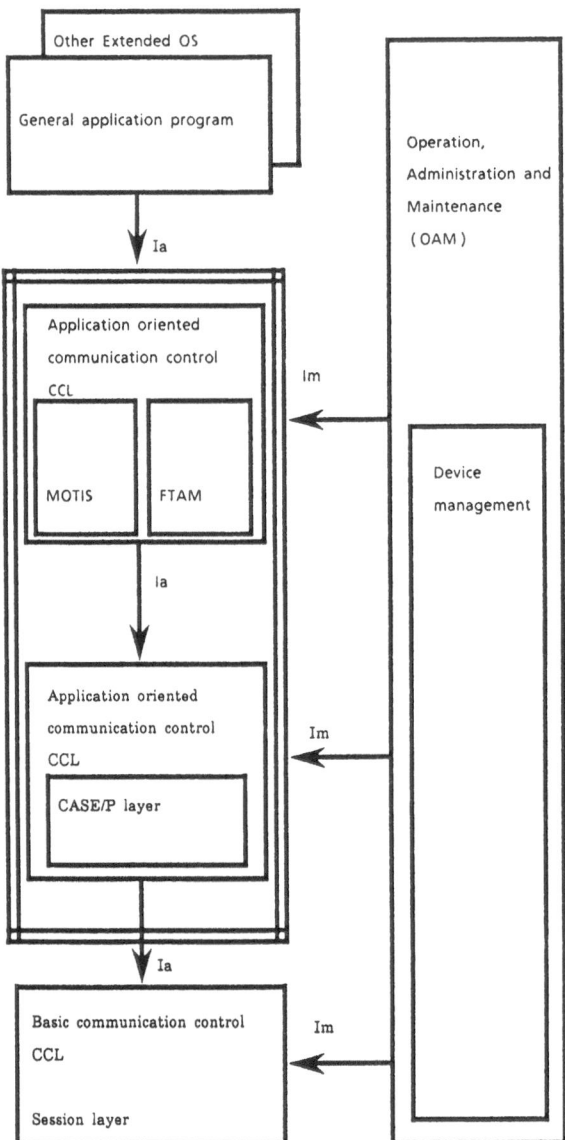

Fig. 8   Relationship between Application Oriented Communication Control and OAM

control. As a fault tolerant system, interface is also required for test, diagnosis, status display functions, etc., but since these are strongly dependent upon implementation, they have not been specified at present.

(b)Application Oriented Communication Control

In application oriented communication control [15] , interfaces are specified for the FTAM, MOTIS, and CASE/P layer at present. The fault tolerance functions for each communication controller (CCL) are discussed below.

1)FTAM (File Transfer, Access and Management)

In FTAM of OSI, two types of service level (internal service and external service) are specified as interface for faults in protocol. Internal service provides an interface which directly controls recovery or management of faults based on communications protocol. With external service, restoration of faults in protocol is carried out automatically by FTAM-CCL itself; an interface for fault direct recovery control is not provided by this service. CTRON is based on external service. Restoration of faults in protocol is performed within FTAM-CCL. For faults except those in protocol, such as faults during actual file access, however, recovery processes such as file retransmission must be performed by the higher-level software.

2)MOTIS (Message Oriented Text Interchange System)

In MOTIS, files are used as buffers for message transceiving and receiving. If a fault arises in a file during access of file buffer within MOTIS-CCL, notice of the fault is given by the notice of completion, and result of transceiving this message becomes an abnormal end. As for message control after fault occurrence, in the case of reception various methods are available. For example, messages are stored temporarily in MOTIS-CCL, and then the messages are transmitted once again or they are all abandoned and only a notice of fault is given. With CTRON, these processing methods are dependent upon implementation.

3)RTSE (Reliable Transfer Server Entity)

The Reliable Transfer Server Entity (RTSE) in CTRON is located in the CASE/P layer. In order to transmit large volume messages such as those of MOTIS with high reliability, this entity provides a checkpoint retransmit function, flow control, a function for reestablishing associations or connections opened by a fault in low layer line or protocol, and a function for retransmitting suspended messages. When restoration is not accomplished with these functions, notice of fault is given to the application program and restoration processing is entrusted to the application program.

(c)ISDN User Control(ISUC)

As shown in *Fig.9*, ISDN user control is comprised of DSS (Digital Subscriber Signaling) protocol control, a call control protocol for the ISDN subscriber, CCS protocol control (ISDN-UP), a call control protocol in the ISDN network, and TC (Transaction Capability), a protocol for data transmission excluding call control between switching systems. As functions pertaining to fault tolerance in each protocol control component, interfaces are specified as well as in other CTRON communications control for collecting statistical information and trace data. In addition, interfaces are specified which have functions for detecting and notifying faults in procedural check based on CCITT standard protocol, and for retransmitting signal messages and congestion control.

When a line fault has been detected in a trunk group, a routing function changes to an alternate route along the same trunk group. It has not yet been specified whether this function should be performed under ISUC or executed as an application program.

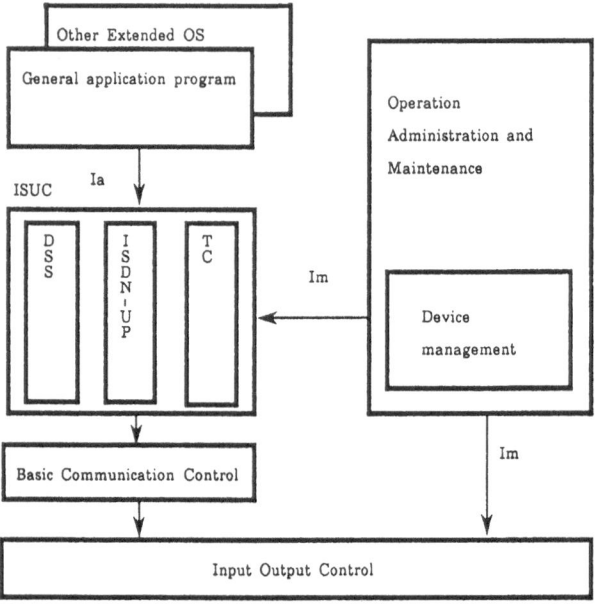

DSS	: Digital Subscriber Signaling
ISDN-UP	: ISDN User Part
TC	: Transaction Capability
ISUC	: ISDN User Control

Fig.9 Relationship between ISDN User Cortrol and OAM

5.5 Execution Control

Execution control [13] provides an execution environment for service or user, and control program execution. Execution control adopts two-layer configuration: common functions to all services including general program control and process control, and service dependent functions in the service control layer, including batch processing control, interactive processing control, and transaction processing control. Interface pertaining to the service control layer is a subject of future investigation. At present, therefore, we shall discuss the fault tolerance functions of general program control and process control.

(a)General Program Control

In general program control [13], the basic functions for invoking general program are specified: namely, program open, close, unload, start and return. Among the functions pertaining to fault tolerance in general program control, first there is a function for forced unloading of abnormal programs. This function deletes the defective program forcefully so that the program which causes a fault will not affect the other running programs. In deletion of the general program, there are two cases: *batch unload and close of all programs* by a task and *unload and close of specific program(s)* among a plural number of programs. Any of these cases are possible with the function of *unload and close of all programs.* In addition, a program *close/unload and close* function are specified and program files can be substituted using these functions during on-line service. This processing is suitable for interactive processing and batch processing in which execution programs open, load and start are grouped together and executed in series. However, it is not suitable for on-line transaction processing in which execution programs are loaded and opened in advance at the system initialization to minimize overhead for invoking program. In standard on-line transaction processing, each unit of service systems are opened or closed in order to substitute programs.

(b)Process Control

1)Process multiplexing
Process multiplexing is a method of achieving fault tolerance by creating a plural number of processes that perform the same procedure. In this way, if a fault occurs in one process, the procedure can be continued by using another multiplexed process. According to process control specifications [13] , the process must be multiplexed by the user of process control.

2)Garbage control
When a process can no longer be executed due to the fault or when a process falls into endless loop status, the process which interrupt continuous operation of the system must be deleted or terminated forcefully so that the fault does not spread. However each resource prepared for the execution environment must be released forcefully when a process is deleted or terminated. This is called garbage processing; there are two objects of garbage processing : the process execution environment and the process itself. In the former case, an interface is specified for registering the garbage routine when a process aborts itself. Resources which can not be released by the garbage routine must be garbaged by the process terminator at the process termination. In the latter case, there are some relationships between the process and its process creator. When the process creator is terminated abnormally, the other processes related to the process creator can never be terminated forever. (They remain as garbage.) In process control, therefore, processes have master/slave attributes to prevent from remaining processes as garbage. Based on this attribute, garbage processing is executed.

5.6Operation, Administration and Maintenance (OAM)

(a)Position

OAM functions in CTRON are shown in *Fig. 3.* OAM functions include the functions provided by each CTRON interface class or unit, and the functions of OAM interface class which must be implemented as the special application program in each application system. OAM interface class includes device management, operation control, fault recovery, maintenance and testing control, accounting control, and operation support [1] [17] . In particular, there are close relationships between fault tolerance functions and device management, fault recovery, maintenance and testing control, etc. Fault tolerance OS is made by adding OAM as the higher-level software using the interfaces provided by each CTRON interface class or unit.

(b)Interface specification

With CTRON, in principle no interface except device management is specified within the OAM interface class because of the strong dependence on hardware architecture or service/operational conditions, as mentioned with regard to interface design principle 4 in section 4. 3. For this reason, as a rule, OAM interface units can be positioned as application programs. With respect to device management, however, only one interface is specified for acquition of logical device identifier in order to promote the circulation of extended OS.

6 .EVALUATION AND SUBJECTS OF FUTURE INVESTIGATION

The interface specifications which have been established at present are each interface class or unit for kernel, input/output control, general file management, database management, basic communications control, application oriented communications control including ISDN user control (ISUC), general program control and process control. What follows is a discussion of the evaluation of each specification at present and the essential subjects to consider in future investigations.

6.1Evaluation

CTRON interface specifications are not only for specific system configuration and specific service condition. All CTRON interfaces are not necessary to specify completely, and some interfaces are unspecified because of implementation dependence. Furthermore, in constructing an actual system, functions unspecified in the CTRON interface specifications, such as OAM, must be added as application programs to each application system. Fault tolerance functions can be considered as the characteristic parts to demonstrate competitive power of implemented products. TRON, as a whole, provides "lose standardization." It's implementation can be made freely thereby enabling implementer's competition. When experience in implementation has been accumulated, consideration should be given to stronger standardization.

6.2Subjects

(a)Distributed processing

Distributed processing is effective for realizing high-level fault tolerance. Such items as guarantee of data consistency, security, and exclusive access control in a distributed resource environment must be investigated. Distributed transaction processing is especially important in CTRON application fields. Synchronization/exclusive control of data update following database access and guarantee of consistency in data are main subject〔14〕.

(b)Transaction processing

An investigation has begun of a transaction processing model for CTRON in which transaction control is positioned in the service control layer of execution control. First of all, transaction recovery should be considered as a fault tolerance function. There are two types of on-line transaction recovery method: checkpoint recovery and transaction recovery. In the former checkpoint technique, the data and conditions of execution at certain points in processing are saved, and if a fault occurs, processing can be recovered from the latest set of data and conditions that were saved. In the latter technique, when data are taken or erased from the update log on a database during a transaction, the conditions immediately prior to generation of the transaction are recovered from the log data. Realization of these methods centers on transaction control and database. These recovery methods are extremely important in transaction processing.

(c)Speech path control

In order to construct a switching system, it is necessary to have ISDN user control, application oriented communications control, which can be positioned in CTRON extended OS, and speech path control, for which CTRON interface specifications are scheduled to be specified in the near future. Among the fault tolerance functions required for speech path control are functions for forced removal of speech path following an anomaly in call control or restoration of the status of the path prior to occurence of the fault, and functions for displaying the conditions of speech path.

(d)OSI management

The OSI management functions are located in the application layer of the OSI reference model, and they consist of configuration management, fault control, directory control, performance management, accounting management and security management. In these function, fault management and security management are especially important for fault tolerance.

The fault management function includes a function for fault analysis and changing management data so that when a fault occurs, the network can be reconstructed. In CTRON communication control including basic and application oriented communication control, it is essential to make possible construction of these OSI management functions.

7.CONCLUSION

This paper has discussed the position of fault tolerance functions in CTRON, requirements, and the design principles, and it has presented an outline of fault tolerance function specifications for each interface class and unit. Interface specifications at present are at the first stage of investigation of fault tolerance functions. In each interface class, the minimum interface necessary for implementation of fault tolerance functions has been specified. Current specifications, however, are loose specifications. In order to define more detailed specifications, factors such as hardware architecture and operational conditions must be limited. For the second stage, in addition to interface investigation by the conventional bottom-up approach, specifications centered on service control will have to be investigated. At present, investigation has begun of on-line transaction processing, taking distributed processing into consideration. These fault tolerance functions are being investigated for CTRON, of course, but they are strongly dependent upon functional assignment with service control. In the near future, these fault tolerance functions centered on transaction processing will be studied, together with fault tolerance functions considered for application in distributed processing.

Table 1   *List of Interfaces for CTRON Operation,*
Administration and Maintenance(included Fault Tolerance) (1/3)

CTRON Interface Name	Type Level	Position
Kernel		
■DEFINE__INTERRUPT__HANDLER	Ia	Common Part
■RAISE__INTERRUPT	Ia	Common Part
■REFER__INTERRUPT__STATUS	Ia	Common Part
■DEFINE__EXCEPTION__HANDLER	Ia	Common Part
■GET__EXCEPTION__HANDLER	Ia	Common Part
■RAISE__EXCEPTION__SELF	Ia	Common Part
■RAISE__EXCEPTION	Ia	Common Part
■CANCEL__EXCEPTION	Ia	Common Part
■EXIT__FROM__EXCEPTION__HANDLER	Ia	Common Part
■REFER__EXCEPTION__CODE	Ia	Common Part
■REFER__STATISTACAL__INFORMATION	Ia	Common Part
■START__COLLECTING__STATISTACAL__INFORMATION	Ia	Common Part
■STOP__COLLECTING__STATISTACAL__INFORMATION	Im	Common Part
■MEMORY__PROTECT__SET	Im [CS]	Architecture dependent Part
■MEMORY__PROTECT__REFER	Im [CS]	Architecture dependent Part
■INTERRUPT__CORRESPONDENCE__DEFINE	Im [CS]	Architecture dependent Part
■INTERRUPT__VECTOR__DEFINE	Im [CS]	Architecture dependent Part
■INTERRUPT__LEVEL__DISABLE	Im [CS]	Architecture dependent Part
■INTERRUPT__LEVEL__ENABLE	Im [CS]	Architecture dependent Part
■INTERRUPT__EXIT__CHANGE	Im [CS]	Architecture dependent Part
■INTERRUPT__DETALL__REFER	Im [CS]	Architecture dependent Part
■MULTIPLE__HARDWARE__CONTROL	Im [CS]	Architecture dependent Part
■PHYSICAL__HARDWARE__CONTROL	Im [CS]	Architecture dependent Part
■SYSTEM__INTIATE	Im [CS]	Architecture dependent Part
■SYSTEM__START	Im [CS]	Architecture dependent Part
Input /Output Control		
■CREATE__DEVICE	Im [CP]	Common Part
■DELETE__DEVICE	Im [CP]	Common Part
■INITIATE__DEVICE	Im [CP]	Common Part
■TERMINATE__DEVICE	Im [CP]	Common Part
■CONTROL__BIO	Im [CP]	Common Part
■GET__DEVICE__CONTROL__INFORMATION	Im [CP]	Common Part
■CHANGE__DEVICE__CONTROL__INFORMATION	Im [CP]	Common Part
■READ__BIO	Ia (Note 1)	Common Part
■WRITE__BIO	Ia	Common Part
■CANCEL__IO__REQUEST	Ia	Common Part
■PHYSICAL__IO__HARDWARE__CONTROL	Im [CP]	Architecture dependent Part
■INITIALIZE__IOC	Im [CP]	Optional Part

Table 1　　　*List of Interfaces for CTRON Operation,*
Administration and Maintenance(included Fault Tolerance)　　(2/3)

CTRON Interface Name	Type	Level	Position
■START_COLLECTING_STATISTICAL_INFORMATION_IOC	Im	[CC]	Optional Part
■STOP_COLLECTING_STATISTICAL_INFORMATION_IOC	Im	[CP]	Optional Part
■REFER_STATISTICAL_INFORMATION_IOC	Im	[CP]	Optional Part
■DEFINE_MULTIPLE_DEVICE	Im	[CC]	Optional Part
■CANCEL_MULTIPLE_DEVICE	Im	[CC]	Optional Part
■START_MULTIPLE_DEVICE_RECOVERY	Im	[CC]	Optional Part
■STOP_MULTIPLE_DEVICE_RECOVERY	Im	[CC]	Optional Part
■COPY_MENBER_DEVICE	Im	[CC]	Optional Part

General File Management

■ATTACH_FILE_SYTEM	Im	[CP]	Common Part
■DETATCH_FILE_SYTEM	Im	[CP]	Common Part
■CREATE_DEVICE_SYTEM	Im	[CP]	Common Part
■DELETE_DEVICE_SYTEM	Im	[CP]	Common Part
■GET_FILE_INFORMATION	Im	[CP]	Common Part
■CHANGE_FILE_INFORMATION	Im	[CP]	Common Part
■SET_JOURNAL_ENTRY	Im	[CP]	Common Part
■CANCEL_JOURNAL_ENTRY	Im	[CP]	Common Part
■RETURN_TO_FILE_MANEGEMENT	Im	[CP]	Common Part
■INITIALIZE_GENERAL_FILE_MANAGEMANT	Im	[CP]	Common Part

Communication Control (Common)(Note 2)

■○○_ACTIVATE_CCL	Im	[CP]	
■○○_DEACTIVATE_CCL	Im	[CP]	
■○○_SUSPEND_FLOW	Im	[CP]	
■○○_RESUME_FLOW	Im	[CP]	
■○○_START_COLLECTING_STATISTICAL_INFORMATION	Im	[CP]	
■○○_REFER_COLLECTING_STATISTICAL_INFORMATION	Im	[CP]	
■○○_STOP_COLLECTING_STATISTICAL_INFORMATION	Im	[CP]	
■○○_START_TRACE	Im	[CP]	
■○○_STOP_TRACE	Im	[CP]	

Data link layer

■DL_ACTIVATE_PLINE	Im	[CP]	
■DL_DEACTIVATE_PLINE	Im	[CP]	
■DL_ADD_PLINE	Im	[CP]	
■DL_DELETE_PLINE	Im	[CP]	

Application Oriented (FTAM, MOTIS)

■△△_INITIATE_SERVICE	Im	[CP]	
■△△_TERMINATE_SERVICE	Im	[CP]	
■△△_INQUIRE_SERVICE	Im	[CP]	

Table 1   *List of Interfaces for CTRON Operation,*
Administration and Maintenance(included Fault Tolerance)   *(3/3)*

CTRON Interface Name	Type Level	Position
<MOTIS>		
■MO_REGISTER_PROFILE	Im [CS]	
■MO_INQUIRE_PROFILE	Im [CS]	
■MO_DELETE_PROFILE	Im [CS]	
■MO_GET_XX (Note 3)	Im [CS]	
■MO_RELEASE_XX (Note 3)	Im [CS]	
ISDN User Control (Note 4, 5)		
■IC_RESET_CIRCUIT	Im [CP]	
■IC_BLOCK_CIRCUIT	Im [CP]	
■IC_BLOCK_LINE	Im [CP]	
■IC_UNBLOCK_CIRCUIT	Im [CP]	
■IC_UNBLOCK_LINE	Im [CP]	
■IC_QUERY_CIRCUIT_STATUS	Im [CP]	
■IC_STOP_CONTROL_CIRCUIT	Im [CP]	
■IC_GET_PARAETER	Im [CP]	
■IC_CHANGE_PARAMETER	Im [CP]	
Process Control		
■TERMINATE_AND_DELETE_PROCESS	Ia	Common Part
■CREATE_PROCESS	Ia	Common Part
■GET_PROCESS_INFORMATION	Im [CS]	Common Part
Genaral Program Control		
■UNLOAD_AND_CLOSE_ALL_PROGRAMS	Ia	Common Part
■OPEN_AND_LOAD_PROGRAM	Ia	Common Part
■OPEN_PROGRAM_IN_LIBRARY	Im [CP]	Unspecified
■CLOSE_PROGRAM_IN_LIBRARY	Im [CP]	Unspecified
■GET_PROGRAMS_INFORMATION	Ia	Optional Part
■GET_SPECIFIED_PROGRAM_INFORMATION	Ia	Optional Part

(Note 1)   Items carried in Ia interface can be also used for operation, administration and management (OAM)

(Note 2)   ○○∈{DL,NL,TL,SL,AC,FO,MO,IC,ID,IT}   △△∈a{FO,MO}

        DL:Data link layer   NL:Network layer TL :Transport layer   SL:Session layer

        AC:CASE/P   FO:FTAM   MO:MOTIS   IC:ISDN-UP

        ID:DSS   IT:Transaction Capability

(Note. 3)   XX∈{MPDU_IDENTIFIER,IPM_IDENTIFIER}

(Note 4)   Trace is specified for only DSS in ISDN user control.

(Note 5)   Statistics are specified for only DSS and TC in ISDN user control.

ACKNOWLEDGEMENTS

We wish to express our deepest appreciation to Dr. Ken Sakamura and Dr. Fukuya Ishino for his helpful suggestions given throughout our investigation of CTRON fault tolerance functions and to the CTRON technical committee. We also want to thank everyone at the following companies for their valuable opinions and comments. Appreciation is especially due also to the members of the Non Stop ad hoc and the Operation, Administration and Maintenance ad hoc: Fujitsu, Ltd., Hitachi, Ltd., Matsushita Communication Industry Co., Ltd., Mitsubishi Electric Corporation, NEC Corporation, Northern Telecom Japan, Inc., and Toshiba Corporation.

REFERENCES

〔1〕 TRON Association, "ORIGINAL CTRON SPECIFICATION SERIES 1 OUTLINE of CTRON, " Ohmsha , Tokyo, 1989

〔2〕 Mukaidono M, "Introduction to Computer System High Reliability Technology," Japan Standards Association, Tokyo, 1989 [In Japanese]

〔3〕 Information Technology Research and Standardization Working Group, "Standardization of Information Technology, "Ohmsha, Tokyo, pp57-60, p130, 1988 [In Japanese]

〔4〕 Wasano T, Ohminami M, Kobayashi Y, Ohkubo T, and Sakamura K, "Design of CTRON," TRON PROJECT 1987, pp157-172

〔5〕 David A.Renels, "Fault-Tolerant Computing Concepts and Examples," IEEE TRANSACTION ON COMPUTER, VOL.C-33,NO.12, December 1984

〔6〕 Daniel P.Siewiorek, Carnegie-Mellon University, "Architecture of Fault Tolerant Computer," IEEE COMPUTER, pp9-18, August 1984

〔7〕 Omri Serlin, ITOM International Company, "Fault-Tolerant Systems in Commercial Applications," IEEE COMPUTER, pp19-30, August 1984

〔8〕 "Technology of System Reliabilty for Electronic Applied Systems, "Japan Standards Association, Tokyo, 1988 [In Japanese]

〔9〕 TRON Association, "ORIGINAL CTRON SPECIFICATION SERIES 2 KERNEL INTERFACE, "Ohmsha, Tokyo, 1989

〔10〕 TRON Association, "ORIGINAL CTRON SPECIFICATION SERIES 3 I/O CONTROL INTERFACE, " Ohmsha, Tokyo, 1989

〔11〕 Kumasaki K, "Design of CTRON File Management," Proceeding of the Third TRON Project Symposium, pp173-182, 1987

〔12〕 Shimizu Y, "Design of CTRON Communication Control Interface, " Proceeding of the Fifth TRON Project Symposium, pp157-166, 1988

〔13〕 Baba Y, Ohminami M, Kusumoto H, Kosugi H, " Design of CTRON Execution Control Interface, " Proceeding of the Fifth TRON Project Symposium, pp167-187, 1988

〔14〕 Japan Information Processing Socity, "Special Issue on Distributed Processing Technology, " VOL.28 NO.4, pp395-401, p373, 1987 [In Japanese]

〔15〕 Nitta T, "Design of CTRON Application Oriented Communication Control, " The 4th TRON Technical Study Group Meeting, Vol. 2 NO.2, July 1989 [In Japanese]

〔16〕 Ohta T, Ishikawa H, and Wasano T, "Software Structure for ESS using CTRON," JC-CNSS'88, pp53-58, November 1988

〔17〕 TRON Association, "ORIGINAL CTRON SPECIFICATION SERIES 8 EXECUTION CONTROL INTERFACE OPERATION, ADMINISTRATION AND MAINTENANCE MANAGEMENT INTERFACE, " Ohmsha, Tokyo, 1989

208

Makoto Fukuyoshi : assistant manager of Software Engineeing Section in Software Engineering Department, Switching Systems Engineering Division, Telecommunications Group at Oki Electric Industry Co., Ltd. He joined the company in 1979 after graduating from Kyushu Institute of Technology in Fukuoka. Since then, he has been engaged in the development of the basic software. He is a member of IPSJ.

Masaru Ishizuka : manager of Software Engineering Section in Software Engineering Department B, Switching Systems Engineering Division, Telecommunications Group at Oki Electric Industry Co., Ltd. He joined the company in 1974 after graduating from Meiji University in Tokyo. Since then, he has been engaged in the development of basic software and switching software. He is a member of IEICE and IPSJ.

Above authors may be reached at : Oki Electric Industry Co., Ltd 10-16, Shibaura 4-chome, Minato-ku, Tokyo 108 Japan

Noboru Furuya : assistant manager of General Planning Office in Computer Systems Division at Oki Electric Industry Co., Ltd. He joined the company in 1975. Since then, he has been engaged in the development of basic software and operating systems. He recieved B. S. degree, M. S. degree from Tohoku University in 1973 and 1975. He is a member of IEICE.

Above author may be reached at : Oki Electric Industry Co., Ltd 16-8, Chuou 1-chome, Warabi-shi, Saitama pref. 335 Japan

Tadashi Ohta : executive engineer at NTT Network Systems Development Center. Since joining the company in 1970, he has been engaged in the research and development of software systems for electronic switching systems. He received the B. S. degree, M. S. degree and Ph. D. degree from the Kyushu University in 1968, 1970 and 1987. He is a menber of the Institute of Electronics, Information and Communication Engineers of Japan (IEICE) and of the Information Processing Society of Japan (IPS).

Above author may be reached at: NTT Network Systems Development Center 2-1,Uchisaiwai-cho 1-chome,Chiyoda-ku, Tokyo 100 Japan

An Experimental Implementation for One Level Storage on CTRON KERNEL

Kazuhiro Oda, Norio Inoue, Tetsuya Murooka
Masamichi Nakata
Toshiba Corporation

ABSTRACT

We have been developing and implementing the CTRON basic operating system as an information processing system for past two years. The goal of our implementation is to realize the KERNEL system based on a virtual storage system.

This paper describes the issues and the solutions in the case of developing and implementing the KERNEL with full functions that subset [C+I] of the CTRON specifications provides for.

Keywords: REAL/VIRTUAL system, ONE LEVEL storage, ODP, virtual space, main/secondary storage

1. INTRODUCTION

The target of CTRON virtual memory interface definition is to make the best use of its merit, while to hide the difference among plural CPU architectures and also the difference between REAL and VIRTUAL storage systems.

Though memory chips become very cheap according to the advance of VLSI technology, a large virtual address space is still desirable. ONE LEVEL storage system is one of ultimate goals of virtual storage operating systems.

It is assumed in CTRON that a program loading is managed by Extended Operating System (EOS). A program loading process consists of reading a file from a secondary storage and expanding it into main storage according to its structural information on REAL storage system, while it consists of mapping its logical address onto the corresponding secondary storage address on VIRTUAL storage system.

The purpose of ONE LEVEL storage system is to enable upper layer software to access files without explicit READ/WRITE requests, and could not be attained without mapping arbitrary files onto virtual storage space. Although these functions are desirable in principle, their early implementations were deeply depending on their CPU architecture or their file system.

It is the goal of our implementation to realize ONE LEVEL storage system on CTRON kernel memory interface definition.

This paper describes our virtual storage system model and an enhanced set of interface definitions which are independent of a certain CPU architecture or a certain file system.

2. ISSUES FROM MEMORY MANAGEMENT

Fig. 1 shows a conceptual diagram that programs are running under a Virtual Storage (VS) system environment.

It is the feature of the virtual memory system that enables programs to run in a large address space with the aid of On-Demand-Paging (ODP) mechanism using main storage and secondary storage.

A program consists of text, data and stack regions of which structures, however, may be different slightly among operating systems. A certain region of text would be shared by plural programs as commonly usable procedures which are registered in shared libraries. A certain region of data might be shared by them as common area to communicate each other. In the latter case, the addresses of the data region in each program may differ.

The categories of each element to construct programs are shown by Table 1 .

category	symbol in Fig. 1	comment
private text	EA-1, EB-1	
private data	EA-3, EB-4	with initial value
	EA-4	without initial value
shared text	EA-2, EB-2	
shared data	EA-5, EB-3	
stack	EA-6, EB-5	

Table 1 Elements of a program

These elements, if they are not shared, exist only when the program is active. The elements that are shared, however, ought to exist even after the program is finished. It is because shared data and/or shared text might be used by other programs simultaneously or because they are expected to be used by the programs born later. In such cases, ODP control information shall not be deleted immediately for managing these situation.

Our design uses subset [I] of CTRON kernel specification to implement VS environment as illustrated in Fig. 1. Functions of VS system can be divided into following three categories:

211

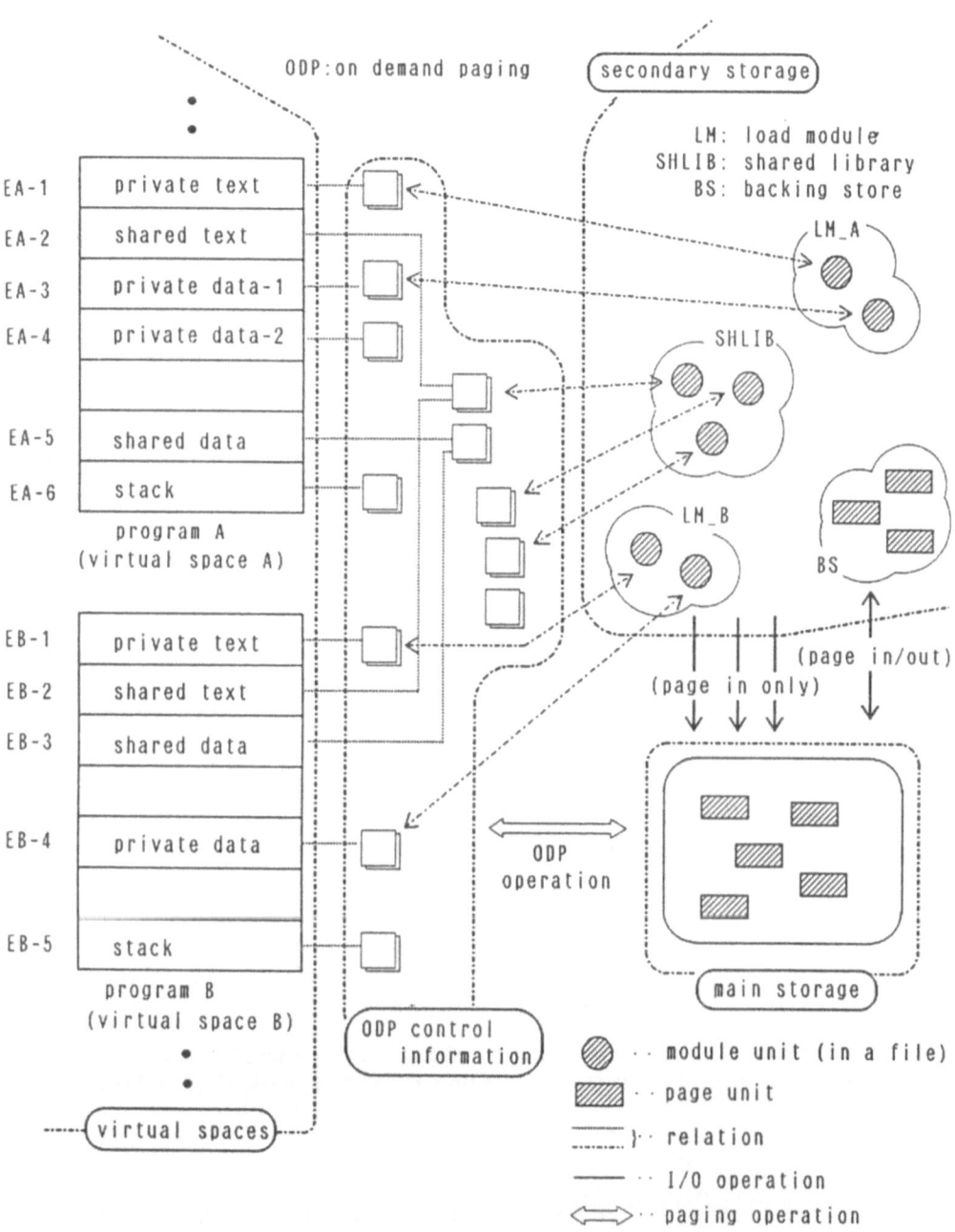

Fig. 1 Program structure and VS operation

1) Logical Segment management
This category of functions manages a region which is allocated to a task.

2) Logical Subsegment management
This category of functions manages an area within a logical segment.

3) Shared space management
This category of functions manages a region which is shared by programs.

In order to understand our approach, it is helpful to examine how to manage the text region. Below, a typical flow that a text region is allocated to a program shall be discussed.

We have an assumption that a program should correspond to a task and its text should correspond to a logical segment. Fig. 2 shows how the text region is created and made ready for execution with the logical segment/subsegment interface.

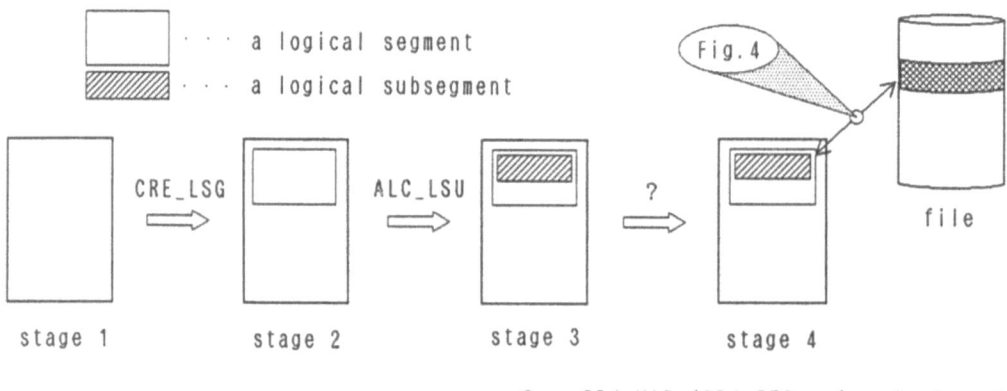

□ ···· a logical segment
▨ ···· a logical subsegment

CRE_LSG ALC_LSU ? file

stage 1 stage 2 stage 3 stage 4

? = OBJ_MAP (OBJ_REG already done)

stage 1: A virtual space as task local is allocated when a task is born.
stage 2: A logical segment is created with CREATE_LOGICAL_SEGMENT.
stage 3: A logical subsegment is allocated in the segment with ALLOCATE_LOGICAL_SEGMENT.
Hereby this area becomes accessible from the task.
stage 4: A mapping between the logical segment and the contents stored in a secondary storage corresponding to the text is established.
(One of the issues to be considered is that there is no mean to do it)

Fig. 2 Logical segment's stages

The program can be ready to execute only after the preceding stages.

The flow of Fig. 2 teaches us two issues from VS system functions of CTRON specifications. The following describes the reason we present the issues.

First, we discuss the necessity of the function that manages the relation between a logical segment and the contents of a secondary storage. There are various types of ODP control information depending on CPU architectures, of which differences should be hidden into KERNEL. Locative information of a file on a secondary storage is maintained by a file system, which belongs to EOS. However, the request's direction between software layers is limited by CTRON specifications, that is, the lower software layer(KERNEL) cannot request any service to the upper layer(EOS).

Therefore, it is necessary to prepare the system calls that EOS tells locative information of them to KERNEL, for the purposes that a program running with ODP mechanism is to be mapped to a file of a file system of EOS, and KERNEL must recognize the contents of a secondary storage.

Second, we discuss the shared memory space management. In the beginning of this discussion, we must analyze the characteristics of shared memory space. Table 2 shows how the state of a task space is influenced by the functions of shared memory space and logical segment/subsegment.

action [system calls]	shared memory space	logical segment/subsegment
c r e a t i o n ⌐CRE _ SHM ⌐ ⌐CRE _.LSG ⌐	the state of task space does not change. the existence of a shared memory space is recognized by the system.	a part of task space is reserved, but not accessible.
a l l o c a t i o n ⌐ALC _ SHM ⌐ ⌐ALC _ LSU ⌐	a part of task space is reserved, and made accessible.	the reserved space is made accessible.

Table 2 the states of task space

A shared memory space can have two conditions after creation, one is that without allocating to any task, the other is that with allocating to tasks. A shared memory space, after creation, must be maintained in the system with no concern of allocating to a task. And, once a shared memory space has been allocated to a task, the state of the task space is the same when a logical segment is created and a logical subsegment is allocated, because shared memory space allocation occupies an accessible part of a task space. A logical segment is born and died on a task space, that is, existence of a logical segment depends on existence of a task. On the other hand, a shared memory space is born and died without concerning a task. Even if a task with a shared memory space allocated vanishes, the shared memory space must stay in the system till it is deleted, regardless of access by any task.

Therefore, a shared memory space has these two characteristics, one is that of a system resource that the system recognizes its existence with no concern of allocation to a task, and the other is that of a logical segment which is created on a task. In this paper, to manage the former is called as "system resource management", and to manage the latter is called as "access management in a task".

The shared memory space management functions of CTRON specifications seem to be designed almost only from the view point of system resource management. Because, for the purpose that EOS can manage virtual spaces, a shared memory space in allocation to a task should be managed in the same way as the logical segment management, and ALLOCATE_SHARED_MEMORY should return a logical segment id better than a virtual address. Therefore, shared memory space interfaces should be designed not only from the view point of system resource management but also from the view point of access management in the task space. (One of the issues to be considered is that the relation between a logical segment and a shared memory space is not defined.)

The following is a summary of the issues that we pick up above.

(a) Difficulty in mapping a logical segment to the contents of a secondary storage.

(b) There is no explicit specification on the relation between a logical segment and a shared memory space.

3. SOLUTIONS

There described are solutions in our implementation for the issues discussed in chapter 2.

(a) Difficulty in mapping a logical segment to the contents of a secondary storage.

To make KERNEL independent of any file system, the system calls are provided as an architecture dependent function based on a concept called object. The object is defined as grouped information consisting of block addresses in the CTRON general input/output interface specification.

KERNEL recognizes the object as a unit to manage a secondary storage space, which may be a file, a part of a file, or a group of files depending on the file system in EOS. To make the object independent of file systems, the object is composed of a list of entries. Each entry corresponds to blocks of the secondary storage, accessible with an input/output operation, and contains a logical device identifier and relative addresses in the logical device. The list is sorted to represent virtual address. Fig. 3 shows a format of mapping information of the object.

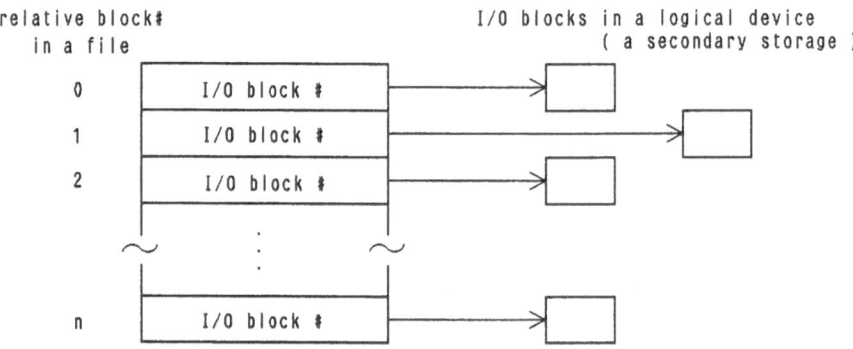

Fig. 3 Mapping information of an Object

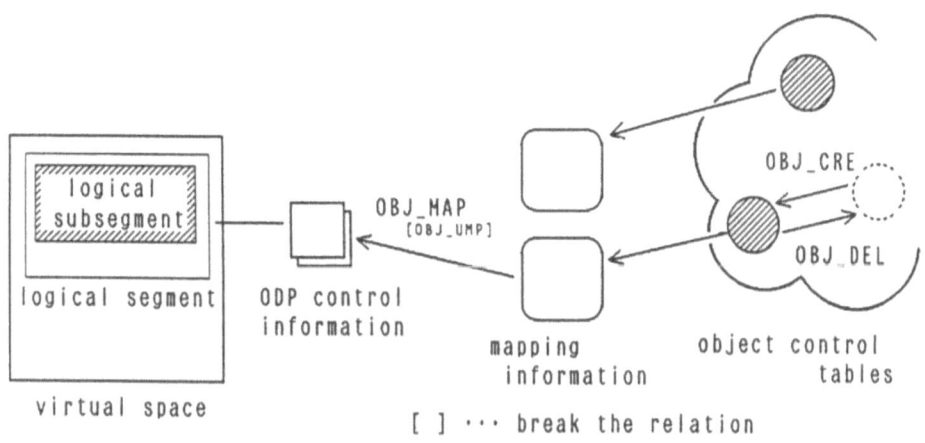

Fig. 4 Object operation

The object management facility is provided with six system calls, detailed in chapter 4. Fig. 4 shows relations among the main four system calls.

(b) There is no explicit specification on the relation between a logical segment and a shared memory space.

The shared memory space in this implementation is managed in the same manner as the logical segment and the logical subsegment management.   This means that the shared memory space management is internally implemented as follows:

To create a shared memory space is -
   a shared space management table and a logical subsegment management table are
   created and linked each other.
To allocate a shared space is -
   a logical segment management table is created and then linked to the related
   logical subsegment management table.

Through this implemented mechanism, the shared memory space allocated to a task can be assumed as a logical segment created and allocated with logical subsegments from the view point of access management in a task space.   The state where a shared memory space is created as a system resource, could be internally regarded as that shared memory space management table and logical subsegment management table are created and linked each other.   Therefore, shared memory space management table itself represents the shared memory space as a system resource.   A shared memory space allocated to a task and also mapped with the object is accessible from other tasks after allocation to them without re-mapping of the object.   Because, mapping information is already reflected in ODP control information representing the logical subsegment.   Fig. 5 shows the relation of a shared memory space and the logical segment.

Above described are the solutions for the issues.   Next are additional proposals for VS systems.

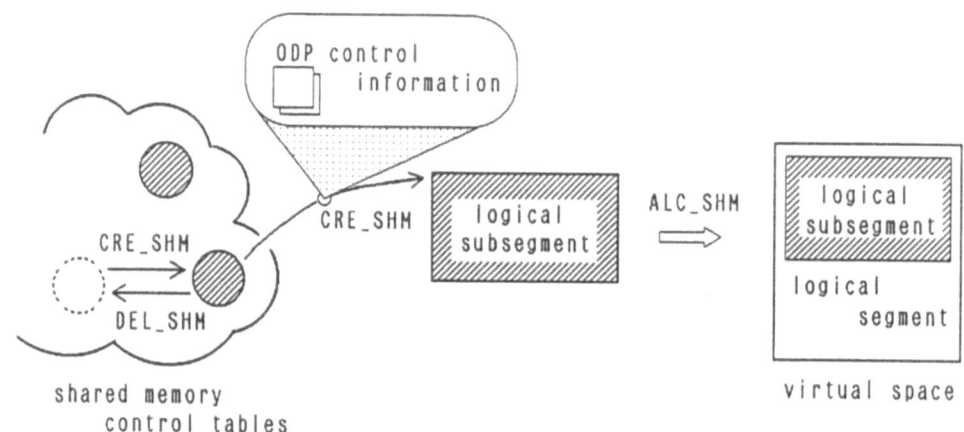

Fig. 5 Shared memory space and Logical segment

(1) Inter-tasks logical segment copy function on VS system with ODP facility.

Although a task in the application layer can't access to spaces of other tasks, information of them should be efficiently utilized under permission of EOS authorization. It is considered as an efficient function to copy logical segments between tasks without sharing the segments.

When the logical segment to be copied has non-ODP attribute, the contents of the physical memory are copied. On the other hand, if the logical segment with ODP attribute is copied, it is enough to copy only the ODP control information to one for the target segment. The required entity of a logical subsegment will be actually copied at the reference from each task. This copy mechanism based on the ODP function, aims at both more efficient memory utilization and faster copy performance.

We propose two kinds of inter-tasks logical segment copy function, one used for logical segments with ODP attribute and the other not. The Fig. 6 shows the illustration of these two functions.
(2) Shared space allocation function with address specified

A shared space can be created at a specified address in CTRON specifications. The virtual addresses are thus forced to be fixed among multiple tasks with the same shared address spaces. If the address can be specified at the shared space allocation, EOS can decide virtual addresses statically or dynamically with more flexible virtual address management. Therefore, addresses should be able to be specified with the shared space allocation function, just like address specification at the logical segment creation.

According to the solution of the issue (b), the shared space allocation function can be equivalent to the logical segment creation function. This means the necessity of address specification at the shared memory space allocation is proved by the definition of address specification at the logical segment creation. Fig. 7 shows the outline of this function.

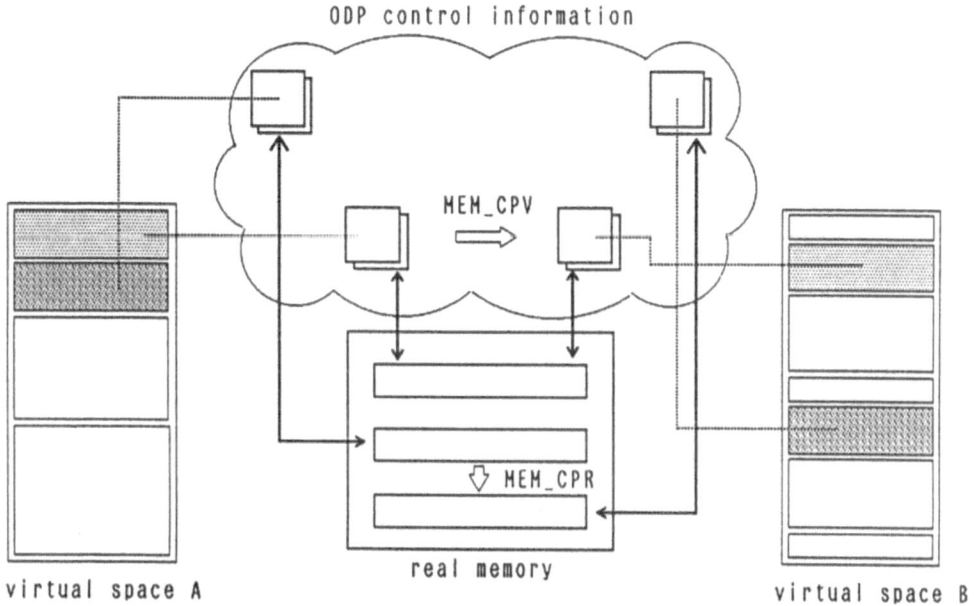

Fig. 6 Concept of copy functions on VS environment

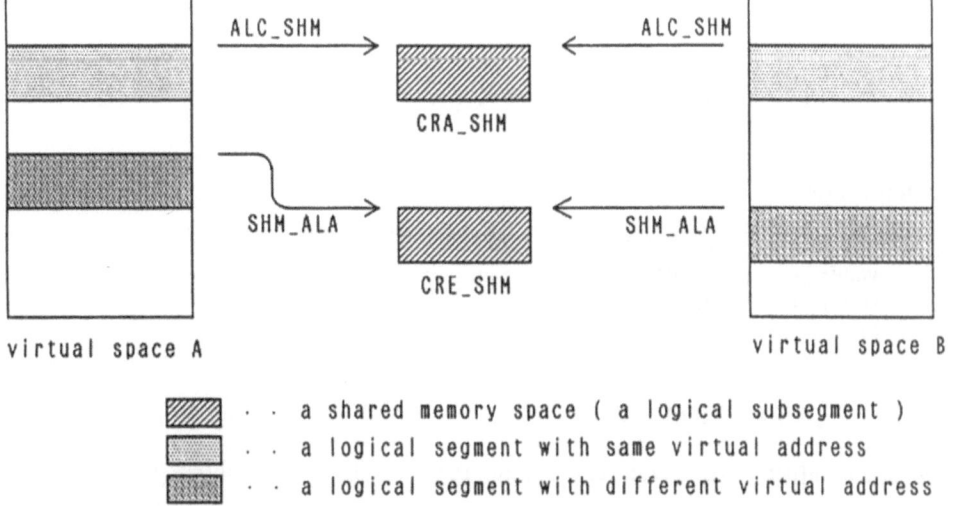

Fig. 7 SHM_ALA operation

4. SYSTEM CALLS

The system calls proposed here are implemented as functions of architecture_dependent interface.

4.1 Object Management

(a) REGISTER_OBJECT_IN_THE_KERNEL(OBJ_REG)

Registers an object. This system call informs the map list of the object to the system.

```
        e_reason_t    OBJ_REG(object_name, device_id, device_block_size,
                                  map_list, list_size, object_id, return_code)
        systag_t      object_name;
        systag_t      device_id;
        long_t        device_block_size;
        map_list_t    map_list;
        long_t        list_size;
        systag_t      *object_id;
        errpt_t       return_code;
```

(b) MAP_LOGICAL_SPACE_WITH_OBJECT(OBJ_MAP)

Maps a registered object to a logical segment.

```
        e_reason_t    OBJ_MAP(vaddr, space_offset, object_id, object_offset,
                                  mapping_size, return_code)
        vaddr_t       vaddr;
        long_t        space_offset;
        systag_t      object_id;
        long_t        object_offset;
        long_t        mapping_size;
        errpt_t       return_code;
```

(c) UNMAP_LOGICAL_SPACE_FROM_OBJECT(OBJ_UMP)

Releases a logical segment from an object. This system call cannot delete the map list of the object from the system.

```
        e_reason_t    OBJ_UMP(vaddr, object_id, return_code)
        vaddr_t       vaddr;
        systag_t      object_id;
        errpt_t       return_code;
```

(d) DELETE_OBJECT(OBJ_DEL)

Deletes an object. This system call deletes the map list of the object registered in the system.

```
        e_reason_t    OBJ_DEL(object_id, return_code)
        systag_t      object_id;
        errpt_t       return_code;
```

(e) GET_ID_OF_OBJECT(OBJ_GID)

Gets the ID of an object defined by a specified name.

```
e_reason_t    OBJ_GID(object_name, object_id, return_code)
systag_t      object_name;
systag_t      *object_id;
errpt_t       return_code;
```

(f) GET_INFORMATION_OF_OBJECT(OBJ_GIF)

Gets management information for a specified object.

```
e_reason_t    OBJ_GIF(object_id, inf_id, inf_block, return_code)
systag_t      object_id;
int_t         inf_id;
inf_block_t   inf_block;
errpt_t       return_code;
```

4.2 Shared Memory Management

(a) ALLOCATE_SHARED_MEMORY_WITH_ADDRESS_SPECIFIED(SHM_ALA)

Allocates a shared memory to the caller's virtual space using the specified address as the location to be allocated.

```
e_reason_t    SHM_ALA(shm_id, location, return_code)
systag_t      shm_id;
location_t    location;
errpt_t       return_code;
```

4.3 Logical Space Copy

(a) COPY_REAL_MEMORY(MEM_CPR)

Copies a logical segment of another task to a logical segment of caller. Both logical segments must not have the ODP attribute.

```
e_reason_t    MEM_CPR(source_task_id, source_vaddr, source_offset, size,
                       destination_vaddr,destination_offset, return_code)
systag_t      source_task_id;
vaddr_t       source_vaddr;
long_t        source_offset;
long_t        size;
vaddr_t       destination_vaddr;
long_t        destination_offset;
errpt_t       return_code;
```

(b) COPY_VIRTUAL_MEMORY(MEM_CPV)

Copies a logical segment of another task to a logical segment of caller. Both logical segments must have the ODP attribute.

```
e_reason_t    MEM_CPV(source_task_id, source_vaddr, destination_vaddr,
                            object_id, return_code)
systag_t      source_task_id;
vaddr_t       source_vaddr;
vaddr_t       destination_vaddr;
systag_t      *object_id;
errpt_t       return_code;
```

5. CONTROL TABLES

Fig. 8 shows the relations among the control tables for the memory management in our implementation based on VS system. The control tables for VS system are divided into the following four types.

Logical Segment Table:
Logical segment tables are prepared to manage the regions of the system space and the user space which includes shared memory space. Each table contains the information about a logical segment. If a logical segment is allocated to the system space, the table is chained to "lsegsys". If it is allocated to a user space, the table is chained to the "TCB".

Logical Subsegment Table:
Logical subsegment tables are prepared to manage the regions of the accessible space in the logical segment. The address of the region is established corresponding to the location where the logical segment is allocated. This table is linked to the ODP control information. If the region has initial value, this table is linked to the object table.

Shared Memory Space Table:
Shared memory space tables are prepared to manage the shared memory space as a system resource. The CREATE_SHARED_MEMORY creates this table and a logical subsegment table, and links them. ALLOCATE_SHARED_MEMORY creates a logical segment table and links it to the logical subsegment table.

Object Table:
Object tables are prepared to manage the objects in the system. REGISTER_OBJECT_IN_KERNEL creates this table and links it to the map information table which shows the arrangement of the object. And MAP_LOGICAL_SPACE_WITH_OBJECT links it to a logical subsegment table.

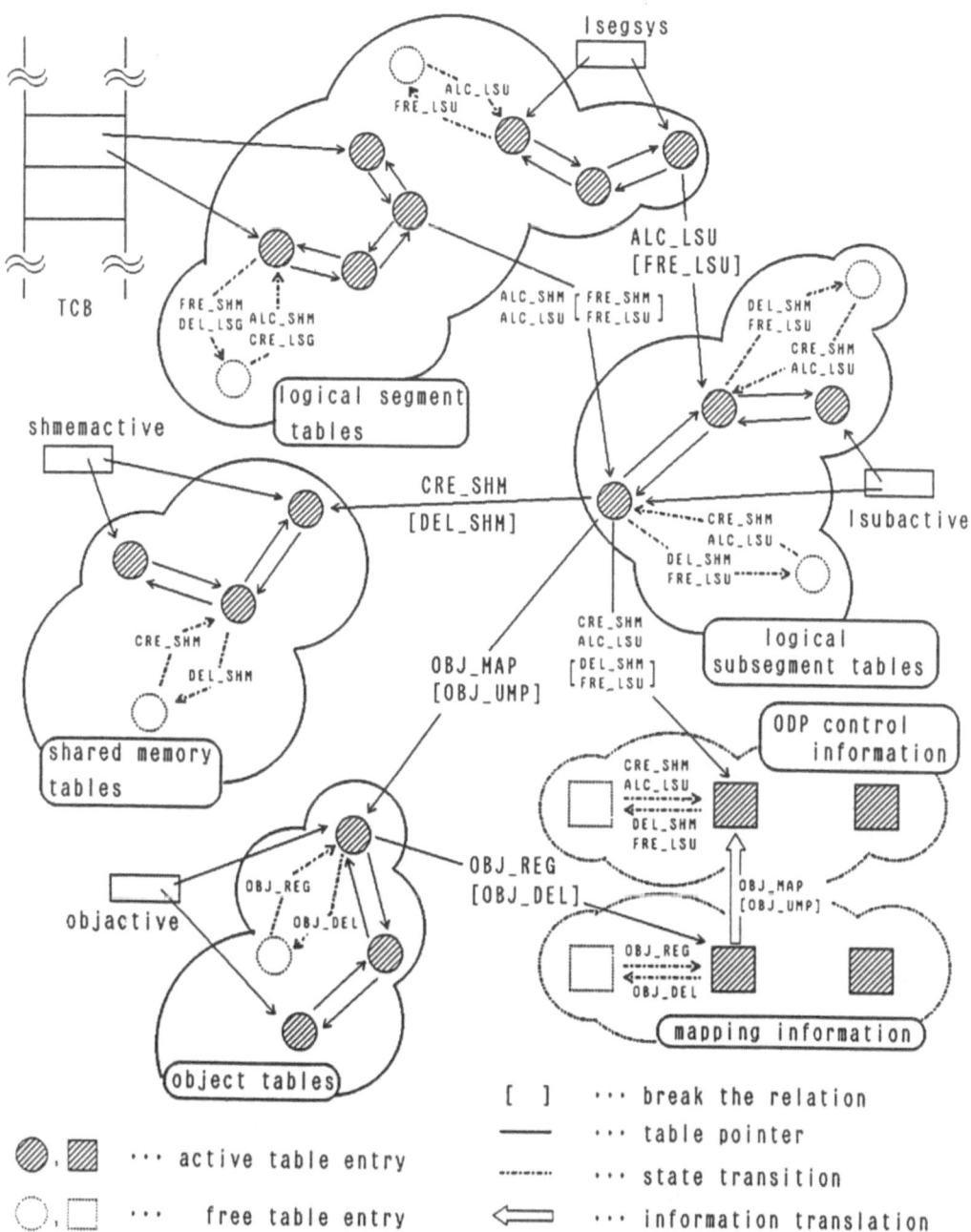

Fig. 8 Relations of control tables

6. CONCLUSION

We have investigated the general model of VS system to realize ONE LEVEL storage on CTRON basic OS. Then we found out two important problems.

The first problem is how KERNEL deals with secondary storage. We have resolved this problem by preparing the object management function as KERNEL interface. Therefore, a program has been able to access files which have different structures and are managed by different file systems in any EOS on KERNEL.

The second problem is that the relation between a shared memory space and a logical segment is ambiguous in the case of accessing the shared memory space as the user space, though the management of a shared memory space as a system resource is defined clearly in CTRON specifications. We have resolved this problem by internally relating the shared memory space function with allocating a logical subsegment and creating a logical segment.

Besides the above, we investigated the necessity of the "copy logical segment between tasks" function and the "allocate shared memory with address specified" function in VS system, and prepared them as KERNEL interfaces.

We have implemented a UNIX interfacer as an EOS on this system. Though the KERNEL is an experimental system for ONE LEVEL storage system, but this UNIX interfacer is a practical syste m which has enough performance and functions to practically use it.

The KERNEL that we have just implemented does not cover all the features of ONE LEVEL storage. The validity of the features has been proved in the program loading field, however not in the data access field this time. We are examining more additional KERNEL features required in a file system for ONE LEVEL storage, and there still remains the problems to be solved in updating the objects corresponding to file closing or file checkpoint operation.

We will continue our further study of CTRON KERNEL based on a virtual storage system, and we should propose CTRON Technical Committee the unresolved problems to realize ONE LEVEL storage, that are the program management (especially the dynamic linking), the file management, and the data_base management.

7. ACKNOWLEDGMENT

The authors wish to express our deep appreciation for the valuable advice given by Dr.Ken Sakamura, Dr.Fukuya Ishino, Toshikazu Ohkubo, Ichizo Kogiku and members of CTRON Technical Committee.

REFERENCES

[1]T.Wasano, Y.Kobayashi, and K.Sakamura "CTRON Reference Model", TRON Project 1988, Springer-Verlag, 1988, pp145-155.

[2]I.Kogiku, T.Ohkubo, and M.Matsushita "Enhancement of the CTRON Kernel Interface", TRON Project 1988, Springer-Verlag, 1988, pp189-211.

[3]K.Oda, N.Shimizu, N.Inoue, and Y.Iba "An Implementation of CTRON Basic OS on a Lap-Top", TRON Project 1988, Springer-Verlag, 1988, pp235-243.

[4]"CTRON SPECIFICATION KERNEL INTERFACE", CTRON Technical Committee, May.1989.

[5]"CTRON SPECIFICATION I/O CONTROL INTERFACE", CTRON Technical Committee, May.1989.

224

Kazuhiro Oda is a chief specialist in Personal Computer Design Department at the Ome Works of Toshiba Corporation. He is now a member of BTRON and CTRON technical committee of TRON Association. He received his BE from Kyuusyuu University at Fukuoka in 1964. He is a member of ACM, the Information Processing Society of Japan(IPSJ) and the Institute of Electronics, Information and Communication Engineers of Japan(IEICE).

Norio Inoue is an engineer in Personal Computer Design Dept. at the Ome Works of Toshiba Corporation after graduated from electric engineering of Tadotsu Technical high school in 1973. He has been engaged in software design and development of large and medium scale general purpose computers and office computers.

Tetsuya Murooka is an engineer in Personal Computer Design Dept. at the Ome Works of Toshiba Corporation. He received his BE in mathematics from Waseda University in 1986. He has been engaged in software design and development of office computers. He is a member of Information Processing Society of Japan.

Masamichi Nakata is an engineer in Personal Computer Design Dept. at the Ome Works of Toshiba Corporation after graduated from electric engineering of Nihon Kougakuin Technical college in 1989. He has been engaged in software design and development of personal computers.

Above authors may be reached at: Personal Computer Design Dept. in Ome Works, Toshiba Corporation 2-9, Suehiro-cho, Ome, Tokyo 198, Japan.

Design of the CTRON Application Oriented Communication Control Interface

Tetsuji Nitta

Oki Computer Systems Division

ABSTRACT

CTRON is a set of operating system interface specifications designed for common applications to be applied to nodes on information and communication networks. A lot of effort for standardization of API (Application Program Interface) is being made by some non-profit bodies.

Interface Specification Ver.1 of Basic Communication Control (layer 2 - 5 in OSI mode) defined in CTRON Extended OS was published in March 1988. Ver.2 was in July 1989.

Interface Specifications defined as Application-Oriented Communication Control, such as FTAM which is serving file transfer, 1988's MOTIS/P1/P2 and related P/CASE, was published in July 1989.

This paper briefly discusses the scope, functional model and detailed specifications of CTRON Application-Oriented Communication Control.

Keywords: CTRON, Communication Control, Application Program Interface, FTAM, MOTIS

1. INTRODUCTION

CTRON[*1] is a set of operating system interface specifications designed for applications to each node in an information communication network.-[1][2][3] Progress is currently being made in the standardization of application program interfaces (API), thanks to the efforts of a number of nonprofit bodies[*2] including the TRON Association.

---

*1; CTRON stands for "Communication and Central TRON."
    TRON stands for "The Real Time Operating System Nucleus."

The first step toward international standardization in the communication field is the standardization of basic standards of service and protocol based on the OSI reference model. In a multivendor environment, the provision of mutual interconnectability is an extremely important user request.

For this reason, as the second step, the choice specified by basic standards of options pertaining to the service and protocol and specification of realization value are being established as implementation specification at ISO/IEC JTC1, this is scheduled to be standardized as ISP (IS Profile).-[4][5][6] However, the demands of end users do not stop at this level; the ultimate demand is the portability of application programs, which are the users of communication service. This is assumed to rank as the third step in standardization. At ISO/IEC JTC1, these activities have just begun as IAP (ISO/IEC JTC1/TSG-1 Interfaces for Application Portability), and detailed results have not yet been reported.

Efforts to develop communication control interfaces for CTRON fall under the third step mentioned above.

The third step may require an overall revision of the current

interface specifications in the sense that it is undesirable that multiple different specifications claim to be international standards in parallel.

As a result of CTRON communication control interface developments, the first edition of basic communication control (accommodation of interface specifications for OSI layers 2 to 5) was published in March 1988 and the second edition in July 1989.-[7] Similarly, the first edition of application-oriented communication control interface specifications prescribing the API for OSI layers 6 and 7 was also published in July 1989.-[8] The scope of the first edition included FTAM (file transfer only), MOTIS (P1. P2 specifications of 1988 edition) and related presentation layer/CASE functions.*3 The first edition of ISUC in which ISDN user interface was specified was also published in the same period.-[9]
This paper introduces the scope of specifications, the design concepts, and the functional model of CTRON Application-Oriented Communication Control, in addition to an outline of each interface as a report of the CTRON Application Oriented Communication Control Working Group.

---

*2; X/Open, POSIX (Portable Operating System Interface),
    X.400/API Industry Committee and others.
*3; ACSE, RTS

2. Design Concepts and Functional Model of Application-Oriented Communication Control

2.1 Common Design Concepts of Communication Control Specifications

The common design concepts of communication control are presented below.-[10][11]

(1) Accordance with OSI

Efforts to standardize service and protocol in accordance with the OSI reference model have been continuing at ISO and CCITT. International standards (IS) have already been established for FTAM, MOTIS (MHS), etc., which are gradually spreading. In the world of multivendors, the spread and promotion of OSI has become an extremely important topic. In CTRON communication control specifications, priority is being put on developing the specification of system call interface for OSI based on the OSI reference model, while consideration is also being given to the expandability to non-OSI.

Interfaces, together with each layer, are prescribed with reference to OSI service primitives, but in actual implementation, this is not sufficient; system call must also be prescribed as necessary.

(2) Aggressive Adoption of Implementation Specifications developed by OSI Promotion Group

It is of course mandatory that products established in accordance with CTRON communication control specifications can be interconnected with computer systems which run non-CTRON products. As pointed out in the introduction, OSI implementation specifications are being stipulated for the purpose of interconnection, and it is unnecessary to develop implementation specifications specifically for CTRON. Aggressive steps should be taken to adopt OSI specifications.

(3) Specifications of Interface for Each Layer

Generally, in a computer node, subordinate layers in the OSI7 Layer are served by communication control devices or FEP (Front End Processor). The question of up to what layer can be served with these devices is a matter of the individual vendor. What is most often seen is support up to the data link within the limit of the conventional manager, or support up to the transport layer for the purpose of concealing communication media dependency.

In CTRON communication control, an interface is specified on a layer-by-layer basis. Taking an overview of the portability of CTRON communication control products as an extended OS, we find the following two characteristics which make it necessary to have the layer-by-layer basis interface specifications.

One is that some applications at layer 7 need to be directly served with services which were originally provided by the layers below layer 7. The kinds of services that should be supplied to an application are application-dependent. Another, is that it is difficult to clearly specify the portable units due to the complicated relationship between the scope of support by the communication control devices.

Nevertheless, it is not always requested that all of these layer interfaces be provided as communication control products conforming to CTRON. Which layer interface(s) should be provided to the user is up to the implementation of the individual enterprise.

Each layer interface consists of two interfaces: one interface (Ia interface) mainly effects data transfer among applications; the other interface (Im interface) mainly provides maintenance and administrative service.

The name of the system call specified in each layer interface is attached with reference to OSI service primitives. The module which provides n layer service is called (n) -CCL (Communication Controller) in CTRON. The relationships between CCL, Ia and Im interface are shown in Figure 1.

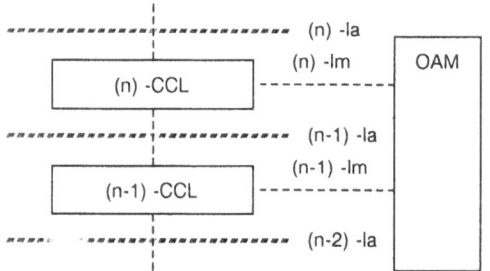

CCL; Communication Controller
OAM; Operation and Management
n; corresponds to (n) layer entity in the OSI
   reference model
Ia; application program interface
Im; maintenance / operation / management
   interface

Figure 1   CCL hierarchical model in CTRON communication control

(4) Subsetting

The OSI implementation specification falls under two categories. The first category refers to low-level implementation specifications, which cover from the physical layer to transport layer for each communication media. The other category comprises the high-level implementation specifications, which cover the profile of each Application Service Element (ASE) from the session layer to the application layer. The subsetting of system calls for CTRON communication control are specified in accordance with these implementation specifications.

2.2 REQUIREMENTS FOR APPLICATION-ORIENTED COMMUNICATION CONTROL

The interfaces provided by application layer have the characteristics indicated below.-[12]

(1) Two sides of OSI reference model and OS/AP model.....

Application layer entities in the OSI reference model purely provide communication service and protocol. In this model, AP (Application Process), the user thereof, is outside layer 7. The service provided by application layer is specified in the form of service primitive or abstract service definition. It is the representation style of the boundary between an application layer and an application process; its purpose is not to describe the boundary of OS and an application program. The interface providing CTRON application-oriented communication control must handle these two boundary problems.

(2) Difference between application layer interface and low-level layer interface.....As indicated previously, with CTRON it is a requirement that the interface be specified for each layer CCL. Direct use of these low-level interfaces at the application layer or below is usually either by CCL directly above or by other extended OS. However, when an old system is replaced with a product based on CTRON specificaitions, there are cases in which the application program must use the low level interface directly. However, when an application program has been newly designed, these low-level interfaces should not be used directly; designing should take place on the basis of interface provided by application layer.

(3) Interface per application service element.....In the OSI reference model, the service primitives provided by the application layer are basically prescribed for each ASE as seen in FTAM and MOTIS. These service primitives, however, lack uniformity among the various ASE.

In this section, we discussed the unique characteristics of the application interface program. In the future, new CTRON interface specifications such as RDA, TP, and DR will have to be developed. In these application program interfaces, prescription will have to be based on a manner which has been made uniform to some extent. In consideration of the aforementioned, the vital topics to consider in the design of application layer CCL interface are presented below.

1) View of OSI layer 7 service at boundary between OS and an application program

-- Whether user friendly interface or OSi service primitive level interface.

-- Visible/invisible distribution control pertaining to distributed resources

-- Protocol concealment

-- Relationship between client agent and server process in a distributed environment

2) Manner of interface provided by application layer CCL

-- Concealment of faults from the standpoint of fault tolerance and garbage processing

-- Uniformity of interface

A more detailed discussion on these topics will follow in the next chapter. As a result, we adopted a two-layer application program interface model as shown in Figure 4. In the first edition, the interfaces of FTAM and MOTIS were presribed as APIp (interface of OSI service primitive level) according to this model.

2.3 FUNCTIONAL MODEL

The functional model of FTAM, MOTIS and related presentation. CASE(common application service element), the subjects of specification in the first edition, is shown in Figure 2.

231

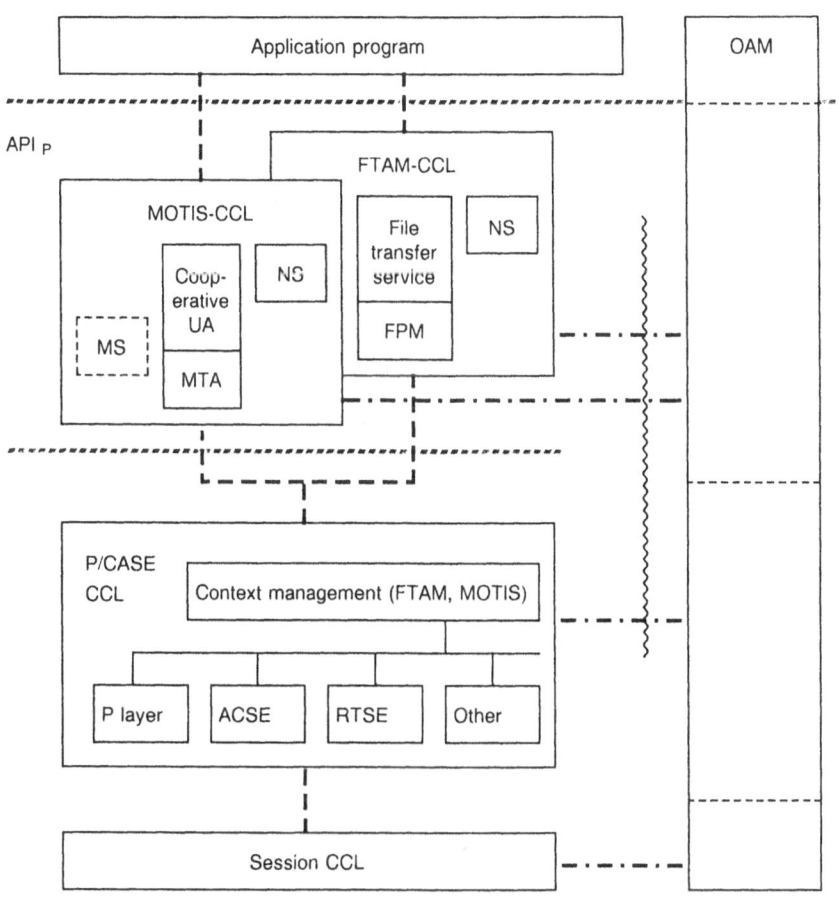

(Note) 1. Abbreviation

    OAM : Operation And Management   , NS : Name Saver

    US   : User Agent   , FPM :File Protocol Machine

    MS   : Message Store   MTA ; Massage   Transfer Agent

2. Interface prescribed in first edition

    ▬▬▬▬▬▬ ; Prescribed la interface

    〜〜〜〜〜〜 ; Prescribed lm interface

3. Implemented / Nonimplemented function block ·············· each corresponds to solid-line block

                                                         / dot-line block

Figure 2 Functional Model of FTAM, MOTIS and P/CASE - CCL

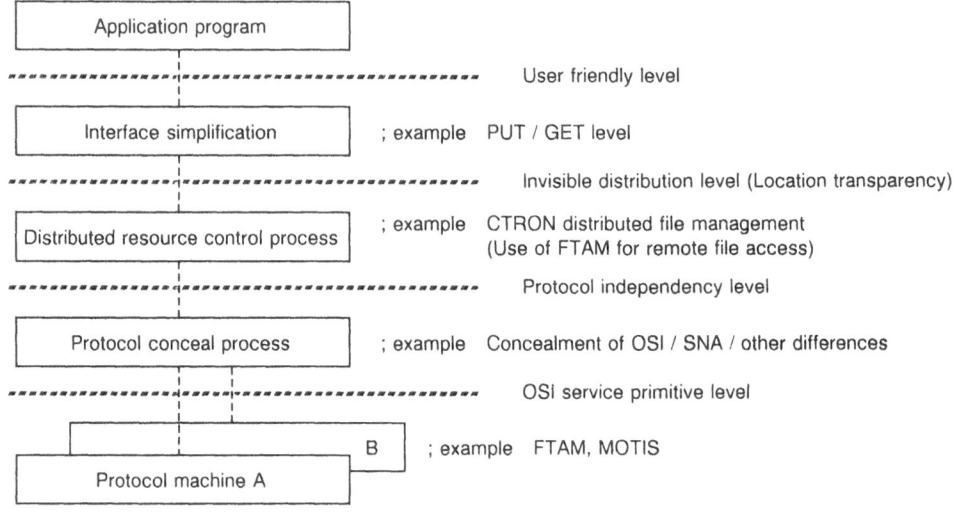

Figure 3 *Processing hierarchy related to user friendly interface, distribution and protocol independency.*

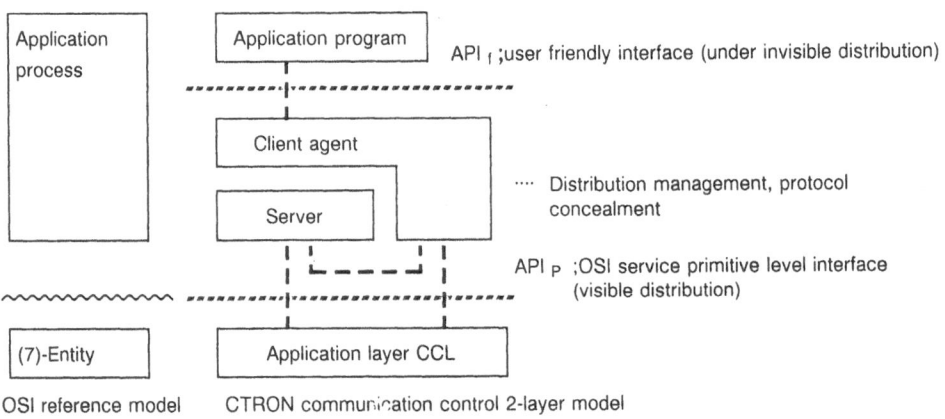

Figure 4 *Model of CTRON application layer specification interface*

(Note) From the standpoint of application layer CCL providing APIp, both server and a client agent are application programs.

3. INTERFACE DESIGN SPECIFICATIONS

In the previous section, we discussed the principles for designing common communication control and the vital topics in specifying application program interface. This section discusses the design concepts which form the basis of specifications made with respect to these topics.

3.1 VIEW OF OSI LAYER 7 SERVICE IN OS AND APPLICATION PROGRAM

At layer 7, we have to organize several vital key words, which intuitively indicate isolated concepts but could be implicated each other from the standpoint of hierarchical processing. Those vital key words are user friendly interface, integrated application interface, location transparency, protocol concealment and OSI primitives. The following is our understanding on the implication among those key words. Figure 3 also depicts this implication having the following upper/lower relationship.

1) In order to realize user friendly interface, there must be concealment at least with respect to protocol and distribution

2) Protocol concealment processing is constructed on individual protocol service.

3) Distribution control means concealment of local/remote resource location, and there must be concealment of protocol at least at this level.

For CTRON application-oriented communication control, the question of the level at which application program interface should be specified in Figure 3 must be answered.

Generally, the distributed application process on the application layer protocol machine is organized by the client/server model.-[13]

For example, if an application program enjoys an electronic mail service, it should be used without awareness of OSI/MOTIS, UNIX mail or mail protocol of SNA network. It is an ideal way for an application program requiring an easy-to-use interface to provide an interface in which these individual mail protocols have been actualized (made to appear as virtual mail machine), an interface which guarantees location transparency. Needless to say, a user friendly interface also should be provided.

For this reason, we used the two-layer API model shown in Figure 4. In the two-layer API model, the client agent provides this easy-to-use interface, which is called APIf (User Friendly Application Interface). On the other hand, there is also a primitive level interface, called APIp (Application Interface of OSi Service Primitive Level), which provides each detailed unique characteristic in order to serve mail service. In essence, this corresponds to the service primitives in the OSI reference model.

In the implementation of application program which places importance on the real-time property, configuration should be over APIp, not over APIf so that OS overhead can be avoided as much as possible.

3.2 IN CONSIDERATION PORTABILITY

A product, either an extended OS or an application program, configured on a CTRON specified interface is not always guaranteed of 100 percent compatibility.

In CTRON interface specifications, some of the specifications are left underfined as implementation-dependent problems. Consequently, with an actual product, this undefined portion of specifications must be determined locally. An actual CTRON product can be regarded as having source programs which are dependent on local specifications to some extent. Accordingly, at the time of transporting, these products, the local portion of the source program must be revised. In CTRON interface specifications, however, utmost attention must be paid to enhance portability. In this case, the items which should generally be considered are as follows.

1) Separation of the portion of specifications dependent upon system or performance scale from the transport target:
2) Clarification of interface for each implement dependent specification segment
3) Provision of a system generation interface

In particular, with respect to maintenance interface (Im) of exceptionally strong system dependency, definition of detailed components are omitted from specifications. There are two reasons for this omission.

The first is that under OSI network management, layer control specifications have not yet been standardized. The second reason is that it is better to define system call names or parameters which can be defined in common rather than to leave definition of all implement-dependent specifications up to local implementation for the sake of smoother transportation.

Accordingly, when progress is made in the standardization of basic standards of OSI network management and the standardization of implement specifications, Im interface specification will have to be reconsidered. This problem has been taken up as a topic of communications control in fiscal 1989.

3.3 ACQUISITION OF FAULT TOLERANCE-[14]

A unique feature of the CTRON OS is its suitability for information communication over a broad range of application fields. For this reason, specifications must be defined with ample consideration given to the variation of faults that are possible. In general, on the other hand, the scope of countermeasures against faults and the recovery specifications, including those of machinery, are very much dependent upon the system. It is difficult to define these specifications.

Nevertheless, the recovery specifications have been defined for the faults handled by application layer CCL, which are relatively system-independent.

In the interface specified by application layer CCL; specifications have been defined in consideration of the following two points.

(a) Concealment of association and low-level connection faults

When noise arises on the transmission route, the network relay node is down, there is intermittent protocol failure, or temporary congestion of partner resource, and the relevant CCL implements the appropriate retry for error freedom. If the retry fails, however, the association or connection is ultimately disconnected. In application layer CCL, specifications are defined so that temporary faults arising from disconnection of these low-level connections are concealed from the application program. Concealment of this fault is realized by the checkpoint function, a session layer function, in accordance with protocol. However, if the fault is not temporary and restart by check point ends in failure, a notice of fault is directed to the application program. In this case, the application program is responsible for recovery from the failure and generally, restarts from the most initial data.

(b) Resource garbage processing

The resources shown by CTRON communication control either directly or indirectly to the application program are listed below. The relationships among them are shown in Figure 5.

1) Connection/association.....Shown indirectly through service port
2) Service port.....This is the service window for an application program, and corresponds to Log-on operation. Service can be received under conditions in which service port was opened by the user.
3) Sending and receiving data buffer, notice message.....In the locate mode, it is possible for application program to exchange buffer/message directly between CCL and the application program.
4) Self service access point (SAP) ..... In the CTRON communication control CCL model, start of service must be declared to the relevant SAP prior to connect request/connect indication.
5) CCL .... CCL module activation/deactivation
6) MBX .... Message box can be used in message synchronous interface. In CTRON communications control, synchronous form by messaging is adopted among CCL and between CCL and application programs.

Activation/deactivation and allocation/deallocation of these resources are carried out directly or indirectly via Ia/Im interface by the application program (in the case of Im interface, the user on the model is OAM). In general, it is essential that the OS should be designed to provide for the case in which the application program exits abnormally while using these resources. This is called resource garbage processing.

If, for example, the CCL providing service detects that the application program has exited abnormally, resources, such as association/connection provided by CCL to the application programs and buffer resource kept within CCL, can be released under the responsibility of CCL. However, when dynamic resources like buffer/message posted to the application program in locate mode are to be released, a controlling mechanism is required to indicate whose context at present these resources are under. It is considered that this mechanism should be realized by the basic OS. Nevertheless, it is better to avoid using such mechanisms as much as possible because of the OS overhead it incurs during normal operations. In other words, when selecting such a locate mode, it should be designed such that release of resources at abnormal exit is part of the responsibility of the application program. For application programs that cannot have responsibility, service should be provided not in the locate mode, but in the more mode.

In consideration of the aforementioned, design of interface for application-oriented communication control was accomplished on the basis of the following allotment of responsibility.

1) resources linked with service port ..... Such resources as connection/association and buffer kept by CCL are released correspond to close the service point.

2) static resources.....CCL, SAP and MBX, etc. are static resources and management of them on our model is the responsibility of the management program shown in Fig. 5. Consequently the application layer CCL has nothing to release these resources even if the application program exits abnormally.

3) Release responsibility in locate mode.....Responsibility for release of resources such as service point and buffer/message posted to the application program in locate mode falls within the scope of application program responsibility.

These functions are offered by process management extended OS.

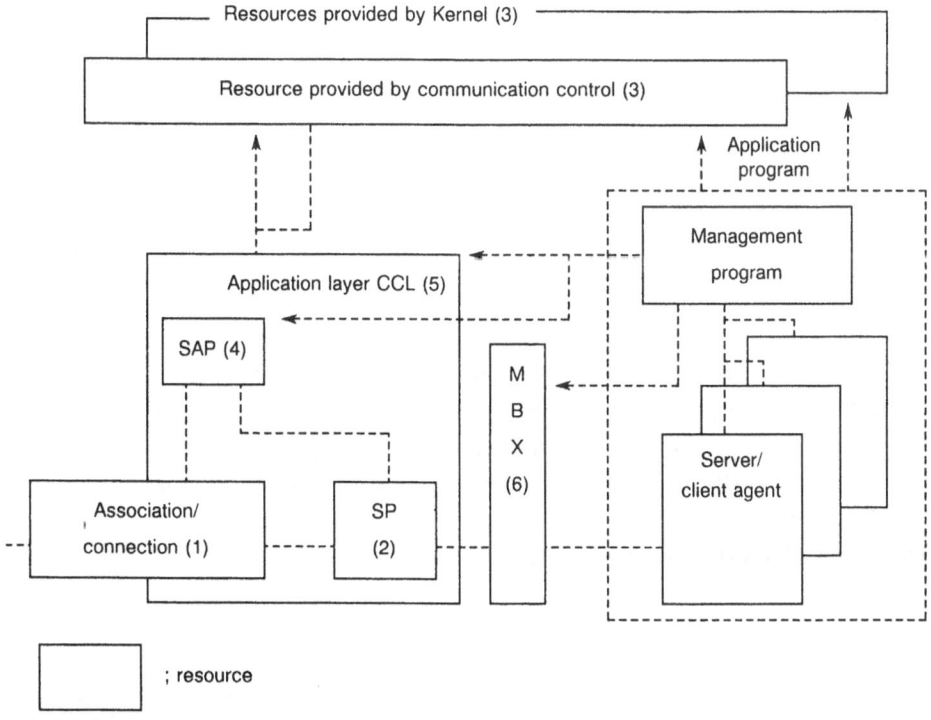

Figure 5   *Resources concerned with CTRON application-oriented communication control environment*

3.4 FLOW CONTROL

In the OSI 7-layer model provision of positive flow control function ranges from data link to transport layer. In order to understand matters more clearly, let us assume, for example, that a server process which receives large amounts of message data is constructed on extended OS for application-oriented communication.

The buffer size for sending and receiving data at the lower layer depends upon the communication media. With DDX (P), for instance, it is 256 byte data, and with LAN (IE^3 802.3) specifications, it is about 1.5K byte data. This media dependency is concealed in the OSI reference model by the transport layer. Consequently, as long as the interface specifications have implemented the OSI model faithfully, the higher-level CCL can operate with the buffer size (e.g., 4K byte) most convenient for them without being aware of buffer size for each communication media. However, when lower level CCL receives data beyond the processing capacity of the server process, the buffer resources pooled for lower level CCL could be exhausted, or the self station node would fall into busy state before becoming exhausted. In any case, the resources cannot be used effectively. This means that the higher layer needs appropriate flow control in order to prevent the aforementioned condition from arising. In order to secure appropriate data flow in the higher layer, it is necessary to operate a synchronization mechanism (minor synchronization), which is a session layer function, although it is not designed originally for flow control function, but for fault recovery methods. In the implementation specifications of MOTIS/RTS, both size of checkpoint and of window on the mirror-synchronization mechanism are prescribed.

Nevertheless, even though such an appropriate data flow can be obtained by checkpoint size, we must assume that application programs would temporary fall into the congestion state. For this reason, as the means of input suppression CASE/P-CCL provides a flow control system call as Ia interface. It is not specified whether request for this flow control undergoes mapping with checkpoint control mechanism or CASE/P-CCL simply queues reception data for a while it is left as a problem of implementation. For a similar reason, flow control system call is provided with FTAM-CCL and MOTIS-CCL.

3.5 CONSIDERATION OF REAL-TIME PROPERTY

In order to improve real-time performance, the following items generally should be considered in implementation.

(1) Avoidance of unnecessary resource allocation/deallocation

(2) Prevention of unnecessary data movement among buffers

(3) Prevention of unnecessary task context switching

(4) Avoidance of use of system calls with large overhead

Items (3) and (4) are clearly problems of implementation and cannot be easily considered in prescribing interface. In prescribing the interface in question, consideration was given to points pertaining to (1) and (2). In other words, use of buffer in the locate mode was permitted. Moreover, by using a buffer chaining mechanism which can submit a plural number of redundant sequences can be accomplished, This chaining mechanism also contributes to the avoidance of segmentation/assembling overhead at the lower level.

3.6 SPECIFICATION OF OPERATION, ADMINISTRATION AND MAINTENANCE INTERFACE

As a common specification on CTRON communication control, system calls pertaining to CCL activation/deactivation, start/stop of trace and collection of statistical information are prescribed as Im interface. The prescription of these Im interfaces is more rough than that of the Ia interface. As discussed previously, specification of these items will be enhanced in the future when layer management functions under OSI network control are made concrete. Specifications of administration and maintenance, however, are highly system dependent, and a complete specification level cannot be anticipated.

4. OUTLINE OF CASE/P-CCL INTERFACE

4.1 SPECIAL FEATURES OF CASE/P-CCL

The special features of CASE/P-CCL provided in the first edition are as follows.

(1) The Presentation layer function and CASE (Common Application Service Element) are realized as one entity, namely CASE/P-CCL. The various elements of CASE included in CCL, however, are limited to ones that have their own protocol context.

(2) As a presentation layer function, abstract syntax/transfer syntax conversion function is not supported within CASE/P-CCL.

(3) ACSE (Association Control) and RTSE (Reliability Transfer Server) have been specified as CASE functional elements which are necessary for both FTAM and MOTIS.

The design concept of CASE/P-CCL is presented below.

4.2 Abstract/Transfer Syntax Conversion Function

In the OSI model, this conversion can be mapped to a presentation layer function, but with CTRON this function cannot be realized for the following reasons. In other words, FTAM-CCL and MOTIS-CCL must assume the burden of encoder/decoder to ASN.1 expressions.

(1) Real time performance accompanying syntax conversion....

Transfer/abstract syntax conversion for each application context is possible logically, but the overhead for conversion cannot be ignored from the stand point of real time performance.

(2) Abstract syntax representation as internal data handling format.... In essence, the representation format of protocol parameter or transferred data in API of CTRON can be thought of as representation by structured table format, which is called the Canonical form. This form is not good for representing a row of variable-length parameters, but it is convenient to access essential parameters directly and in real time. This form is widely used for implementation s in fields requiring the real-time property. Given this point, it has been judged that data representation based on abstract syntax is not the appropriate format for representing transferred data in API.

(3) Use of proposal for blending ASN.1 and canonical form.... or ISO basic standard, some parameters are of completely variable length, but the maximum length of parameters is prescribed in implementation specification. Hence there is no need to use a variable-length format in actual implementation. This means that adequate representation can be made with the Canonical form. There is also data which can be treated as fixed data of ASN.1 representation; an example is O/R_Address in MOTIS-CCL. This type data needs not be always converted to Canonical form at the interface. In other words, the Canonical form was used to represent data which should be

accessed dynamically, and ASN.1 coded form was used to represent data which can be operated as relatively static. In this way, the presentation layer in CTRON is specified in a highly formal configuration.

4.3 INDEPENDENCE OF CASE/P-CCL

The background of CASE/P-CCL designed as independent CCL was aimed at releasing the higher-level AP from the dispatch processing of CASE function.

For example in the RTS used with MOTiS, dispatch of the association is as follows. The AC_Connect_Reliable_Association request system call corresponds to RT_OPEN, which is an OSI service primitive for RTSE, and when its system call is accepted at RSTE, RTSE next issued an association request for ACSE. Notice of completion of association request is returned via the opposite route.

Consequently, in the MOTIS system, notice of a fault in the association is sent from ACSES to RTSE, and after RTSE reestablishes the association, recovery is executed according to checkpoint control protocol. In this way, concealment of association faults in RTSE is realized by closing CASE/P-CCL.

On the other hand, in control of FTAM association under this CASE/P-CCL, request for association and notice of disconnection are made directly between FTAM-CCL and CASE/P-CCL.

4.4 TOPICS

The following two points are to be considered as topics.

(a) Treatment of ROSE (Remote Operation Service Element).. Essentially, this is a function which should be classified as a CASE function, but in ROS basic standards, ROS has been specified as not having a native context identifier. For example, RDA is constructed on ROS, but on the contest there is an RDA context, and ROS is realized within it. Accordingly, it is considered impossible under present circumstances to incorporate ROSE into CASE/P-CCL.

(b) Provision of encoder/decoder library for ASN.1 representation.... This library does not have the characteristics of system call, but for blocks described by ASN.1 representation, provision of a function for conversion to an internal representation format easy to process is now being considered.

5. OUTLINE OF FTAM-CCL INTERFACE SPECIFICATIONS

5.1 CHARACTERISTICS OF FTAM-CCL

The characteristics of FTAM-CCL specified in the first edition are as follows.

(1) Interface specifications were made concerning the scope of file transfer function within file transfer, file access and file management.   ....Access function and others are scheduled for extension in the second 'edition.

(2) File view from the application program is an FTAM virtual file specification. In other words, a real file access interface has not been incorporated.

(3) There are the following three functional subsets: client, server and client/server subset.

(4) FTAM entity, application entity and presentation address information are managed by the name server.

What follows is a discussion of the FTAM-CCL design concept.

5.2 USE OF FTAM VIRTUAL FILE INTERFACE

The first edition of FTAM-CCL specifications uses FTAM virtual file interface.   We had two alternatives in making a choice of the way to view a file at API.   The choice was whether real file access should be incorporated into FTAM or not.   We decided that real file access would not be incorporated because of the following reasons.

(1) Requirement of OSI standards based extension... There are many functions in CTRON file management specification that cannot be completely mapped to the current OSI FTAM protocol.   Investigation of file store management shown in CTRON file management specification is still undergoing at ISO FTAM.

(2) Conformity to the distributed file management model... Distributed file management in CTRON is presently still under development and cannot be incorporated in the first version of FTAM-CCL.

(3) Organization in the API two-layer model... In the API two-layer model illustrated in Figure 6, either the FTAM client agent or server accesses the real file.

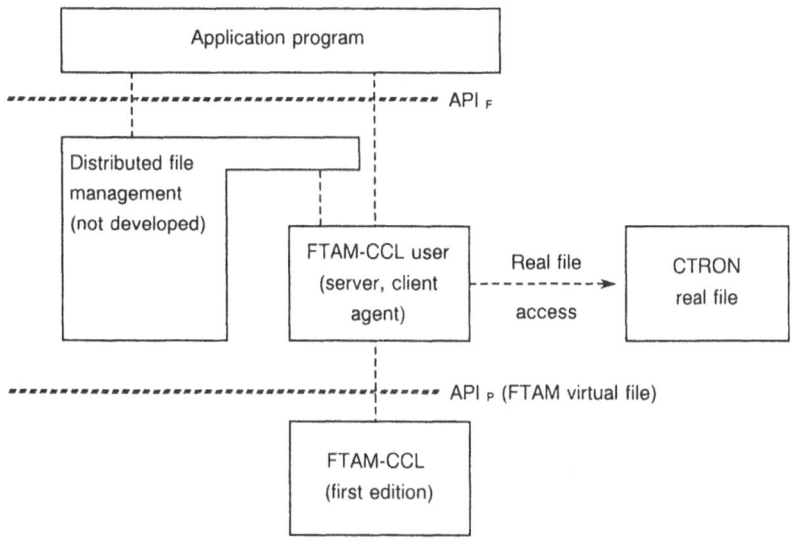

Figure 6   Display method of CTRON/FTAM virtual file in 2 layer   API model

5.3 FAULT RECOVERY SPECIFICATIONS

The first edition of specification does not adopt the interface via file in API, which limits the choice of restart methods, if the restart is implemented within the scope of FTAM-CCL. This limitation necessitates saving all file data to storage media as long as the recovery is performed within the FTAM-CCL specifications, because in some cases, file recovery must be performed from the head of the file.

In CTRON, however, this method of implementing recovery is not expected. It is necessary to save at least checkpoint sized data (in the memory buffer). An application is responsible for restart beyond the checkpoint range which cannot be automatically recovered by means of FTAM-CCL. This decision is made for the following three reasons. First, it is only rarely that CCL makes a notice of a failed restart (most troubles caused by connection/association faults are resolved by checkpoint restart.) Second, in general, application programs, including a server and a client agent, are equipped with a file recovery function from the head of the file. Finally, performance deterioration due to unnecessary file saving is impossible.

5.4 CONCATENATION OF F-DATA

The F-DATA unit usually has a meaning corresponding to file format, and in general, it's size is smaller than that of P-DATA (Presentation Data). Consequently, FTAM basic standard specifications includes a function which transceives concatenated F-DATA at one time.

In FTAM-CCL, the transferring data unit of application program is the F-DATA unit. A plural number of F-DATA are concatenated by the buffer chainging mechanism discussed in section 3.5.

6. OUTLINE OF MOTIS-CCL INTERFACE SPECIFICATIONS

6.1 CHARACTERISTICS OF MOTIS-CCL

The characteristics of MOTIS-CCL provided in the first edition are as follows.

(1) Protocol and service....Conforming to MHS/P!.P2 specifications in 1988 edition

(2) Built in specifications for interconnection with MHS in the 1984 edition... Basic service specifications conform to the 1984 edition MHS implementation specifications with consideration of interconnection.

(3) Applicable range... The applicable range of interface under these specifications is the MTA node which mounts US's. The lack of interface for realizing relay MTA does not cause any problem to have such a function locally in MOTIS-CCL.

(4) Message box function..... Although the message box function specified by P7 protocol scheduled for extension in the second edition) is not available, MOTIS-CCL provides a temporarily queuing mechanism for arrived MOTIS messages.

(5) Data transferring.... In addition to memory buffer, data transferring via file is available.

What follows is a discussion of MOTIS-CCL design concepts and topics.

6.2 SYSTEM CALL SPECIFICATION POINT

MOTIS base standard specifications have two service definitions; one is the service primitive provided to UA by MTA; the other is the abstract service definition which is aware of mapping to ROS (Remote Operation Service).

The APIp boundary of MOTIS-CCL is located between common UA and local UA. Consequently, with respect to the message transferring interface, specifications have been based on submit/deliver service primitive specified by MTA. On the other hand, the individual information management interface has been specified on the basis of the abstract service definition. The relationships among these OSI service primitives, abstract service and system call specified by MOTIS-CCL are shown in Table 1.

6.3 ADDRESS MANAGEMENT IN TWO-LAYER API MODEL

MOTIS (MHS) is most standardized pertaining to directory service. In the 1988 edition of MHS, the recipient can be designated by designating DN(Director Name) corresponding to user friendly name (such as a nickname). For relay between MTA, however, the O/R_Address of the recipients and the address of P-SAP (Presentation Service Access Point) of the relay MTA are necessary. The conversion process model of theses addresses in the two-layer API model is shown in Figure 7.

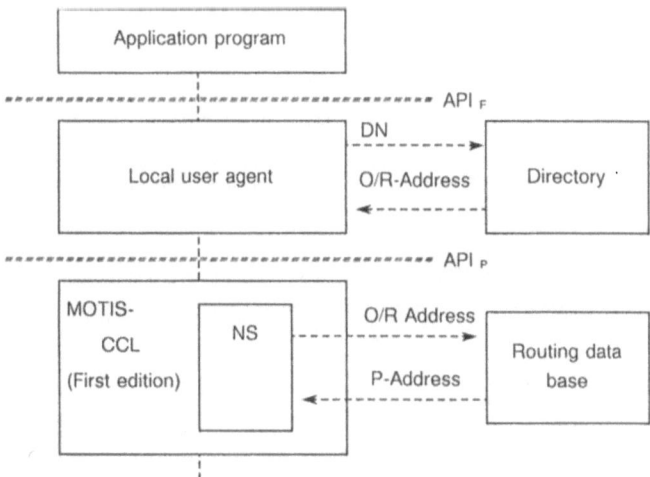

Figure 7   Address Management in 2-Layer API Model

Table 1   Relationships Among OSI Service Primitive, Abstract   Service and MOTIS-CCL System   Call

Service	OSI Service Primitive	CTRON System Call	la/m
Initiate/Terminate Service of MOTIS		MO_INITIATE_SERVICE MO_TERMINATE_SERVICE	la
Open/Close Service Port	MTS_BIND*** MTS_UNBIND***	MO_OPEN_SERVICE_PORT MO_CLOSE_SERVICE_PORT	
Data reception	DELIVERY_CONTROL Req. DELIVERY_CONTROL Cnf. DELIVER ,NOTIFY Ind.	MO_RECEIVE_DATA MO_DELIVERY_CONTROL * MO_RESPOND-RECEIPT **	
Data transmission	SUBMIT Req. SUBMIT Cnf. PROBE Req. PROBE Cnf. SUBMISSION_CONTROL***	MO_SEND_DATA * MO_SEND_PROBE * MO_RESPOND_SUBMISSION_CONTROL MO_CANCEL_DELIVERY	
Suspend flow/Resume flow		MO_SUSPEND_FLOW ,MO_RESUME_FLOW	
Register/delete individual information	REGISTER_ /CHANG_CREDENTIALS***	MO_REGISTER_PERSONAL_PROFILE MO_INQUIRE_PERSONAL_PROFILE MO_DELETE_PERSONAL_PROFILE *	
Name server		MO_INQUIRE_ADDRESS MO_GET_MPDU_IDENTIFIRE MO_RELEASE_MPDU_IDENTIFIRE MO_GET_IPM_IDENTIFIRE MO_RELEASE_IPM_IDENTIFIRE	
UA register/delete		MO_REGISTER_PROFILE, MO_INQUIRE_, MO_DELETE_	lm
CCL activation/deactivation		MO_ACTIVATE_CCL- MO_DEACTIVATE_CCL	
Acquisition of trace information		MO_START_TRACE, MO_STOP_	
Acquisition of statistical information		MO_REFER_COLLECTING_STATISTICAL_ DATA,MO_START_ ,MO_STOP_	

*   notice upon completion of system call
**   notice upon completion of MO-RECEIVE-DATA/asynchronous event
***   abstract service

Conversion from DN to O/R_Address at local user agent is achieved by accessing the MHS directory (this does not apply in the case of having address information as internal data).

In addition, at MTA, the NS (Name Server) interface is used to get the presentation address of relevant relay MTA from the recipient O/R_Address.

As discussed in section 3.2, NS is an interface specification adopted in order to enhance portability. The method of implementating address management strongly depends on whether or not there is a request to dynamically get routing addressed. If dynamic routing is not required, implementation can be realized in a simpler manner. In other words, in the approach where"large is a combination of small," it is difficult to expand the applicable fields of extended OS designed for portable software. The best choice is to establish specifications in which components can be exchanged in accordance with system scale and utility objective.

7. CONCLUSION

7.1 TOTALING OF SYSTEM CALL

The total of system calls specified in the first edition of CASE/P-CCL, FTAM-CCL and MOTIS-CCL are shown in Table 2. In total, there are 61 system calls as Ia interface and 24 system calls as Im interface.

Table 2 Total of System Calls Developed in First Edition

CCL category	Functional scope	Number of system calls Ia	Im	Remarks
CASE/P	P,ACSE,RTS	15	7	
FTAM	File transfer	25	7	
MOTIS	P1·P2/'88	21	10	
Total		61	24	

8. FUTURE TOPICS

(1) topics for FTAM-CCL

- - Provision of a user friendly interface which shows CTRON real files in APIf ....Comparable objective scheduled for the second edition.
- - Extensions pertaining to file access and management
- - Integration with CTRON distributed file management

(2) topics for MOTIS-CCL

- - Support of interfaces for message store service and for P7 protocol (MOTIS application interface on terminal)....Scheduled for second edition.
- - Provision of user friendly interface with APIf
- - Incorporation of 1988 edition MHS service and reexamination of subsetting.
- - Liason and adjustments with other organization developing standards covering IAP.

(3) implementation and evaluation

Internal efforts will have to be directed in the future toward processing claims against implementation by each company and developing APIf interface of FTAM and MOTIS. Evaluation tests of the portability of CTRON extended OS and application programs are scheduled from fiscal 1990. Reexamination of specifications from the implementation side is also necessary.

(4) adjustment to other standard specifications

Meanwhile, there is also the topic of adjusting our specification to the details of standardization covering IAP on an international level.

(5) APIf for OSI=TP

Provision of OSI-TP (Transaction Processing) interface specifications (APIf) in the second edition is also scheduled.

ACKNOWLEDGMENTS

We wish to express our sincerest appreciation to Dr. Fukuya Ishino for his thoughtful suggestions given throughout our investigation of CTRON application-oriented communication control interfaces and to everyone in the CTRON Technical Committee and CTRON Application Oriented Communication Control Working Group.

REFERENCES

[1] ;CTRON Technical Committee, *"ORIGINAL CTRON SPECIFICATION SERIES OUTLINE OF CTRON"* OUT LINE OF CT, OHM SHA, LTD.

[2] ;CTRON Technical Committee, *"ORIGINAL CTRON SPECIFICATION SERIES OUTLINE OF CTRON KERNEL INTERFACE"*, OHM SHA, LTD.

[3] ;CTRON Technical Committee, *"ORIGINAL CTRON SPECIFICATION SERIES OUTLINE OF CTRON I/O CONTROL INTERFACE"*, OHM SHA, LTD.

[4] ;*"Implementation Specifications for Common Upper Layers (V1. 0)"* INTAP (Interoperability Technology Association for Information Processing)

[5] ;*"Implementation Specifications for Message Oriented Text Interchange Systems"* , INTAP (Interoperability Technology Association for Information Processing)

[6] ;*"Implementation Specifications for File Transfer, Access and Management"*, INTAP (Interoperability Technology Association for Information Processing)

[7] ;Special Committee on CTRON, *"ORIGINAL CTRON SPECIFICATION SERIES COMMUNICATION CONTROL INTERFACE, BASIC COMMUNICATION CONTROL"*, OHM SHA, LTD.

[8] ;Special Committee on CTRON, *"ORIGINAL CTRON SPECIFICATION SERIES COMMUNICATION CONTROL INTERFACE CASE/P LAYER, FTAM AND MOTIS"*, OHM SHA, LTD.

[9] ;Special Committee on CTRON, *"ORIGINAL CTRON SPECIFICATION SERIES COMMUNICATION CONTROL INTERFACE ISDN USER CONTROL"*, OHM SHA, LTD.

[10];Mikio Tabe, *"Design of CTRON Communication Interface"*, TRON Technical Research Study Group, 1988.6 VOL1.1/NO1

[11];Yutaka Simizu, *"Design of CTRON Communication Control Interface"*, tron Project 1988

[12];Paul J. Fortier, Junichiro Kuroda, *"Design of Distributed Operating Systems (1986)"*, Nikkei Business Publications, Inc.

[13];ISO/IEC JTC1 SC18/WG4/N865, *"Information processing system - Text and Office Systems - Distributed-office-application Model"*

[14];Masayoshi Matsushita, *"A study of fault tolerant Processor with CTRON"*, The Institute of Electronics, Information and Communication Engineers, SE87-163

Tetsuji Nitta : is a manager of Computer System Division, OKI Electric Industry Co. , Ltd. He joined the company in 1972 after graduating from the University of Tottori with a B. E. degree.

Above author may be reached at : Software Development Dept, Computer System Division, OKI Electric Industry Co. , Ltd, 16-8, Chuou 1-chome, Warabi-shi, Saitama pref. , 335, Japan

Chapter 4: TRONCHIP

Advanced Optimizing Compilers Boost Performance on TRON Specification Chip Pipelined CISC Architectures

Craig Franklin, and Mike Haden
Green Hills Software, Inc.

ABSTRACT

Green Hills Software, Inc. introduces a new family of four optimizing compilers (C, C++, Fortran, Pascal) for the TRON Specification Chip architecture. The TRON Architecture is an advanced example of a Complex Instruction Set Computer (CISC).

The TRON Specification Chip architecture presents some novel challenges to the compiler writer. The TRON Specification Chip has many powerful but complicated instructions and addressing modes. The TRON Specification Chip has only 16 integer registers and 16 floating point registers. In addition, most TRON Specification Chip implementations are pipelined.

Using each of these features efficiently is difficult. During the implementation of the Green Hills family of TRON Specification Chip compilers, Green Hills confronted all these problems. We present our solutions, with examples.

Keywords: optimizing conpiler, TRON specification chip, CISC, pipeline optimization

1. The Pipelined CISC Challenge

The new generation of pipelined CISC (Complex Instruction Set Computer) architectures, such as the TRON Specification Chip architecture, needs a new generation of advanced optimizing compilers to wring out maximum performance.

The new CISC chips simplify compiler design in some ways and greatly complicate it in others. Because they usually have an orthogonal instruction set, CISC chips make it easy to generate naive code. But generating efficient code requires more work. CISC chips have variable size instructions. They have many instruction formats and addressing modes. Many instructions can access memory, not just Load and Store. Because so many of the instruction bits are used for the opcode and the addressing modes, there are fewer bits left for the register field. Most RISC chips have 32 or even 64 registers. The new TRON chips, however, have 16 integer registers and 16 floating point registers. Therefore, careful register allocation is even more important.

And there also new challenges. The new generation CISC chips are *pipelined* for maximum performance. There can be several instructions executing in the CPU simultaneously, each at a different stage of execution: instruction fetch, instruction decode, execute operation, and store the result into a register. (See Figure 1.) The compiler must perform resource scheduling to minimize pipeline resource conflicts.

Example: suppose a load instruction takes 4 cycles to execute. Any subsequent instruction which uses the loaded value should be inserted in the code stream at least three cycles later to avoid pipeline interlock delays. This leaves three empty slots for other, non-conflicting instructions to be put into. The combinatorial explosion of possible permutations makes building an efficient code generator for a pipelined architecture a non-trivial task.

Instruction Fetch: ————————

Instruction Decode: ————————

Operand Fetch: ————————

Instruction Execution: ————————

Store Result: ————————

Figure 1

1.1. The CISC Compiler Response

All of these properties mean that compiler writers must do a better job. The register allocator, peephole optimizer, and pipeline optimizer are all much more complicated than for a RISC chip.

An advanced optimizing compiler system has now solved these problems, allowing software developers to port their application programs from older architectures to pipelined CISC architectures, just by recompiling, while still achieving near optimal CPU performance. The first implementation of the new solution is a quartet of Green Hills Software compilers (C, C++, Fortran-77, and Pascal) for the TRON Specification Chip. See Figure 2.

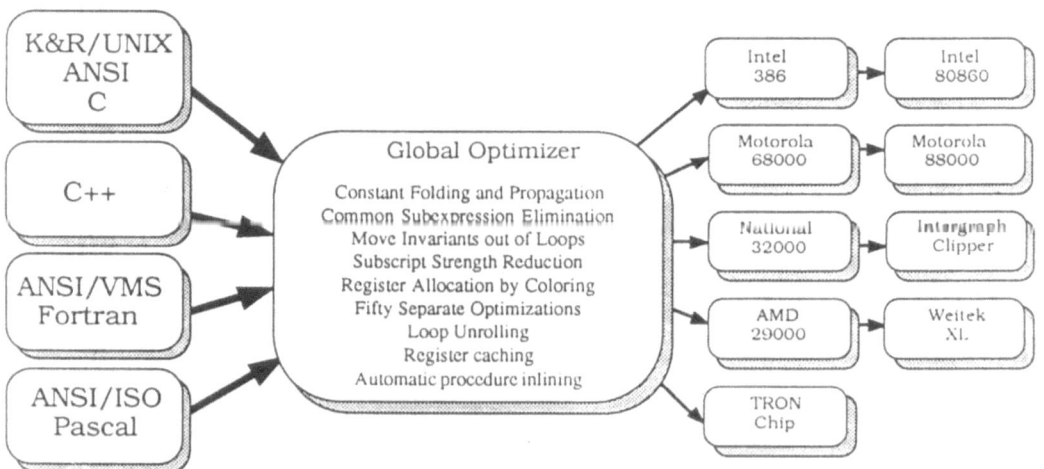

Figure 2

2. Compiler Structure And Flow Of Control

The Green Hills compiler design combines three standard compiler elements:

- Four language-specific front ends (C, C++, Fortran, Pascal)
- One global optimizer for all languages and all target architectures
- One code generator for each architecture

The front end processes the source language, using a lexical analyzer, a parser, and a symbol table. It produces an intermediate representation of the program in the form of a tree, plus the information stored in the symbol table.

The Green Hills C and Pascal front-ends each have a complete C preprocessor built into the lexical analyzer. The strategy of integrating the preprocessor means that the compiler runs much faster, since it does not need to preprocess the source, write it out, and then read it back in again to the front end. Of course, it makes the implementation of the front-end lexical analyzer slightly more complex, but the performance gain is significant and well worth the additional effort.

The control flow of the Green Hills compilers is very efficient and designed to reduce I/O, which is slow, to the minimum possible: each time the front-end has lexed and parsed a procedure, it pauses in reading the input source and calls the optimizer (optional) and code generator. The optimizer optimizes the tree for the current procedure. The code generator generates code for the current procedure. The front-end then frees the tree back to free storage, frees the symbol table entries back to free storage, and then continues with the next procedure in the source file.

The effect of this strategy is that Green Hills compilers can compile an arbitrarily long source file, provided that there is enough memory to compile the largest single procedure within the source file.

3. Global Optimizer Features

If the compiler has been invoked with the OPTIMIZE option, the global optimizer optimizes the tree. It modifies the tree in place, leaving a new program which computes the same values as the old program, but which may often execute much faster.

The tree passed from the front end to the optimizer to the code generator contains some high-level operators, including those for case switching and block entry and exit. The optimizer and code generator can make use of these high level operations to generate more efficient code.

For example, the optimizer looks at case statements. If there are three or fewer cases, it changes the tree to be a series of IF... THEN... ELSE IF... statements, because that is faster. If the cases are sparse, it changes the case operator to a sparse-case operator, which uses a binary search. If the cases are fairly dense, which is the most common case, the code generator will generate the usual jump table.

Typical optimizations include moving invariant computations out of loops (these are often generated by the address computations associated with subscripting), strength reduction (changing a subscript multiply by the loop index to an add to a running pointer), common subexpression elimination, etc.

The Green Hills Software globally optimizing compilers perform all standard optimizations:

- Dead code elimination
- Constant folding
- Passing arguments in registers
- Optimal data alignment
- Loop rotation
- Branch tail merging
- Extensive peephole optimizations
- Reducing a constant multiply to adds and shifts
- Reducing an add to increments
- Short circuit boolean expression evaluation
- Entry and exit code optimization
- Memory allocation by size and use

The Green Hills Software globally optimizing compilers also perform advanced optimizations that are not available in most other microprocessor compilers. These optimizations include:

- Register allocation by coloring
- Subscript strength reduction
- Dead store elimination
- Tail recursion
- Loop invariant removal
- Global constant propagation
- Global common subexpression elimination
- Nearly optimal pipeline instruction scheduling
- Register caching over loops
- Loop unrolling
- Local and global inline procedure expansion

These optimizations can decrease the size of a program by up to 30% compared to the Unix pcc (Portable C Compiler) and can increase its speed by up to four times. Green Hills compilers perform up to fifty separate optimizations on each program.

4. Code Generator Structure

The code generator is language independent, but specific to a particular CPU. The code generator translates the optimized tree into machine language.

There is an old saying among compiler writers that code generation is trivial if optimal register allocation has already been done, and that register allocation is trivial if optimal code generation has already been done. Some compilers do one or the other very well. The Green Hills compilers attempt to do both well.

Here's how Green Hills breaks the cycle: do simple code generation first, then do register allocation, then do the code generation again for certain cases, then peephole optimize. This strategy has proven itself to generate near optimal code on nine different machine architectures so far. Finally, if there is a pipeline, optimize again, this time for maximum pipeline throughput.

The Green Hills code generator structure involves several sub-modules. Two of these are optional: PIPE is only used if the architecture is pipelined, and FIXUP is only used if the architecture is not perfectly orthogonal. (See Figure 3.)

| GEN | → | REG | → | FIXUP | → | PEEP | → | PIPE | → | JUMP | → | EMIT |

Code Generator Phases

Figure 3

4.1. The GEN Phase -- Generate Optimistic Code

The GEN module in the code generator generates the first try at good code. It assumes that there are an unlimited number of registers. This makes code generation simple: initially assume that all scalar variables which can be put in registers are in fact allocated to registers. Now walk the tree, and for each operator, emit the machine code to perform the operation.

In a certain sense, GEN is optimistic. By this we mean that it tries to generate excellent code and ignores some of the constraints. Since most code is straightforward, GEN can often generate quite excellent code. Most code generators take the opposite approach: they generate code that they know will always work, and then try to find special cases in which they can generate better code. They are "fail-safe" but pessimistic.

4.2. The REG Phase -- Allocate Registers

REG, the register allocator assigns registers to variables and to compiler created temporaries. Registers are classified by type -- for example, integer registers and floating point registers -- and the register allocator maintains information about the current status of each register. During compilation, this information is constantly updated to reflect the value of the registers at run time.

The optimizer has already computed the lifetime of each variable throughout the program. The register allocator uses this information, plus a popularity count of which variables are referenced most often, weighted by loop depth, to allocate the most popular scalar variables permanently to registers. The register allocator uses what is called a coloring algorithm to perform register allocation. Think of each register as a color, and the program and variable lifetime information as a big graph. Now color the graph, in accordance with the lifetime information, reusing old colors when possible, but avoid any conflicts: a computation where two different variables are assigned the same color at the same time. The register allocator is actually smart enough to assign two popular variables, say I and J, to the same register at different times, if their lifetimes do not overlap.

The register allocator is pretty efficient, especially when given lots of registers to work with, as on most RISC machines. However, in the TRON Specification Chip architecture, there are only 16 integer registers and 16 floating point registers. Also, many of the integer registers are already reserved for other uses. R14 is FP, the Frame Pointer. R15 is SP, the Stack Pointer. The calling convention specifies that R0, R1, R2, and R3 are temporary registers which are not saved or restored across calls. This means that a leaf procedure (one which does not call any other procedures) can use them to hold local variables, but non-leaf procedures cannot (unless the lifetime analyzer finds a lifetime which does not span any calls). This leaves only R4 through R13, only 10 registers free. Furthermore, we need to reserve one of these free registers (R4 -- see the discussion of FIXUP below) for use by the compiler. This leaves only 9 integer register to hold all popular scalar variables.

4.3. The FIXUP Phase -- Correct For Excessive Optimism By GEN

Since the TRON Specification Chip now has only 9 free registers, it is especially important to be frugal with them. The register allocator tries to make true the code generator's assumption that scalar variables were in registers, at least in the case where it really counts -- deep in the innermost loop. For the other cases, the FIXUP routine will change the addressing mode of the instruction operand, if possible, from register to memory. If this change is not possible, FIXUP will insert the necessary Load and Store instructions to move values from memory to registers and back.

The TRON Specification Chip architecture is very orthogonal. The instruction set and addressing modes are so regular that we only need to reserve one register (R4) for FIXUP to do its job. On most of our other code generators, we need 2 or even 3 FIXUP registers.

So FIXUP is the phase that corrects for the cases where the optimistic approach of GEN and REG failed, where some things were not in registers or an assumed addressing mode was not available for a particular instruction. But the philosophical approach of optimistic code generation and register allocation followed by correcting when necessary has proved to generate consistently better code than that generated by pessimistic code generators. The key is to make sure you can always FIXUP any errors that may have been introduced by excess optimism.

4.4. The PEEP Phase -- Peephole Optimization

Now the peephole optimizer PEEP gets a chance to work over the code. It scans the code looking for simple, machine-dependent code patterns, and replaces them with more efficient code patterns. The Green Hills peephole optimizers are all hand coded, not table driven, which makes them both fast and easy for customers to extend or to suggest extensions to Green Hills.

4.5. The PIPE Phase -- Pipeline Reorganization

If the architecture has a pipeline, the PIPE optimizer now reorders the code for maximum throughput, subject to data dependencies.

To do this, it mimics in software the hardware resource and timing constraints. It builds a table called a *scoreboard* (named after the corresponding Cray hardware pipeline interlock mechanism) which has a row and a column for each instruction. Each bit in a row/column intersection tells whether the row instruction has a resource conflict with the column instruction. The scoreboard is used to check whether one instruction can be moved past other instructions.

The pipeline reorganizer PIPE then reorders the instructions in a basic block to maximize total throughput: wherever it finds an empty slot in the instruction pipeline, it tries to find an instruction from before or after that it can move into the slot. This moving may create more opportunities, and so it continues for the entire basic block.

It has been shown that instruction scheduling is a non-polynomial time (NP) problem, that is, the time required to find the optimal general solution is exponential in the number of instructions involved. Knowing this, Green Hills did not try for a theoretically optimal solution, but rather for something far more useful: good heuristic algorithms that produce almost optimal code most of the time on real programs.

After the PIPE module comes the JUMP module, which optimizes jumps. It replaces a jump to jump by a jump to the final destination. On machines with two different sizes of jump displacement, it performs short/long jump optimization. It can also reverse the sense of conditional jumps if that will improve the speed of the program.

4.6. The EMIT Phase -- Assembler And/Or Binary COFF Output

The final phase, EMIT, emits the assembly language source or the binary COFF object module output.

5. Sample Program

Matrix multiply is a short (12 line) subroutine that illustrates many of the Green Hills Software compiler optimizations.

Here is the original Fortran source code:

```
C
C    Matrix Multiply: A = B * C, where A, B, and C are N x N matrices.
C
     SUBROUTINE MATMUL(A,B,C,N)
     INTEGER I,J,K,N
     REAL     A(N,N),B(N,N),C(N,N)
     DO 10 I=1,N
       DO 10 J=1,N
         A(I,J) = 0.0
         DO 10 K=1,N
10          A(I,J) = A(I,J) + B(I,K) * C(K,J)
     END
```

We will write the rest of the examples in pseudo-C or assembly code, since Fortran cannot represent many of the compiler optimizations at the source level. The pseudo-C is just like ANSI C except that we permit an array declaration with lower and upper bound, and either bound can be an argument variable, and we also permit the "noalias" keyword (see discussion below).

For simplicity of exposition, we ignore the fact that Fortran stores arrays in column-major order and C stores them in row-major order. For clarity, we present the optimizations in a different order than the compiler actually performs them.

Here is the original program transformed into pseudo-C:

```
void  MATMUL(A,B,C,N)
int N;
float noalias A[1:N,1:N],B[1:N,1:N],C[1:N,1:N];
{
for(i=1; i<=N; i++)
    {
    for(j=1; j<=N; j++)
        {
        A[i,j] = 0.0;
        for(k=1; k<=N; k++)
            A[i,j] = A[i,j] + B[i,k] * C[k,j];
        }
    }
}
```

5.1. Register Caching Over Loops

An lvalue is a memory location or register which can be stored into and fetched from. It is called an lvalue (in C) because the left hand side of an assignment must be an lvalue (a left-value), that is, something that can be assigned to.

Sometimes the compiler can find an lvalue, like A[i,j], which must be in memory (because A is an array), but which is used heavily enough in a loop to justify putting the lvalue into a register, if we could do that, which we can't. BUT, if the loop satisfies certain conditions, we can temporarily move the memory value to a register before the loop, use the register lvalue in place of the memory lvalue during the loop, and, after the loop is done, store the register value back into the original memory location, without changing the meaning of the program at all, but possibly speeding it up.

We call this transformation is called Register Caching Over Loops. Although this optimization appears in some vectorizing compilers, we believe it is a new optimization for microprocessors. We have called it register caching because we are temporarily *caching* the memory lvalue in a register. The optimization can also be done outside of loops (and our compiler does it in both cases), but it is most useful in a loop context, since loops are executed more than non-loop code.

When is this Register Caching transformation possible? When the loop body makes no calls which could access the original memory lvalue, and when the loop body makes no stores which could alter the original memory lvalue and no loads which could fetch from the original memory lvalue. We not only need to look at all the loads and stores in the loop, we need to make sure that none of their sources or targets could alias the original memory lvalue.

The compiler performs register caching of A[I,J] over the k-loop:

```
void  MATMUL(A,B,C,N)
int N;
float  noalias A[1:N,1:N],B[1:N,1:N],C[1:N,1:N];
{
for(i=1; i<=N; i++)
    {
    for(j=1; j<=N; j++)
        {
        register float aij;            /* register cache A[i,j] */
        aij = A[i,j];                  /* redundant -- deleted later */
        aij = 0.0;
        for(k=1; k<=N; k++)
            {
            aij = aij + B[i,k] * C[k,j];
            }
        A[i,j] = aij;
        }
    }
}
```

The compiler can perform register caching in this case because of the special Fortran rule that no two arguments can be aliases. Therefore, a store into A[i,j] cannot alter B or C, which are used on the right hand side of the assignments statement. In ANSI C, one would need to use the keyword "noalias" on arguments A, B, and C to convey the same information. However, after introducing the "noalias" keyword into ANSI C, the ANSI committee deleted it at the next meeting.

5.2. Subscript Strength Reduction

Now the compiler examines all the subscripts. If any subscript is also the loop index variable, then the compiler tries to strength reduce the subscripted reference. Note that the A[i,j] subscript is inside both the i-loop and the j-loop, and so it is strength reduced twice. Note also another optimization: we have folded aij = aij + ... into aij += ....

```
void  MATMUL(A,B,C,N)
int N;
float  noalias A[1:N,1:N],B[1:N,1:N],C[1:N,1:N];
{
register float *ap1,*ap2,*bp,*cp;        /* strength reduced pointers */

ap1 = &A[1,1];

for(i=1; i<=N; i++)
    {
    ap2 = ap1;
    for(j=1; j<=N; j++)
        {
        register float aij= 0.0;        /* register cache A[i,j] */

        bp = &B[i,1];
        cp = &C[1,j];

        for(k=1; k<=N; k++, bp++)
            {
            aij += *bp * *cp;
            bp++;                    /* &B[i,k++] */
            cp += N;                 /* &C[k++,j] */
            }
        *ap2 = aij;
        ap2++;                       /* &A[i,j++] */
        }
    ap1 += N;                        /* &A[i++,j] */
    }
}
```

5.3. Move Loop Invariants Out Of Loops

But now &B[i,1] is inside both the j-loop and the i-loop, but it only depends on i. Therefore, it is a loop invariant with respect to the j-loop, and we can move it out of the j-loop. But once we do that, the reference can now be strength-reduced on the i subscript in the i-loop:

```
void  MATMUL(A,B,C,N)
int N;
float  noalias A[1:N,1:N],B[1:N,1:N],C[1:N,1:N];
{
register float *ap1,*ap2,*bp1,*bp2,*cp; /* strength reduced pointers */

ap1 = &A[1,1];
bp1 = &B[1,1];

for(i=1; i<=N; i++)
      {
      ap2 = ap1;
      bp2 = bp1;
      for(j=1; j<=N; j++)
            {
            register float aij= 0.0;        /* register cache A[i,j] */

            cp = &C[1,j];

            for(k=1; k<=N; k++, bp++)
                  {
                  aij += *bp2 * *cp;
                  bp2++;                  /* &B[i,k++] */
                  cp += N;                /* &C[k++,j] */
                  }
            *ap2 = aij;
            ap2++;                  /* &A[i,j++] */
            }
      ap1 += N;                    /* &A[i++,j] */
      bp1 += N;                    /* &B[i++,1] */
      }
}
```

5.4. Loop Unrolling

Note that the body of the innermost loop is very short, really just aij += ... and two pointer increments. We would like to have a larger inner loop body, for two reasons: we can use our register allocator better on larger pieces of straightline code, and we can overlap instructions better for pipelined execution. One technique for making a larger loop body is called Loop Unrolling. The Green Hills compilers, if requested, unroll the inner loop, if it is not too large, by a factor of four:

```
void  MATMUL(A,B,C,N)
int N;
float  noalias A[1:N,1:N],B[1:N,1:N],C[1:N,1:N];
{
register float *ap1,*ap2,*bp1,*bp2,*cp; /* strength reduced pointers */

ap1 = &A[1,1];
bp1 = &B[1,1];

for(i=1; i<=N; i++)
    {
    ap2 = ap1;
    bp2 = bp1;
    for(j=1; j<=N; j++)
        {
        register float aij= 0.0;             /* register cache A[i,j] */

        cp = &C[1,j];

        for(k=1; k<=N/4; k += 4)      /* unrolled loop */
            {
            aij += *bp2 * *cp;
            aij += *(bp2+1) * *(cp+1);
            aij += *(bp2+2) * *(cp+2);
            aij += *(bp2+3) * *(cp+3);
            bp2 +=- 4;                        /* &B[i,k++] */
            cp += 4*N;                        /* &C[k++,j] */
            }
        for(; k<=N; k++)                      /* final loop */
            {
            aij += *bp2 * *cp;
            bp2++;                            /* &B[i,k++] */
            cp += N;                          /* &C[k++,j] */
            }
        *ap2 = aij;
        ap2++;                                /* &A[i,j++] */
        }
    ap1 += N;                                 /* &A[i++,j] */
    bp1 += N;                                 /* &B[i++,1] */
    }
}
```

Note that the unrolled loop, at least in this case, adds very little to the overall code size, but it decreases the loop bookkeeping overhead by a factor of four, while, as we shall see, giving the code generator a chance to do a much better job.

5.5. Unoptimized Code

This is the code generated by the Green Hills TRON-Fortran compiler for the inner loop of matrix multiply without any optimization.

```
/
/ This is one iteration of the inner loop of matrix multiply.
/ Note that the loop rotation optimization has been performed
/ (by the Front End) so that the loop test is at the bottom of the loop.
/
$L19:
/
/ start of inner loop
/
        mov:l       r12,r2
        sub:q       #1,r2
        mov:l       r2,r3
        mul:g       @(-16,fp),r3
        mov:l       r3,r0
        add:l       r11,r0
        fmov        @(@(-8,fp),-4,r0*4).s,fr2.s
        mov:l       r11,r3
        sub:q       #1,r3
        mov:l       r3,r0
        mul:g       @(-12,fp),r0
        mov:l       r0,r1
        add:l       r13,r1
        fmul        @(@(-4,fp),-4,r1*4).s,fr2.s        / B[i,k] * C[j,k]
        mov:l       r12,r0
        sub:q       #1,r0
        mov:l       r0,r1
        mul:r       r5,r1
        mov:l       r1,r2
        add:l       r13,r2
/
/ now add the product of B[i,k] and C[k,j] to A[i,j] (inside the inner loop)
/
        fmov        @(r7,-4,r2*4).s,fr1.s              / aij = A[i,j]
        fadd        fr2.s,fr1.s                        / aij += ...
        fmov        fr1.s,@(r7,-4,r2*4).s              / A[i,j] = aij
        add:q       #1,r11                             / k++
/
/ decrement the loop iteration count, test, and branch
/
        sub:q       #1,r8
        cmp:z       #0,r8
        bne:g       $L19
```

5.6. Optimized Loop Unrolled Code With Good Register Allocation

This is the code generated by the Green Hills TRON-Fortran compiler for the inner loop of matrix multiply with all machine independent optimizations applied, including loop unrolling, but no machine dependent optimizations.

```
/
/ The compiler unrolled the inner loop of matrix multiply four times.
/
        fsub        fr2.s,fr2.s                   / aij = 0.0
$L65:
/
/ iteration 1
/
        fmov        @r12.s,fr1.s
        fmul        @r7.s,fr1.s                   / B[i,k] * C[k,j]
        fadd        fr1.s,fr2.s                   / aij += ...
/
/ iteration 2
/
        fmov        @(4,r12).s,fr1.s
        fmul        @r8.s,fr1.s                   / B[i,k+1] * C[k+1,j]
        fadd        fr1.s,fr2.s                   / aij += ...
/
/ iteration 3
/
        fmov        @(8,r12).s,fr1.s
        fmul        @r9.s,fr1.s                   / B[i,k+2] * C[k+2,j]
        fadd        fr1.s,fr2.s                   / aij += ...
/
/ iteration 4
/
        fmov        @(12,r12).s,fr1.s
        fmul        @r10.s,fr1.s                  / B[i,k+3] * C[k+3,j]
        fadd        fr1.s,fr2.s                   / aij += ...
/
/ increment the strength reduced column pointer (remember Fortran is column-major)
/
        add:l       #16,r12
/
/ increment the four strength reduced row pointers by the loop invariant row length in r3
/
        add:l       r3,r10
        add:l       r3,r9
        add:l       r3,r8
        add:l       r3,r7
/
/ decrement the loop iteration count, test, and branch
/
        sub:q       #1,r13
        cmp:z       #0,r13
        bne:g       $L65
/ restore the register cached value aij to A[i,j] in memory
        fmov        fr2.s,@@(-4,fp).s             / A[i,j] = aij
```

5.7. Optimized Loop Unrolled Code With Good Register Allocation After PEEP

This is the code generated by the Green Hills TRON-Fortran compiler for the inner loop of matrix multiply with all machine independent optimizations applied, including loop unrolling, and all machine dependent optimizations except pipeline reorganization.

```
/
/ The compiler unrolled the inner loop of matrix multiply four times.
/
        fsub        fr2.s,fr2.s              / aij = 0.0
$L65:
/
/ iteration 1
/
        fmov        @r12.s,fr1.s
        fmul        @r7.s,fr1.s             / B[i,k] * C[k,j]
        fadd        fr1.s,fr2.s             / aij += ...
/
/ iteration 2
/
        fmov        @(4,r12).s,fr1.s
        fmul        @r8.s,fr1.s             / B[i,k+1] * C[k+1,j]
        fadd        fr1.s,fr2.s             / aij += ...
/
/ iteration 3
/
        fmov        @(8,r12).s,fr1.s
        fmul        @r9.s,fr1.s             / B[i,k+2] * C[k+2,j]
        fadd        fr1.s,fr2.s             / aij += ...
/
/ iteration 4
/
        fmov        @(12,r12).s,fr1.s
        fmul        @r10.s,fr1.s            / B[i,k+3] * C[k+3,j]
        fadd        fr1.s,fr2.s             / aij += ...
/
/ increment the strength reduced column pointer (remember Fortran is column-major)
/
        add:l       #16,r12
/
/ increment the four strength reduced row pointers by the loop invariant row length in r3
/
        add:l       r3,r10
        add:l       r3,r9
        add:l       r3,r8
        add:l       r3,r7
/
/ decrement the loop iteration count, test, and branch
/
        scb:q       #1,r13,#1,$L65          / PEEP compressed 3 instructions to 1
/
/ restore the register cached value aij to A[i,j] in memory
/
        fmov        fr2.s,@@(-8,fp).s / A[i,j] = aij
```

5.8. Optimized Code With Good Register Allocation After PEEP and PIPE

This is the code generated by the Green Hills TRON-Fortran compiler for the inner loop of
matrix multiply with all machine independent optimizations applied, including loop unrolling, and
all machine dependent optimizations, including peephole optimzation and pipeline reorganization.

```
/
/ The compiler unrolled the inner loop of matrix multiply four times.
/ Note how the integer operations have been moved to overlap
/ with the floating point operations.
/
        fsub        fr2.s,fr2.s             / aij = 0.0
$L65:
/
/ iteration 1
/
        fmov        @r12.s,fr1.s
        fmul        @r7.s,fr1.s             / B[i,k] * C[k,j]
        add:l       r3,r7                   / PIPE moved this here
        fadd        fr1.s,fr2.s             / aij += ...
/
/ iteration 2
/
        fmov        @(4,r12).s,fr1.s
        fmul        @r8.s,fr1.s             / B[i,k+1] * C[k+1,j]
        add:l       r3,r8                   / PIPE moved this here
        fadd        fr1.s,fr2.s             / aij += ...
/
/ iteration 3
/
        fmov        @(8,r12).s,fr1.s
        fmul        @r9.s,fr1.s             / B[i,k+2] * C[k+2,j]
        add:l       r3,r9                   / PIPE moved this here
        fadd        fr1.s,fr2.s             / aij += ...
/
/ itcration 4
/
        fmov        @(12,r12).s,fr1.s
        add:l       #16,r12                 / PIPE moved this here
        fmul        @r10.s,fr1.s            / B[i,k+3] * C[k+3,j]
        add:l       r3,r10                  / PIPE moved this here
        fadd        fr1.s,fr2.s             / aij += ...
/
/ decrement the loop iteration count, test, and branch
/
        scb:q       #1,r13,#1,$L65          / PEEP compressed 3 instructions to 1
/
/ restore the register cached value aij to A[i,j] in memory
/
        fmov        fr2.s,@@(-8,fp).s       / A[i,j] = aij
```

6. Portability And Compatibility

The modular design of the Green Hills compilers has allowed Green Hills to maintain absolute compatibility of languages across microprocessor systems and absolute compatibility between languages on the same microprocessor system. If you can compile a program with one Green Hills compiler, you can compile it with any other Green Hills compiler for the same language. If you can mix languages on one system using Green Hills compilers, you can mix languages on any other system using Green Hills compilers.

This means that a wide variety of programs which run on eight other microprocessors (Intel 386 and 860, Motorola 68000 and 88000, AMD 29000, Weitek XL, Intergraph Clipper, and National 32000) can now run on the TRON Specification Chip architecture, provided only that they have been previously compiled with a Green Hills compiler for one of the other eight microprocessors.

Each Green Hills Software compiler conforms to the applicable ANSI and ISO standard and is a superset of the most widely used Unix implementation of that language.

But it is not enough any more to have compilers that merely conform to an industry or ANSI standard. Real programs come from many different environments, and use many different language dialects and extensions.

Green Hills Fortran implements ANSI Fortran 77, the DOD Mil Std 1753 extensions, and almost all of the VAX/VMS Fortran extensions. This gives maximal portability when moving Fortran programs to Green Hills Fortran.

Green Hills Pascal is ANSI Pascal and ISO Level 1 Pascal, plus most of the Berkeley Unix Pascal extensions for separate compilation.

Green Hills C is K&R C from AT&T Unix, plus the C language extensions from Berkeley Unix, plus an ANSI C compiler option which tracks the draft ANSI C standard, and which will be released when the Standard is finally approved.

Green Hills C is powerful enough to recompile the entire Unix kernel and all of the Unix utilities and has done so for five different architectures. This is the true test of an industrial strength C compiler.

Green Hills C++ is compatible with the AT&T Version 1.2 C++ translator. In addition, it includes all the AT&T Version 2.0 C++ features except multiple inheritance, which will be added in early 1990. Unlike the AT&T C++ implementation, however, Green Hills C++ is a true compiler, not a translator. This means faster compilation, better error messages, and better debugger support.

Summary

The Green Hills compilers are able to use such TRON architecture features as the scb instruction to replace three normal instructions and also the multiple indirect addressing mode and indexed addressing mode to generate efficient code -- certainly more compact code than for a RISC architecture. And the Green Hills compilers are able to exploit the pipelined implementation of the TRON architecture to overlap instruction execution and improve throughput.

The Green Hills Software compilers meet the challenge of generating near-optimal code for the new generation of pipelined CISC architectures, such as the TRON Specification Chip family.

Acknowledgements

The authors would like to acknowledge the founders of Green Hills Software: Dan O'Dowd, President and Carl Rosenberg, Vice-President of Engineering, who personally created the compiler technology described here over a period of seven years. We would like to thank George Williams, who implemented C++ single-handedly in less than a year. We would also like to thank Dr. Ken Sakamura of Tokyo University for creating an interesting architecture as a target for our efforts, and also Mitsubishi, Hitachi, and Fujitsu for their implementations of that architecture. We owe a special debt to Mr. Norihiko Ito of Hitachi, who first introduced Green Hills to the TRON architecture in 1986 and who has worked with us since then to make this project a success.

References

[1] Sakamura, K., "TRON VLSI CPU: Concepts and Architecture," TRON Project 1987, Springer-Verlag, pp. 199-238.

[2] Sakamura, K., "Architecture of the TRON VLSI CPU," IEEE Micro, Volume 7, Number 2, pp. 17-31, April, 1987.

Craig Franklin has been Vice-President of Marketing for Green Hills Software, Inc. since 1986. After graduating with a BS in Mathematics from Stanford university in 1966, Mr. Franklin spent two years on the Apollo program at North American Rockwell, five years at MIT on the Multics project, five years at Data General in charge of PL/I, and five years as President of his own company, Carolina Software. Mr. Franklin has produced ten commercially successful compilers, in ten tries, for languages including PL/I, Fortran, C, Pascal, Basic, and SAS for organizations including MIT, Data General, Plessey, Brandeis University, SAS Institute, Digital Research, and Microtec Research.

Mike Haden is a Software Engineer at Green Hills Software, Inc. Prior to joining GHS he worked with the Green Hills compilers for several years at Ridge Computers. He has worked on compilers and language related tools since graduating from San Diego State University in 1979 with a B.A. in Computer Science.

The authors may be reached at Green Hills Software, Inc., 425 East Colorado Street, Suite 710, Glendale, California 91205, USA.

Design of Microcomputer Systems Using the TX1 Family LSIs

Takashi Miyamori, Toshiya Yoshida,
and Hidechika Kishigami
Toshiba Corporation

Abstract

The TX1 family LSIs consist of a 32-bit microprocessor TX1 based on TRON specifications and dedicated peripheral LSIs including a clock generator (CG), interrupt controller/timer (ICT), and DMA controller (DMAC). This paper outlines the features of the TX1 family LSIs and explains how to design microprocessor systems using these LSIs. We give two examples of the TX1-based computer systems and discuss the evaluation results of the TX1 used in these systems. Here, we examine the relationship between memory speed (with or without a cache) and system performance by executing typical benchmark programs.

Keywords: Microprocessor, Peripheral LSI, VME board computer, Benchmark program

1. Introduction

We have been developing a 32-bit microprocessor TX1[1][2][3][4][5] based on TRON specifications[6], as well as dedicated peripheral LSIs such as a clock generator (CG), interrupt controller/timer (ICT), and DMA controller (DMAC). The TX1 family consists of these microprocessors and peripheral LSIs. The peripheral LSIs are designed to take full advantage of the TX1's capabilities to enable the easy configuration of high-performance, high-function microcomputer systems.

In this paper, we outline the features of the TX1 family LSIs and explain how to design microcomputer systems with the TX1. The interface circuits between the TX1 and peripheral LSIs are described.

We then give two examples of the TX1-based computer systems. One is a VME board computer which is a relatively small system. The VME board computer has two ROM sockets, a 256K bytes SRAM memory accessible with 0 wait cycles, and an external interface consisting of two serial ports and one parallel port. In this system, the ICT is also used as a VME bus interrupt handler and a 32/16-bit timer.

The other system is a large size computer system. In addition to the 32M bytes large-capacity main memory, this system incorporates 128K bytes cache memory to increase system performance. The cache memory system consists of four dedicated cache memory LSIs. The model computer system has Ethernet and SCSI interfaces in addition to a serial port.

In the last section of the paper, we discuss the results of TX1 performance in these systems. We examine the relationship between memory speed (with or without a cache) and system performance by executing typical benchmark programs.

Table 1 Outline of TX1

Performance	5MIPS (average), 12.5MIPS (max.)
Address bus / Data bus	32 bits / 32 bits (separate)
Number of instructions	93 instructions
Address space	4G bytes
Minimum bus cycle	2 clock cycles
Interrupt levels	15 levels
Maximum operating frequency	20MHz / 25MHz
Manufacturing process	1μm 2-layer AL CMOS
Package	155-pin PGA

2. TX1 Family LSIs
2.1 TX1

(a) Outline

The TX1 is designed primarily for real-time and embedded applications such as robots, high-speed facsimiles, laser beam printers, and so on. Table 1 lists the features of the TX1. The TX1 has 93 instructions, operates at a maximum frequency of 25MHz, and can execute instructions at an average rate of 5MIPS. Both address and data buses of the TX1 are 32 bits wide. The TX1 supports a 4G-byte physical address space. It has a vectored interrupt processing function with 15 priority levels. Its dynamic bus sizing function allows peripheral LSIs with 8-bit or 16-bit data bandwidths to be easily interfaced to the TX1.

(b) Bus Operation

Table 2 lists the signals used for the TX1's bus operation. Various control signals are provided to allow external devices to be easily connected to the TX1.

Fig. 1 shows a bus cycle timing diagram. The bus operation of the TX1 is synchronized to the single-phase clock (CLK). The first clock of the bus cycle is called "TA cycle" in which address information is output. The last clock of the bus cycle is called "TD cycle" in which data is transfered. The minimum bus cycle consists of two clock cycles: the TA cycle and TD cycle. If an access speed of the external devices is slow, one or more wait cycles (TW) can be inserted between the TA and TD cycles. Fig. 1 shows an example of a 1 wait read bus cycle and a 1 wait write bus cycle. The description of the bus cycle is as follows:

<Read bus cycle>
1) When the TA cycle starts, the TX1 outputs the address on the address bus A00-31 along with the BC0-3# and BAT0-2 signals. It drives the WR# signal "High" for the read bus cycle. The BSTART# signal is "Low" for one clock period.
2) The AS# signal is driven "Low" from the second half of the TA cycle.
3) The DS# signal is driven "Low" in the TW and TD cycles.
4) External hardware outputs data on the data bus D00-31, then asserts the bus cycle terminate signal DSIZK0#-1#.
5) When the DSIZK0#-1# are sampled active, the data is read into the TX1 at the next rising edge of the clock signal CLK.

Table 2 Signals Used for Bus Operation

Signal name	Type	Number of signal lines	Functions
CLK	Input	1	Clock input to the TX1.
A00-31	Output	32	Indicates the address for data to be transferred.
BC0#-3#	Output	4	Indicates data validity for each byte.
BAT0-2	Output	3	Indicates such bus cycle modes as instruction fetch, operand read / write, and interrupt vector fetch.
WR#	Output	1	Indicates the direction of data transfer done by TX1.
BSTART#	Output	1	Indicates that a bus cycle has started.
AS#	Output	1	Indicates that the address is valid.
DS#	Output	1	In the read bus cycle, it indicates that an external device is granted control of the data bus; in the write bus cycle, it indicates that the TX1 is driving the data bus.
D00-31	Input / Output	32	A data bus signal used to transfer data to and from external devices.
DSIZK0#,1#	Input	2	Indicates termination of a bus cycle. It also indicates the port size of the external device.

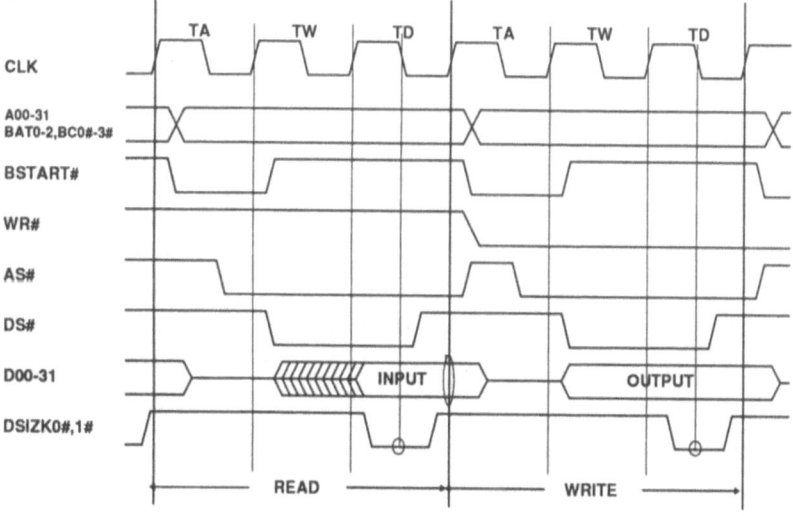

Fig. 1 TX1 Bus Timing

<Write bus cycle>

1) When the TA cycle starts, the address are output on the address bus A00-31 along with the BC0-3# and BAT0-2 signals. The WR# signal is driven "Low" for the write bus cycle. The BSTART# signal is "Low" for one clock period.

2) The AS# signal is driven "Low" from the second half of the TA cycle.

3) The DS# signal is driven "Low" in the TW and TD cycles, and data are output on the data bus D00-31.

4) The bus cycle terminate signals DSIZK0#-1# are sampled at the falling edge of the clock in the TD cycle.

5) When the DSIZK0#-1# are sampled active, the DS# signal is driven "High".

6) The data bus D00-31 is placed in a high-impedance state at the rising edge of the clock.

2.2 Clock Generator (CG)

The CG supplies stable clock pulses to the TX1-based microcomputer system. Either the internal quartz oscillator or an external TTL-level clock signal can be selected as a clock source. The maximum output frequency is 50MHz. In addition to the basic clock, the CG outputs double period and quadruple period clocks and the inverted-phase clocks of each. These clock outputs can be used to provide timing signals to peripheral LSIs and other system components.

The CG also outputs bus cycle terminate signals DSIZK0#-1# which indicate the transfer byte size, as well as the bus cycle termination. The CG generates the DSIZK0#-1# from the bus size signals (BSZ0-1) and bus timing signal (BTM#). The DSIZK0#-1# signals are output synchronously at the rising edge of the basic clock (CLK1) to guarantee the TX1's setup time for the DSIZK0#-1#. Table 3 shows the relationship between the BSZ0-1, BTM#, and DSIZK0#-1#.

Fig. 2 shows an example of interfacing the CG to the TX1. The basic clock CLK1 of the CG is used as the TX1's clock (CLK). The chip select signal and the bus size signals BSZ0-1 that indicate the port size of the selected device are generated in the address decode

Table 3 Bus Cycle Terminate Signals

BTM#	BSZ0	BSZ1	DSIZK0#	DSIZK1#	Transfer byte size
LOW	HIGH	HIGH	LOW	LOW	4 bytes
LOW	HIGH	LOW	LOW	HIGH	2 bytes
LOW	LOW	HIGH	HIGH	LOW	1 byte
LOW	LOW	LOW	HIGH	HIGH	Bus cycle continued
HIGH	—	—	HIGH	HIGH	Bus cycle continued

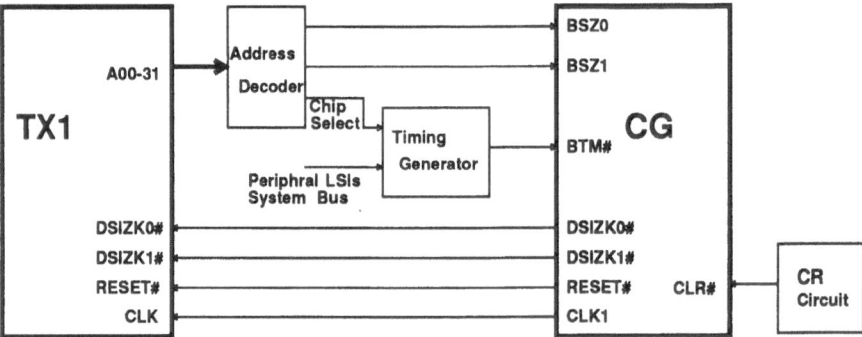

Fig. 2 Interface for TX1 and CG

circuit, then are input to the CG. The timing generator produces the bus timing signal BTM# from the chip select signal in such a way that appropriate wait cycles are inserted to match the speed of the selected device. The CG produces bus cycle terminate signals DSIZK0#-1# from the BSZ0-1 and BTM#, then outputs them to the TX1 synchronously with the CLK1. When peripheral LSI or system bus is accessed, the bus timing signal BTM# is generated based on the acknowledge signal output from these devices.

When the system is going to turn on, there is a possibility that system may malfunction because the supply voltage and clock are not stable yet. The CG can output a reset signal RESET# to a system at power-on by fitting a simple CR circuit to the CLR# pin of the CG.

2.3 Interrupt Controller/Timer (ICT)

The ICT provides efficient interrupt processing functions. Because a number of peripheral devices are connected to a high-performance 32-bit microprocessor system, it is necessary to handle multiple interrupt requests generated from these peripheral devices according to their priorities. Therefore, the TX1 can handle interrupts with up to 15 priority levels. Correspondingly, the ICT allows 15-level interrupt priorities to be set for individual interrupt requests.

Fig. 3 shows an interface circuit between the TX1 and ICT. The ICT outputs encoded interrupt request signals IRP0-3 to the TX1. In response to the interrupt vector fetch cycle, the ICT outputs interrupt vectors. In this cycle, because the TX1 outputs "Low, High, Low" to BAT0-2, an external decode circuit can produce interrupt acknowledge signals IACK#, RACK# by decoding the BAT0-2 signals. The data acknowledge signal DACK# output by the ICT can be used to generate bus cycle terminate signals. After being synchronized with

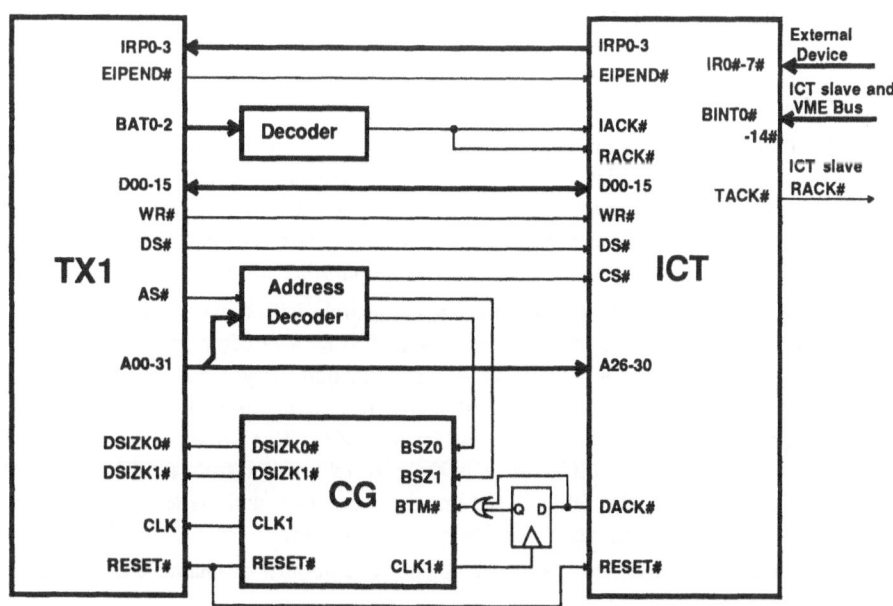

Fig. 3 Interface for TX1 and ICT

the clock at a F/F, the DACK# signal is input to the BTM# of the CG. In order to access the internal control register of the ICT, the ICT's chip select signal CS# must be active. The CS# signal is generated by decoding the upper bits in the address bus A00-31 and the AS#. In the write bus cycle, the ICT reads data at the rising edge of DS#. Because the TX1 guarantees data after the rising edge of the TX1's DS# signal, the TX1's DS# signal and ICT's DS# signal can be directly connected.

An ICT can process up to eight interrupt requests. The number of requests can be easily expanded by daisy chaining two or more ICTs. In a daisy chained system, the transfer interrupt acknowledge signal TACK# is cascaded to the receive interrupt acknowledge signal RACK# of the next ICT.

Generally speaking, it is necessary for interrupt controllers to process a interrupt request in real time. This is especially important when the TX1 is used in real-time and embedded applications. The ICT only requires about 50ns for level-triggered interrupts from when it receives an external interrupt request to when it outputs the IRP0-3 to the processor. In addition, the ICT has a dynamic priority processing function to guarantee real-time response when multiple interrupts occur. This function works in such a way that if the interrupt level, at which the ICT attempted to interrupt the TX1, is a level inhibited for the TX1, the ICT is able to output the highest interrupt level at that time. It, therefore, prevents pending high-level interrupts when a low-level interrupt which is inhibited by the TX1 is requested first, thus making it possible to build a fast-responding, real-time interrupt processing system. The dynamic priority function can be implemented by connecting the EIPEND# terminals of the TX1 and ICT.

The ICT incorporates internal 32-bit timers so that it can count the falling edges of an interrupt request signal. Because it is possible to generate interrupts when predetermined numbers of falling edges are detected, the ICT can be used as a timer to generate interrupts at certain intervals by entering clock to the interrupt request signals IR#.

2.4 DMA Controller (DMAC)

In the TX1-based microcomputer systems, the DMAC executes a high speed data transfer between memory and I/O devices instead of the TX1. The DMAC has a 32-bit wide data bus and address bus. It supports data transfer on 4G-byte address space. Its minimum bus cycle consists of two clock cycles, and the maximum data transfer rate is 50M bytes per second, providing sufficient high-speed capability as a DMA controller for 32-bit MPUs.

The signal lines used for bus operation are compatible with those of the TX1, and can be connected directly to the TX1. All devices designed to be accessible from the TX1 can also be accessed directly by the DMAC, making it easy to build any microprocessor system. In addition, because the DMAC also has the dynamic bus sizing function, 8-bit and 16-bit I/O devices can be connected in the same way as for the TX1. When transfer byte sizes between the source and destination are different as in the case of transfer from an 8-bit or 16-bit I/O device to 32-bit memory, the DMAC buffers the data once and writes it. Therefore, the number of bus cycles is minimized to enable efficient transfer.

The DMAC has four DMA transfer channels. The number of channels can be expanded by daisy chaining multiple DMACs.

3. Example of Application Systems

In this section, we show a VME board computer system and model computer system as two examples of microcomputer systems built by using the TX1 family LSIs.

3.1 TX1 VME Board Computer

The following describes the outline features of the TX1 VME board computer and its on-board SRAM interface circuit.

(a) Outline

Table 4 outlines the specifications of the VME board computer. The photograph of the board is shown in Photo.1. The TX1 VME board computer was initially developed to evaluate TX1 performance. It includes the CG and ICT. The ICT handles the interrupt requests from serial and parallel ports and it is also used as a VME bus interrupt handler and 32/16-bit timer. The VME board computer has 0 wait SRAM as main memory to take full advantage of TX1 performance In addition, it has RS-232C and Centronics I/O interfaces and a system bus interface based on the VME bus specifications. For the evaluation of the TX1 by using the VME board computer, a "TX1 Debug Monitor", one of the TX1 application development tools[7], can be used. The debug monitor is manipulated from a host computer such as the AS3000 series workstation or J3100 series lap-top computer.

(b) SRAM interface circuit

Fig. 4 shows the SRAM interface circuit. In order to achieve 0 wait access at 25MHz, a 256K-bit SRAM device that can be accessed in 20ns is adopted.

Here the circuit operation is explained by referring to the operation timing diagram shown in Fig. 5. For the bus cycle to be terminated with 0 wait state, the bus cycle terminate signals DSIZK0#-1# signals and the data D00-31 setup times are critical. In the TX1's specification, the DSIZK0#-1# must be asserted 5ns before the falling edge of CLK pulse in the TD cycle. In the SRAM circuit, the DSIZK0#-1# signals are valid 7.8ns before (t_{ZSU}). The other critical timing is that the TX1 requires 10ns as a data setup time before the rising edge of CLK pulse at the end of TD cycle. The data setup time (t_{DSU}) is 18.8ns in the circuit. From the calculation in Fig. 5, the setup times satisfy the timing requirements of the TX1.

Table 4 Outline of TX1 VME board Computer

ROM	512K bit EPROM socket x 2
RAM	256K Bytes SRAM (0 wait)
Serial Port	RS232C x 2
Parallel Port	Centronics x 1
VME bus I/F	Address 32 bits / Data 32 bits Single level bus arbiter Interrupt handler
Timer	32/16 bit timer

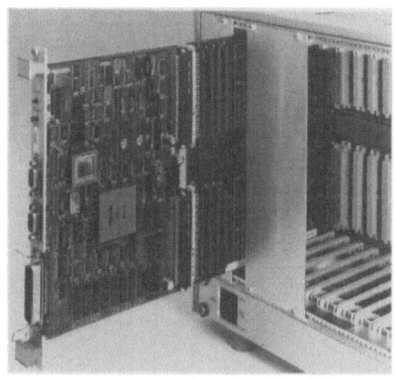

Photo. 1 Photograph of VME Board Computer

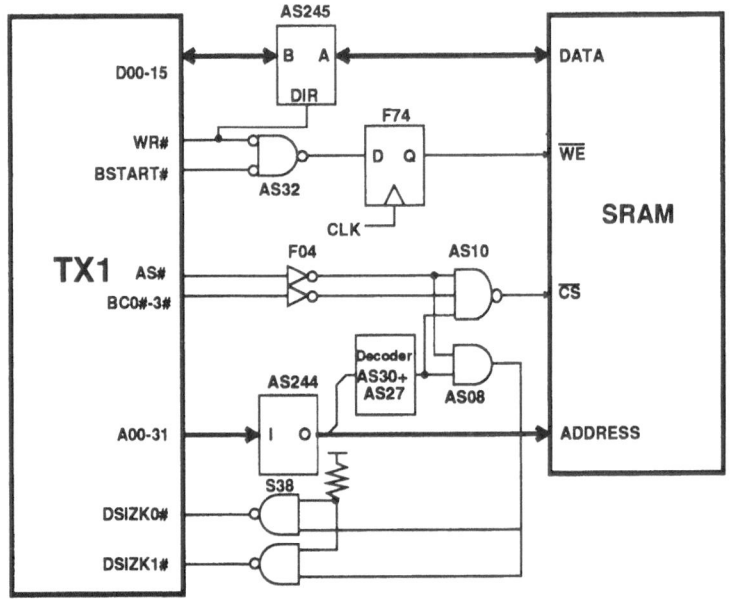

Fig. 4 SRAM Circuit

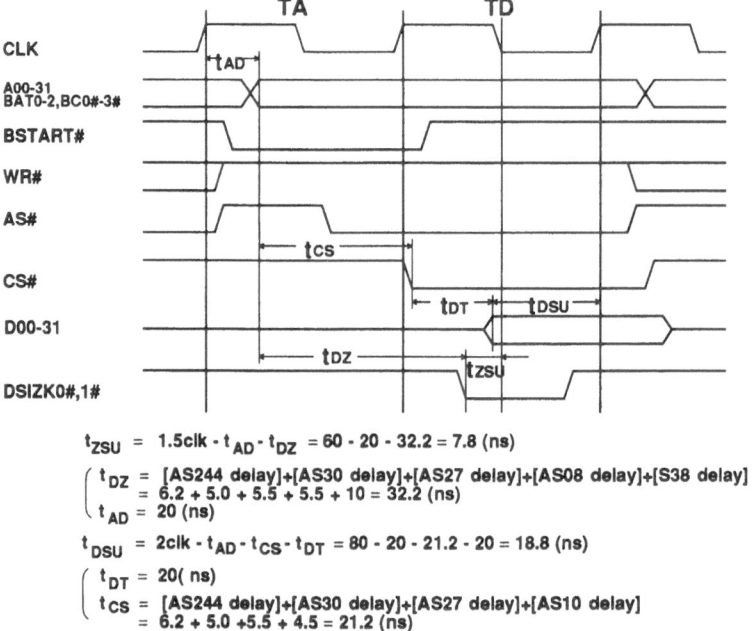

$t_{ZSU} = 1.5clk \cdot t_{AD} \cdot t_{DZ} = 60 - 20 - 32.2 = 7.8 \ (ns)$

$\begin{cases} t_{DZ} = [\text{AS244 delay}]+[\text{AS30 delay}]+[\text{AS27 delay}]+[\text{AS08 delay}]+[\text{S38 delay}] \\ \quad = 6.2 + 5.0 + 5.5 + 5.5 + 10 = 32.2 \ (ns) \\ t_{AD} = 20 \ (ns) \end{cases}$

$t_{DSU} = 2clk \cdot t_{AD} \cdot t_{CS} \cdot t_{DT} = 80 - 20 - 21.2 - 20 = 18.8 \ (ns)$

$\begin{cases} t_{DT} = 20 \ (ns) \\ t_{CS} = [\text{AS244 delay}]+[\text{AS30 delay}]+[\text{AS27 delay}]+[\text{AS10 delay}] \\ \quad = 6.2 + 5.0 + 5.5 + 4.5 = 21.2 \ (ns) \end{cases}$

Fig. 5 SRAM Read Timing

Photo. 2 Photograph of Model Computer

Table 5 Outline of TX1 Model Computer

Cache Memory	128K Bytes
RAM	32M Bytes
ROM	256K Bytes
Video Memory	256K Bytes
Kanji ROM	6353 Characters
Keyboard	TRON Spec. / ASCII Std.
Floppy Disk Drive	4M Bytes Vertical Magnetic-recording
Hard Disk Drive	100M Bytes
Serial Port	RS232C/RS423 (Max. 19.2K bps)
Ethernet	1 Channel
SCSI	1 Channel
Plasma Display	1024 x 768 Dots

3.2 TX1 Model Computer

This section outlines the features of the TX1 model computer (Photo.2) and its cache memory interface circuit.

(a) Outline

Table 5 outlines the specifications for the TX1 model computer. Fig. 6 shows its block diagram. This computer is a prototype model designed by considering TX1 use in future personal computers and workstations. It has the dedicated peripheral LSIs such as the CG, ICT, and DMAC. In addition to the 32M-byte large-capacity main memory, it incorporates 128K-byte 0 wait accessible cache memory to improve system performance. This cache memory consists of four dedicated LSIs. For external interface, the computer has Ethernet and SCSI interfaces, as well as a serial port. All these functions are integrated on a 40cm × 29cm, 4-layered printed circuit board.

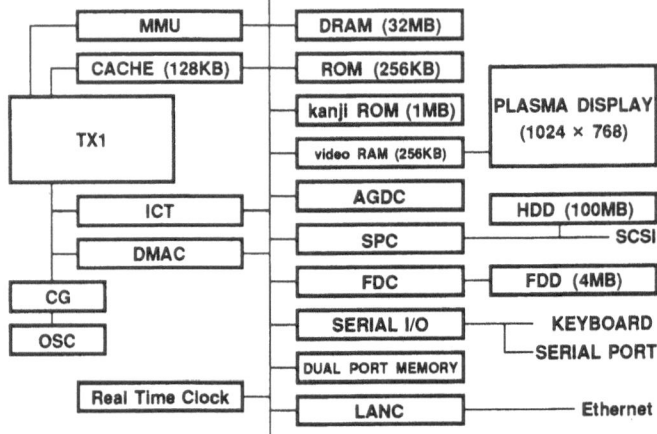

Fig. 6 TX1 Model System Block Diagram

Table 6 Outline of T9490

Cache size	32K bytes (16 bytes × 2,048 set)
Block size	16 bytes (4 × 4 lines)
Line length	4 bytes
Address tag	17 bits × 2,048
Method	Direct mapping 2-way set associative
Refresh algorithm	LRU (Least Recently Used)
Main memory update	Write through

(b) Cache memory (T9490) circuit

The dedicated LSI (T9490) used as the cache memory of the TX1 model system is briefly explained here. The T9490 is a cache memory LSI developed for use with the Intel 80386 microprocessor. It has 32K-byte memory, address tag, comparator, and cache memory control circuits integrated on a single chip. The cache size can be expanded up to 128K bytes by using two- or four-piece combinations of this LSI, and a 2-way set associative cache system can be easily configured. Table 6 summarizes the features of the T9490.

Fig. 7 shows a cache system block diagram in the TX1 model computer. The cache section uses four T9490 chips to configure a 128K bytes, 2-way set associative system. The cache control circuit updates main memory and cache memory according to cache hits or misses. The main memory consists of 72 4M-bit DRAM chips (including parity bits) to provide 32M bytes of memory capacity. Caching is enabled only when the TX1 accesses the

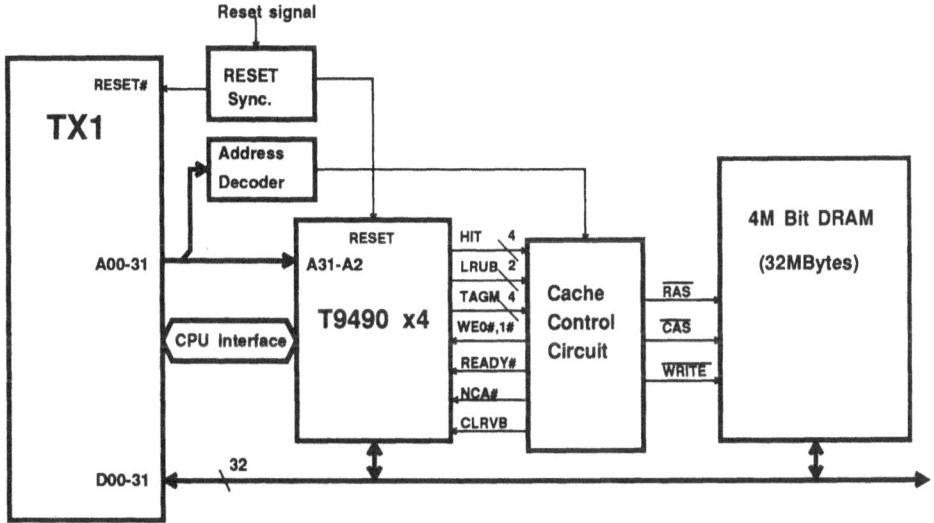

Fig. 7 Cache System Block Diagram

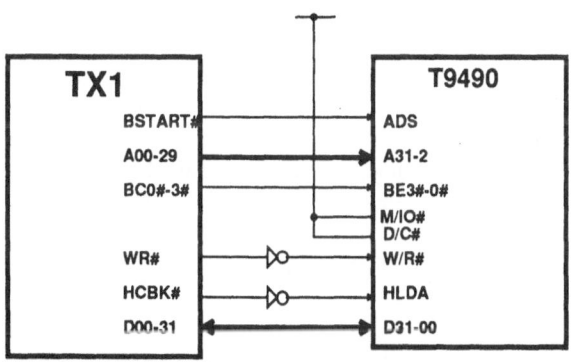

Fig. 8 Interface for TX1 and T9490

DRAM area. In addition, this system supports programmable cache enable/disable mode and allows the entire cache to be purged. Fig. 8 shows a CPU interface for the TX1 and T9490.

When the required data is stored in the cache (a hit), the read cycle can be terminated with 0 wait states by generating the bus cycle terminate signals DSIZK0#-1# from the HIT signal output by the T9490. On the other hand, if the data is not stored in the cache (a miss), 3 wait states are inserted in the bus cycle because DRAM must be accessed. Because a write-through method is used in the write cycle, data is written to DRAM regardless of a cache hit or miss.

4. Performance Evaluation with Actual System

We now show the results of performance evaluations in actual systems as described in Section 3. For this evaluation, we executed such typical benchmark programs as Dhrystone[8] and Stanford[9] and measured the time required for the execution. Note that in running the Stanford benchmark program for our evaluations, we only used the Integer benchmark portion, and not the Floating Point benchmark.

We measured the performance of the VME board computer with the 0 wait memory system. Performance with this system is the highest one that can be achieved by the TX1.

For the model computer, we evaluated performance with and without a cache memory. When the cache is used, two cycles are required for a read when caching is hit (0 wait); five cycles are required when caching is missed (3 wait). On the other hand, five cycles are required for a write regardless of cache hit or miss because a write-through cache is used. When the cache is not used, five cycles are required for both read and write because DRAM is accessed for all memory references.

Table 7 lists the results of the Dhrystone benchmark evaluation and Table 8 lists the results of the Stanford Integer benchmark evaluation.

The results of two benchmark evaluations show the same tendencies. A 3 wait memory system shows approximately half the performance of a 0 wait memory system. DRAM with an access time of 100ns requires 3 wait states to be inserted in the memory cycle. Therefore, if the main memory is configured entirely with DRAM, only half the highest performance of the TX1 can be achieved. On the other hand, when the cache is used, approximately 90% the performance of a 0 wait system can be obtained, demonstrating that the cache is very effective for improving performance. The capacity of the cache used in the model computer is 128K bytes, which is large enough to load the entire benchmark program (Dhrystone or Stanford) executed for our evaluations. We assume that the cache hit rates with the benchmark programs are rather high if compared to those we can expect in case of executing actual applications. We feel it necessary to evaluate performance by using actual application programs in the future.

Table 7 Results of Dhrystone(Ver.1.1) Benchmark

Number of memory waits	Dhrystone / Sec.	Performance ratio
0	10286	1
Cache operation (read hit 0/miss 3, write 3)	8908	0.87
3	5714	0.56

Table 8 Results of Stanford Integer Benchmark

Number of memory waits	Execution time(Sec.)	Performance ratio
0	3.11	1
Cache operation (read hit 0/miss 3, write 3)	3.31	0.94
3	5.44	0.57

5. Conclusion

The features of the TX1 family LSIs have been outlined above. The 32-bit MPU TX1, clock generator (CG), interrupt controller/timer (ICT), and DMA controller (DMAC) in the TX1 family are all designed to enable high-performance, high-function microcomputer systems to be easily configured.

We explained the VME board computer and the model computer as two examples of microprocessor systems built by using the TX1 family LSIs. For these systems, we described the actual design of memory systems by using the SRAM memory system and cache memory system as examples. In the last section of this paper, we discussed the relationship between memory access speed (with or without cache memory) and system performance by actually running typical benchmark programs. We found that if the main memory was configured entirely with 3 wait DRAM, we could only obtain about half the performance of a 0 wait memory system. We also found that performance could be improved up to about 90% of a 0 wait memory system by adopting a cache memory. As a result, we clarified that performance was greatly affected by memory speed, and that cache memory was very effective in improving performance.

6. Acknowledgement

The authors would like to thank Dr. Ken Sakamura of University of Tokyo for his many helpful suggestions.

References

[1] K. Namimoto et al.,"TX series Based on TRONCHIP Architecture", TRON Project 1987, Springer-Verlag, pp.291-308.

[2] M. Miyata, H. Kishigami, K. Okamoto, and S. Kamiya,"The TX1 32-bit Microprocessor: Performance Analysis and Debugging Support", IEEE Micro, vol.8, no.2, pp.37-46, April 1988.

[3] T. Tokumaru, E. Masuda, C. Hori, K. Usami, M. Miyata, and J. Iwamura, "Design of a 32-bit Microprocessor, TX1", 1988 Symposium on VLSI Circuits Technical Digest, III-5, August 1988.

[4] J. Iwamura et al., "Implementation and Evaluation of the TRONCHIP Specification for the TX1", TRON Project 1988, Springer-Verlag, pp.285-300.

[5] H. Kishigami et al., "The Effectiveness of TRONCHIP Instructions in the TX1 System", Compcon spring 89, pp.43-47.

[6] K. Sakamura,"TRON VLSI CPU : Concepts and Architecture", TRON Project 1987, Springer-Verlag, pp.199-238.

[7] S. Ishimaru et al., "Development Support System for TX Series", TRON Project 1988, Springer-Verlag, pp.351-361.

[8] R. P. Weicker, "Dhrystone : A Synthetic System Programming Benchmark", Communications of the ACM, vol.27, no.10, October, 1984, pp.1013-1030.

[9] B. A. Naused et al., "A 32-Bit 200MHz GaAs RISC", IEEE MICRO, December, 1987.

Takashi Miyamori: He is a researcher of VLSI design in the department of Advanced Microprocessor Development at the Semiconductor Device Engineering Laboratory(SDEL) of Toshiba. He received his BS and MS degrees in electronics engineering from Keio University in 1985 and 1987. Since joining the department, he has been engaged in research and development of 32-bit microprocessor and peripheral LSIs. He is a member of the information Processing Society of Japan.

Toshiya Yoshida: He is a researcher in the same laboratory. After he received his BS in electrical engineering from Meiji University in 1984, he joined the computer design division of Toshiba Corporation. Now, he engages in development and design of application hardware system of 32-bit microprocessor.

Hidechika Kishigami: He is a researcher in the same laboratory. He received his BS and MS degrees in electronics engineering from Kyoto University in 1983 and 1985, respectively. Since joining the department, he has been engaged in research and development of 32-bit microprocessor design. His current interests include performance analysis of 32-bit microprocessors. He is a member of the information Processing Society of Japan.

Above author may be reached at: Advanced Microprocessor Technology, Semiconductor Device Engineering Laboratory, 580-1, Horikawa-cho, Saiwaiku, Kawasaki, 210 Japan.

Implementation and Performance Evaluation of the M32/100

Jun-ichi Hinata, Toyohiko Yoshida, Yuichi Saito,
Akira Ohtsuka, Toru Shimizu, and Osamu Tomisawa
Mitsubishi Electric Corporation

ABSTRACT

A high performance 32-bit microprocessor M32/100 has been developed. The M32/100 is a microprocessor based on the TRON specification for real addressing memory systems. The chip was fabricated in 1.0 micron CMOS technology containing over 340k transistors. In order to achieve high performance, a five-stage pipeline and an advanced pre-jump mechanism were adopted. The performance was evaluated by a single board computer. The results of the Dhrystone 1.1 benchmark showed 16K Dhrystones/second at 25 MHz clock rate.

Keywords: M32/100, Microprocessors, Core processor, Pipelining, Pre-jump, Branch prediction

1. INTRODUCTION

The M32/100 is one of the 32-bit GMICRO family microprocessors based on the TRON architecture specification [1]. The applications of this chip will include embedded system controllers, small personal workstations, and core processors for an ASIC (application specific IC). These applications require less expensive microprocessors with high performance. One of the design goals is to realize a small die size. Another goal is to achieve high performance. Instruction pipelining has become a widely used technique for microprocessor design. The M32/100 uses advanced technology, called "pre-jump mechanism", in conjunction with the instruction pipelining. This paper describes the implementation of the chip focussing on the pipeline structure and the pre-jump mechanism and also reports the performance evaluation.

2. OUTLINE OF THE M32/100

Table 1 shows the architectural features of the M32/100 [2][3]. The chip supports 92 instructions including many high-level instructions to support efficient execution of high-level languages and has a rich set of addressing modes. The M32/100 provides powerful bit-map manipulation instructions [4]. The bit-map instructions are useful for bit-map display control. The chip supports both options /F (processing forward) and /B (processing backward) of variable-length bit-field manipulation instructions. The M32/100 features high speed bit-map operations. BVCPY instruction has a function of bit-map transfer. The transfer rate of the BVCPY instruction is maximum 200 Mbit/second at 25 MHz clock rate. BVMAP instruction provides bit-map operations having sixteen logical functions. The chip also achieves 133 Mbit/second operation rate of the BVMAP instruction. Although the chip does not provide either a virtual memory environment or a co-processor interface, the compact design allows the M32/100 to be used for a core processor of an ASIC.

It is important to reduce debugging time in program development. The M32/100 provides useful on-chip system debug capabilities. The chip has five system debug registers as shown in figure 1. The first register DBC contains debug control and status information. The other four registers store the required break point addresses. XBP0 and XBP1 are for execution break. OBP0 and OBP1 are for operand break. The chip provides a single-step instruction operation on trace mode. These capabilities enable application programmers to debug systems without in-circuit emulators.

Table 1 Architectural features of M32/100

General purpose registers	16 (32-bit)
Number of instructions	92 instructions
Addressing mode	14 types (general format)
	12 types (short format)
Data types	bit, bit field, integer, string, and queue
Addressing space	4G bytes

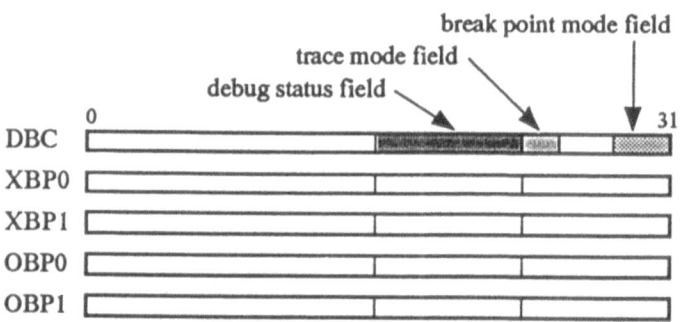

Fig. 1 System debug registers

3. IMPLEMENTATION

3.1 PIPELINING

The M32/100 uses a five-stage pipeline for instruction execution. As illustrated in figure 2, the pipeline scheme consists of IF (instruction fetch) stage, D (instruction decode) stage, A (operand address generation) stage, OF (operand fetch) stage and E (execution) stage. Each stage performs one operation during two clock cycles. The effective execution rate of basic instructions is two clock cycles per instruction so that the chip's peak throughput is 12.5 MIPS (million instructions per second) at 25 MHz clock rate.

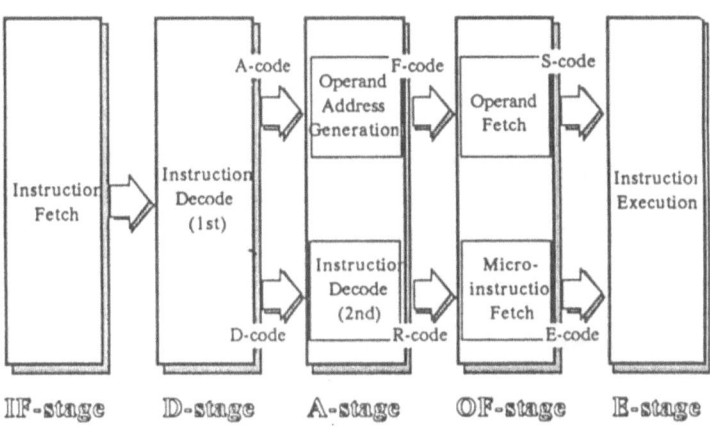

Fig. 2 Pipeline scheme

IF stage: The IF stage contains a instruction queue (16 bytes) and a branch buffer (256 bytes). The branch buffer is a special purpose instruction cache with a direct-mapping scheme. When the queue holds no instructions, the branch buffer stores the instructions fetched from an external memory. For example, when the queue is flushed, caused by a jump instruction, the branch buffer caches the instruction called by the jump instruction. The branch buffer is also available to be used for a general cache memory. The IF stage fetches instructions from the external memory or the branch buffer, and stores the instructions to the instruction queue. An instruction is sent to the D stage via the instruction queue.

D stage: The D stage decodes an operation code of the instruction into a control code (D-code) which specifies operation. Using an address offset and addressing mode in the instruction, an operand address code (A-code) is generated and is sent to the A stage. When two operands must be fetched from memory for a memory-to-memory instruction, the D stage sends A-code twice.

A stage: In the A stage, two processings which are the operand address generation and the second decoding of the instruction are performed in parallel. An operand address is generated from the A-code and is sent to the next OF stage as a F-code. The D-code sent from the D stage is decoded for obtaining a microprogram address (R-code). The R-code presents the entry address of the microprogram.

OF stage: The OF stage fetches operand data specified by the operand address (F-code). The OF stage also fetches a micro-instruction from a ROM which stores the microprogram. If the instruction requires some micro-instruction steps to complete the instruction, the micro-instruction fetching is repeated.

E stage: The execution stage (E stage) includes a 4-byte store buffer. The E stage is controlled by the microprogram. Instructions are executed in one or more steps. The result is written into the external memory via the store buffer. Therefore, the E stage can perform the following execution without completion of it's memory write cycle.

3.2 PRE-JUMP MECHANISM

In addition to the pipeline scheme, advanced pre-jump mechanism was applied to minimize the penalties related with jump instructions. Pipelining increases performance by executing multiple instructions in parallel. Generally, however, jump instructions work against performance increase. When a jump instruction is executed at execution stage of pipelining, an instruction stream on pipe should be flushed. A new instruction stream is fetched. Performance degradation may result from the jump instructions. In order to reduce the performance degradation caused by the jump instructions, the chip utilizes the pre-jump mechanism. The pre-jump mechanism of the M32/100 is built into the decode stage of the pipeline. This mechanism works effectively for seven kinds of jump instructions as shown in Table 2. There are two types of pre-jump processings: pre-branch processing for branch instructions and pre-return processing for return instructions from subroutines.

(a)Pre-branch processing

The pre-branch processing for BRA (branch) and BSR (branch to subroutine) instructions is simple. When these instructions are decoded at the D stage, pre-branch is always taken. While with a conditional branch instruction (Bcc), dynamic branch prediction mechanism is used, and pre-branch is taken in accordance with a branch history. The M32/100 contains a branch prediction table for the

Table 2 Pre-jump instructions

instructions	pre-jump processing	
BRA BSR	taken always	
ACB SCB	taken always	pre-branch
Bcc	taken based on prediction table	
RTS EXITD	taken always	pre-return

pre-branch processing of Bcc instruction. This branch prediction table is constructed by 1-bit x 256 entry direct mapped configuration. A prediction, whether the Bcc instruction will take or not, is made based on the history of the most recently executed branch instruction.

Figure 3 shows the pre-branch mechanism. If pre-branch is detected, the branch address is calculated by adding the branch displacement to the PC (program counter) value using the PC adder in the D stage. And the following instruction's address is also calculated by adding the instruction length to the PC value using the Address adder in the A stage for a miss of branch prediction. When branch is taken with Bcc instruction in the E stage, the bit of the branch prediction table specified by the 8 bits, from bit 23 to bit 30, of the preceding instruction's address (PC) is set. After that, when Bcc instruction is arrived in the D stage, branch prediction table is checked by the preceding instruction's address (PC). If the bit of specified address is set, pre-branch is taken.

ACB (add, compare and branch) and SCB (subtract, compare and branch) instructions are always predicted to branch. Since these instructions are for loop sequence controls, they have a high probability of branch. M32/100 always executes the pre-branch processing for these instructions.

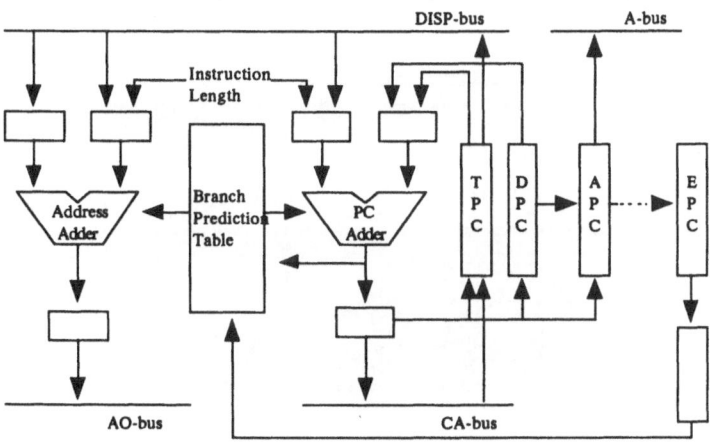

Fig. 3 Pre-branch mechanism

(b)Pre-return processing

For return from subroutine instructions, RTS and EXITD instructions, M32/100 takes pre-returns at the D stage using a on-chip PC-stack memory. The PC-stack is the stack memory consisting of 32-bit x 8 entry configuration. The return address of these instructions depends on the call instruction which calls the subroutine. Consequently, above mentioned methodology of using the branch history is not effective. An instruction which calls a subroutine, such as BSR instruction, saves the address of the next instruction to the stack on memory. M32/100 stores it not only to the main memory but to the on-chip PC-stack. That is, M32/100 holds the copy of the return address in the PC-stack.

When RTS instruction is decoded, the on-chip PC-stack is popped up to obtain the return address (PC1) and the pre-return is performed. In detail, the chip prefetchs the instruction specified by the address obtained from the PC-stack. At the operand fetch stage, the return address (PC2) is fetched from the memory by popping the external stack. The value of PC1 is compared with the value of PC2 at the execution stage. If the both values are equal, the pre-return is successful and the jump processing is not required at the execution stage. If not, the jump processing is performed. As the results, the instruction stream on the pipeline is flushed and new instruction specified by PC2 is fetched.

3.3 CHIP DESIGN

Photo 1 shows a photomicrograph of the M32/100. The chip is organized into three major strips. The upper strip contains the instruction fetch unit, the instruction decode unit, and the microprogram ROM. The middle strip contains the control logic. The lower strip contains the 32-bit datapath with 32-bit ALU. 32-bit barrel shifter, and the bus interface unit. The bus interface unit interfaces the M32/100 to the external system bus and controls address, data and control signals to and from the chip. The bus interface unit is located in two separated sections. One is for address and the other is for data.

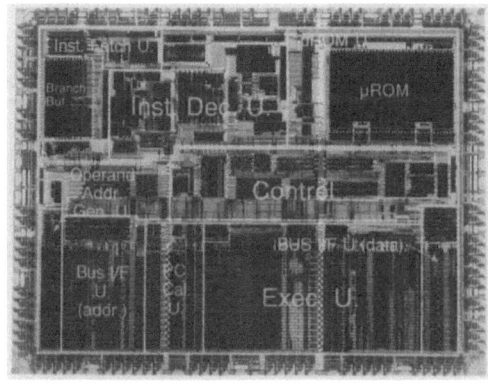

Photo 1 Photomicrograph of M32/100

The characteristics of the M32/100 are summarized in Table 3. The chip was fabricated in 1.0 micron double-level metal CMOS process technology. The chip contains over 340k transistors on 11.47 x 8.89 square millimeters die size. The chip was mainly laid out by hand-craft design method. Most of the control logics were designed by standard cell approach. These standard cells were placed and routed automatically. The chip is housed in a 135-pin pin grid array (PGA). The power dissipation of the chip is less than 1.5 watts under worst-case condition at 25 MHz rate. Therefore, a quad flat packaged device (QFP) will be available.

Table 3 M32/100 characteristics

Operating frequency	20 MHz / 25 MHz
Performance	max. 12.5 MIPS (at 25 MHz)
	ave. 8 MIPS (at 25 MHz)
Address bus / data bus	32 bits (separated)
Min. bus cycle	2 clocks
Number of transistor	340k
Pipeline	5 stages
Buffer memory	
instruction queue	16 bytes
branch buffer	4-byte x 64 entry
store buffer	4 bytes
Branch prediction table	1-bit x 256 entry
Process	1.0μm, double-level metal CMOS
Die size	11.47 x 8.89 mm^2
Package	135-pin PGA
	135-pin QFP (under development)
Power dissipation	max. 1.5W

4. PERFORMANCE EVALUATION

There are many benchmarks for evaluating the microprocessor performance. Dhrystone is one of the benchmark programs and is widely used. The fabricated M32/100 operated on a single board computer at 25 MHz clock rate. The chip performance was evaluated by the single board computer using Dhrystone version 1.1 program written in C language [5]. The results of the Dhrystone 1.1 benchmark showed 16K Dhrystones per second at 25 MHz clock rate with no wait state access. Based on the results, the average performance of the M32/100 is rated at 8 MIPS. Figure 4 shows the chip performance as a function of the memory wait and clock rate. A low-end computer system often uses a slow speed memory system. In the case of one wait state access at 25 MHz, benchmarks of 12k Dhrystones/second was measured.

The effects of the dynamic branch prediction mechanism was measured by the single board computer using the benchmark programs. The experimental results are shown in Table 4. The performance are normalized by the case of which the branch prediction is off mode and the branch buffer is set on standard chache mode. The performance improvement of 30 percent has been achieved by Sieve benchmark with the branch prediction. While, the Dhrystone benchmark did not show significant improvement.

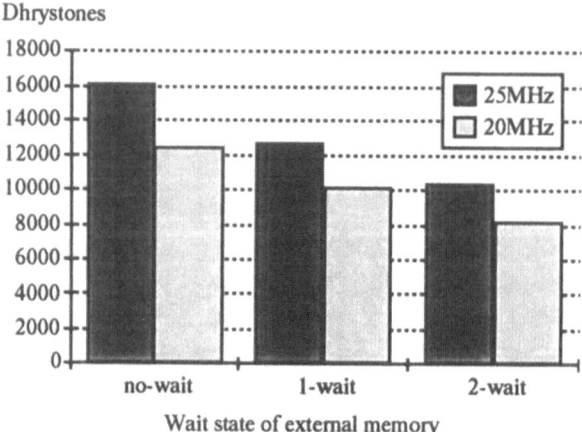

Fig. 4 Dhrystone benchmark results

Table 4 Efect of dynamic branch prediction

	Relative performance	
	without Branch Prediction	with Branch Prediction
Sieve	1.00	1.30
Quicksort	1.00	1.01
Dhrystone	1.00	1.00

5. CONCLUSION

The M32/100 was designed to provide high performance by using the pipeline scheme and the pre-jump mechanism. The chip, running on the board computer at 25 MHz clock rate, achieved 16k Dhrystones/second. The chip containing over 340k transistors was implemented in the effective die size to be used as the core processor for system integration of applications based on TRON architecture.

ACKNOWLEDGMENTS

The authors gratefully acknowledge associate professor Ken Sakamura for helpful discussions and the GMICRO members of Hitachi Ltd. and Fujitsu Ltd. for their useful comments.

REFERENCES

[1]   K. Sakamura,:"TRON VLSI CPU:Concepts and Architecture", TRON Project 1987, Springer-Verlag, pp.199-238, 1987.

[2]   O. Tomisawa,et al,: "Design Considerations of the GMICRO/100", Proceedings of the Third TRON Project Symposium, pp.249-258, November, 1987

[3]   T. Shimizu,et al,:"A 32-bit Microprocessor Based on the TRON Architecture Design of the GMICRO/100", COMPCON Spring 1988, pp.30-33

[4]   T. Shimizu,et al,:"A 32-Bit Microprocessor with High Performance Bit-map Manipulation Instructions", Proceedings of ICCD '89, October, 1989, pp.406-409

[5]   A. Ohtsuka,et al,:"The bus-interface in M32/100", Technical papers of 3rd TRON Technical Study Group Meeting, Vol.2, No.2, pp.11-25, 1989 (in Japanese)

[6]   T. Yoshida,et al,:"32-bit MPU GMICRO/100 improving pipeline efficiency by pre-jump scheme", Nikkei Electronics, No.477, pp.185-196, 1989 (in Japanese)

Jun-ichi Hinata : He is a assistant manager of advanced microprocessor group in advanced microprocessor development department at LSI research and development laboratory. He joined Mitsubishi Electric Corporation in 1974. Since then, he has been engaged in the design of small computers, the development of VLSI custom processors and a 32-bit microprocessor. He received his B.E. degree in electrical engineering from Hokkaido University, Sapporo, Japan, in 1974. He is a member of the Information Processing Society of Japan.

Toyohiko Yoshida : He is a researcher of advanced microprocessor development group at LSI Research and Development laboratory. He joined Mitsubishi Electric Corporation in 1983. Since then, he has been engaged in the design of 32-bit microprocessors. He received his B.E. and M.E. degrees, both in electronics engineering from Kyoto University, Kyoto, Japan in 1981 and 1983 respectively. Mr. Yoshida is a member of IEEE and the Institute of Electronics, Information and Communication Engineering of Japan.

Yuichi Saito : He is a researcher of advanced microprocessor group in advanced microprocessor development department at LSI research and development laboratory. He joined Mitsubishi Electric Corporation in 1982. He has been engaged in the design of a 16-bit microcontroller and a 32-bit microprocessor. He received his B.E. degree in electrical engineering from Yokohama National University in 1982. Mr. Saito is a member of the Institute of Electronics, Information and Communication Engineers of Japan.

Akira Ohtsuka : He is a researcher of advanced microprocessor group in advanced microprocessor development department at LSI research and development laboratory. He joined Mitsubishi Electric Corporation in 1983. Since then, he has been engaged in the research of 32-bit microprocessor. He received his B.E. and M.E. degrees in electrical engineering from Tokyo university of agriculture and technology, Tokyo, Japan, in 1981 and 1983, respectively. He is a member of IEEE and the Institute of Electronics, Information and Communication Engineering of Japan.

Toru Shimizu : He received his B.S., M.S. and Ph.D. degrees both in computer science, from University of Tokyo, Tokyo, Japan, in 1981, 1983, and 1986, respectively. He joined Mitsubishi Electric Corporation in 1986. Since then, he has been engaged in the research of VLSI microprocessor architecture and basic software for the microprocessor at LSI Research and Development Laboratory. Dr. Shimizu is a member of ACM, IEEE, the Institute of Electronics, Information and Communication Engineers of Japan, and Information Processing Society of Japan.

Osamu Tomisawa : He received the B.S. and M.S. degrees in electric Engineering from Kyoto University,Kyoto, Japan, in 1969 and 1971, respectively. He received Ph.D degree in electrical engineering in 1980 from Osaka University, Osaka, Japan. He joined Mitsubishi Electric Corporation in 1971, Since then he has been working on logic LSI/VLSI design. In 1980, he stayed one year at University of California, Berkeley as a visiting scholar, where he was involved in the research of VLSI computer architecture. He is currently a manager of Advanced Microprocessor Group in LSI Research and Development Laboratory, Mitsubishi Electric Corp. Dr. Tomisawa is a member of IEEE and the Institute of Electronics, Information and Communication Engineers of Japan.

Above authors may be reached at : Advanced Microprocessor Development Department, LSI Research and Development Laboratory, Mitsubishi Electric Corporation, 4-1, Mizuhara, Itami, Hyogo, 664 Japan

Generation and Debugging of Optimized Code for the TRON Architecture

Durga Agarwal and Fu-Hwa Wang
Microtec® Research, Inc.

Manoochehr Ghiassi
Department of Decision and Information Sciences
Santa Clara University

ABSTRACT

Microtec Research, Inc. (MRI) has developed an integrated set of software tools to support both the fast generation of highly optimized code and subsequent high-level/low-level debugging of this code for embedded and native UNIX® applications. This paper discusses the global and TRON architecture-specific optimization techniques used to produce this highly space/time efficient object code. The use of optimization information to provide source-level debugging of optimized code is also discussed.

Keywords: Compiler optimization, debugging, TRON architecture, GMICRO, TX1

1. INTRODUCTION

Since the early part of 1987, Microtec Research, Inc. has been developing toolkits for two members of the TRON family: the GMICRO and the TX series of microprocessors. Currently, these toolkits include an ANSI C optimizing compiler, assembler, linker, object librarian, simulator, and the high-level/low-level XRAY debugger™ for the GMICRO/100/200/300 and the Toshiba TX1 microprocessors. These toolkits are now available for the VAX™/ULTRIX™, VAX/VMS™, IBM®-PC/MS-DOS™, and Sun™/UNIX computer systems. Figure 1 shows the GMICRO/200 toolkit and how its components communicate with each other (Bigazzi 1988).

This paper discusses the technology used to develop the ANSI C optimizing compiler and emphasizes:

- the optimization techniques used to achieve the highest performance from the execution of high-level application programs
- the use of additional debugging information generated by the compiler to allow debugging of optimized code with the powerful XRAY source-level debugger.

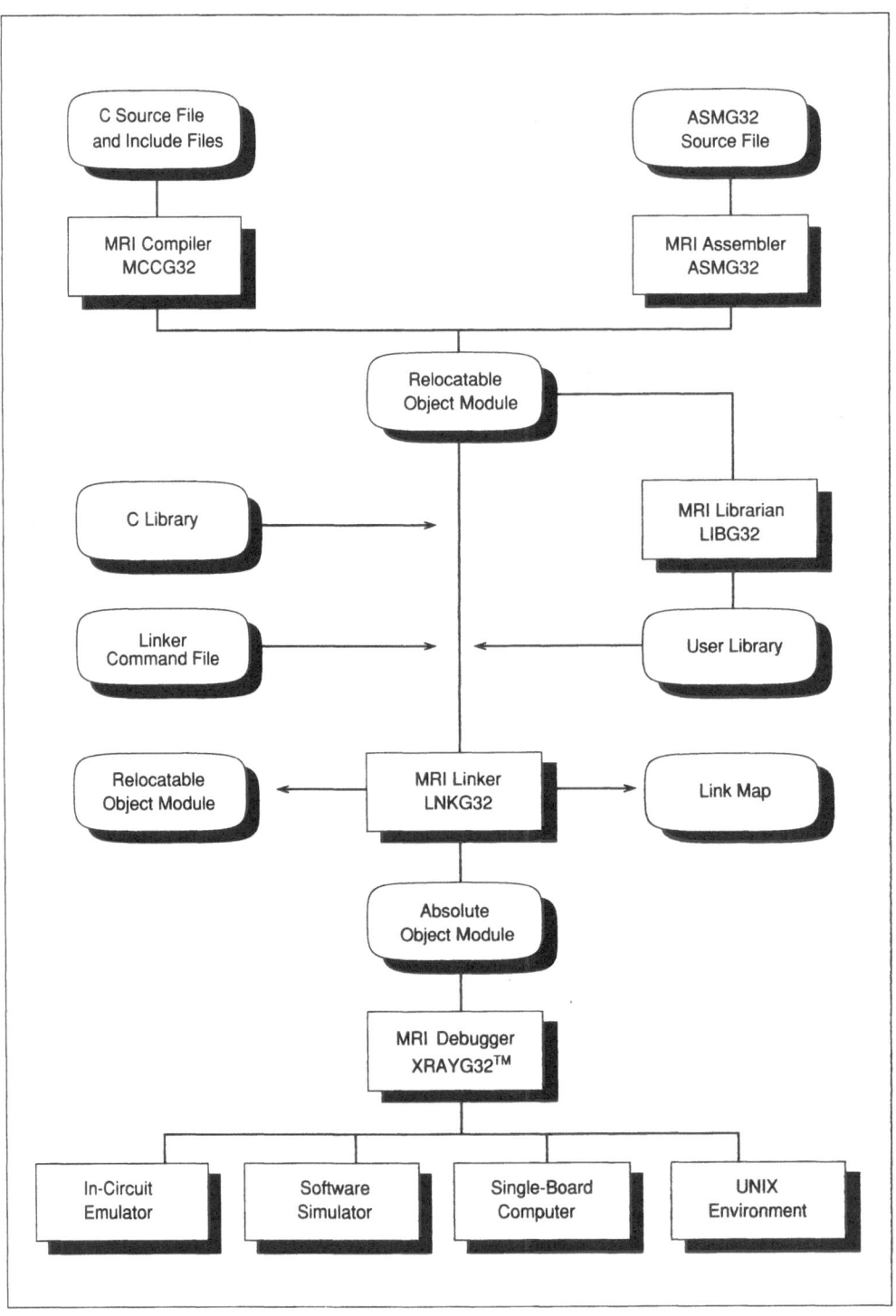

Fig. 1 Microtec Research GMICRO/200 Toolkit

The ANSI C optimizing compiler is a full implementation of the ANSI (American National Standard for Information Systems) proposed standard for the C programming language (ANSI 1988). MRI's ANSI C optimizing compiler provides features that are targeted toward embedded application programs such as the generation of ROMable code, re-entrant code, position independent code, in-line assembly, and interrupt handlers. These features give the embedded applications programmer flexibility and complete control over the object programs for the intended target.

Additionally, the C compiler produces compact and efficient code by taking advantage of several features of the TRON . architecture that facilitate high-level programming language implementation. The orthogonal design of the TRON instruction set, for example, lets efficient code be generated because every addressing mode can be used with every opcode. By combining the power of a globally optimizing compiler with the strength of the TRON architecture, an efficient development environment is produced. In this environment, the powerful XRAY debugger/simulator gives debugging support both at the high-level and the assembly-level.

The optimizing compiler, which is one of the focuses of this paper, is designed to reduce compile time, produce compact code, maintain portability across several hosts, and to tune the compiler to the TRON architecture for the highest performance. To achieve these goals, many optimization techniques were implemented. These optimization techniques are discussed in the following sections.

Note, however, that optimized code can be vastly different in organization although not in functionality from the original source program. Debugging such code becomes at best a difficult task. MRI compilers have been extended to provide additional debugging information so that it is possible to debug optimized code. This concept, the debugging of optimized code, is the second focus of this paper and is discussed in section 4.

2. OPTIMIZING COMPILERS

Most compilers make two passes through the source program. During the first pass, called the front end, the compiler reads in the program, verifies the code for syntactic and semantic correctness and, if successful, translates the source code into an intermediate language. During the second pass, the compiler takes the intermediate representation as input and produces machine code. The optimizing compiler also provides an optimization stage that generates more compact and/or faster code. Both the optimizer and the code generator use a binary tree representation of the program for optimization. Specifically, the MRI C optimizing compiler is partitioned into five components: the driver, the C preprocessor, the C language front end, the global optimizer, and the code generator (back end). The driver parses and interprets the command line; the C preprocessor is an implementation of the ANSI C preprocessor; the C language front end performs the syntactical and semantical analysis; the global optimizer performs language and machine-independent optimizations; and the code generator or back end translates the intermediate language into TRON (GMICRO or TX) assembly language and performs many local and machine-dependent optimizations.

3. MRI OPTIMIZATIONS

The MRI ANSI C optimizing compiler uses state-of-the-art optimization techniques to improve code density and code execution. The optimization techniques used are shown in Table 1.

Table 1 MRI Optimizations

Local and Global Optimizations	Code Generator and TRON Architecture-Specific Optimizations
Register allocation	Instruction scheduling
Loop invariant code motion	Dead code elimination
Common subexpression elimination	Chained addressing
Local/global constant propagation	Jump optimization
Local/global copy propagation	Loop by ACB and SCB instruction
Strength reduction	Loop rotation
Index simplification	Redundant load and store elimination
Dead block elimination	In-line run-time functions
Unused definition elimination	Switch statement optimization
	Function prologue and epilogue
	Group stack adjustment
	String operation instructions

To demonstrate the effect of these optimizations, several benchmark programs were executed on a Sun 3/50 host computer using the GMICRO toolkit. Tables 2 and 3 show the results when the code is optimized for speed and space, respectively. Execution speed improved from 5% to 228%, and code sizes as a result of space optimizations were 5% to 29% smaller than the non-optimized versions. These benchmarks were executed using the XRAYG32 Simulator.

These optimizations techniques are discussed in more detail in sections 3.1 and 3.2.

Table 2 Speed Benchmarks for the Optimizing Compiler (Speed/Cycles)

Benchmark Program	No Opt.	With Opt.	% Change
Ackerman	4810	4534	6
BenchE	38689	28839	34
Bubble	361279	290048	25
Matrix	167295	51001	228
Puzzle	34922039	22641875	54
Qsort	84254	79744	6
Queen	824794	784596	5

Table 3 Size Benchmarks for the Optimizing Compiler (Size/Bytes)

Benchmark Program	No Opt.	With Opt.	% Change
Bubble	292	268	9
Dhrystone	1294	1186	9
Fibonacci	82	76	8
Hanoi	806	640	26
Matrix	274	212	29
Permutation	262	242	8
Stanford	6482	6154	5

3.1 Local and Global Optimizations

The optimization process can be viewed as a multi-step process with each step performing a certain type of optimization. In the first step, the compiler reads the intermediate representation of the program produced by the compiler front end and partitions it into "basic blocks". A basic block is defined as a sequence of consecutive program statements which may be entered and executed in sequence without a halt or the possibility of a branch except at the end of the basic block. No program branch may enter the block except through its first statement. Local optimization techniques are a class of optimization techniques performed within a basic block.

Global optimization techniques are implemented by constructing the program "flow graph". A program is partitioned into basic blocks. Each basic block is considered to be a "node" in the flow graph. The branches in the graph represent the interrelations among the basic blocks. Therefore, the existence of an arrow or branch between two nodes implies a possible flow of information between the two nodes. Global optimizations occur between and within basic blocks. The global optimizer establishes the flow graph for each function and analyzes it during the compilation process. This analysis uses both "control flow" and "data flow" analysis techniques to achieve its goals. Control flow analysis traces the many patterns of possible execution paths in a program, and data flow analysis provides traces of possible "definitions" and "uses" of data in the program. It is during the construction and analysis of the flow graph that additional optimization opportunities may be discovered. These optimization opportunities and the flow of information concepts will be discussed later.

3.1.1 Definitions and Terminologies

Before discussing the local and global optimization techniques used in this paper, the following definitions and terminologies are presented first (Aho 1985, Fischer 1988):

Dominance In a flow graph, a node B1 dominates node B2, if every path from the initial node of the flow graph that reaches B2 also goes through node B1.

Precedence If there is a conditional or unconditional jump from basic block B1 to basic block B2, then B1 is a predecessor of B2, or B2 is a successor of B1.

Live Variable Given variable x at a point p in a basic block, if the value of variable x could be used along some path from p, then variable x is alive at p; otherwise, it is dead at p.

Use and Definition The use of a variable x occurs when a statement explicitly or implicitly references variable x. A definition of a variable x is a statement that assigns, or may assign, a value to variable x.

Depth-First Ordering (DFO) DFO is a particular ordering of the basic blocks that speeds up the iterative data flow algorithm used by the global optimizer. It provides additional information that lets the global optimizer detect loops and dead blocks as well. The DFO is created by starting at a function entry and searching all the basic blocks. It tries to visit blocks as far away (depth first) from the function entry as possible.

The global optimizer uses data flow and control flow information and the concepts just introduced to perform several optimizations. For example, the live-variable analysis is used for register coloring and unused definition elimination, and the use-definition analysis is used for loop optimization, common subexpression elimination, and constant and copy propagation.

3.1.2 Steps in the Global Optimization Process

The global optimizer partitions a program into functions and performs optimizations using the concepts introduced in the previous section. These optimizations are performed as follows:

1. The input to the global optimizer is the symbol table information and the tree representation for each function.

2. The global optimizer partitions this tree into a linked list that consists of basic blocks. Each basic block may contain a number of subtrees.

3. A special linked list (DFO) of basic blocks is constructed and, by using this order, the global optimizer collects all the necessary control flow and data flow information for each function.

4. The optimizer then builds the control flow information for each basic block (for example, the predecessors, successors, and dominators).

5. The local data flow information is collected for each basic block. This information includes the definition, use, use-definition, live-variables, and conflict graph.

6. The optimizer propagates the local data flow information for each basic block to its successors and predecessors.

7. The optimizer performs common subexpression elimination (CSE) and loop optimizations which could generate temporary variables.

8. The optimizer allocates registers to local and temporary variables using the register coloring algorithm described in section 3.1.3.

9. Local/global copy propagation, local/global constant propagation, and unused definition elimination optimizations are performed.

10. The optimized trees are passed to the code generator for additional code generator and TRON architecture-specific optimizations as well as code generation.

Several examples follow that show how the optimizer performs some of the optimization techniques described earlier.

3.1.3 Register Allocation by Priority-Based Coloring Algorithm

The optimizer uses register coloring algorithms and graph reducibility concepts to perform its optimization. The basic algorithm for this optimization was designed using the concepts described by Chaitin (1981, 1982), Chow (1983, 1984), and Sites (1979). Basically, the algorithm creates a "conflict graph". A conflict graph is constructed by assigning nodes to every local or temporary variable that is a candidate for a register. Two nodes are connected by an arc if and only if the corresponding variables are alive simultaneously at any point in the program. Since two nodes (variables) cannot be allocated to the same register, mapping of the registers is made through a map coloring assignment. In this assignment, each color is represented by a register, and no two nodes in the conflict graph having a common link can have the same color (register). When a conflict graph needs more colors (registers) than there are available colors (registers), the registers must be "spilled".

The global optimizer register allocation includes enhancements for computing priorities. The priority weight is assigned to a variable based on the frequency with which that variable is referenced. A penalty function for not allocating a register to a variable is also used as a weight in some cases.

For example, consider Figure 2a which shows a source program and execution points within the program. Execution points refer to and are numbered according to the order in which the expressions are executed. Without optimization, variables i1, i2, and i3 require three registers during program execution. However, with optimization, the optimizer uses the live-variable information shown in Figure 2b and the conflict graph to serialize register requirements. In this example, only one register is required for program execution because the lifetimes of these three variables never overlap.

3.1.4 Loop Optimizations

The global optimizer detects natural loops using the following control flow information.

For a basic block B1 and its successor B2, if B2 dominates B1, then:

1. B1 and B2 form a loop.

2. B2 is the beginning, and B1 is the end of the loop.

3. All the blocks between B2 and B1 are also part of the loop.

The global optimizer uses the collected data flow information to perform loop invariant code motion, strength reduction, and index simplification optimizations. Expressions inside the detected loops are examined for the following:

1. An invariant variable. A variable x is invariant (i.e., does not change) if all the definitions reaching the use of x are outside the loop.

2. An invariant expression. An expression is invariant if all the operands in the expression are either invariant variables, constants, or invariant expressions.

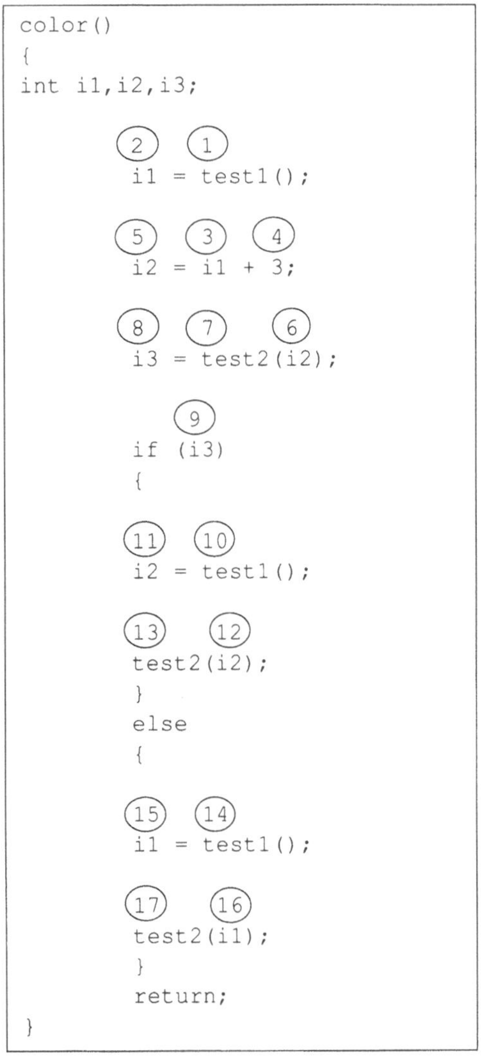

```
color()
{
int i1,i2,i3;

      (2)  (1)
      i1 = test1();

   (5)  (3)  (4)
   i2 = i1 + 3;

   (8)  (7)  (6)
   i3 = test2(i2);

         (9)
   if (i3)
   {

   (11) (10)
   i2 = test1();

   (13) (12)
   test2(i2);
   }
   else
   {

   (15) (14)
   i1 = test1();

   (17) (16)
   test2(i1);
   }
   return;
}
```

```
                          Variables
                        i1    i2   i3
             Execution
             Point #
   (1)

   (2)
                              |
   (3)

   (4)

   (5)
                                    |
   (6)

   (7)

   (8)
                                         |
   (9)

   (10)

   (11)
                                    |
   (12)

   (13)

   (14)

   (15)
                              |
   (16)

   (17)
```

Fig. 2a Register Coloring Optimization

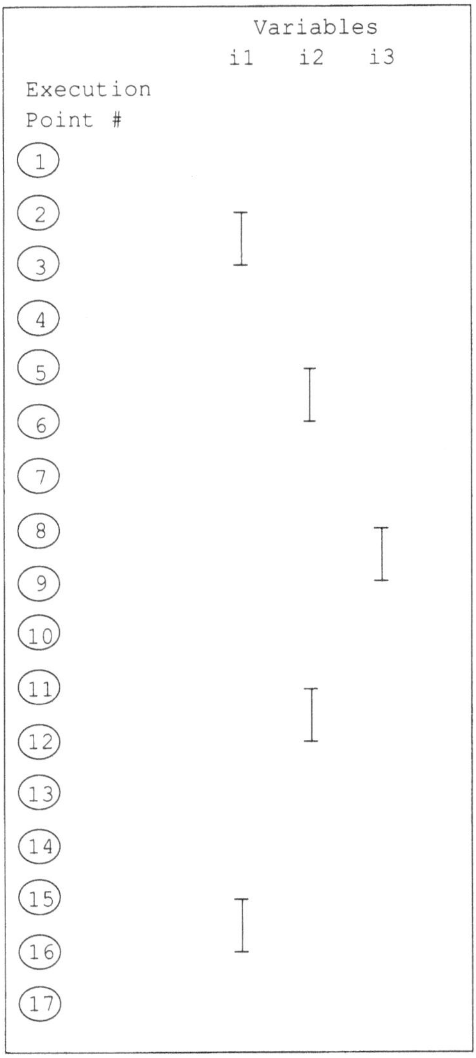

Fig. 2b Live-Variable Analysis for Register Coloring Optimization

3. Induction variables. Induction variables are variables whose values form an arithmetic progression within the loop. These variables are often used to count or index an array.

4. An induction expression. An induction expression is an induction expression if all of its operands are invariant expressions except for one induction variable.

The loop invariant code motion optimization searches loops for expressions which yield the same results regardless of the number of times a loop is executed. Invariant expressions are placed before the loop to save execution cycles inside the loop. With strength reduction and index simplification (induction variable elimination), the optimizer replaces multiplications with additions and eliminates recalculation of array indices for each loop iteration. Figure 3a shows the source code for matrix multiplication. Figure 3b shows the loop-optimized GMICRO assembly code for statement 1 in Figure 3a, and Figure 3c shows the non-optimized version of this code.

The address of c[i][j] (see Figure 3a) is an invariant expression in the innermost loop because i and j are invariant for the innermost loop. The invariant code motion optimization will allocate a temporary variable in r4 (see Figure 3b) for the invariant expression (i.e., the address of c[i][j]). This temporary variable is initialized outside the loop.

The variable k is an induction variable in the innermost loop. It is incremented by 1 for each iteration of the loop. The induction variable elimination optimization first detects two related induction expressions. These expressions are the addresses of a[i][k] and b[k][j]. The optimization allocates two temporary variables in r6 and r7 for the expressions. Before incrementing k, the temporary variable containing the address of a[i][k] is incremented by 4, and the temporary variable containing the address of b[k][j] is incremented by 400.

For example, the Matrix benchmark in Table 2 shows a performance improvement of 228%. This improvement is due mostly to the implementation of loop optimizations.

3.1.5 Local/Global Common Subexpression Elimination

By using hashing, the optimizer recognizes identical expressions. The optimizer uses dominance and use-information to determine if the two identical expressions are common subexpressions. For example, consider:

```
B1:     x+y
        . . .
        . . .
B2:     x+y
```

If block B1 dominates block B2, and the x and y values do not change in between these two blocks, the global optimizer will assign the first x+y to a temporary variable. Reference to the second x+y will be replaced later with the value of the temporary variable.

Note that the register allocation and common subexpression elimination (CSE) optimizations are coordinated to get optimum results. For example, if x and y are already allocated to registers and there are no registers available, CSE is not performed for the two occurrences of x+y. CSE is not performed because the temporary storage required in CSE must be stored at some memory location and recomputation of x+y is cheaper than the "store" and "load" operations.

```
int i,j,k;
int a[100][100],b[100][100],c[100];
for (i=0; i<100; i++)
{
    for (j=0; j<100; j++)
    {
      c[i][j] = 0;
      for (k=0; k<100; k++)
      {
        c[i][j]=c[i][j]+a[i][k]*b[k][j]   ;  statement 1
      }
    }
}
```

Fig. 3a Source Code for Matrix Multiplication

```
B17:
        mov     @(r6),r0  ; r0 contains the value of a[i][k]
        mul     @(r7),r0  ; r0 contains the value of a[i][k]*b[k][j]
        add     r0,@(r4)  ; add a[i][k]*b[k][j] to c[i][j]
        add     #400,r7   ; increment address of b[k][j]
                          ; by 400 every time k increments by 1
        add     #4,r6     ; increment address of a[i][k]
                          ; by 4 every time k increments by 1
        add     #1,r5     ; increment k by 1
        cmp     #100,r5
        blt:d   B17
                          ; total number of cycles
                          ; for each iteration is 46
```

Fig. 3b Loop-Optimized GMICRO Assembly Code for Statement 1

3.1.6 Local/Global Constant and Copy Propagation

By using the dominance and use-definition information, the global optimizer propagates a constant value which has been previously assigned to a variable to all the occurrences of that variable. Similarly, given the assignment x=y, the copy propagation uses y for x whenever possible and gives an opportunity to eliminate the assignment.

3.1.7 Dead Block Elimination

A dead block is a basic block which will never be reached during program execution. The DFO analysis results in identification of dead blocks which will be removed from the trees and thus will not become a part of the data flow analysis.

```
B17:                              ; the following 6 instructions calculate
                                  ; the address of a[i][k].
        mov     r5,r0
        mulu    #H'190,r0
        mova    @(fp,-40000,r0),r0
        mov     r6,r1
        shl     #2,r1
        add     r1,r0
        mov     @(r0),r0    ; r0 contains the value of a[i][k].
                                  ; the following 6 instructions calculate
                                  ; the address of b[k][j].
        mov     r6,r1
        mulu    #H'190,r1
        mova    @(fp,-80000,r1),r1
        mov     r4,r2
        shl     #2,r2
        add     r2,r1
        mul     @(r1),r0    ; r0 contains the value of a[i][k]*b[k][j].
                                  ; the following 6 instructions calculate
                                  ; the address  of c[i][j].
        mov     r5,r1
        mulu    #H'190,r1
        mova    @(fp,-120000,r1),r1
        mov     r4,r2
        shl     #2,r2
        add     r2,r1
        add     r0,@(r1)    ; add a[i][k]*b[k][j] to c[i][j].
        add     #1,r6       ; increment k by 1.
        cmp     #100,r6
        blt:d   B17
                                  ; total number of cycles
                                  ; for each iteration is 150.
```

Fig. 3c   Non-Optimized GMICRO Assembly Code for Statement 1

3.2 Code Generator and TRON Architecture-Specific Optimizations

The TRON architecture is designed with software efficiency as one of its design goals (Sakamura 1987). This architecture provides many features that facilitate the efficient implementation of high level languages. The ANSI C optimizing compiler has been further tuned to take advantage of the GMICRO and TX1 architectural features such as instruction pipelining and the chained addressing mode.

3.2.1 Instruction Scheduling

The TRON architecture allows implementation of the pipelining concept in the design of the TRON-based microprocessors. A pipelined processor is one in which several sequential instructions are simultaneously executed in different stages. One component of an instruction may refer to a value that is computed in an earlier instruction. Because the earlier instruction may still be executing, the value may not be available, and a pipeline interlock occurs.

Instruction scheduling optimization orders instruction execution to avoid interlocks and to fully use the pipelining facilities of the processor. Instruction scheduling was implemented as follows (Gibbons 1986, Hennessy 1983):

1. For each basic block, the optimizer constructs a dependency graph. The dependency graph is a directed acyclic graph with nodes representing instructions and arcs representing resource dependencies. Existence of an arc between nodes x and y indicates that an instruction corresponding to x must be executed prior to the execution of an instruction corresponding to y. This execution order preserves correctness.

2. The instructions are then scheduled to minimize delays in the pipeline.

Figures 4a and 4b show a code sequence and its dependency graph.

For any resource, such as a register, memory, or condition code, the dependency graph serializes:

- definition versus definition (instruction 3 versus instruction 4)
- definition versus use (instruction 6 versus instruction 7)
- use versus definition (instruction 1 versus instruction 2)

For the GMICRO/100 pipeline architecture, address generation conflicts occur between instructions 1 and 2, 6 and 7, 7 and 8, and 8 and 9. Each conflict will cause 4 cycle interlock delays in the pipeline. Address generation conflicts occur when the generation of the effective address of an operand requires a reference to the content of a general register which has been modified by a prior instruction.

The optimizer uses the dependency graph to select instruction ordering using the following rules:

A. A node cannot be selected before all its predecessors have been selected.

B. A node will be selected that will not interlock with the one just selected.

C. A look ahead approach is used to select a node that will interlock with the next node in order to minimize future interlocks.

```
;       st->i = 2;
1       mov       @_st,r0
;                           interlock
2       mov       #2,@(4,r0)
;       e = a+b*a;
3       fmov.d    fr6,fr9
4       fmul.d    fr8,fr9
5       fadd.d    fr8,fr9
;       st->next->next->i = 2;
6       mov       @_st,r1
;                           interlock
7       mov       @(r1),r1
;                           interlock
8       mov       @(r1),r1
;                           interlock
9       mov       #2,@(4,r1)
;       f = c+d*c;
10      fmov.d    fr7,fr5
11      fmul.d    fr4,fr5
12      fadd.d    fr4,fr5
;       g = d+c-b;
13      fmov.d    fr7,fr10
14      fadd.d    fr4,fr10
15      fsub.d    fr6,fr10
```

Fig. 4a GMICRO Code Sequence Sample

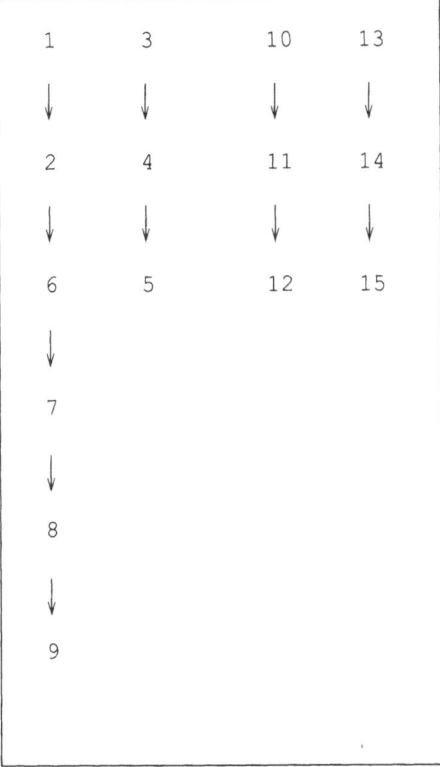

Fig. 4b Dependency Graph

The optimizer then assigns weights to each individual path in the dependency graph based on:

- The current length of the path
- The number of the interlocks in the path
- The number of cycles of delays in the pipeline

The weights determine which node will be selected next. These weights are recalculated after each selection. The instruction scheduling optimization is applied to the code in Figure 4a as follows:

1. Selection starts from node 1 which has both the longest path and the most interlocks.

2. Nodes 3, 10, and 13 are the next candidates. (Node 2 violates Rule B because node 2 interlocks with node 1).

3. The next selections include node 13 followed by node 10.

4. Now we can select node 2 which has the longest path and the most interlocks.

This selection removes pipeline delay between nodes 1 and 2.

5. By applying the same rules to the rest of the code, all the interlocks will be removed.

When this optimization is applied, all interlocks are removed thereby saving a total of 16 cycles as shown in Figure 4c.

```
1        mov      @_st,r0     ; no interlock
13       fmov.d   fr7,fr10
10       fmov.d   fr7,fr5
2        mov      #2,@(4,r0)
3        fmov.d   fr6,fr9
14       fadd.d   fr4,fr10
6        mov      @_st,r1     ; no interlock
11       fmul.d   fr4,fr5
4        fmul.d   fr8,fr9
7        mov      @(r1),r1    ; no interlock
15       fsub.d   fr6,fr10
12       fadd.d   fr4,fr5
8        mov      @(r1),r1    ; no interlock
5        fadd.d   fr8,fr9
9        mov      #2,@(4,r1)
```

Fig. 4c Optimized Instruction Scheduling Result

3.2.2 Chained Addressing Mode Optimization

The chained addressing mode is a high-level addressing mode that can specify multiple levels of register indirection, index, and displacement with a single instruction. This feature is particularly useful for embedded applications by providing a much more compact code than basic instructions. For example:

```
x[i+2] = y[i+3];       /* x and y are local int arrays */

mov @(fp,-16,r4*4),@(fp,-40,r4*4)
```

More complicated address calculations can be constructed with the chained addressing mode. However, this is not always desirable since no intermediate results are saved in registers for possible future optimizations. For example, the opportunity for CSE optimization is checked before the selection of the chained addressing mode. Sometimes, an instruction with the chained addressing mode can be broken into two or more instructions with the same overall size and execution cycles. This separation of instructions lets the instruction scheduler rearrange instructions in order to minimize pipeline delays.

Consider the following two instruction sequences for multiplying a variable in a register by the constant 10:

Sequence 1:

```
mova @(r2*2,r2*8),r0
```

Sequence 2:

```
mova @(r2,r2*4),r0
add r0,r0
```

The above two instruction sequences use the same number of bytes (i.e., 8 bytes). However, the second sequence of instructions provides an opportunity for additional pipeline optimization by intermixing the second sequence with other instructions.

3.2.3 Machine-Dependent Optimizations

The code generator performs additional optimizations that are architecture-implementation specific. These are:

1. Optimizing function prologue and epilogue.

   The compiler generates a full prologue or epilogue only when it is absolutely necessary. A prologue will not be generated if the stack frame is not needed. For example, a prologue will not be generated if the function has no local stack variables and does not return a structure.

2. Group stack adjust instructions.

   The GMICRO calling convention requires the calling routine (caller) to remove the function arguments from the stack after the call. The stack pointer is adjusted by adding a constant which equals the total size of the function arguments pushed. The compiler will try to combine two or more stack adjust instructions by accumulating the adjustments to the last instruction, thereby saving two ADD instructions as shown in Figure 5.

```
;       test2(i1);
        mov     r4,@-sp
        bsr     _test2          ; no adjustment yet
;       test3(i1);
        mov     r4,@-sp
        bsr     _test3          ; no adjustment yet
;       test4(i1);
        mov     r4,@-sp
        bsr     _test4
        add     #12,sp          ; adjustment for all 3 calls
```

Fig. 5 Group Stack Adjustment

6. Replacing multiplication by shift and addition.

The code generator will replace a multiplication instruction by a combination of shift, addition, and register indirect with index as shown in Figure 6. This optimization is controlled by a compiler option for speed/space trade off.

```
;          i3 = i1 * 180;
           mov       r4,r5
           mov       r5,r0
           shl       #4,r5
           sub       r0,r5
           mova      @(r5,r5*2),r5
           shl       #2,r5
                              ; total of 18 cycles
                              ; (21 cycles without optimization)
```

Fig. 6 Multiplication Optimization

7. Use of ACB and SCB for loop statement.

The code generator will use TRON's powerful ACB (add, compare, branch) and SCB (subtract, compare, branch) instructions for loop statements (instead of the traditional ADD/SUB, CMP/BR instructions) whenever applicable. The ACB/SCB instructions increment/decrement the loop count, compares the loop count with the loop limit, and branches to the beginning of the loop based on the result. ACB/SCB instructions produce code that is 2 to 4 bytes smaller and 0 to 2 cycles faster than the traditional instructions.

8. Use of string operation instructions.

The SMOV (string move) instruction performs structure assignments. It is also used in the in-line expansion of the memcpy and strcpy functions. The SSCH (string search) instruction generates code for SWITCH statements and also for in-line expansion of the strlen function. The SCMP (string compare) instruction is used in the in-line expansion of the strcmp function. In particular, in-line expansions improve execution speed by as much as 200% when compared with the equivalent code that uses the strcp, strlen, and strcmp function calls.

Finally, the code generator of the optimizing compiler performs additional optimizations generically referred to here as the "code generator optimizations" which are machine- or architecture-dependent. TRON microprocessors provide several opportunities for such optimizations. The additional optimization techniques implemented in the code generator include:

1. Dead and redundant code elimination

2. Constant folding

3. Redundant load and store elimination

4. Switch statement optimization

5. Loop rotation

6. In-line run-time functions such as strcpy, strcmp, strlen, and memcpy

7. Jump optimizations:

    a. Redundant jump elimination

    b. Jump to jump elimination

    c. Branch tail merging

    d. Cross-jump optimization

    e. Short/long displacement optimization

One result of the optimization techniques described earlier is the generation of code which is functionally equivalent to the original source but different in code organization. Debugging such optimized code is a difficult task. The ANSI C compiler is designed to generate additional debugging information to make it easier to debug optimized code. MRI's XRAY debugger is discussed next along with how it uses this additional debugging information about optimized code.

4. SOURCE-LEVEL DEBUGGING OF OPTIMIZED CODE

Most optimizing high-level language systems use optimization techniques to generate efficient object code, but they support source-level debugging of only non-optimized programs. For time-critical embedded applications, debugging non-optimized versions of the object code is unacceptable since timing problems found with optimized object code may not appear with less optimized equivalents. MRI has developed an interactive debugging environment (XRAY) for the TRON architecture which supports source-level debugging of highly optimized code for both embedded and native UNIX applications (Agarwal 1988).

Typical optimization transformations that create problems for the debuggers include:

- register allocation by priority-based coloring
- loop invariant code motion
- common subexpression elimination
- unused definition and dead code elimination
- instruction scheduling optimizations
- code merging optimizations (branch tail merging, cross jump optimization)
- function prologue and epilogue optimization (frameless functions)

The major debugger problems introduced by the above optimizations are:

- Displaying the values of program variables is not straightforward since they can exist in registers, on the stack, or they may not be alive.
- It is difficult to correctly show the current execution point. More than one source line may correspond to an object address because of common subexpression elimination and code merging optimizations.

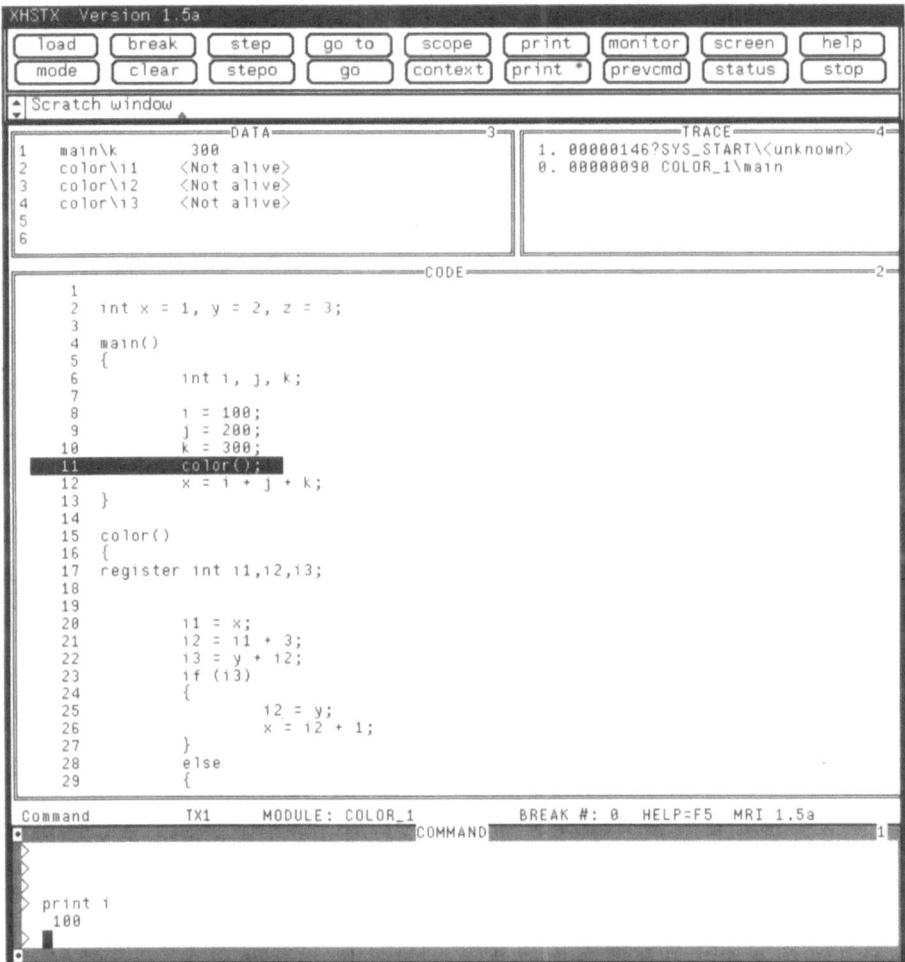

Fig. 7 Variables i1, i2, and i3 are Not Alive

- It may be difficult to find the object address at which to set a breakpoint for a given source line. The mapping from source lines to object code addresses becomes very complex because of optimizations. In many cases, a source line may map to multiple target addresses because of common subexpression elimination, code motion, and instruction scheduling optimizations. In some cases, a source line may not have a corresponding object address because of unused definition or dead code elimination.

4.1 Transparent versus Correct Debugger Behavior

The ideal debugger will have transparent behavior for optimized programs (Zellweger 1983). With such a debugger, the responses to the user requests concerning the execution of optimized and non-optimized versions of a program will be identical. However, it is not practical to have completely transparent behavior when the generated machine instructions have been reordered by

```
XHSTX  Version 1.5a
  ┌──────┐ ┌──────┐ ┌──────┐ ┌──────┐ ┌──────┐ ┌──────┐ ┌───────┐ ┌──────┐ ┌──────┐
  │ load │ │break │ │ step │ │ go to│ │scope │ │print │ │monitor│ │screen│ │ help │
  └──────┘ └──────┘ └──────┘ └──────┘ └──────┘ └──────┘ └───────┘ └──────┘ └──────┘
  ┌──────┐ ┌──────┐ ┌──────┐ ┌──────┐ ┌───────┐ ┌───────┐ ┌───────┐ ┌──────┐ ┌──────┐
  │ mode │ │clear │ │stepo │ │  go  │ │context│ │print *│ │prevcmd│ │status│ │ stop │
  └──────┘ └──────┘ └──────┘ └──────┘ └───────┘ └───────┘ └───────┘ └──────┘ └──────┘
```

```
Scratch window
                    ═══════DATA═══════════════════3═     ══════════TRACE══════════════4═
 1   main\k      ? 300                               2. 00000146?SYS_START\<unknown>
 2   color\i1    1                                   1. 00000094 COLOR_1\main
 3   color\i2    <not_alive> 1                        0. 000000AE COLOR_1\color
 4   color\i3    <not_alive> 1
 5
 6
                              ═════════════CODE══════════════════════════════════2═
 1
 2   int x = 1, y = 2, z = 3;
 3
 4   main()
 5   {
 6           int i, j, k;
 7
 8           i = 100;
 9           j = 200;
10           k = 300;
11           color();
12           x = i + j + k;
13   }
14
15   color()
16   {
17   register int i1,i2,i3;
18
19
20           i1 = x;
21           i2 = i1 + 3;
22           i3 = y + i2;
23           if (i3)
24           {
25                   i2 = y;
26                   x = i2 + 1;
27           }
28           else
29           {
```

```
Command          TX1    MODULE: COLOR_1        BREAK #: 0   HELP=F5   MRI 1.5a
                                  ═══════════COMMAND═══════════════════════════1═
     color\i1             : Type is Living Register int.
                            Register = @r4
>  printsymbols i2
     color\i2             : Type is Living Register int.
                            Register = @r4
> ▮
```

Fig. 8 Variable i1 is Alive

instruction scheduling optimizations. An acceptable alternative is to provide correct behavior with respect to optimizations. This means that the debugger should be able to present, in source program terms, those changes caused by the optimization transformations. The primary objective of the XRAY debugging environment is to provide correct behavior by presenting optimization information to the user in a manner that can be easily understood.

4.2. Tracking Locations of Program Variables

As explained in section 3.1.3, the MRI ANSI C Compiler for the TRON architecture assigns variables to registers in a most efficient manner. A single register can hold multiple variables if their live ranges are disjoint. Conversely, a single variable can reside in different locations in different parts of the code. The XRAY debugger tracks the location of each variable at all times even if the variable is moved to the

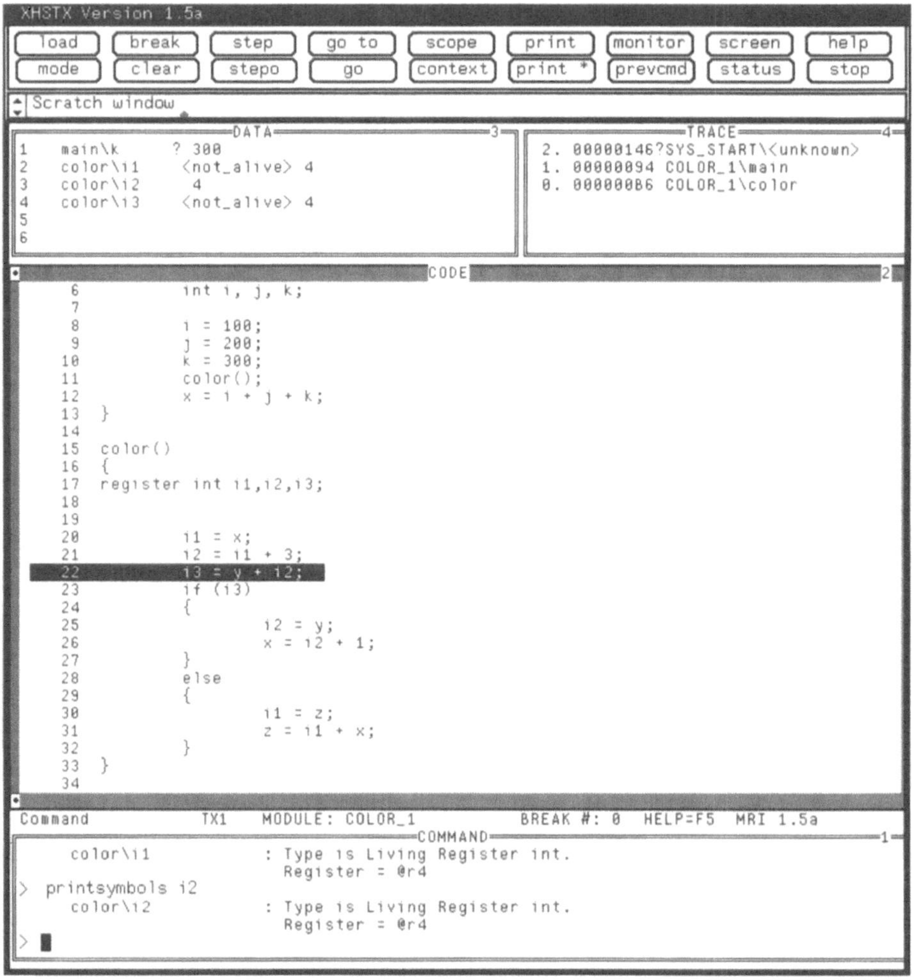

Fig. 9 Variable i2 is Alive

stack as the result of a call.

Figures 7, 8, and 9 show examples of how the XRAY debugging environment correctly displays the values of the variables in a program that has been optimized using priority-based register coloring. Each XRAY screen in these figures, produced using the TX1 toolkit, contains a number of viewports or windows. The code viewport displays the lines of high-level source code, the data viewport displays the values of monitored variable expressions according to their types, and the command viewport lets the user enter commands and display the resulting output. The highlighted line indicates the next source line to be executed.

The data viewport of each screen contains monitored values of the variables k, i1, i2, and i3. When program execution is suspended at line 11 (see Figure 7), the debugger displays the value of k and indicates that the variables i1, i2, and i3 are not alive yet. The local variable k of the function main is in a register assigned by the register coloring optimization. The debugger can get the correct value of k because it knows the register location of k. When control is at line 21 (see Figure 8), the local variable i1 is alive, and its value is contained in register r4 (see the output of the printsymbols commands in the command viewport). The value of variable k of the function main is now on the stack, but XRAY can display its correct value because it tracks the location of k. The local variable i2 becomes alive when the execution stops at line 22 (see Figure 9). The value of i2 is also in register r4 since i1 is not alive anymore. The variable i3 becomes alive when the program control moves to line 23.

Thus, the XRAY debugger uses the location of the control flow of a program to track the locations of the variables for both display and assignment. This is possible only if the compiler has transmitted the relevant optimization information to the debugger. Most current object formats do not have facilities for transferring such optimization information. MRI has extended the IEEE 695 (IEEE 1985) and AT&T COFF (Gircys 1988) object formats to include the optimization information about register usage. The extensions are such that existing software tools and applications are not affected.

4.3 Debugging of Control-Flow Optimized Programs

A conventional high-level debugger not supporting the debugging of optimized programs uses a simple one-to-one mapping between source statements and object code locations. This mapping information is typically included in the object code.

The MRI ANSI C optimizing compiler performs code motion, instruction-scheduling, and code merging optimizations. As a result, the object code address ranges for source statements overlap, and the mapping between source statements and object code locations becomes complex. Setting a breakpoint at a given source statement requires an accurate mapping from the source line to all the object locations that represent the object code for that statement. If a single object location represents the beginning of several source statements, the debugger should be able to indicate this condition to the user (not transparent but correct debugger behavior). Reporting the current execution point requires an accurate mapping from each machine instruction to all the source statements on whose behalf it executes. MRI has enhanced its XRAY debugging environment to construct this many-to-many mapping between source lines and object code locations. In a program that has been optimized with instruction scheduling, the execution of one statement may begin before the execution of a previous statement is complete. In fact, several statements may be executing at the same time. For this reason, MRI is enhancing the XRAY debugger to indicate to the user, in the code viewport, all the source lines whose execution is partially complete. In addition, more research and development will continue to support the debugging of code that has been optimized with interprocedural optimizations.

5. CONCLUSIONS

This paper reported on the implementation of a highly optimizing ANSI C compiler targeted toward the TRON-based GMICRO and TX1 microprocessors. The high-level language orientation of the TRON architecture and the MRI language tool development technology has resulted in an efficient compiler which incorporates state-of-the-art optimization technology. The optimization techniques used (local, global, code generator, and TRON-architecture specific) were discussed. Implementation of these techniques has resulted in a compiler that can generate optimal code with respect to both speed and space as controlled by the user. Moreover, the toolkit includes a powerful debugger that can debug optimized code. In the future, MRI will include additional optimization techniques for the TRON architecture such as "interprocedural" optimization and optimizations utilizing information feedback that is generated by the profiling feature of the debugger. In addition, research and development is continuing that will further improve the ability of the software tools to debug highly optimized code.

REFERENCES

[1]   Agarwal D, Kimelman P (1988) An Adaptable High-Level Debugging
      Environment for Embedded Systems. In: Proceedings of BUSCON 1988, pp
      223-233

[2]   Aho AV, Sethi R, Ullman JD (1985) Compilers: Principles, Techniques, and
      Tools. Addison-Wesley

[3]   ANSI Accredited Standards Committee X3 (1988) Draft Proposed American
      National Standards for Information Systems - Programming Language C. The
      American National Standards Institute. Washington, D.C.

[4]   Bigazzi A, Lillge JE, Jaskolski DE (1988) An Integrated Software Development
      Toolkit for the GMICRO/200. In: Sakamura K (ed) TRON Project 1988.
      Springler-Verlag, pp 363-380

[5]   Chaitin GJ, Auslander MA, Chandra AK, Cocke J, Hopkins ME, and Markstein
      PW (1981) Register Allocation via Coloring. Computer Languages 6:47-57

[6]   Chaitin GJ (1982) Register Allocation & Spilling via Graph Coloring. In:
      Proceedings of the SIGPLAN '82 Symposium on Compiler Construction,
      pp 98-105

[7]   Chow FC (1983) A Portable Machine Independent Global Optimizer -
      Design and Measurements. Computer Systems Laboratory Technical Note
      No. 83-254. Stanford University

[8]   Chow FC, Hennessy JL (1984) Register Allocation by Priority-Based Coloring.
      In: Proceedings of the SIGPLAN '84 Symposium on Compiler Construction,
      pp 222-232

[9]   Fischer CN, LeBlanc, Jr. RJ (1988) Crafting a Compiler. Benjamin Cummings

[10] Ghiassi M (1987) Validating Optimizing Compilers. In: Proceedings of the 1987 IEEE/WESCON Conference 31(2),1-13

[11] Gibbons PB, Muchnick SS (1986) Efficient Instruction Scheduling for a Pipelined Architecture. 1986 ACM

[12] Gircys GR (1988) Understanding and Using COFF. O'Reilly and Associates, Inc.

[13] Hennessy JL, Cross TR (1983) Postpass Code Optimization of Pipeline Constraints. ACM Trans on Programming Language and System 5(3):422-448

[14] IEEE Trial Use Standard for Microprocessor Universal Format for Object Modules (IEEE Std 695) (1985) IEEE Technical Committee on Microcomputers and Microprocessors of the IEEE Computer Society

[15] Sakamura K (1987) TRON VLSI CPU: Concepts and Architecture. In: Sakamura K (ed) TRON Project 1987. Springer-Verlag

[16] Sites RL (1979) Machine Independent Register Allocation. 1979 ACM

[17] Zellweger PT (1983) An Interactive High-Level Debugger for Control-Flow Optimized Programs. In: Proceedings of the SIGPLAN '83 Software Engineering Symposium on High-Level Debugging

Durga Agarwal: joined Microtec Research, Inc. in 1988. He is currently Managing Director responsible for research and product development. He received a BSEE from B.I.T.S., Pilan, India in 1968, an MSEE from I.I.T., Bombay, India in 1970, and an MSCS from Carnegie-Mellon University in 1972. From 1974 to 1976, he pursued graduate research in computer architecture and Ada language implementation at Rutgers University, New Jersey. Prior to joining MRI, he was Director of Software Development at Pyramid Technology. At National Semi-conductor and Perkin-Elmer Data System, he was involved in the development and management of several optimizing compiler projects.

Fu-Hwa Wang: joined Microtec Research, Inc. in 1985. He is currently a Senior Software Engineer and is responsible for the global optimizer. He is also conducting research in language-related software tools. Fu-Hwa received a B.S. from Chao-Tung University in Taiwan in 1979, and an M.S. in Computer Science from West Virginia University in 1982.

Above authors may be reached at: Microtec Research, Inc., 2350 Mission College Blvd., Santa Clara, CA 95054, USA

Manoochehr Ghiassi: is currently an associate professor in the Department of Decision and Information Sciences at Santa Clara University. He received a B.S. from Tehran University, IRAN, in 1970 and an M.S. in economics from Southern Illinois University at Carbondale, Illinois, in 1974. He also received an M.S. in Computer Science in 1979 and a Ph.D. in Industrial Engineering in 1980 both from the University of Illinois at Urbana-Champaign. His current research interests involve software engineering and simulation modeling. He is a member of IEEE, ACM, and a senior member of AIIE.

Above author may be reached at: Manoochehr Ghiassi, 213 Kenna Hall, Santa Clara Univesity, Santa Clara, CA 95053, USA

List of Contributors

The page numbers given below refer to the page on which contribution begins.

Keywords Index

TRON TOTAL ARCHITECTURE

Designed by ken Sakamura

New Computer Systems Construction

In TRON (The Realtime Operating system Nucleus) project, we try to build new computer systems architecture by foreseeing the technological breakthroughs in the future together with the demands on computer systems and then designing new systems accordingly. We feel the existing computer systems have many problems not fit for the future.

The Objectives of the TRON Project

The TRON project aims to support a society structure where computers are used in every conceivable places and where these computer systems talk to each other without difficulty. The TRON project will support HFDS (Highly Functionally Distributed System), which will connect many computer controlled objects and is an important infrastructure of the future society, by providing methodology of how to build such computer systems and plan for acceptance of the computer systems by the society. The reason the TRON project covers many fields is to realize such environment.

The 21st century will come within two decades. It is certain that the number of computers used then will be much larger than today's figure. Because the computer will be used very widely, any problem associated with it, however small, should be eliminated as soon as possible. Not all the criticisms about today's computer systems are about technical matters but are about socioeconomical matters as well. Hence, the preparation for eliminating or reducing the problems of the computer systems in the future must be planned in a very broad context.

TRON Subprojects

The TRON project covers many fields of computer system construction and application. Activities of the TRON project are divided into subprojects. The following software subprojects are running currently; ITRON (Industrial-TRON) for embedded computer systems, BTRON (Business-TRON) for workstations, CTRON (Central-TRON) for large file and communication servers, and MTRON (Macro-TRON) for distributed control of TRON computer systems in a large network. The TRON VLSI CPU CHIP subproject to design VLSI microprocessor which can support various TRON systems is also underway.

The Features of the TRON Project

The TRON computer systems are designed as hierarchy of system layers. The TRON project provides specifications for interfaces among these layers. However, the realization of each layers is left to each implementor. While following the TRON Design Guideline, each implementor can freely compete in creating a concrete computer system based on the general TRON concept and specifications.

The TRON computer systems has the data compatibility and the program compatibility. In addition, the TRON computer systems have man-machine interface compatibility, which has rarely been discussed before.

The man-machine interface compatibility together with other TRON design principles have make it possible to use uniform design principles in computer systems and application design. These principles are valid for all TRON-based computer systems.

TRON Association

TRON Association is an organization to provide a forum for discussions about the future computer systems among TRON project members and any interested parties. Please contact the address below if you are interested in joining the TRON Association. Annual membership fee is 500,000 YEN.

TRON Association
5th floor, Tomoecho Annex-II
3-8-27, Toranomon, Minato-ku
Tokyo 105 JAPAN
TEL. 81-3-433-6741
FAX. 81-3-433-5003